RESIDENTIAL MORTGAGE LENDING

Third Edition

Marshall W. Dennis

Prentice Hall
Englewood Cliffs, New Jersey 07632

Library of Congress Cataloging-in-Publication Data

Dennis, Marshall W.
   Residential mortgage lending / Marshall W. Dennis. — 3rd ed.
     p. cm.
   Includes index.
   ISBN 0-13-755406-0
   1. Mortgage loans—United States. I. Title.
HG2040.5.U5D46 1991
332.7′22′0973—dc20

                                      91–26580
                                          CIP

Acquisitions editor: Jim Boyd
Editorial/production supervision and
   interior design: Tally Morgan, WordCrafters Editorial Services, Inc.
Cover Design: Rosemarie Paccione
Prepress buyer: Ilene Levy
Manufacturing buyer: Ed O'Dougherty

© 1992, 1989, 1985 by Prentice-Hall Inc.
A Simon & Schuster Company
Englewood Cliffs, New Jersey 07632

Printed in the United States of America
10 9 8 7 6 5 4 3 2 1

ISBN 0-13-755406-0

Prentice-Hall International (UK) Limited, *London*
Prentice-Hall of Australia Pty. Limited, *Sydney*
Prentice-Hall Canada Inc., *Toronto*
Prentice-Hall Hispanoamericana, S.A., *Mexico*
Prentice-Hall of India Private Limited, *New Delhi*
Prentice-Hall of Japan, Inc. *Tokyo*
Simon & Schuster Asia Pte. Ltd. *Singapore*
Editora Prentice-Hall do Brasil, Ltda. *Rio de Janeiro*

CONTENTS

LIST OF FIGURES ══════

PREFACE

The first book in what became a series, *Fundamentals of Mortgage Lending*, was published in June 1978. During 1977 when I was writing that book, it was my expectation that revisions would be necessary every three or four years. I was completely wrong. More change has occurred in residential mortgage lending since that first book was written than had occurred during all the years since the Great Depression. This is the sixth revision of that first book in fourteen years: strong evidence of the magnitude of change.

The first book and its successor, *Mortgage Lending, Fundamentals and Practices* (first and second editions), were primarily concerned with residential mortgage lending, but not exclusively. Two chapters in those earlier books were devoted to the basics of income-property lending. Because of the importance and extent of recent changes in residential mortgage lending, I decided to concentrate on residential mortgage lending in the three editions of the current book.

The basic purpose of this book remains the same as prior editions: to communicate and explain the fundamentals of mortgage lending in as simple and concise a manner as possible. It is designed for either a new employee of a mortgage lender or a college student studying real estate finance who wants to supplement that study with practical mortgage lending fundamentals.

A new employee of any mortgage lender will probably need at least the first six months to understand both the specific job requirements and some of the fundamentals of mortgage lending. This book is for that individual, whether the employing mortgage lender be a commercial bank, a savings and loan institution, a credit union, a savings bank, or a mortgage banker.

The backgrounds of those entering the mortgage lending field today range from those with solid real estate finance training to those with no formal academic training. Whatever the background, all of these students can and will succeed if they have the ability to learn and apply what they have learned. No prior knowledge of finance or of any part of mortgage lending is assumed in this book. The reader is assumed to possess only the ability and willingness to learn.

This book will discuss each topic beginning with the fundamentals and will develop them to the point where the reader will have a basic understanding of that topic. Not all topics will be applicable to every mortgage lender, nor even be of interest at the time to all readers, but to understand the basics of modern residential mortgage lending each subject included needs to be comprehensively understood. Changes occur so rapidly in this segment of the economy that an area in which a particular mortgage lender is not involved today may be where the growth and profit potential are tomorrow. All mortgage lenders should prepare for this growth and change by either employing suitably educated personnel or providing that education.

While explaining the fundamentals of residential mortgage lending, this book also examines the similarities and differences which exist among mortgage lenders. Basically, therefore, this text is designed to fulfill the need all mortgage lenders have for a basic text to prepare new employees for the important job of helping finance the growing housing needs of this country.

ACKNOWLEDGMENTS

I am deeply indebted to a number of experts for their valuable advice and assistance in preparing this book. These individuals were most generous with their time and their experiences in mortgage lending. Some of those named assisted in the preparation of the preceding book, *Mortgage Lending, Fundamentals and Practices*, but I would like to acknowledge them again.

Kathleen J. Brace, president, Brace Financial Group; Agoura Hills, California

John P. Brady, executive vice president, Staten Island Savings Bank; Staten Island, New York

Jeffrey L. Briggs, senior vice president, Centerbank; Waterbury, Connecticut

David L. Chapman II, executive vice president, Lomas & Nettleton; Dallas, Texas

John D. Fitzmaurice, president, Investors Mortgage Insurance Company; Boston, Massachusetts

Edwin R. Goodwin, senior vice president, Mortgage and Trust, Inc.; Houston, Texas

Gary Hammond, vice president, First Federal Savings and Loan of Arizona; Phoenix, Arizona

Stuart M. Lopes, senior vice president, General Electric Mortgage Insurance Companies; Raleigh, North Carolina

Robert F. MacSwain, vice president, Guilford Transportation Industries; Boston, Massachusetts

Brian L. McDonnell, director, mortgage department, Navy Federal Credit Union; Vienna, Virginia

Ted A. Miller, vice president, General Electric Mortgage Insurance Companies; Raleigh, North Carolina

Donna J. Pillard, senior vice president, Thomson-McKinnion Mortgage Securities, Inc.; Memphis, Tennessee

Michael J. Robertson, vice president, CUNA Mortgage; Madison, Wisconsin

A special thanks to Systems and Forms, Chicago, Illinois for supplying many of the mortgage forms.

For any possible errors, omissions, or faulty analysis, the author assumes full and sole responsibility.

Finally, a special thank you to my wife, Marilyn, for her many hours of tedious reading of the proofs.

Marshall W. Dennis
Monroe, Connecticut

HISTORY OF MORTGAGE LENDING

1

Today's student or practitioner of residential mortgage lending may be hard-pressed to keep pace with this rapidly changing business. This is a segment of our society and economy that indeed changes from year to year, if not monthly. The extent of the recent changes in residential mortgage lending is major and is reflected in the following topics:

- rapid deregulation of financial institutions
- dramatic growth in the use of mortgage-backed securities
- evolution in alternative types of mortgage instruments
- increase in the use of delegated underwriting
- failure of many mortgage lending institutions
- rise and fall of high ratio mortgages

These developments could lead one to assume that all meaningful changes have occurred in the past couple of years or so. That assumption would be wrong. Mortgage lending is, and always has been, a constantly changing part of our economic life and history. The basic concepts of mortgage lending have developed over centuries, and the use of mortgages can be traced to the beginning of recorded history.

This chapter is divided into two parts. Part One describes the historical development of mortgage lending from its beginning in Babylonia until the Great Depression of the 1930s. Part Two begins with the federal government's intervention in real estate and mortgage lending activity in the 1930s. This decade is often identified as the beginning of the modern period of residential mortgage lending. The chapter ends with an examination of the issues facing residential mortgage lending today.

Many of the complexities of today's mortgage lending are the result of problems that existed not only half a century ago but hundreds of years ago. To truly understand how and why residential mortgage lending works today, an understanding of this history is essential.

PART ONE: MORTGAGE LENDING, A DEVELOPING CONCEPT

The underlying product in all real estate activities is land. Some sociologists claim that the use of land, the desire to acquire it, and the need to regulate its transfer were among the fundamental reasons for the development of governments and laws. As government units developed, laws were formulated to govern the ownership and use of land. Because of the importance of land in an agrarian society, it was soon being used as security for the performance of such obligations as debt repayment and the fulfillment of military service.

Evidence of transactions involving land as security has been uncovered in such ancient civilizations as Babylonia and Egypt. Many of the basic principles of mortgage lending—including the essential elements of naming the borrower, naming the lender, and describing the property—were developed in these early civilizations. For example, there is evidence that the Egyptians were the first to use surveys to describe mortgaged land. This practice was undoubtedly necessitated by the annual flooding of the Nile River, which often obliterated property markers.

During the period when Greek civilization was at its peak, temple leaders often loaned money with real estate as security. In fact, throughout history organized religion has taken a strong interest in real estate and related activities.

ROMAN LAW

The Roman Empire developed mortgage lending to a high level of sophistication, beginning with the *fiducia*. This transaction was an actual transfer of possession and title to land. It was subject to an additional agreement which stated that if the borrower fulfilled the obligation a reconveyance would occur. As Roman government became stronger and the law more clearly defined, a new concept of security called the *pignus* was developed. No title transfer occurred. Instead, the land was "pawned." According to this concept, title and possession remained with the borrower, but the lender could take possession of the property at any time if it was deemed that a possibility of default existed.

The most important Roman development regarding mortgages, however, was the *hypotheca,* which was a pledge. The hypotheca is similar to the lien theory (described later) that exists in most states in this country today. The title remained with the borrower, who was also allowed to retain possession of the property. Only if an actual default occurred (a failure on the part of the borrower to perform) was the lender entitled to take possession of and title to the land.

As the Roman Empire receded throughout Europe during the Dark Ages, a Germanic law introduced a new concept. A borrower was given the choice of fulfilling an obligation or losing the security. If the mortgagor defaulted, the mortgagee had to look exclusively to the property itself. This security system was called a *gage* in Germanic law: something was deposited for the performance of an agreement. As the Dark Ages continued and the governmental authority of Rome weakened to such a degree that lenders were not sure they would have support from the central authorities in securing their debts, the hypotheca system decayed and died, and the more primitive concept of the fiducia returned.

ENGLISH DEVELOPMENTS

Later, in Europe, a new system of government and social structure, the feudal system, became widespread. The essential characteristic of the feudal system was the totality of the king's control. He was the owner of all lands, and granted their use to certain lords in return for their military fealty. Lords given the use of the land were permitted to continue on the land as long as they fulfilled a military obligation to the king. If this obligation was not fulfilled, or if the lord died, the use of the land was revoked and given to others. In this situation, land served as a security for the performance of an obligation—military service.

Along with the feudal system of land tenure, the Germanic system of the *gage* was introduced into early English law by William of Normandy in 1066 following the successful invasion of England. The word *mortgage* was not found in English literature until after the Norman invasion. It derives from the French words *mort,* meaning "dead" (the land was "dead" since the mortgagor could not use or derive income from it), and *gage,* meaning "pledge." During the years after the Norman invasion, the Catholic Church established civil law in England. The Church's policy at this time was that the charging of any interest for money loaned was usury.

As the common law evolved in England, there occurred a gradual shift from a concept of favoritism or protection of the mortgagee to favoritism or protection of the mortgagor. Finally, the common law reached a more balanced position. The initial concept of mortgagee favoritism was dictated by the realities of the economic and legal systems that existed at this early stage of mortgage development.

Mortgage lending was not a common occurrence during this period for two reasons: first, there was very little need for it; and second, no incentive to lend existed without the ability to collect interest. The mortgage lending that did occur was not for the purpose of providing funds to purchase real estate, but was usually provided to finance large purchases (such as a new mill or livestock) or perhaps to prepare a dowry for a daughter. Since lenders could not collect interest on these loans, they would take both title and possession of a designated portion of the borrower's land and thus be entitled to all rents and profits. When the obligation was fulfilled, title was reconveyed to the mortgagor. If the mortgagor defaulted, the mortgagee would permanently retain title and possession of the mortgaged land. The mortgagee was also still entitled to expect performance of the underlying obligation.

During the 15th century, courts of equity allowed the mortgagor to perform the obligation, even after the required date, and redeem the property. This concept was expanded, and by 1625 nearly all existing mortgage lending practices had ended because a mortgagee never knew when a mortgagor might perform and thus redeem the property. To alleviate this problem, mortgagees would petition the court for a decree requiring the mortgagor to redeem the property within six months or lose the right to do so.

AMERICAN DEVELOPMENTS

Westward expansion in America following the Revolutionary War was financed by land development banks which borrowed primarily in Europe to finance their land purchases in the developing West. Much of this land acquisition was speculative and eventually culminated in the bankruptcy of nearly all these land development banks. Thereafter little, if any, real estate financing was done on an organized basis until after the Civil War.

During the first 75 years of this country's history, most of the population lived on small farms whose ownership was passed down through families. Little need existed for mortgage lending in this society except for an occasional purchase of new land or for seed money. The small amount of mortgage lending that did occur during this period was provided primarily by family and friends. It is important to realize that until the 1920s, the largest category of mortgage lenders in the United States was composed of individuals, not financial institutions.

Thrift Institutions

The birth of various thrift institutions provided an opportunity for change in mortgage lending. The first thrift institution formed was a mutual savings bank, the Philadelphia Savings Fund Society, which was established in 1816. Of greater long-term importance to mortgage lending was the organization of the first building society in the United States. Modeled after societies that had existed in England and Scotland for 50 years, the Oxford Provident Building Association was organized in 1831 in Frankfort, Pennsylvania. This association, like the ones that soon followed, was intended to exist only long enough for all the organizers to obtain funds to purchase homes. Ironically, the first loan made by this association became delinquent and another member of the association assumed the debt and took possession of the house. Later, other associations were formed, providing a popular means of financing home purchases across the United States.

Even with these new financial institutions, mortgage lending was still not an important part of the economy in the first half of the 19th century. Most families still lived on farms which met basically all their requirements. No urgent need for savings existed. Away from the farm there were few employment opportunities where excess cash could be accumulated for savings. The concept of saving was still new, and the number of active savers was very small. Then, as now, the impetus for mortgage lending was the inflow of savings to the institutions that would lend funds.

Mortgage Companies

After the Civil War, the nation's expansion continued and developments in mortgage lending resumed. Starting with a new westward expansion which opened virgin lands for farming, a regular farm mortgage business developed in the predominantly rural Midwest. The Midwest is an area where many mortgage companies began, and it still has one of the heaviest concentrations of mortgage companies.

These companies did not originate mortgage loans for their own portfolios, as did the thrift institutions. Rather, these loans were for direct sale to wealthy individuals or to institutional investors such as life insurance companies. Most of these individual and institutional investors were located on the East Coast and needed local mortgage companies to originate loans for them. This need developed into the mortgage loan correspondent system.

The bulk of the mortgage business consisted of financing farms, usually with a prevailing loan-to-value ratio of 40 percent. An occasional 50 percent loan might be made on a farm in a well-developed area. The term of the loan was short (less than five years), with interest payable semi-annually and the principal paid at the end of the term. By 1900, outstanding farm mortgages originated by these mortgage companies totaled more than $4 billion.

During this period of time, the population movement to urban areas began to increase, swelled by the ever-mounting numbers of immigrants. In 1892, the United States League of Savings Associations, a trade organization, was founded in response to the expanding savings and loan industry. These institutions provided urban residents a place to save money and a source of funds to use in purchasing homes. Some of these mortgages made by savings and loan associations were repaid on an installment basis, not at the expiration of the term as were mortgages from other types of lenders.

Commercial Banks

Commercial banks made few real estate loans until the Civil War, when a sudden demand for loans to finance new farmsteads encouraged state-chartered commercial banks to make low-ratio farm mortgages. Except for a brief period of time, federally chartered commercial banks could not make real estate loans.

This competition from state-chartered banks eventually forced a change in federal banking law. In 1913 the Federal Reserve Act authorized federally chartered banks to lend money on real estate. This initial authorization limited mortgage loans to improved farms for a five-year term with the loan-to-value ratio of 50 percent. This authorization was extended in 1916 to include one-year loans on urban real estate.

Many changes have occurred in both state and federal laws relating to the types and terms of mortgage loans made by commercial banks. These changes have tended to lag behind advances made by other mortgage lenders. However, the contribution made by commercial banks to mortgage lending has been meaningful, especially in those areas of the country where they function as the principal mortgage lender.

Turn of the Century

During the period from 1870 to the early 1900s, a few mortgage companies in or near urban areas began to make loans on single-family houses. Initially, such loans constituted a very small percentage of their business, but they gradually grew to account for more and more total origination volume. The Farm Mortgage Bankers Association, a trade organization formed in 1914, changed its name in 1923 to the Mortgage Bankers Association to reflect the increasing emphasis on residential lending.

In the first two decades of this century the typical loan made by a mortgage company on a single-family dwelling called for no more than a 50 percent loan-to-value ratio, with a three-to-five-year mortgage term. There were no provisions for amortization of the loan and interest was generally payable semi-annually. The majority of these mortgages were renewed upon maturity, since few families had the money to retire the debt. The mortgage companies originating these mortgages charged the borrower from one to three percent of the amount of the loan as a fee. Upon renewal, an additional one percent fee would be charged.

As the 20th century progressed, thrift institutions—especially savings and loan associations—continued to expand. The mutual savings banks, which had their greatest growth after the Civil War, remained principally in the New England states, but savings and loan institutions continued to grow and spread across the country. During this time, thrift institutions were originating short-term mortgage loans for their own portfolios.

All mortgage lenders participated in the real estate boom years of the 1920s. This was a period of unrestrained optimism. Most Americans believed growth and prosperity would continue forever. Real estate prices appreciated as much as 25 to 50 percent per year during the first half of the decade. Many lenders forgot their underwriting standards, believing that inflating prices would bail out any bad loan. As with any speculative period, the end came, and along with it, many personal fortunes were dissipated.

Depression Era

The real estate boom of the 1920s began to show signs of weakening long before the stock market crash. By 1927, real estate values that had appreciated excessively in the early 1920s began to decline dramatically. Following the disastrous dive of the stock market in 1929, the entire economy of the United States was in danger of collapse. Real estate values plunged to less than half the level of the year before. The ability of both the individual borrower and the income-property mortgagor to meet quarterly or semi-annual interest payments was reduced by the large-scale unemployment that followed the collapse of the stock market and the loss of economic vitality throughout the nation.

Because periodic amortization of mortgages was not common, a six-month lag often occurred before an institutional investor realized a mortgage was in trouble. In addition, the various financial institutions were faced with a severe liquidity crisis which required them to sell vast real estate and mortgage holdings under very unfavorable conditions. This need to sell real estate holdings to obtain cash, coupled with a rise in foreclosures and tax sales, severely depressed an already crumbling real estate market. Many individual home owners were threatened with property loss even if they retained their jobs because when their five-year mortgages expired, many were unable to refinance their mortgages: lenders were caught in the liquidity crisis and did not have the funds to lend.

Thrift institutions also experienced problems during this period even though some of their mortgagors had installment-type mortgages. As many workers lost their jobs and unemployment reached 25 percent, the savings inflow to thrifts diminished drastically. All types of financial institutions began to fail, and as a result savers withdrew funds and the liquidity crisis worsened for all lenders. In the early 1930s, many commercial banks and savings and loan institutions failed due to massive withdrawals of savings and the high foreclosure rate. By 1935, 20 percent of all mortgage assets were in the "real estate owned" category.

The vast majority of all foreclosures during the 1930s were made by second and third mortgagees who needed to foreclose immediately in order to protect what little security they had. The highest number of foreclosures occurred from 1931–35, averaging 250,000 each year. The increasing number of foreclosures, especially on family farms in the Midwest, forced the beginning of compulsory moratoria. In the Midwest, where economic deterioration was aggravated by the dust bowl storms, the cry for a moratorium reached the stage of near rebellion, and some violence occurred. Reacting to the hysteria sweeping the farm belt and some of the larger cities, many mortgagees voluntarily instituted forbearance, some for as long as two years. The first law requiring a mortgage moratorium became effective in Iowa in February, 1933. Over the next 18 months, 27 states enacted legislation suspending nearly all foreclosures. Most of the moratorium laws enacted during this period were intended to last for two years or less, although many were reenacted and allowed to continue as law until the early 1940s.

It is important to note that during the period when these laws were in effect, some foreclosures did occur. The determining factor on whether to grant relief was the soundness of a debtor's fundamental economic position. If it were determined that a debtor would eventually lose the land anyway, postponing the foreclosure or granting a moratorium was considered a waste of time and an injustice to the creditor. The moratoria of the early 1930s did not provide an actual solution to the underlying economic problems, but they did provide a respite during which public unrest could be soothed and the federal government could introduce some economic remedies.

PART TWO: GOVERNMENT INTERVENTION

In the early 1930s, the federal government realized that the drop in real estate values would continue to add to the growing depression of the entire economy, preventing its revitalization. Therefore, the government instituted a series of programs designed to help stabilize real estate values and, it was hoped, the entire economy. This marked the beginning of a drastic reversal in previous governmental–political philosophy, which had been generally laissez-faire.

FEDERAL LEGISLATION

Beginning in the last year of the Hoover Administration, federal legislation usurped, in large measure, control over real estate and mortgage lending activities which previously had been left to the states.

The first legislation designed to meet the threat of the Depression created the Reconstruction Finance Corporation (RFC) in 1932 which, among other things, provided liquidity to commercial banks. Shortly thereafter, the Federal Home Loan Bank (FHLB) was created to provide a central credit facility to home finance institutions, primarily savings and loan institutions. The next major legislation was the Home Owners Loan Act (HOLA) in 1933. This act provided for federal charters for savings and loan institutions and created the Home Owners Loan Corporation (HOLC), which was designed to provide emergency relief to home owners by refinancing or purchasing defaulted mortgages. This program kept many tens of thousands of families from losing their homes in the 1930s.

One of the most far-reaching enactments of this period was the National Housing Act (1934) which created the Federal Housing Administration (FHA) and the Federal Savings and Loan Insurance Corporation (FSLIC). FSLIC and the Federal Deposit Insurance Corporation (FDIC) were instrumental in encouraging depositors to return desperately needed deposits to financial institutions. FHA has provided the framework and the impetus necessary for the development of a true national mortgage market. FHA has also been credited with either initiating or making popular many innovations in mortgage lending, such as mortgage insurance and the long-term, self-amortizing mortgage.

THE GROWTH ERA

A minimal amount of single-family housing construction occurred from 1926 to 1946 as a result of the Depression and World War II. At the end of the war, however, five million servicemen returned home, and a tremendous demand for housing was created. The government, as part of its responsibility to returning veterans, as well as a way of stimulating housing, passed the Servicemen's Readjustment Act (1944). One of the major features of this act was a guaranty program which provided a desirable way of financing homes for veterans. The most distinguishing characteristic of this guaranty program (then and now) is the lack of a down payment requirement for eligible veterans. Under this program no mortgage insurance premiums are collected from veterans; instead, the government absorbs the cost of the mortgage guaranty.

The highly liquid position of financial institutions was the second great impetus to the rapid expansion of single-family housing construction following World War II. In 1945, more than half of the assets of financial institutions were tied up in the no-risk but low-yielding government securities that institutions were obligated to purchase during World War II. At the end of the war, these bonds could be sold and the cash converted into mortgages, which provided a higher yield.

The greatest boom in housing construction in the history of this country, and possibly the world, occurred from 1945 to 1955. The two government housing programs (FHA and VA), the built-up demand for housing, and the liquid position of lenders were instrumental in this dramatic growth in housing. Since the end of World War II, mortgages have been the largest user of long-term credit in the entire American economy.

Housing Act of 1949

The Housing Act of 1949 is one of the most important pieces of social legislation in the past 50 years because of the national commitment made to provide "...a decent home and suitable living environment for every American family." Much of the legislative action in the housing and mortgage lending field since then has been an attempt to fulfill that commendable but probably unrealistic goal.

The 1950s and early 1960s were a period of national optimism, economic growth and, as far as mortgage lending is concerned, a relatively quiet period in the legislative arena. This period of tranquility soon dissipated in the face of an onslaught of such national crises as political assassinations, civil rights demonstrations, urban blight, and the war in Vietnam.

HUD

The lack of adequate housing, a situation often associated with poverty, was partially addressed in 1965 by the consolidation of the many federal housing agencies into a new cabinet-level department, the Department of Housing and

Urban Development (HUD). HUD was to be the focal point of much of the new legislation in the years to come as it assumed a dominant position in regulating real estate and mortgage lending.

The avalanche of legislation and regulation that was to so change mortgage lending began a few years after HUD was created, when the Housing and Urban Development Act (1968) was enacted. This was the first major legislation in the mortgage lending field in over a decade. The act committed the government to a goal of 26 million new housing starts in the next decade. At the time, many argued that this goal was not practical on either fiscal or political grounds. However, the act introduced a new concept in government programs for residential real estate by adopting the principle of subsidizing interest rates. The two major subsidy programs of the 1968 act were:

1. section 235, which encourages home ownership for low- and moderate-income families by providing special mortgage insurance and by subsidizing the mortgage interest rate in excess of one percent.
2. section 236, which is basically the same as 235 but is geared to multifamily rental units.

These government subsidy programs, combined with national economic growth, stimulated housing production in 1972 to more than three million units—the highest ever. With political pressure to increase housing production, the inevitable problems developed almost immediately. Report of possible scandals in subsidized housing began to appear in 1971, involving FHA officials and some mortgage lenders. These scandals were followed by congressional investigations which spotlighted the unforeseen high costs of these programs.

In January of 1973, President Richard Nixon ordered a freeze on all subsidy programs. This was partially lifted later, but only after a thorough review of government programs by a special task force created by HUD. This task force reviewed the history of government involvement in real estate and analyzed the impact of the various subsidy programs on housing. The task force concluded that the goal of providing home ownership for everyone was neither practical nor desirable when weighed against the cost.

The government's concept changed from subsidizing home ownership to subsidizing rent. The Housing and Community Development Act (1974) formalized this change with the Section 8 program. This program allows low- and moderate-income families to choose the rental unit in the community in which they want to live, with the government subsidizing the amount of fair market rent that is in excess of 25 percent of the family's monthly income. This program provides assistance both to families who could not afford the minimal housing expenses stipulated in prior programs and to families whose incomes were just over the maximum income limit to qualify for assistance in home purchasing.

CONSUMER PROTECTION

The way residential mortgage lending is conducted today is strictly controlled by a series of federal laws and regulations. These are discussed in detail in Chapter 6, but a brief description of these laws and regulations at this point of the book will be helpful in understanding the role of the federal government in residential mortgage lending.

Truth-in-Lending and Fair Housing Legislation

The Consumer Protection Act (1968) was the first in a series of legislative acts which redefined the concept of consumer protection regarding mortgage lending, thus changing forever the way in which residential mortgage lending is conducted. The major features of this bill were:

- Truth-in-Lending. The Federal Reserve Board was given the authority to draft regulations implementing this law and to monitor compliance. This law became known to mortgage lenders as Regulation Z. The key provisions are that a lender is required to provide a borrower with complete written information about the terms of the loan and a disclosure of the annual percentage rate (APR).
- Fair Credit Reporting Act. This important development in how credit reports are to be handled by consumer credit reporting agencies and lenders helped to resolve most abuses that had occurred. This regulation also limits the use of so-called investigative credit reports.
- Fair Housing Act. This 1968 civil rights law was designed to prohibit racial discrimination in the sale and financing of real estate. Many of the provisions were enhanced by the Equal Credit Opportunity Act in 1974.

Flood Disaster Protection Act, Real Estate Settlement Procedures Act, and Equal Credit Opportunity Act

The 1970s is often described as the decade of the consumer. In many areas of society, consumer protection was a cresting wave, but nowhere was it as strong or as pervasive as in mortgage lending. The year 1974 witnessed much of this movement coming to fruition in Congress with three important legislative acts:

1. Flood Disaster Protection Act. This act requires all lenders to ascertain before loan closing whether real estate securing a mortgage is located within a designated flood hazard area. If so located, this fact must be disclosed to a borrower before closing. A borrower then must obtain flood

insurance from the National Flood Insurance Administration and the flood insurance policy should remain in the loan file.

2. Real Estate Settlement Procedures Act. This act, known as RESPA, was originally enacted in 1974 and extensively amended in 1976. The act requires mortgage lenders to provide mortgage borrowers with advance disclosures regarding loan settlement costs and charges, as well as information regarding the settlement itself—the latter to be found in a booklet prepared by HUD. Limits were also set on the amount of real estate tax and insurance escrows required by a lender. The 1976 amendments require mortgage lenders to supply both a "good faith estimate of settlement costs" and the HUD booklet within three business days after the loan application is received. The amendment also requires the use of a document prepared by HUD, the complex Uniform Settlement Statement (HUD-1), at closing.

3. Equal Credit Opportunity Act. This act, known as ECOA or Regulation B, was originally enacted in 1974 and then extensively amended in 1976. This act further extended the original Consumer Protection Act of 1968. The law, as it applies today, prohibits discrimination based on age, sex, race, marital status, receipt of public assistance, color, religion, national origin, and good faith reliance on any consumer protection legislation.

Home Mortgage Disclosure Act and Community Reinvestment Act

In 1975, Congress attempted to address the "redlining" issue with this act. Redlining is the policy of a financial institution of not lending in a certain geographical area because of a perceived increase in risk due to the racial make-up of the area or other factors.

- Home Mortgage Disclosure Act. This act requires all mortgage lenders to make disclosures regarding the geographical distribution of loans within a standard metropolitan statistical area. These disclosures must be available for any interested group to review and, at least once each year, the mortgage lender must notify depositors of this information.

- Community Reinvestment Act. This act, effective in 1979 and amended in 1988, requires regulated financial institutions (but not credit unions) to meet their communities' need for credit for low- and moderate-income neighborhoods "consistent with safe and sound operation" of the institution. In order to accomplish this, an institution must define its community, publish a CRA statement listing the types of credit available to the community, and, finally, maintain a public file for inspection of written comments in regard to the institution's CRA statement.

Other consumer protection acts of lesser impact include the Fair Debt Collection Practices Act and the Right to Financial Privacy Act.

The government's role in the management of the nation's economy in general, and mortgage lending in particular, is one that has been analyzed and debated many times—and undoubtedly will continue to be in the future. There seems to be little argument that government, regardless of whether it is federal, state, or local, has an obligation to its citizens to provide adequate shelter for all—even if they cannot afford it themselves. There are many arguments, though, regarding how to provide this basic necessity. Over the past decade, the federal government tried helping people in need of shelter in a variety of ways, first by providing rent assistance, then mortgage assistance so people could purchase rather than rent, and, finally, by returning to subsidizing rent payments.

Recently, some commentators have suggested that excessive governmental interference has resulted in fewer families being able to afford the average-priced home. That may be true, but most governmental laws and regulations have had a commendable impact on real estate and mortgage lending. The Interstate Land Sales Full Disclosure Act (1968), which helped to prevent fraudulent land sales, is an obvious example. Many of these new laws and regulations were necessitated by excesses and failures on the part of the lending community. The contribution of some of these laws cannot be overstated. In fact, one governmental creation, the Federal Housing Administration, has provided the framework for a modern, vibrant mortgage lending system that has made this the best-housed nation in the world. Following is a listing of the more important federal legislative acts impacting mortgage lending.

> 1913—*Federal Reserve Act.* Established the Federal Reserve System and authorized federally chartered commercial banks to make real estate loans.
>
> 1916—*Federal Farm Loan Act.* Provided for the formation of Federal Land Bank Associations as units of the Federal Land Bank System which was given authority to generate funds for loans to farmers by the sale of bonds.
>
> 1932—*Reconstruction Finance Act.* Created the Reconstruction Finance Corporation which was designed, among other things, to provide liquidity to commercial banks.
>
> 1932—*Federal Home Loan Bank Act.* Established the Federal Home Loan Bank Board and 12 regional banks to provide central credit facilities for home finance institutions which were members of the FHLB.
>
> 1932—*Home Owners Loan Act.* This act produced two results: (1) created the Home Owners Loan Corporation with authority to purchase defaulted home mortgages and to refinance as many as prudently feasible; (2) provided the basic lending authority for federally chartered savings and loan associations.

1934—*National Housing Act.* Authorized the creation of the Federal Housing Administration and Federal Savings and Loan Insurance Corporation.

1938—*National Mortgage Association of Washington.* This governmental agency, soon renamed Federal National Mortgage Association, was authorized to provide secondary mortgage market support for FHA mortgages.

1944—*Servicemen's Readjustment Act.* Established within the Veterans Administration a mortgage guarantee program for qualified veterans.

1949—*Housing Act.* Stated that the national housing goal was to provide "...a decent home and suitable living environment for every American family." Consolidated past lending programs of the Farmers Home Administration.

1961—*Consolidated Farmers Home Administration Act.* Extended authority for the agency to make mortgage loans to non-farmers in rural areas.

1965—*Housing and Urban Development Act.* Consolidated many federal housing agencies into a new Department of Housing and Urban Development with expanded authority.

1966—*Interest Rate Adjustment Act.* Authorized the setting of maximum savings rates and the creation of a differential between the savings rates of commercial banks and thrift institutions.

1968—*Fair Housing Act.* Prohibited discrimination in real estate sales and mortgage lending based on race, color, national origin, and religion.

1968—*Interstate Land Sales Full Disclosure Act.* Required complete and full disclosure of all facts regarding interstate sale of real estate.

1968—*Consumer Credit Protection Act.* Contained Title I, better known as Truth-in-Lending, which authorized the Federal Reserve Board to formulate regulations (Reg Z) requiring advanced disclosure of the amount and type of finance charge and a calculation of the annual percentage rate. Title VI, better known as the Fair Credit Reporting Act, established disclosure requirements, regarding the nature of credit information used in determining whether to grant a loan.

1968—*Housing and Urban Development Act.* This act put the existing Federal National Mortgage Association in private hands and authorized it to continue secondary mortgage market support. The act created a new governmental agency, the Government National Mortgage Association, and authorized it to continue the FNMA special assistance function and guarantee mortgage-backed securities.

1969—*National Environmental Policy Act.* Required the preparation of an Environmental Impact Statement for the Council on Environmental Quality in order to determine the environmental impact of real estate development.

1970—*Emergency Home Finance Act.* Created a new secondary mortgage market participant, the Federal Home Loan Mortgage Corporation, which had as its stated objective providing secondary mortgage support for conventional mortgages originated by thrift institutions. The act also gave FNMA authority to purchase conventional mortgages in addition to FHA/VA.

1974—*Flood Disaster Protection Act.* Effective in 1975, mortgage loans could not be made in a flood hazard area unless flood insurance had been purchased.

1974—*Real Estate Settlement Procedures Act* (RESPA) (as amended in 1976). This act as amended required mortgage lenders to provide mortgage borrowers with an advance disclosure of loan settlement costs and charges. Further, this act prohibited kickbacks to any person for referring business. The 1976 amendment required lenders to provide applicants with a Good Faith Estimate of Settlement Costs and a HUD booklet. A Uniform Settlement Statement (HUD-1) must be furnished to the borrower before or at the settlement.

1974—*Equal Credit Opportunity Act* (ECOA) (as amended in 1976). This act as amended prohibited discrimination in lending on the basis of sex, marital status, age, race, color, national origin, religion, good faith reliance on consumer protection laws, or the fact that a borrower receives public assistance. In addition, if an application is rejected, the borrower must be notified within 30 days of the reason for rejection.

1975—*Home Mortgage Disclosure Act.* This act required disclosure, in order to prevent redlining, of geographic distribution of loans in standard metropolitan statistical areas.

1976—RESPA amendments (see 1974).

1976—ECOA amendments (see 1974).

1978—*Fair Lending Practices Regulations.* These FHLB regulations required members to develop written underwriting standards, keep a loan registry, not deny loans because of age of dwelling or condition of neighborhood, and to direct advertising to all segments of the community.

1978—*Community Reinvestment Act.* This act required FSLIC-insured institutions to adopt a community reinvestment statement which delineates the community in which they will invest; maintain a public comment file; and post a CRA notice.

1979—*Housing and Community Development Amendments.* This legislation exempted FHA-insured mortgages from state and local usury ceilings. (Other concurrent legislation exempted VA and conventional mortgages.)

1980—*Depository Institutions Deregulation and Monetary Control Act.* Congress extended the savings interest rate control and thrift institution's ¼ of 1 percent differential for six years. The act also extended the federal override of state usury ceilings on certain mortgages. Other changes included: simplified truth-in-lending standards, eased lending restrictions, including geographical limitations, loan-to-value ratios, and treatment of one-family loans exceeding specified dollar amounts.

1980—*Omnibus Reconciliation Act.* Limited the issuance of tax-exempt housing mortgage revenue bonds.

1982—*Garn–St. Germain Depository Institutions Act.* Preempted state due-on-sale loan restrictions; mandated phase-out of interest rate differential by 1/1/84; provided FSLIC and FDIC assistance for institutions with deficient net worth; and allowed S&Ls to make consumer, commercial, and agricultural loans.

1984—*Deficit Reduction Act.* Extended the tax exemption for qualified mortgage subsidy bonds; created new reporting procedures for mortgage interest.

1986—*Tax Reform Act.* Reduced top corporate tax rate from 46% to 34%; reduced taxable income bad debt deduction from 40% to 8%; provided for three-year carrybacks and 15-year carryforwards for savings institution net operating losses.

1987—*Competitive Equality Banking Act.* Set the FSLIC $10.8 billion recapitalization in motion, kept intact Savings Bank Life Insurance, and gave thrifts flexibility to form different types of holding companies.

1989—*Financial Institutions Reform, Recovery and Enforcement Act (FIRREA).* Restructured the regulatory framework by eliminating FHLBB, FSLIC, and FADA; created the Office of Thrift Supervision (OTS) under the Treasury Department; enhanced FDIC to supervise safety and soundness of financial institutions, the Savings Institutions Insurance Fund, and the Bank Insurance Fund; created the Resolution Trust Corporation (RTC) to dispose of failed savings and loans; established new capital standards for thrifts.

RECENT MORTGAGE LENDING

The most productive boom in real estate construction and financing in the United States has occurred during the past 50 years. More housing units and other types of buildings have been constructed during this period than in all the years since this country was founded. Much of the credit for this boom can be attached to the availability of capital at a reasonable rate and the corresponding creation of the secondary mortgage market. For example, FNMA was given expanded purchasing authority in 1970, and was joined by the Federal Home Loan Mortgage Corporation (FHLMC) in that year to provide secondary market facilities for conventional mortgages originated by savings and loan institutions. While the housing boom changed the landscape of the American countryside, new office buildings, apartment complexes, and shopping centers provided the amenities and services needed by the families in these new homes.

In the 1970s, providing or stimulating housing for low- and moderate-income families was not the exclusive province of government at the federal level. Before 1960, the state of New York had the only state housing agency, but by 1975 nearly all states had some type of housing agency. Although some states have used tax-exempt bonds to raise revenue to lend to home buyers at below-market interest rates, many have fulfilled their social responsibility by providing financing for multi-family units.

During the 1970s, the rapid growth and equally rapid decline of a new mortgage lender—the real estate investment trust, or REIT—occurred. Authorized by a 1960 amendment to the tax laws, REITs were originally designed to provide a type of mutual fund interest or equity ownership in real estate for the investing public. By purchasing a share of stock, a shareholder had an interest in a trust that owned and managed real estate. A combination of inexperienced management, poor underwriting of loans, the oil embargo, a recession, and the unforeseeable dramatic increase in the prime interest rate brought disaster to the REITs. Most short-term trusts charged an interest rate that floated from 3 to 5 percent above the prime rate. The increase in the prime rate to 12 percent in 1974 forced many builder/developers into default, since few projects could carry an interest rate of 17 percent. The result was massive foreclosures and losses to REITs. Although only a few trusts became bankrupt, most had substantial portions of their assets in an interest non-accrual category for a period of time. Most REITs will probably survive past reversals, but the public's confidence in them may have been shattered by the spectacular drop in REIT share prices.

1980s—THE DECADE OF HISTORIC CHANGE

The decade of the 1980s will be remembered as the decade when the economy went through startling changes and, as a result, changed residential mortgage lending and mortgage lenders. This period witnessed positive developments such as the rapid growth of mortgage-backed securities, the evolution of alternative mortgage instruments, and, in general, more sources of needed capital. All of these positive developments, combined with much lower interest rates, produced historic 1-4 family originations in 1986 and 1987 which total over $440 billion each year. However, the decade also witnessed double-digit inflation, a major recession, a record for the stock market, and then a crash exceeding that of 1929. The decade ended with the near total collapse of the savings and loan industry and the related taxpayer bailout of the Federal Savings and Loan Insurance Corporation (FSLIC).

All of these events produced drastic changes for the nation's economy in general and for mortgage lending in particular.

The 1980s began with the nation's economy clearly out of control. The Federal Reserve, responsible for managing and regulating interest rates and monetary supply, was forced in the fall of 1979 to bring about some order to the economy. Its fundamental decision was to stop attempting to regulate short-term interest rates, and instead, to exercise control over growth in the money supply. The theory was that control of the money supply would help reduce inflation, and that this in turn would decrease upward pressure on interest rates as investors decreased their need for inflation protection.

The immediate result of this action was sharply higher interest rates. The most visible rate, the so-called prime rate, peaked at 21½ percent in 1981. Interest rates did come down fairly rapidly after that peak, partially as a result of the Federal Reserve action but primarily because of a serious recession which followed this action. The recession which followed, the worst since the Great Depression, resulted in unemployment reaching over 10 percent.

This recession and the action of the Federal Reserve deflated the inflation balloon to the point where inflation in the mid-1980s fell to about 1 percent per year before turning up at the end of the decade. As a reaction to control over inflation, the prime interest rate dropped sharply to 7½ percent by the spring of 1987 before turning up slightly. In 1986 interest rates on 30-year home mortgages fell below 10 percent for the first time in the 1980s and as a result 1–4 family mortgage originations totalled $442 billion for that year. That was a staggering $200 billion increase over the record totals of the previous year.

Crash of '87

With inflation under control and interest rates declining, the stock market rocketed to levels only dreamed of by the most optimistic of market watchers. On August 25, 1987 the Dow Jones industrial average hit a record of 2722, and some market watchers were calling for 3000 by the end of the year.

What happened instead was a crash that exceeded (in points, but not percent) the 1929 crash. On October 19, 1987 Wall Street was shocked by a 508-point drop in the Dow Jones industrial average. A week later the market dropped another 175. The sound heard around the world was the hard landing of other stock exchanges as they followed the lead of Wall Street.

The reasons for the crash of '87 are many and varied, but the two principal ones are that the market was simply over-valued and that investors in the United States and abroad had lost faith in the ability of the United States government to control its huge deficits. The federal deficits for the second half of the 1980s averaged approximately $150 billion a year. These huge deficits have turned the United States into the world's largest debtor nation, owing hundreds of billions of dollars to foreigners. With interest payments rising faster and faster it is projected that the amount owed to foreigners could place a severe strain on the entire United States economy in the 1990s.

The obvious result of deficits of such magnitude is that the economy of the United States becomes hostage to the willingness of foreign investors to finance our deficits. This dependence must result in the long run with a lower standard of living in the United States. An important barometer of the economic health is the value foreign investors and governments place on the currency of a country. During the early 1990s the value of the dollar continued to erode, reaching the lowest levels since the end of World War II. This decline in the value of the dollar was viewed in two ways. In a positive manner, it would help shrink the large trade imbalance existing in our foreign trade by making products produced in the United States more competitive in foreign markets. Looked at negatively, it probably would increase inflation in this country because foreign goods will become more expensive.

The impact of the crash of '87 and the 1990–1991 recession chilled the home purchasing plans of many Americans. The impact of this on mortgage lenders is that the record originations of 1986 and 1987 will probably not be duplicated for a few years.

Deregulation of Financial Institutions

During the 1970s, the topic of deregulation of financial institutions was extensively debated within the executive and legislative branches of the federal government as well as among the representatives of the various financial institutions. The resulting Hunt Commission reached some conclusions and made recommendations, but the actual beginning of deregulation was marked by the passage in 1980 of the Depository Institutions Deregulation and Monetary Control Act (DIDMCA). One of the driving forces behind the passage of the DIDMCA was a Congressional desire to help the faltering savings and loan industry.

Immediately after the passage of DIDMCA, a committee was established to control interest rates at financial institutions. One of its first acts was to set a date (January, 1986) when all limits on interest rates on savings would be eliminated. The consumers benefited from this action, but it resulted in a higher cost of funds to lending institutions and, in some situations, a decrease in profits.

Some commentators have concluded that the failure of hundreds of savings and loans in the 1980s was the direct result of deregulation. They believe that the loosening of the reins of regulation, without a corresponding increase in supervision, allowed many savings and loans to engage in high-risk mortgage lending for which they had no competency. Whether deregulation of the financial institutions was the proximate cause of the failure of the savings and loan industry as has been suggested is open to debate, but deregulation and the changes that followed have changed financial institutions and the way they engage in mortgage lending.

FIRREA

By 1988, the problems of the savings and loan industry, which had been festering since the late 1970s, reached a climax. Many of the savings and loans in the 1980s were characterized by speculative lending, negative earnings, low capital, and poor management. These problems eventually culminated in the failure of many savings and loans and the insolvency of the Federal Savings and Loan Insurance Corporation (FSLIC)—the deposit insurance fund for savings and loan associations.

The failure of FSLIC precipitated a massive federal bailout of the insurance fund and the closing of hundreds of failed savings and loans. The 1989 law which mandated these changes was called the Financial Institutions Reform, Recovery, and Enforcement Act (FIRREA). The cost of this federal bailout is projected to be as high as $400–500 billion over the life of the bonds sold to finance the bailout.

The 1990s

The 1990s began with a recession that purged much of the spending excesses of the 1980s from the United States economy. This change in attitude toward spending combined with the restored faith in the country after the smashing success of Desert Storm may produce an environment for increased real estate activity and thus mortgage lending, which has been missing since the boom years of 1986–1987. Many of the disappointed potential home buyers of the 1980s may be able to start the mortgage lending ball rolling again in the early 1990s as interest rates begin to dip to their lowest level in a decade and home prices drop for the first time in years.

THE ROLE OF MORTGAGE LENDING IN THE ECONOMY

2

The importance of housing, and therefore mortgage lending, to the nation's economic health is unquestionable. The sharp drop in housing construction in 1989 and 1990 certainly contributed to the recession experienced in that time frame. Many economic commentators contend that housing construction and all of the related activities such as sales, financing, furnishings, among others are the engine of the economy of the United States.

The National Association of Home Builders estimates that housing construction, sales, and financing accounts for one out of every twelve jobs in the United States. The Home Builders calculates that economic impact of the construction of 1,000 single-family houses creates nearly 1,800 man-years of employment and over $60 million in wages.

Housing drives economic growth by the multiplier effect that results from construction and financing. It is generally assumed that housing generates about $4 in Gross National Product (GNP) for every $1 of activity. The Home Builders expands the economic impact this way: "...The servicing of housing in place—broadly defined to include brokerage services, rental housing management, mortgage lending and servicing, and repair and maintenance services—contributes another 7 percent to GNP."

This economic impact is derived from the fact that the wages earned by home builders are spent on food, clothing, cars, furniture, schooling, and taxes in addition to many other products and services. Obviously, the ripple effect of a healthy home building industry stimulates the entire economy. And there can not be a healthy home building industry without mortgage lending.

Mortgage lending, in addition to being an important part of our nation's economy, also allows for the fulfillment of certain sociological demands, principal among them being the attainment of the "American Dream"—owning one's own home. Those who reach this status in life have a more substantial stock in their community and our nation's society, with many resulting benefits.

Another positive result of the mortgage lending process is that it provides a means whereby an attractive return on savings can be generated for those individuals who are in the savings cycle of their lives.

Mortgage lending could not fulfill these functions without many and varied types of mortgage lenders. These lenders are discussed in detail in Chapter 3.

A VAILABILITY OF CREDIT

The health of the home building industry and mortgage lending is determined by the availability of credit for home buyers and by its cost. It is estimated that mortgage lending will require over $400 billion a year from the capital markets in the 1990s in order to meet the projected housing demands. This chapter examines how this money for mortgage lending is created and then made available to home buyers.

The common requisite for all residential mortgage lenders is the accumulation of sufficient savings to produce the capital needed for mortgage loans. Unless financial intermediaries have access to sufficient savings, capital shortages result and credit restraints occur that affect all mortgage lenders, often with disastrous results. This was the situation in 1973–74 and 1979–89 when housing starts and resales dropped dramatically. Secondary mortgage markets can assist during these periods of credit restraint but cannot solve the basic problem of a lack of savings inflow to mortgage lenders. On the other hand, the dramatic fall-off in housing starts in 1989–1991 was not the result of a shortage of capital but a drop in consumer confidence because of the war and recession.

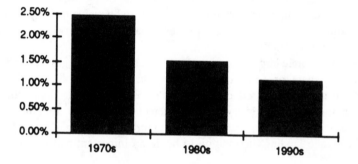

Annual rate of household growth

Capital Formation

The funds required for capital formation are derived primarily from the savings of individuals and businesses. This process of capital formation produces most of the capital used by various segments of our economy. Business savings are defined as retained earnings and capital consumption allowances. They exceed personal savings by a substantial amount. However, the savings generated by individuals, either as deposits at financial institutions or as reserves that accumulate in whole life insurance policies, account for approximately 90 percent of funds for residential mortgage lending.

Savings

The importance of savings to residential mortgage lending cannot be over-emphasized. Since the end of World War II, the national personal savings rate has ranged from a low of about 3 percent to a high of about 9 percent and has (except for brief periods of disintermediation) permitted borrowers to obtain needed funds at reasonable rates. Through this process, the percentage of Americans who own the home they live in reached an all-time high of 65 percent in the early 1980s. This has since slipped to about 63 percent.

Savings inflows are not constant, and the savings function must compete with food, shelter, clothing, transportation, recreation, and other real or perceived demands for an individual's after-tax income. Those who do save are motivated by such needs and desires as accumulating funds for retirement, future security, major purchases, or a college education.

In recent years the percentage of disposable income the American public has put into savings has decreased alarmingly. The reasons for this decline include the

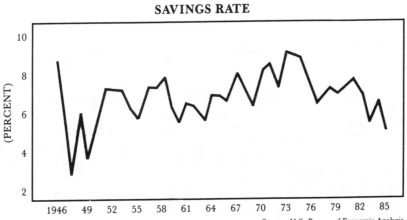

SAVINGS RATE

(PERCENT)

Source: U.S. Bureau of Economic Analysis

relatively low interest paid on passbook savings in past years, as well as the fact that the interest received was subject to federal, state, and (in some situations) city income taxes. During the high inflation period of the late 1970s and early 1980s, many sophisticated individuals realized it was more prudent to borrow and pay back the loans later with deflated dollars rather than save. That attitude over a period of time led to an actual negative savings flow at thrift institutions in 1981–82.

Of course, it must be recognized that today's society offers fewer reasons for some to save. Many individuals rely on pensions or social security to provide for retirement, or believe they need no further savings because inflation has dramatically increased the equity in their home. After the crash of '87, savings did turn up, but the rate is still insufficient.

Changes in the economy directly affect savings in many ways. For example, if the business cycle is down and unemployment increases, individuals may increase savings because of uncertainty over their employment. The result could be a savings inflow which theoretically should cause interest rates to decline as more dollars chase less demand. On the other hand, with a downturn in the business cycle and an increase in unemployment, those who are unemployed may have to withdraw savings for living expenses. If the economy is expanding, savings may also accumulate, since the demand for funds could reach a point where high interest rates attract more savings.

For a period of time, depository institutions could not attract savings during periods of high interest because limits were placed on the amount of interest that could be paid to savers. This is no longer a problem since all limits on savings have been deregulated and now move with the market. This change in itself will have a major impact on future availability of funds for residential mortgage lending.

MORTGAGE MARKETS

In our economy, the total financial market consists of the capital market and the money market. These two markets compete with each other for funds. The basic difference between the two markets is the maturity of the financial instruments. Money market instruments (U.S. treasury bills, corporate commercial paper, etc.) mature in less than one year. The mortgage market is only a part of the complete capital market. Within the capital market, a specific demand for funds (e.g., mortgages) must compete with other instruments, such as corporate bonds. The competition is determined by the price a user of funds is willing to pay. The price of money is stated as the interest rate.

In today's economic environment, the demand for credit is derived from four major areas:

1. business loans
2. mortgage loans
3. consumer loans
4. government borrowing

Business loans are always needed for financing inventory, accounts receivable, plant expansion and modernization, and occasionally for research and development. The magnitude of business loan demand is normally tied to the business cycle. Consumer loans are also impacted by the business cycle and employment. These loans are used to purchase automobiles, furniture, clothing, and other durable and nondurable goods. Finally, all levels of government have experienced insatiable appetites for borrowed funds in recent years. These have been used primarily to finance the federal government's deficits, in addition to other local needs such as mortgage revenue bonds. Mortgages are competing for the same funds at the same time as the users of credit (see page 30 for more detail).

GROWTH IN SELECTED TYPES OF CREDIT
(In Billions of Dollars)

Type of Credit	1960	1989	Increase
Total credit outstanding	$779	$12,406	$11,627
Residential mortgage debt			
1–4 family mortgage debt	142	2,384	2,242
apartments	20	306	286
total	162	2,690	2,528
Corporate and foreign bonds	90	1,550	1,469
State and local government debt	71	558	517
Consumer debt	65	790	725
Commercial mortgages	32	745	713
Federal debt	243	3,567	3,324

Source: Federal Reserve Board

INTEREST RATES

If the composite demand for available funds is high, the price for these funds (the interest rate) will probably be high as well. Therefore, the price of money is subject to supply and demand like any other commodity. For example, if those who are demanding funds for mortgages are willing to pay the price for the funds, credit will be made available. But if business demand is also high and businesses are willing to pay a price equal to that offered by mortgages, funds will generally flow to bonds to the detriment of mortgage lending.

The explanation for this relative attractiveness of corporate capital instrument lies in the unique characteristics of mortgage debt. Mortgage debt requires a higher yield because of the longer maturity, lack of uniformity in mortgages, lower liquidity, and the problems and delays of foreclosure. Although inflation and demand and supply of funds are most important factors in the rise and fall of interest rates, the degree of risk inherent in a mortgage loan or a bond offering also is influential. Of course, if the other major consumers of capital—the various levels of government—are also active in the capital markets, they will take all they need. More about that later.

COUNTERCYCLICAL NATURE OF REAL ESTATE

During periods of high demand for credit (normally the apex of a business cycle), the capital markets are usually unable to satisfy the combined demands for credit of individuals, government, and business. Mortgage lending usually suffers during such periods because the price of money, as indicated by the interest rate, is too high for most home buyers to qualify for a mortgage. In some situations mortgage interest rates may even be forced up against a state's usury ceiling, if one exists. Because real estate in general and mortgage lending in particular are the losers in a credit crunch, they have often been classified as countercyclical. This means that real estate activity, and consequently mortgage lending, usually expands when the general business cycle is down and credit demand is low. The result of this situation is lower interest rates which allows more borrowers to qualify for a mortgage. Conversely, as the economy begins to improve and demand for credit from other users increases, real estate activity begins to slow down as interest rates increase. This somewhat simplified explanation demonstrates the direct relationship between the availability of credit and real estate activity.

FINANCIAL INTERMEDIARIES

The more modern, and clearly more descriptive term, *financial intermediaries* describes that classification of economic units that previously were called financial institutions. The principal economic function of financial intermediaries is to serve as the middleman, the intermediary, between the saver and the borrower. Both saver and borrower benefit from this arrangement. The saver, as will be explained, is able to earn a higher return on savings, while the borrower can obtain needed funds at a more reasonable rate. The term financial intermediaries includes these major economic units, among others:

- commercial banks
- savings and loan institutions
- life insurance companies
- savings banks
- finance companies
- investment companies
- credit unions
- pension funds
- money market funds
- stockbrokers

Financial intermediaries are essential to the entire economy but are especially crucial to mortgage lending, since they lend practically all of the funds required by home buyers, and those funds are accumulated almost exclusively from individual savers. The characteristics of these lenders will be examined later, but let us first examine how savers benefit from using these intermediaries.

Many of the benefits to savers are obvious, such as higher yield, safety, and diversification. Others, such as economies of scale, variety of maturities, and specialization, are not. Higher yields result from the increased level of knowledge and experience intermediaries have over the average saver. The experts know where, how, and when to make safe, profitable investments. Safety is derived both from federal deposit insurance and from the informed investment decisions of the experts. Diversification is also an element of safety that for a smaller saver can only be reached, without sacrificing yield, by the use of an intermediary.

The cost to a mortgage borrower in need of a large loan is made lower by dealing with an intermediary. Instead of having to solicit many savers for funds, this mortgage borrower need only deal with one financial intermediary which has been able to pool the funds of many savers. The benefit to savers in this arrangement is a higher yield since a part of the saved cost of borrowing can be passed on to them while a borrower will also benefit from this economy of scale. Each saver has different objectives in mind for savings deposited. Since financial intermediaries can also lend to borrowers with differing needs and for differing maturities, the match is beneficial to both parties. Finally, since many financial intermediaries specialize in a selective type of lending, they can provide that type of lending more cheaply than competitors, with a resulting benefit to both saver and borrower. An example of this type of specialization is thrift institutions and single-family mortgage lending.

Gross Profit Spread

Financial intermediaries are able to fulfill their important economic function by operating on a spread between their cost of funds (generally the interest on savings of individuals) and their portfolio yield (the interest earned on loans outstanding). As a general rule, savings institutions require a gross profit spread of from 2 or 3 percent (200 or 300 basis points). Credit unions, on the other hand, may require 3 or 4 percent since they don't have the benefit of economies of scale. As an example, if the average interest rate paid by a savings bank on all savings deposits is 8 percent, the average portfolio yield would need to be between 10 and 11 percent for that institution to be profitable.

The primary economic danger to financial intermediaries that are portfolio lenders, like credit unions and some savings institutions, is that interest rates will begin a rapid increase. The financial institution would have to match the rising rates on savings deposits in order to retain its deposits. It could then lend these funds out at what should be an increased mortgage rate. The problem is that even with the increased interest rate on current mortgage production, the entire mortgage portfolio may not have a sufficient yield to generate a profitable spread. Thus, even though an institution is currently lending 200 to 300 basis points above its cost of funds, the portfolio yield may not be sufficient for a profitable spread; in fact, it may even be negative, as it was for savings institutions during the high interest rate period of 1981–83.

PUBLIC DEBT VERSUS PRIVATE DEBT

When any government—federal, state, or local—spends more money than it collects, it must borrow in the same markets in which other users of credit borrow. This includes issuers of corporate bonds and home buyers. In this manner government competes with other users of credit for the limited capital available. The federal government in particular has been in a severe deficit position recently, a condition which many economists believe was the basic cause of the persistent inflation of the late 1970s and early 1980s. This inflation and the continuing credit demands of the federal government resulted in high interest rates which played

FEDERAL DEBT AS A PERCENT OF GNP 1981–1988

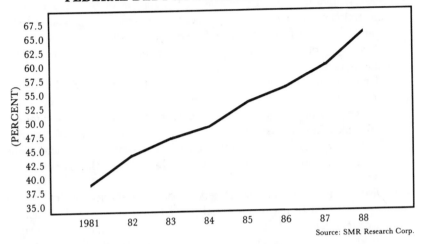

Source: SMR Research Corp.

havoc in both the money markets and the capital markets. As a result, all users of credit suffered during this period.

The reason why the federal government's borrowing has such a negative impact on other borrowers is that the federal government will always get as much money as it needs because of its unquestioned credit. Therefore, unless available credit is expanding at a rate which allows for the accommodation of all users of credit, excessive federal borrowing will have a crowding-out effect on less credit-worthy borrowers.

As bad as the deficits of the 1970s and 1980s were, they pale in comparison to the projected deficits of the 1990s. An example of the magnitude of this problem in the past is the $200 billion deficit for 1983 which exceeded the total residential mortgage originations for that year. The deficits for the early 1990s apparently will be in the range of $150–200 billion per year. Excessive federal deficits require massive borrowing, and the result is usually higher rates that have a negative impact on all borrowers, especially home buyers.

Many times the fiscal policy of the federal government forces the Federal Reserve to act in an attempt to moderate the impact of federal borrowing on the nation's economy.

Federal Reserve

In addition to its banking functions, the Federal Reserve has credit control responsibility over the nation's economy through financial institutions. The Federal Reserve has several methods of implementing this control:

- Reserve requirements. By increasing the amount of money a member institution must have in its reserve account, less money is available to be loaned. Conversely, if the Federal Reserve policy is to increase the amount of money in order to make credit easier to obtain, it can lower the reserve requirement.
- Open-market operations. This commonly used method allows the Federal Reserve to decrease the supply of money by selling treasury securities on the open market. The securities are paid for by checks drawn on commercial banks. This decreases their reserves, therefore reducing the amount of funds which can be loaned. If the Federal Reserve intends to increase the supply of money, it will buy the securities by issuing a check drawn upon itself.
- Discount rate. The Federal Reserve operates a service of discounting (paying less than par) commercial paper from member institutions. By discounting, the Federal Reserve provides funds which can be loaned. If the discount rate (considered to be the interest rate that a member institution pays the Federal Reserve) is increased, it becomes more difficult for an institution to borrow to obtain necessary reserves. Consequently, the interest rate a member institution must then charge a borrower increases. If the discount rate is lowered, borrowing is easier for a financial institution and the interest rate charged to a borrower could be lowered.

MORTGAGE LENDERS AND THE PRIMARY MORTGAGE MARKET

The primary economic function of a residential mortgage lender is to lend money for the purchase or refinancing of residences of all types in the primary mortgage market. This would include single-family detached, condominiums, and cooperative housing. These loans are secured by either a first or second mortgage. The primary mortgage market is that market where funds are loaned directly to a borrower. This market is contrasted with the secondary mortgage market where mortgages originated in the primary market are bought and sold. The secondary mortgage market will be discussed in detail in Chapter 10.

Those financial intermediaries which are usually involved in the residential primary mortgage market include:

- savings and loan institutions
- mortgage bankers
- mortgage brokers
- commercial banks
- savings banks
- credit unions

These mortgage lenders, along with a few nontraditional mortgage lenders (such as Sears and GMAC), originate nearly all residential mortgage loans each year. Some of these mortgage lenders also hold mortgages in their own portfolio. Others, such as mortgage bankers, sell all of their originations. Some of these same lenders are also very active in commercial mortgage lending. These lenders obtain the money for mortgage loans form the following sources:

- funds deposited by savers
- funds borrowed from other financial intermediaries
- sale of commercial paper
- proceeds from the sale of mortgages or mortgage-backed securities

Normally, all of the residential mortgage lenders are active on a day-to-day basis in the primary market but during some stages of the economic cycle one or more may temporarily drop out. When this occurs it is usually because of lack of funds to lend. By bringing together borrowers and savers from different economic sectors and geographic locations, mortgage lenders as financial intermediaries contribute to a more efficient allocation of the economy's resources. All of the mortgage lenders will be discussed individually in detail in Chapter 4.

MORTGAGE INVESTORS

In addition to those mortgage lenders which hold mortgage debt in their own portfolio, a number of other financial institutions are important holders of mortgage debt. These only hold debt; they do not originate any loans. Classified as mortgage investors, they include the following:

- Federal National Mortgage Association (Fannie Mae)
- Federal Home Loan Mortgage Corporation (Freddie Mac)
- retirement and pension funds
- federal agencies
- state housing agencies
- life insurance companies
- individuals

These investors acquire the mortgages they hold either directly from the mortgage lenders that originated them or through the operation of the secondary mortgage market. For a discussion of the secondary mortgage market, see Chapter 10.

TRENDS IN MORTGAGE LENDING

More changes in residential mortgage lending are occurring today than at any other time since the 1930s. These changes affect:

- who the lenders are in the primary market
- how funds for mortgages are generated
- how interest rates are calculated
- how mortgages are sold
- how mortgages are serviced
- how borrowers are qualified
- who the mortgage investors are

Some of these changes are discussed in this text. Others, such as who the lenders of tomorrow will be, are beyond the scope of a text of this type. The most meaningful changes over the past ten years include the following:

- the massive failures of thrift institutions
- the widespread use of mortgage-backed securities to access the capital markets for additional funds for residential loans
- the adoption of alternative mortgage instruments by financial intermediaries to spread the risk of mortgage lending

These subjects are discussed in detail in later chapters.

THE MORTGAGE LENDERS

3

The objective of this chapter is to examine those financial intermediaries, the mortgage lenders, that originate mortgage loans in the primary mortgage market. Care should be taken to understand that originators of mortgage debt are not necessarily holders of mortgage debt. Some mortgage lenders, such as credit unions, hold in their portfolio most of the mortgage debt they originate. On the other hand, mortgage bankers sell all of the loans they originate.

The term financial intermediary is applied to all of these mortgage lenders even though not all are depository institutions. Mortgage bankers, for example, do not take deposits, but instead borrow for their mortgage lending activities from other financial institutions, or they acquire funds for lending by the sale of commercial paper.

Before the Great Depression, individuals were the largest classification of holders of residential debt. Although individuals still hold billions of dollars of residential debt, this chapter will focus on a discussion of the major residential lenders in order of their origination volume, starting with savings and loan institutions.

HOLDERS OF 1–4 FAMILY MORTGAGE DEBT BY LENDER
(In Billions of Dollars)

	Savings & loans	Savings banks	Commercial banks	Federal agencies	All others	Total
1980	$411.0	67.5	160.4	183.2	144.0	965.1
1985	485.8	75.9	213.4	492.5	233.8	1,501.4
1987	505.6	94.1	276.3	825.8	257.8	1,959.6
1989	557.7	117.5	359.2	1,044.8	304.8	2,384.0

SAVINGS AND LOAN INSTITUTIONS (S&Ls) _____

The historical role of savings and loan institutions in the nation's economy is the pooling of savings of individuals for investment primarily in residential mortgages. This major type of financial intermediary is still fulfilling that role even though S&Ls have had great difficulty over the past five or so years. In 1989, for example, S&Ls helped finance nearly 1,500,000 one- to four-family homes.

Although the name may be different in some states (e.g., homestead associations, building and loan, cooperatives, etc.), their role remains the same. S&Ls operate in all 50 states and number approximately 2,000 (with about 20,000 branches) employing 400,000 people at the end of 1990. This number has decreased rapidly over the previous ten years from about 4,100 as the savings and loan crises and the resulting federal bailout closed many failed S&Ls.

S&Ls are still the largest private holder of residential mortgage debt and originate about 30–35 percent of total residential mortgage debt each year. Before the recent decrease in the number of S&Ls, this origination percent was closer to 50 percent each year.

The mortgage portfolio of S&Ls at the end of 1989 consisted of approximately $558 billion of 1–4 family mortgages, $86 billion of multi-family, and $118 billion of commercial mortgages for a total mortgage portfolio of $762 billion. At year-end 1989, the total mortgage portfolio plus mortgage-backed securities ($170 billion) equalled approximately 74 percent of assets ($1,252 billion). The percentage of 1–4 family mortgages to total mortgage debt is still a high 73 percent.

Historical Development

From the founding of the first association in 1831 (Oxford Provident Building Association in Frankfort, Pennsylvania), S&Ls have spread across the United States, providing funds for the housing growth of the nation. For example, S&Ls provided much of the institutional financing of urban homes for middle-income Americans before the 1930s. Although the largest number of S&Ls was reached in 1927 when more than 12,000 were in existence, the contribution S&Ls have made toward providing financing for housing has continued to increase since then.

The 1930s were years of dramatic change for S&Ls. More than half of those in existence failed during this decade and more than 25 percent of S&L mortgage assets were in default. In addition to the general economic depression, the major problem for S&Ls during the 1930s was a lack of liquidity. This liquidity crisis was caused by the panic of the American public following the stock market crash and the failure of some banks, precipitating a rush to withdraw savings from all financial institutions. As nonamortized, short-term mortgages came due, many creditworthy mortgagors were unable to refinance their mortgages because banks and S&Ls had no funds. Many homes were lost as a result. To help alleviate this liquidity problem, the Federal Home Loan Bank System (FHLB) was created by Congress in July, 1932. The FHLB provided liquidity during periods of credit restraint for member S&Ls and served the industry in the way that the Federal Reserve System served the needs of commercial banks. The law provided for the creation of 12 regional banks to serve each geographic area. Many of the functions of the FHLBs were stripped away with the enactment of the Financial Institutions Reform, Recovery, and Enforcement Act (FIRREA) in 1989. FIRREA is discussed further in a section to follow.

Another important step toward the development of the modern S&L occurred with the creation of the Federal Savings and Loan Insurance Corporation (FSLIC) as authorized by Title IV of the National Housing Act of 1934. This step was vital for the restoration of faith in the safety of deposits in S&Ls and paved the way for new deposits which were needed before any new mortgage loans could be made. Today, as a result of changes mandated by FIRREA, deposits in savings institutions are insured up to $100,000 by a successor to FSLIC called the Savings Association Insurance Fund (SAIF), which is a part of the Federal Deposit Insurance Corporation (FDIC).

Savings and loan associations were exempt from federal income tax until 1951. Although subject to taxation, S&Ls were able to avoid this tax by deducting up to 100 percent of taxable income through a bad-debt reserve. By 1987, most of these deductions were removed.

An Institution in Trouble

The 20 years before the enactment of FIRREA in 1989 was a period of highs and lows for S&Ls. The 1970s witnessed steady growth in total assets and profitability, but during the 1980s, the S&L industry struggled for survival and many didn't make it.

The reasons for the collapse of many S&Ls and of their insurance fund (FSLIC) with the resulting federal bailout have been debated in many forums. The experts agreed that the reasons for the collapse included the following:

- low-yielding, fixed-rate mortgages which created interest rate risk that was exacerbated by high inflation
- disintermediation which required more interest rate sensitive deposit instruments, resulting in
- increases in the cost of funds and negative earnings

These problems were addressed by the S&L industry seeking and winning federal government/regulatory approval for:

- deregulation of depository institutions
- creative accounting changes which differed from GAAP (generally accepted accounting procedures)
- approval to expand into high-yield/high-risk lending

ASSET GROWTH AT SELECTED FINANCIAL INSTITUTIONS, 1980–1990
(Assets in Billions of Dollars)

	1980	1983	1986	1989	1990
Commercial banks	$1,482	$1,884	$2,610	$3,231	$3,300*
Thrifts	785	1,013	1,380	1,516	1,500*
Credit unions	69	98	166	199	210*
Finance companies	202	264	410	518	525*
Money market mutual funds	76	179	292	338	350*

*Preliminary
Source: Flow of Funds Accounts, Federal Reserve Board

All of these changes were to occur without an increase in supervision. For a few years, these changes assisted S&Ls in improving their bottom line. But the changes proved to be the undoing of many struggling S&Ls. The Tax Reform Act of 1986 probably was the beginning of the end. This act eliminated many of the tax benefits from real estate which had made real estate an attractive investment for many. As a result of these tax law changes, builders and developers could not sell their property and many S&Ls which had financed these properties had to take them back. Earnings were once again under pressure and regulators were starting to look very carefully at earnings and loan portfolios. For example, the S&L industry lost $20 billion in 1989 alone. The last profitable year was 1986 when $132 million was earned.

The National Association of Realtors recently summed up the problem this way: "Deregulation and new investment powers made financial and managerial demands that most thrift executives had not contemplated. Speculative investments, a regulatory system which failed to exercise controls, basic mismanagement, and an unprecedented level of fraud and abuse perpetrated by many thrift executives resulted in the inevitable legislative backlash." That legislative backlash was FIRREA which is estimated will cost the American taxpayer up to $500 billion over the life of the bonds sold to finance the S&L bailout.

Organization and Regulation

Savings and loan institutions may be chartered either by a state or by the federal government and can be either mutual or stock institutions. In 1990, about an equal number were chartered by the states and by the federal government, and an equal number were stock and mutual institutions.

The enactment of FIRREA in 1989 completely changed the way S&Ls were regulated. FIRREA restructured the regulatory structure by abolishing the Federal

Home Loan Bank Board (but not the Federal Home Loan Banks) and FSLIC. FSLIC was replaced with SAIF, a part of FDIC. The FHLBB was replaced by the Office of Thrift Supervision (OTS) under the Treasury Department. FDIC was given extensive new powers to ensure the safety and soundness of financial institutions (but not credit unions) and was given the supervision of separate S&L (SAIF) and bank deposit insurance funds (BIF). Finally, this major piece of legislation created the Resolution Trust Corporation (RTC) to dispose of failed S&Ls and their assets.

S&Ls Today

Over the years, S&Ls have loaned hundreds of billions of dollars to millions of borrowers at the prevailing market rate for the purchase of homes. During the past decade as the problem at S&Ls multiplied, the share of originations has decreased. But, notwithstanding all of these problems, S&Ls are still a major source of mortgage money. The surviving institutions (probably about 1,500) will probably once again place greater emphasis upon residential mortgage lending and less on commercial lending.

Today, many S&Ls are active in the secondary mortgage market, both as buyers and as sellers. Beginning in 1987, S&Ls have been net sellers of mortgages in the secondary mortgage market. This development is significant in that it demonstrates a change in lending philosophy from one dominated by local concerns to one affected and shaped by the nation's economy. Some S&Ls have even formed mortgage banking subsidiaries to originate all types of loans for sale into the secondary mortgage market.

Because of their historical local focus and previously existing legal limitations on their lending area, many S&Ls did not become involved in either FHA-insured or VA-guaranteed mortgages. Instead, S&L deposits were invested in local conventional mortgages originated either for their own portfolio or for sale. Today, changes in the marketplace have forced S&Ls to originate all types of residential loans, including second mortgages.

In 1989, S&Ls closed $133 billion in 1-4 family loans, $30 billion in construction loans, $11 billion in apartments, and $15 billion for other real estate loans for a total mortgage lending activity of $189 billion. In addition to these loans closed, S&Ls also purchased another $41 billion of mortgages. As an example of the diversity of S&Ls, in this same year, S&Ls sold mortgages worth $107 billion.

COMMERCIAL BANKS (CBs)

Commercial banks have both the largest collective membership at about 12,500 (with 30,000 branches) and the greatest total assets ($3,300 billion in 1990) of all financial institutions. The assets of all CBs are more than twice those of all savings and loans, savings banks, and credit unions combined. CBs are second only to savings and loans in their holdings of the total outstanding mortgage debt. In 1990, CBs originated more 1-4 mortgages than any other lender replacing savings and loans as the largest lender for the first time. They are also first in origination of income-property loans and construction mortgages.

A commercial bank is a private financial institution organized to accumulate funds primarily through time- and demand-deposits and to make these funds available to finance the nation's commerce and industry. Over the past twenty years, commercial banks have expanded their real estate finance operations from mostly short-term mortgage loans to include many long-term loans.

Historical Development

Except for a one-year period following the enactment of the National Bank Act of 1863, federally chartered commercial banks were not allowed to make real estate loans until 1913. During the period from 1863 to 1913, state-chartered banks thrived since they were able to make real estate loans. Then in 1913, the Federal Reserve Act provided the authorization for federally chartered commercial banks to make mortgage loans. The typical CB mortgage loan during this early period was similar to those made by other lenders: a 50 percent loan-to-value ratio for a five-year term, with the principal payable at the end of the term and with interest payable semi-annually.

Commercial banks in the 1930s were in a position similar to that of other financial institutions—lack of liquidity—and consequently many failed. (In fact the number of commercial banks decreased during this period from more than 30,000 to about 16,000.) During the early months of President Franklin D. Roosevelt's first term, many new federal laws affecting the economy were enacted. The Federal Deposit Insurance Corporation (FDIC), authorized by the Banking Act of 1933, helped restore confidence in commercial banks and encouraged badly needed funds to flow back into bank vaults to provide liquidity for new loans. Currently, the Bank Insurance Fund (BIF), a part of FDIC, insures deposits in all commercial banks up to $100,000.

Organization and Regulation

Commercial banks are chartered either by the federal government through the comptroller of the currency, or by a state banking agency. State-chartered banks outnumber federally chartered banks by about two to one, although more assets are in the federally chartered CBs. State-chartered CBs may be members of the Federal Reserve System, but only 1,000 (10 percent) are members. All federally chartered CBs must be members, however. This central banking system, comprising 12 Federal Reserve Districts, provides many services to its members such as issuing currency, holding bank reserves, discounting loans, and serving as a check clearing house. (For a discussion of how the Federal Reserve operates to control economic developments, see pages 31 and 32.)

Mortgage Lending Activity

Commercial banks are quite different from other major mortgage lenders in that, as a general rule, they are neither organized for nor economically inclined toward mortgage lending. Commercial banks historically have been interested in maintaining a balance in the maturity of their source of funds and their loan portfolio. CB funds are primarily short-term and derived from passbook savings and deposits in checking accounts. Because of the maturity of their funds, long-term lending of any type is generally not attractive.

Most CBs are interested in commercial loans which are normally short-term and provide a better match between the maturity of assets (loans) and liabilities (deposits). When commercial loan demand is high, practically all CB funds flow to meet that demand and mortgage loans are neglected. During those periods in the business cycle when commercial loan demand is light, CBs have placed excess funds in real estate. This real estate financing activity has been very profitable to banks during certain phases of the business cycle. But, it has also been very damaging to banks at times because some of the mortgage loans that were made probably should not have been. For example, many of the commercial banks' problem loans in the 1970s, such as real estate investment trusts, can be traced directly to 1972–1973 when CBs had excess funds as a result of little commercial loan demand. That money went into real estate loans. In the second half of the 1980s, CBs once again made a major move into real estate. For example, in 1988–1990, Citicorp was the largest originator of mortgage debt in this country. For some of the banks, this recent experience with real estate lending was not profitable. Many bank failures of the late 1980s and early 1990s have been the result of poor real estate lending according to FDIC.

Currently, CBs make all types of mortgage loans, but construction loans on residential and income properties comprise a large percentage of mortgage financing activity. On the bank's books, these loans are normally classified as ordinary commercial loans, not real estate loans. The interest rate is generally two to five points above the prime rate, depending on the borrower. These loans are attractive to CBs because of the yield and because the loan is short-term (6 to 36 months), making it similar to the term of the bank's source of funds.

The board of governors of the Federal Reserve System issues regulations affecting real estate lending activity by member banks. State-chartered banks are governed by the regulations of the responsible state agency. These regulations usually are similar to those of the Federal Reserve. Current Federal Reserve regulations allow loans up to 90 percent of value to be amortized up to 30 years with no limit on the loan amount, although they are subject to the maximum loan limit in the secondary market. A bank can lend up to 70 percent of its deposits or 100 percent of capital and surplus, whichever is greater. CBs may have up to 10 percent of real estate loan units in a "basket," or nonconforming classification. Leasehold loans are allowed if the lease extends at least ten years past the date of full amortization.

The mortgage lending activity of commercial banks is more diverse than that of other lenders. Banks not only engage in both government and conventional residential mortgage lending, but also are the largest income-property lender. They are the largest mortgage lender for construction loans and help finance other lenders, especially mortgage bankers, by issuing lines of credit which allow for the warehousing of loans until needed for delivery to an investor.

Commercial banks, like other mortgage lenders, both originate loans for their own portfolio and for sale to others. In 1989, CBs sold to others mortgages worth about $37 billion.

SAVINGS BANKS (SBs)

Savings banks have often been categorized as commercial banks and sometimes as S&Ls. Although a SB has some of the characteristics of both, it is actually a thrift institution. At the end of 1989, approximately 490 existed with more than 60 percent of the total located in New York and Massachusetts. Savings banks, which had total assets of $280 billion at the end of 1989, hold about 8 percent of the total outstanding mortgage debt. Since SBs are thrift institutions, this percentage is quite cyclical, depending on savings inflow.

Historical Development

Like the first savings and loan, the first savings bank was founded in Pennsylvania. The Philadelphia Savings Fund Society (now called Meritor Savings Bank), the nation's largest savings bank, began in 1816 and was followed in 1817 by the Provident Institute for Savings in Boston.

Unlike the early building societies, these institutions were organized to provide ongoing facilities to encourage savings by the small wage earner, who had been virtually ignored by the other financial institutions. They were well received and began to spread throughout the New England states. By 1875 the number of SBs had reached a peak of 674. The SB concept never spread far from its origins, though, probably due to the development of S&Ls that encouraged savings and housing, and the development of savings accounts at commercial banks.

Organization and Regulation

Until the early 1980s, all savings banks were mutual organizations and as such had no stockholders. Beginning in the early 1980s, many savings banks realized that they needed additional capital if they were going to be able to compete in the new, deregulated environment. By the end of 1989, nearly one out of three savings banks were stock institutions, and the trend appears to be in the direction of more mutuals converting to stock.

If an SB remains a mutual organization, all depositors share ownership, and it is managed by a self-perpetuating board of trustees, usually made up of prominent local business leaders. If the SB is a stock organization, then it is managed by a board of directors, representing the stockholders of the bank.

In 1979 changes in federal law allowed savings banks to be federally chartered. Before this time all SBs were state chartered. The majority of SBs are still state chartered but that may change as federal laws evolve regarding capital requirements and portfolio structure. With the vast majority of SBs chartered by the various states, the regulations that govern their operations vary from state to state. State regulations establish guidelines for deposits, reserves, and the extent of mortgage lending allowed, as well as maximum loan amounts, loan terms, and loan-to-value ratios. These limits are usually similar to those of S&Ls and are governed to a great extent by what the markets require, especially the secondary mortgage market. SB's deposits are all insured by FDIC up to the $100,000 maximum.

Mortgage Lending Activity

Savings banks differ somewhat from S&Ls in that they were never encouraged by regulators to invest a set amount of money in mortgages. At the end of 1989, SBs had 50 percent of their assets in mortgage loans. Savings banks have had the authority longer to make other types of loans than S&Ls, and today most make consumer loans and commercial loans. Other assets include corporate stocks and bonds, U.S. Treasury and federal agency obligations, and state and local debt obligations.

In the current mortgage market, SBs originate both conventional and FHA/VA mortgages for their own portfolios. Since the majority of SBs are located in capital-surplus areas and therefore have more funds than are demanded locally, they often purchase low-risk FHA/VA and conventional mortgages from other mortgage lenders, particularly mortgage bankers, in capital-short areas of the country. Recently, much of this purchase has been in the form of mortgage-backed securities.

In 1989 SBs closed nearly $43 billion in mortgages and purchased another $2.5 billion from other lenders. During this same year, SBs sold mortgage loans worth nearly $19 billion.

CREDIT UNIONS (CUs)

A credit union is a specialized thrift institution that serves nearly one out of every four Americans. Credit unions are one of the fastest growing financial intermediaries in the American economy. At the end of 1990, the approximately 14,000 credit unions had more than $220 billion in assets and were becoming very sophisticated. Nearly 62 million Americans belong to a credit union which normally represents a specific industry group or community—a common bond. The largest CU is the Navy Federal Credit Union with 830,000 members and assets of nearly $4 billion.

Historical Development

Credit unions began in Germany during the middle of the 19th century. The principal objective of the founding fathers of the credit union movement was to combat usurious rates and to provide consumers with an opportunity to borrow at reasonable rates. The first credit union in the United States was organized in New Hampshire in 1908. Credit unions were chartered only by state law until the Federal Credit Union Act was passed in 1934. Slowly, various states enacted enabling legislation until in 1969, the number of CUs in the United States peaked at 23,876. Since then the number of credit unions has declined as many smaller credit unions merged into larger ones.

Many state-chartered CUs have had the authority to make real estate loans for many years, but federally chartered credit unions only acquired that right in 1978.

Credit unions operate somewhat differently than other thrift institutions. After providing for operating expenses and reserves, credit unions return their earnings to their members. Credit unions pay, on average, about 80 basis points more in dividends than competitors' savings products. This is one of the primary reasons for their popularity.

Organization and Regulation

All credit unions are mutual organizations and, as such, are directed by a board of directors elected by the membership. The members of the board are all volunteers except in the situation where one member from management serves on the board. The management (excluding the board) of a CU consists of professionals who, as a general rule, are paid.

Approximately 60 percent of CUs are chartered by the federal government and as a result are regulated by the National Credit Union Administration (NCUA). State-chartered CUs are regulated by the state and usually have greater leeway in what they may do and how. Nearly all credit unions are insured by the National Credit Union Share Insurance Fund (NCUSIF) with the amount of insurance being the same as with FDIC. A small percentage of CUs are insured privately.

One recent problem CUs have experienced is the decline in the percentage of the assets invested in consumer loans, automobile loans in particular. This decrease in consumer loans is the result of increased competition from automobile manufacturers and other financial intermediaries. In the face of this increased competition and the resulting sea of liquidity, CUs turned to mortgage lending in earnest in the 1980s. Of course, the tax law changes introduced in 1986 encouraged many credit unions to enter into mortgage lending.

Mortgage Lending Activity

Residential mortgage originations at CUs totaled $12 billion in 1990, representing just over 3 percent of total originations for that year. By the end of 1990, first mortgage loans totaled 35 percent of credit union loans outstanding, up from 6.4 percent in 1984. According to the data compiled by NCUA, 50 percent of all credit unions were offering first-mortgage loans at the end of 1990, and nearly all of those with assets over $50 million were offering these loans.

As with most new entrants to residential mortgage lending, most of the mortgages being originated by credit unions are for their own portfolios. At the end of 1990, CUs held about $48 billion in mortgage loans in the portfolios. Estimates are that only $1.25 billion in loans were sold by CUs into the secondary mortgage market in 1990. This small amount of sales is probably the result of their liquidity problems, but also of their not originating standardized mortgage products.

As credit unions continue to grow in total assets and in sophistication, it can be expected that they will increase their mortgage lending activities. These activities will naturally expand to increase sale of mortgages into the secondary mortgage market.

MORTGAGE BANKERS (MBs)

A mortgage company is usually identified as a mortgage banker. The term *mortgage banker* is somewhat misleading since it implies that this lender is a depository for funds like the other lenders. Mortgage bankers are not depositories but are classified as intermediaries since they serve as a financial bridge between borrowers and lenders. The MB borrows money to make loans on residential properties and keeps those loans in its warehouse line until an investor purchases a group of them. After the sale, the MB continues to service the mortgages for the investor.

Fewer than 1,000 actual mortgage bankers exist throughout the United States, although many more belong to the trade association. The majority are located in traditional capital-deficit areas such as the South and West. They render a valuable service to both borrowers and ultimate investors by moving funds for mortgages from capital-surplus areas to areas where insufficient capital exists for needed growth.

Unlike other lenders, a mortgage banker does not intentionally hold mortgages for its own benefit. All mortgages originated are sold to mortgage investors either directly or through the secondary market. MBs originate about 20–30 percent of residential mortgages each year. These percentages vary according to the economy and interest rates, but primarily they depend on the lending activity of S&Ls. When S&L activity is down, MB activity is usually up. MBs originate about 80 percent of each year's FHA/VA mortgages, most of which are pooled in mortgage-backed securities guaranteed by GNMA. Only commercial banks originate more income-property loans than mortgage bankers.

Organization and Regulation

The mortgage banking function is performed primarily by mortgage companies, although some commercial banks and savings and loans serve basically the same function. Some of these institutions have even purchased mortgage companies in order to better compete with MBs.

Unlike other lenders, MBs are not chartered by either the state or federal governments but follow either the partnership or incorporation laws of the state in which the respective company is located. MBs are also unique in that they are not subject to direct regulation or supervision of any agency. If an MB is an FHA-approved lender or an FNMA-approved seller/servicer, it is subject to periodic audits by these entities. HUD has attempted to exercise some control by issuing regulations governing several areas of concern, among them how a mortgagee handles delinquency problems with a mortgagor. During the early 1970s when merger activity between commercial banks and MBs was common, the Federal Reserve exercised some control by requiring approval prior to ownership changes.

Mortgage Lending Activity

The manner in which a mortgage banker conducts its residential lending business differs considerably from that of other lenders. The principal reason for this difference is that MBs usually do not use their own funds to close residential loans. S&Ls and other depository institutions can attract funds needed for mortgage lending directly, but MBs must borrow before they can lend.

Financing the MB

MBs finance lending activity either by the sale of commercial paper or by drawing on a line of credit with a commercial bank. Historically, the latter was the primary way of obtaining funds. Commercial paper is a short-term debt instrument with a maximum term of 180 to 270 days which carries a fixed rate of interest for a fixed term. MBs use this alternative during those periods in the economic cycle when the rate for commercial paper is lower than the prime rate. In addition to the lower cost of borrowing, the use of commercial paper removes the need for compensating balances—funds left on deposit with a commercial bank to provide increased incentive to lend funds. If a commercial bank lends its support to the commercial paper by backing it with an irrevocable letter of credit, the bank will require a fee and some compensating balances. On the other hand, if commercial paper is sold under the name of the holding company of a mortgage banker, no compensating balances are required. For this alternative to be used, the parent company must have an acceptable credit rating. The problem with selling commercial paper is that the market is quite volatile. During periods of tight money only high-cost funds can be obtained and then only by those companies with the highest credit ratings.

The second alternative for obtaining funds is by drawing on a line of credit with a commercial bank. This process is called *warehousing*, and refers to a revolving line of credit secured by the pledge of first mortgages on residential property. This process finances the MB's inventory of closed residential loans. The loan from the commercial bank will require that it be fully collateralized by closed mortgage loans retained by the MB until enough are grouped for sale to investors. The commercial bank is repaid from the proceeds of periodic sales of mortgages to investors. Warehousing aptly describes the flow of closed mortgages into the MB which are used to secure the bank loan. There the closed mortgages remain for 30–60 days until a group or pool of mortgages, typically in million-dollar units, is sold to an investor.

Commercial banks are attracted to this type of loan because it is short-term and involves little risk. The risk is minimal because the mortgages serving as collateral are usually pre-sold to an investor who is obligated to purchase by a commitment it issued. Commercial banks usually require that this line of credit be supported by compensating balances typically of 20 percent of the maximum line of credit. These required compensating balances may consist of tax and insurance escrows collected by the MB and deposited with the lending bank until needed.

The MB pays the prime rate or higher for the borrowed funds, depending on its credit rating and the money market. This often allows for a small warehousing profit between the cost of the borrowing and the interest rate of the underlying mortgage.

Because of its unique financial characteristics, the MB usually first obtains a commitment from either a permanent investor, such as a savings bank, or a government-related agency, such as FNMA, before it originates any mortgages. The investor, by a commitment, agrees to purchase the originated mortgages. A commitment is a contractual agreement between an *investor*, who agrees to purchase a certain amount of mortgages on certain types of properties at a stated interest rate with certain maturities, and a *lender*, who agrees to supply them. The commitment agreement may also stipulate whether servicing is to be granted, how it is to be handled, and the fee involved. A commitment, depending on the terms, can require delivery (a *take-out* commitment) either immediately or in the future (usually within four months), or it may not require delivery at all, in which case it is called a *stand-by* commitment. A commitment may be supported by a fee payable by the lender to the investor, which may be refunded if the commitment is fulfilled. In the case of a stand-by commitment, the fee is not refunded.

Mortgage bankers earn revenue from four sources:

1. Origination fees charged to each borrower.
2. Servicing fee charged to investors.
3. Any marketing difference between the interest rate of the underlying mortgage and the rate required by the commitment.
4. Any warehousing difference between interest rate of funds borrowed and loaned.

Since MBs are not directly regulated on mortgage limits, ratios, lending areas or types of loans, their only limitations are those imposed by investors of mortgages or insuring or guaranteeing agencies or companies.

Mortgage Banking Today

In the 1980s, the term mortgage banking has taken on additional meaning as more traditional and nontraditional mortgage lenders conduct their mortgage lending business in the same way that mortgage bankers conduct their lending business. In 1986, for example, many thrifts acted like mortgage bankers as the thrift industry sold more of their originations into the secondary mortgage market than they added to their portfolios. A further example of the explosive growth of financial institutions engaged in mortgage banking is the over 2,500 members of the Mortgage Bankers Association of America. Many of these members are commercial banks, savings banks, and savings and loan associations.

At the end of 1987, the mortgage banking industry was servicing in excess of $700 billion in mortgages for investors. This represented nearly 25 percent of the total outstanding mortgage debt. The largest independent MB (as determined by size of servicing portfolio) is Lomas and Nettleton, headquartered in Dallas, Texas. At the end of 1987, they were servicing more than $23 billion for over 1,000 investors.

RESIDENTIAL LOAN ORIGINATION   *4*

The beginning of the residential mortgage lending process is the receipt of a completed application for a mortgage loan. Mortgage lenders refer to this activity as loan origination. Residential mortgage loans are originated in the primary mortgage market, i.e., that market where a mortgage loan is entered into or agreed to by a lender and a borrower. This market is contrasted with the secondary mortgage market where loans already originated are bought and sold. (See Chapter 10.)

Introduction

All mortgage lenders perform the origination function. They may use different methods or employ alternative strategies to originate loans according to their own unique sources of funds, portfolio possibilities, fee income needs, staff resources, or other considerations, but to varying degrees they all perform the origination function. Mortgage investors, on the other hand, hold only mortgages that they have purchased from one of the many types of mortgage lenders or from other investors.

First Step

The first step in originating the residential loan is getting the applicant in the door. The process of getting the applicant in the door will be discussed in greater detail below, but how the applicant is treated once in the door can determine whether that applicant will stay with the lender for this particular loan. This is as important to a mortgage lender as is whether this applicant would come back for another mortgage or recommend the lender to another. As a general rule, mortgage lenders are

49

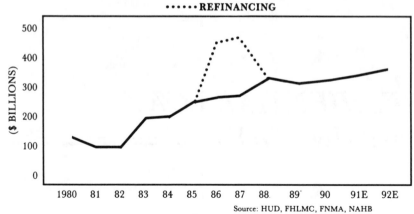

MORGAGE ORIGINATIONS, 1980–1992

Source: HUD, FHLMC, FNMA, NAHB

not very sympathetic or accommodating to the mortgage applicant who really is a lender's life blood.

Mortgage lenders must be sensitive to the stress that most applicants are under when they enter a mortgage lender's office. Lenders also need to understand that the process of applying for a residential loan is often an intimidating experience for many applicants. Lenders are often looked upon as adversaries, and if the function or process is not explained clearly and fully, it can further alienate an applicant. Lenders should understand that most applicants have either never applied for a mortgage loan before, or have done so only rarely. Applicants must be treated with care and understanding, and the reasons for the various verifications, appraisal, survey, insurance, or any other documentations fully explained.

Some lenders have the attitude that they are doing mortgage applicants a favor by considering them for a mortgage loan. Those lenders who have been able to increase their market share over the past few years have been those who have recognized that a mortgage applicant is a customer and is entitled to be treated as one. With the entry of so many new residential mortgage originators into the market, the ability to treat customers correctly will be an important factor in determining a lender's market share.

A fairly recent innovation has been the willingness of some mortgage lenders to meet with applicants any time and any place that will be most convenient for the applicant. This often takes the form of an originator meeting at the applicant's home at night or at the applicant's office. This accommodating approach really gets the attention of real estate sales people. A related issue is whether the origination personnel consider themselves "order takers" or "salespeople." Today's competitive residential lending market places a premium on salespeople, whereas order takers are a relic of the past. See the table on page 53 for a breakdown of originations by lending institutions in 1990.

In a real estate transaction, time is usually of the essence; any delay can destroy the transaction. Since most real estate transactions involve a mortgage of one type or another, time is often critical in a mortgage transaction. Many lenders handle this potentially serious problem by providing potential applicants with a booklet or marketing brochure which explains what information they should bring with them when they come into the lender's office to apply for a loan. This booklet can also be used to explain about income ratios, loan-to-value ratios, and other pieces of information a potential applicant should be aware of before completing an application. If the applicant has all or most of this information at application, the process can be moved rapidly toward a decision.

Once application has been completed, inquiries about the progress of the application or other questions may develop while the application is being processed. Some lenders advise the applicant to talk to the loan originator when questions develop. Other lenders designate a loan processor with whom an applicant should discuss the mortgage loan.

WHAT ATTRACTS CONSUMERS?

Recently, the Mortgage Bankers Association conducted a survey of its membership to determine what attracted consumers to their respective institutions for a residential mortgage loan. The survey confirmed some old ideas and introduced some new ones. An old idea confirmed was the importance of the realtor in determining where an applicant would seek a mortgage. A new idea was that advertising in the media was not all that important. The three "attributes" considered the most important in attracting consumers were:

1. referral by real estate broker
2. low rate of loan
3. good company reputation

The next four were of about equal importance:

4. friendliness of loan officers
5. previous experience with company/institution
6. recognition of company/institution name
7. availability of various loan products

Finally, this survey established the importance of attracting the potential applicant while still "shopping around." Once an applicant has submitted an application elsewhere it is extremely difficult to get him or her to drop that application and apply with another lender.

METHODS OF ORIGINATION

In today's rapidly evolving primary mortgage market, these strategies or methods of loan origination are used:

- retail loan origination
- wholesale loan origination
- combination of retail and wholesale

Recent data indicates that about 75 percent of mortgage lenders follow the retail strategy, about 10 percent the wholesale strategy, and the remaining 15 percent a combination of the two.

These three strategies will be discussed in some detail, with particular emphasis placed on the advantages and disadvantages of each.

Retail Loan Origination

Most borrowers are familiar with retail loan origination. It is still the strategy or method used by most mortgage lenders today and, as had been mentioned, about 75 percent of mortgage lenders use this origination strategy exclusively. This method of loan origination occurs when a lender performs all of the steps in origination directly: application, processing, underwriting, and closing a loan. Historically, most mortgage loan originations have been of this type.

The primary customer or client of most mortgage lenders is the local realtor. Ultimately, of course, the customer is the mortgage borrower, but initially the realtor is the one who directs most borrowers to a mortgage lender. For the retail lender, good relations with realtors are essential. The National Association of Realtors and others have estimated that 80 to 90 percent of home buyers follow the recommendation of the broker who sold them their home as to which lender to apply to for a home mortgage. Realtors will recommend only those mortgage

1–4 FAMILY MORTGAGE ORIGINATIONS, 1982–1991
(In Billions of Dollars)

1982	$ 97	1987	$459
1983	202	1988	384
1984	204	1989	352
1985	247	1990	370
1986	446	1991	340 (estimate)

Source: HUD

lenders who act promptly and who treat the applicants sent to them in a courteous manner. Once a lender has developed a negative image with the real estate sales community, it is difficult to change that image and convince realtors to send new applicants.

Except in small markets or in refinancing situations, borrowers seldom seek out or identify a lender on their own. For this reason, it is essential to a lender that it maintain good working relationships with local real estate salespeople.

Commission Loan Agents

In today's highly competitive primary mortgage marketplace, most retail lenders employ commissioned loan officers or loan representatives to solicit business from realtors or in some cases, builders. Mortgage bankers have traditionally used this approach for compensating their originators. Other lenders, primarily smaller thrifts and credit unions, pay their originators a salary only. Some lenders will use a combination of salary and commissions.

The commission normally given to a retail mortgage loan originator is ½ of 1 percent of the loan amount (or as normally stated, 50 basis points). This commission is payable, of course, only if the loan can be made according to the policies and procedures of the lender and finally closes. Some lenders will give a smaller commission per loan until a certain quota has been reached, and then increase the commission to a higher amount, say 60 basis points.

With the introduction of many new nontraditional mortgage lenders (e.g., Sears and GMAC) into an already crowded marketplace, meeting the competition has become the backbone of all mortgage lenders' game plan. This concern for market share has forced many lenders to change their lending philosophy from being simply an order taker to being an aggressive seller of their mortgage products. Lenders with commissioned loan agents logically seem to be the lenders who will succeed in holding on to their market share and probably grow at the expense of lenders with only salaried loan officers. Increased compensation is still the best reward for increased productivity and as an incentive for additional effort.

MARKET SHARE OF ORIGINATIONS

	Commercial banks	Savings banks	Savings & loans	Mortgage companies	Others
1988	26%	7%	42%	22%	3%
1989	34%	8%	38%	18%	2%
1990[1]	36%	5%	30	25%	4%

[1]1990 date is preliminary.
Source: HUD

1990 TOP THREE LEADERS IN 1–4 FAMILY
MORTGAGE ORIGINATIONS
(In Billions of Dollars)

1. Fleet/Norstar	$11.99
2. H.F. Ahmanson (parent of Home Savings)	11.95
3. Citicorp	10.50

Source: Real Estate Finance Today, February 25, 1991. The totals include both retail and wholesale originations.

Functions Performed

The retail mortgage lender directly performs the following origination functions:

- completes application with borrower
- orders all verifications
- orders appraisal
- orders credit report
- prepares loan for underwriting
- underwrites the loan application
- approves or rejects the loan application
- closes and funds approved loan
- maintains in portfolio or sells (warehouse) loan

Origination Income

Most retail lenders charge both an application fee and origination points to offset some or all of the expenses incurred in performing the various origination functions. The application fee generally is large enough to pay for the credit report, appraisal, and any other direct out-of-pocket expense a lender has in processing the loan application.

Origination points are often used by lenders for revenue to:

- offset personnel and office expenses
- increase yield on mortgages to secondary market requirements
- produce current income

Estimated costs of processing a loan (not including the 50 basis points paid to a loan originator) range from 60 to 120 basis points. Obviously, increased loan volume should help to keep this figure low.

In its Statement of Financial Accounting Standards (#91), the Financial

Accounting Standards Board (FASB) has stated any origination points that are not offset by actual expenses incurred in originating the loan must be amortized over the loan contract period or, if it can be clearly established, the expected life of the loan. This ruling has changed the way many lenders look at origination points. Those lenders that sell loans immediately into the secondary mortgage market (e.g., mortgage bankers and others) are the least affected since they can take any fee income into current income immediately after the sale of any loan. But portfolio lenders (e.g., thrifts and credit unions) will have to amortize much of that fee income over the expected life of the loan. Thrifts in particular may be hurt by this ruling since many have become used to using these fees to boost current income.

Points and Interest Rate Trade-offs

The long-term result of this FASB ruling may be a return to low- or no-point lending of the 1970s. No-point lending does not necessarily interfere with a lender's overall yield since it can increase the interest rate to offset the loss of fee income. As a general rule, a 1 percent origination fee equals an increase in yield of ¼ of 1 percent; thus, a quote of 10 percent and 2 points is approximately the same to a borrower as a 10½ percent quote with no points.

Retail Branch Office

A retail mortgage lender is primarily interested in giving the best possible service to local realtors and, through them, the mortgage applicants. A convenient location for loan origination offices is probably the most basic "service" to applicants, but it can be one of the most important rendered. Location is also important to a retail lender in regard to walk-in business.

Although the percentage of this type of business to total originations is generally small, walk-in business for new mortgages and refinancings can be just the additional business that makes a branch profitable. Therefore, each branch origination office should be easily reached by automobile or public transportation and be in a highly visible location, preferably on a ground floor.

Depending on whether loan processing is centralized or not, a branch office houses the loan origination personnel and appropriate staff support. If loan processing is not centralized, loan processors will also be at each branch office. Mortgage loan volume per retail office varies widely depending on many factors, but a valid goal is to produce 30 to 40 loans per production employee (including loan processors) per year. An office with a staff of nine—a branch manager who handles closings, a secretary, three loan originators, three loan processors, and one underwriter—should produce 300 to 350 loans a year. At an average loan balance of $80,000, annual loans would exceed $25 million.

WHOLESALE LOAN ORIGINATION

Over the last ten years, the natural cyclicality of mortgage lending has been magnified by a number of unpredictable factors. These factors have changed the way many mortgage lenders approach residential mortgage origination.

These factors include, among others:

- mortgage interest rates which climbed from 9 percent in 1979 to 16 percent in 1982 and fell back to 9 percent in 1991.
- 1–4 family mortgage originations dropped from $187 billion in 1979 to $97 billion in 1982 and then shot up to $446 billion in 1986 before slipping again to an estimated $360 billion in 1991.
- geographical cyclicality of originations as one area then another became hot then cooled off.
- an increase in local competition from traditional and nontraditional lenders.
- recognition of the off-balance sheet value of servicing.

All of these factors have contributed to the growth of wholesale mortgage lending by some mortgage lenders. In recent years, approximately 10 percent of mortgage lenders have adopted this origination strategy. This method of loan origination occurs when a mortgage lender acquires a processed loan from another lender that originated the loan. The extent of the loan processing varies depending on the needs of the originating lender and the acquiring lender.

Functions Performed

In most situations the originating lender completes the application with the borrower and orders the various verifications. This material is then shipped to the acquiring lender (sometimes referred to as a wholesaler) who will then make the underwriting decision. In other situations, the originating lender completes the loan processing and makes an underwriting decision. The acquiring lender, upon purchase, re-underwrites some or all of the mortgages in the package. The extent of underwriting by the acquiring lender will depend to a great extent on the amount of business it has done with the originating lender before. The originating lender is most concerned with the turnaround time for underwriting decisions. In most situations, the originating lender is looking for a 48-hour decision time. This is important to the originating lender since it may have to renegotiate with the applicant if the loan is declined as originally submitted. The ability of the wholesaler to fund quickly is also of great importance to the originating lender.

The originating lender retains the application fee and will probably collect as large an origination fee as the market will bear. It is the originating lender's responsibility to pay the originating agent the 50 basis point commission and also to have the staff necessary to process the loan. The originating lender is not interested in holding the loans or in selling them into the secondary mortgage market. This lender has determined that it can operate more profitably by originating loans for other lenders without the inherent interest rate risk associated with holding mortgages for a short or long period of time. This lender will almost always be originating against commitments that have been obtained from those lenders who rely on them for production. In addition to the fee income generated from the origination process, an originating lender often also receives a fee called a "servicing release premium" from the acquiring lender. This fee is a recognition that value (the value inherent in servicing a mortgage) is being transferred to the acquiring lender.

After the loans have been acquired and underwritten, if necessary, the acquiring lender will close the loan in its own name and either put the loan in its portfolio or sell it in the secondary mortgage market.

Affinity Groups

Another variation on the wholesale theme is the growth of the concept of affinity groups. This variation works whereby a mortgage lender hooks up with a large corporation or membership group (such as a credit union) as the preferred provider of mortgage loans. The benefits of this type of arrangement are mutual: the mortgage lender is endorsed by the sponsor, and the borrowers usually are treated better and may get a more attractive deal. Mortgage lenders are also interested in an arrangement of this type because the new business is usually on top of their own business, thus the economies of scale become even more attractive. As a general rule, the arrangement between the mortgage lender and the affinity group contains provisions which prevent the lender from selling the servicing rights to another lender.

Advantages and Disadvantages of Wholesale Lending

As with most types of business strategies or methods of doing business, there are advantages and disadvantages for each. This is particularly true for the wholesale method of loan origination. Possibly, the greatest advantage of wholesale lending is that it provides most lenders with an inexpensive method of originating high volumes of mortgage loans. This method is less expensive for a number of reasons including the ability to acquire loans without the need for a large loan processing staff. Some experts indicate that from 60–70 percent of the cost of originating a mortgage loan involves personnel expenses. If the loan processing function is performed by another organization, it can produce a loan at a much lower cost for a wholesale lender.

An important item to be considered in determining which approach is most appropriate for a particular lender is the expected number of loans produced per production employee. The rule of thumb for retail mortgage lending is yearly production of approximately 30–35 loans per production employee. For wholesale lending, the same approximation is 100–110 loans per production employee. This major difference in productivity is explained by the need for many more employees to take applications and process them in a retail lending operation. Of course, this need for more employees is offset to a major degree by the higher fees earned by a retail lender.

Another important advantage a wholesale lender has is the ability to move quickly into and out of markets that are changing. Since a wholesale lender does not have to be concerned with brick and mortar nor with acquiring personnel, it can quickly move into a geographical area that is attractive even if it is on the other side of the country. In addition, if a market deteriorates quickly, a wholesale lender can simply decide not to purchase any loans in that area; it does not have to be concerned with either selling its physical assets or relocating its personnel.

Unlike the retail lender, the wholesale lender does not have to be concerned with the attractiveness or the location of its offices. Not only will this lender need far fewer offices (each office can serve a very large geographic region), none are needed for direct face-to-face contact with applicants. As a result, offices can be less visible and thus less costly.

Wholesale lenders are usually quite interested in rapid growth in their servicing portfolio. These institutions desire large portfolios in order to obtain the economies of scale that can produce profits approaching 40–50 percent of servicing revenue. To these lenders the quickest way to increase their servicing portfolios is to acquire large blocks of loans through the wholesale approach and then sell them into the secondary mortgage market.

The strongest negative factor to wholesale lending is the issue of quality control. If your institution does not process a loan, your ability to control problems is greatly reduced. Many wholesale lenders have addressed this issue by dealing only with well-established reputable brokers or correspondents. As a result of this potential problem, wholesale lenders generally have higher underwriting and quality control expenses than a retail lender. They face the need of increased spot checking of appraisals and verifications in order to manage quality. Since these loans are probably sold in the secondary mortgage market, the wholesale lender could see its servicing profits greatly diminished with increased servicing expenses if quality controls are not in place and strictly adhered to.

Unlike the retail lender, the wholesale lender (the acquiring lender) does not receive any application or processing fee and normally receives only a 50 to 100 basis points origination fee. This reduced fee is not a critical item to the wholesale lender since it does not have the expenses of a retail lender. The best example of lower expenses is that the wholesale lender does not have to pay the 50 basis points commission to an origination agent.

ALTERNATIVE MORTGAGE INSTRUMENTS

5

The recent explosive growth of the many types of alternative mortgage instruments is the result of fundamental changes in the way homes are financed today. During the period between the Great Depression and the early 1980s practically all residential real estate loan transactions were financed with the use of the standard fixed-rate mortgage. Today, residential real estate is financed by either the standard fixed-rate mortgage or by one of the various alternative mortgage instruments. Depending on interest rates, alternative mortgage instruments will be used for as many as 60 percent of all residential mortgages, or as low as 20 percent. Before reviewing these new instruments, a discussion of the standard fixed-rate mortgage is required.

STANDARD FIXED-RATE MORTGAGE

The standard fixed-rate mortgage was the product of an earlier financial upheaval, the Great Depression of the 1930s, which changed the way homes were financed at that time. Before this innovation, most homes were financed by a term mortgage with the entire principal due at the end (or term) of the loan. It was normal practice for these loans to be rolled over into another loan at the end of the term. However, as a result of this practice, many home owners lost their homes during the economic emergency of the early 1930s because traditional lenders were unable to refinance these mortgages as they came due. This inability to refinance was the result of a severe national liquidity crisis.

The liquidity crisis was brought about by massive bank and thrift failures caused by a combination of bad loans and savers' panic withdrawals of their deposits. The resulting losses to depositors during this predepositor insurance period destroyed savers' confidence in financial institutions until deposit insurance arrived a few years later. As a means of addressing the national wave of foreclosures, the Home Owners Loan Corporation (HOLC), a federal agency, began exchanging government bonds for defaulted mortgages. If HOLC believed a loan it received was basically a sound one and only in default because of the liquidity crisis, that loan would be reconstituted as a 20-year loan with a self-amortizing monthly payment of principal and interest. This became the standard fixed-rate mortgage which was used almost exclusively until recently and which allowed this nation to have such a high ownership rate.

Direct Reduction Instrument

The standard fixed-rate mortgage is a monthly amortized, direct reduction instrument. This means that equal monthly payments for the term of the loan are used to reduce directly the amount owned by first paying interest on the loan due since the last payment and then using the remainder to reduce principal. This periodic reduction of principal combined with the fact that a borrower knows exactly how much is due each month are the two most important features of the standard fixed-rate mortgage.

The direct reduction of principal is also important for another reason. It allows for a considerable savings in the total amount of interest a borrower would have to pay if interest were calculated on the entire amount of principal, as occurs with a term loan. As noted earlier, term loans allow for no principal repayment during the term—only periodic interest payments, with the entire principal due at the end of the term. The savings to a borrower (before taxes) using an amortized loan as opposed to a term loan are seen in the following example.

Example: $1,000 loan at 10 percent interest to be repaid in 5 years with annual year-end payments compared to the same loan repaid on an amortized basis.

	Term loan				Amortized loan		
Year	Interest	Principal	Total	Year	Interest	Principal	Total
1	$100.00	-0-	$100.00	1	$100.00	163.80	$263.80
	100.00	-0-	100.00	2	83.62	180.18	263.80
3	100.00	-0-	100.00	3	63.60	198.20	263.80
4	100.00	-0-	100.00	4	45.79	218.01	263.80
5	100.00	1000.00	1,100.00	5	23.99	239.81	263.80
	$500.00	$1,000.00	$1,500.00		$319.00	$1,000.00	$1,319.00

Thus, with the standard fixed-rate mortgage, the monthly mortgage payment would remain the same from the first payment until the next to last (the last could be slightly different), even though much of the first payment went to interest and practically all of the last went to principal. If the example was for a longer term, say 30 years, practically all of the first payment would go to interest.

This type of mortgage served both borrower and lender well from the 1930s until the middle 1970s. For those who obtained one of these mortgages in the early 1970s or before, the fixed nature of their monthly mortgage payment was an obvious beneficial feature during the high inflation period of the late 1970s and early 1980s. What was good for those fortunate borrowers was nearly ruinous for mortgage lenders after 1978. The billions of dollars in these fixed-rate mortgages was also a deterrent to new borrowers who had to pay higher rates for mortgages than would have been expected in order to help offset low-yielding mortgages.

_____ *MORTGAGE LENDERS' DILEMMA*

For those portfolio lenders active in residential lending, primarily savings and loan, savings banks, and some commercial banks, the path which eventually led to financial ruin for some was initially quite smooth and profitable. These institutions had served savers and borrowers well over the past 50 years as they borrowed money at 5 or 5½ percent and loaned it out to home buyers at 7 or 7½ percent. The 150 to 250 basis points spread between a lender's cost of funds and the yield on its portfolio allowed for all operating expenses and an attractive profit. Through the process of financial intermediation, these institutions built up loan portfolios of 20–30 year mortgages worth hundreds of billions of dollars. It was this huge portfolio of low-yielding mortgages that became the nearly fatal characteristic of thrift institutions in the early 1980s.

Two events occurred during the late 1970s and early 1980s that changed how mortgage lenders would operate: rapid increases in inflation and increased competition for depositors' savings. The result was a doubling of the costs of funds to lenders in just a period of months. Since thrifts were primarily mortgage lenders and did not have the benefit of a variable-rate asset structure, as did many commercial banks with commercial loans, they suffered greatly.

Many portfolio lenders found themselves paying more for deposits than they were earning on the mortgage portfolios. Many lenders that normally worked with a positive spread of 200 to 250 basis points were now faced with a negative spread of over 100 basis points. As a direct result of these unforeseeable events, many lending institutions were forced to close their doors or to merge with other institutions. All mortgage lenders were forced to reexamine how they would lend on mortgages in the future.

As a consequence of this near disaster for those mortgage lenders which portfolioed mortgage loans, many surviving mortgage lenders retreated from the standard fixed-rate mortgage to one of a number of alternative mortgage instruments. These alternative mortgage instruments were attractive because they would allow for some periodic adjustment to interest rates in a changing financial environment. Even those mortgage lenders which sold some or all of their production into the secondary mortgage market needed new mortgage instruments so that their investors would be protected from interest rate risk. The feature that lenders were looking for in these alternative mortgage instruments was a way of sharing with borrowers some of the risk of lending in an uncertain economic environment.

Sharing the Risk

In order for traditional mortgage lenders to remain active in the mortgage market on a daily basis, they must have a way of meeting interest rate shifts in a profitable manner. Borrowers, if they want mortgage money available at all and at reasonable rates, will have to share some of the interest rate risk with their lenders.

All mortgage lenders must expect that future lending activity will produce a sufficient spread between its cost of funds and its portfolio yield to cover the following:

- cost of funds/interest expenses
- cost of loan processing
- operating expenses
- reasonable profit

In the past, many mortgage lenders borrowed short and loaned long by using market-sensitive savings to finance 20–30 year mortgages. Hopefully, with the bitter lesson of the 1980s behind them, lenders have become more sophisticated and have learned how better to match the maturity of their liabilities with their assets. The improvement in lenders' asset/liability management is evidenced by the increased use of certificates of deposit of longer maturity and by the use of alternative mortgage instruments. Many different types of alternative mortgage instruments have evolved since the first type was used in California in the early 1970s. The more common are discussed in the following sections.

ALTERNATIVE MORTGAGE INSTRUMENTS

Adjustable Rate Mortgage (ARM)

The most popular form of alternative mortgage instruments is the adjustable rate mortgage (ARM). Over the past ten years, the percent of residential mortgage loans which were ARMs has been as high as 60 percent when interest rates were high, and as low as 20 percent when interest rates were low. An ARM is basically an alternative mortgage instrument with the interest rate adjusting periodically to some predetermined index, and with the payment increasing or decreasing accordingly.

Alternative mortgage instruments, familiar around the world, were first used in this country in the early 1970s by state-chartered savings and loan institutions in California. These thrifts had qualified success with these instruments, but many borrowers who were afraid that their interest rates would increase rapidly stayed with the fixed-rate mortgage. Only after mortgage lenders began putting caps on how far interest rates could adjust each year and over the life of the loan were borrowers willing to try these new instruments.

Structure of an ARM

Adjustment period. The period of time in which the interest rate and payment can change is called the "adjustment period." ARMs can have adjustment periods of varying length, but most common are one-year, three-year, and five-year adjustment periods. Therefore, an ARM with a one-year adjustment period is called a one-year ARM. The one-year ARM is, by far, the most popular of the various ARMs today. One of the reasons for the popularity of this ARM is that it usually has the lowest interest rate of all the various ARMs. As a general rule, the shorter the interval between adjustments, the lower the initial interest rate.

Index. The concept behind an ARM is that it will produce an interest rate that moves as interest rates in general move, thus providing the portfolio lender with some protection against interest rate risk. In order to accomplish this, the interest rate for the ARM is tied to an "index." The index must be beyond the control of the lender; thus it can not be the lender's cost of funds. As a general rule, the index is tied either to a general cost of funds (e.g., the 11th district of the FHLB), or to a treasury security with a like period of maturity (e.g., a one-year ARM indexed to the one-year treasury bill). The most common index is the one-year treasury bill (adjusted to a constant maturity).

The following are some representative ARM indices:

- *Six-month treasury bill.* Based on the weekly auction rates on six-month (26-week) treasury bills. Generally considered the most responsive of all indices to changes in market interest rates and thus the most volatile.
- *One-year constant maturity treasury.* The index is calculated by taking the average of all treasury securities having one year remaining until maturity. This index is very responsive to market interest rate changes and therefore is volatile. Most popular of all indices.
- *Three- and five-year treasury.* Similar to the one-year treasury in that each is adjusted to a constant maturity. These have become less popular over recent years because the discount from a fixed-rate mortgage is much less with these indices.

- *Federal home loan district bank cost of funds.* Based on the total of all interest/dividends paid or accrued by thrift institutions in a particular district. The most common COF index is the 11th district (west coast) of the FHLB index. This index has lost some appeal since it is now understood as a trailing index in that it lags behind recent interest rate movements.
- *National contract rate on purchase of previously occupied homes.* Based on a weighted average of initial contract mortgage rates charged by major lenders on newly originated, conventional, fixed- and adjustable-rate mortgages on previously occupied homes. Probably the least volatile of indices. Not used very often.

Other indices are used occasionally, such as LIBOR (London Inter-Bank Offering Rate), used for ARMs sold in Europe, and a fairly new CD interest rate index which is the average of commercial bank certificates of deposit. All of the indices can be tracked by use of the Federal Reserve Board's statistical release H.15.

Margin   The margin originally was to correspond to that lender's operating expenses, but it is now market driven. Recently the margin has been averaging between 200 and 300 basis points. This is an important number for a consumer to establish before entering into any ARM transaction. Once the margin is established, it is set for the life of the loan.

Index Rate + Margin = ARM Interest Rate

Interest rate caps   In addition to the requirement (Truth-in-Lending amendment) that all ARMs entered into after December 8, 1987 must have an interest rate ceiling, most ARMs today have other "caps." Interest rate caps place a limit on the amount the interest rate can increase. The introduction of caps was what made ARMs acceptable to most consumers. Two types of interest rate caps are used today to make ARMs attractive to consumers:

- periodic caps, which limit the interest rate increase from one adjustment period to the next—a 2 percent cap is the most common
- life-time cap, which limits the interest rate increase over the life of the loan—a 6 percent cap is the most common life-time cap

Some ARMs have payment caps which limit the monthly payment increase at each adjustment period, usually to a certain percentage of the previous payment. A payment cap that has been recently used is a 7½ percent payment cap which means that payment can not increase more than that amount each adjustment period. Payment caps are not very popular because they usually produce "negative amortization" (deferred interest). This occurs when the monthly mortgage payment is not sufficient to pay all the interest due on the mortgage, thus the mortgage balance is increasing, not decreasing as would be expected. These loans may not be saleable on the secondary mortgage market because of investors' concerns that these mortgages have increased risk of delinquency.

Discounts   In order to make ARMs more attractive to more consumers, most lenders lower the initial interest rate (and thus the payment rate) from that called for by adding together the index and the margin. This initial rate is called a "discounted" rate and may be as much as 200 basis points below the fixed-rate mortgage. If the rate is 300 basis points or more, the rate is called a "teaser" rate. Mortgage borrowers should be wary of teaser rates since they often require large loan fees or have larger than normal margins.

Offering a discounted ARM is important to a lender if that lender wants to originate ARMs. There must be enough of a difference between what the fixed-rate mortgage is offered at and the rate for the ARM. If no difference exists, no borrower would select an ARM because that borrower would be taking on the risk of interest rates increasing. Therefore, lenders must compensate borrowers by making the ARM attractive as compared with the fixed-rate mortgage. This normally requires a discount from the interest rate called for by adding together the index and the margin. This discount is usually from 150 to 200 basis points below what the fixed-rate mortgage is offered at. As interest rates increase, the amount of discount necessary to attract borrowers will decrease since lenders see the opportunity for rates to drop in the future.

Sometime a seller or builder will pay a lender money so a borrower can get a lower initial rate. A transaction of this type is called a "buy-down" and is discussed in detail on page 67. The reason these buy-downs occur is that the borrower will be able to qualify for the mortgage at the payment rate rather than the FIAR rate (fully indexed accrual rate).

The risk to a borrower with an ARM with a discounted rate is that that payment rate may still go up at the adjustment period even if the index does not. See the example below.

Example: A borrower wants to buy a house by putting 10 percent down and borrowing $100,000. The mortgage lender is offering two mortgage choices:

1. a one-year ARM indexed to the one-year treasury with a 250 basis point margin and 2 and 6 percent caps, and
2. a 30 year fixed-rate mortgage at 10 percent.

If the one-year treasury index is at 7 percent, the situation will be as follows:

One-year treasury index	7.00 percent
Margin	2.50 percent
Fully indexed accrual rate	9.50 percent

But, the 30 year fixed-rate is at 10 percent and the lender realizes no borrower will select the ARM since it carries interest rate risk. The lender therefore offers the

ARM at a 200 basis point discount from the 30 year fixed-rate. As a result, the payment rate will be 8 percent and not the 9.50 percent fully indexed accrual rate.

One year later, however, even if the one-year treasury index stays the same, the payment will change. The payment rate the second year will be 9.50 percent. (Note, the new payment rate is established by adding the index, 7 percent, to the margin, 250 basis points, producing the new payment rate, 9.50. The increase of 1.5 percent is less than the 2 percent adjustment period cap and is, as a result, the correct rate.)

In order the protect the public, Congress passed an amendment to Regulation Z (Truth-in-Lending) which requires that lenders provide the following information if an ARM is applied for on a borrower's principal dwelling:

- the interest rate ceiling
- a booklet explaining ARMs (Consumer Handbook on Adjustable Rate Mortgages)
- 15-year historical example of how rates would have changed
- worst-case example assuming a $10,000 loan

Biweekly

Developed during the middle of the 1980s, a popular instrument that some home owners use for shortening the life of their mortgage debt is the biweekly mortgage. The obvious benefit of such a payment schedule is that it better fits the budget of those who are paid on a weekly or biweekly basis, as many American families are. Another meaningful benefit of a more frequent payment schedule is the substantial reduction in the total interest paid over the life of the loan and a reduction in the life of the loan.

Example: Assume a $50,000 mortgage for 13 percent for 30 years.

		Mortgage life	Total interest paid
Monthly payment	$533.10	30 years	$149,113
Biweekly payment	$276.55	17.9 years	$ 78,813

The mortgage life is shortened and interest paid substantially decreased because with biweekly payments a borrower is paying off more of the mortgage principal in a year than would occur with monthly payments. The payment is calculated on a 30-year amortization schedule at the market rate for a biweekly mortgage which usually is at a 25–50 basis-point reduction from regular 30-year mortgages. The biweekly mortgage payments total 26 (52 weeks divided by 2) during the year rather than the 12 payments for the regular 30-year mortgage. The increased number of payments allow for more principal to be paid before the next scheduled payments, thus reducing the interest and the effective mortgage life.

The negative aspects of the biweekly mortgage are minor as far as the borrower is concerned. These negative aspects mainly center around coordinating the mortgage payment with the borrower's payday. Lenders have helped to make this easier for borrowers by setting up checking accounts which are debited every two weeks for the mortgage payment. Many borrowers have their pay checks deposited directly into these checking accounts thus making the payment process even easier.

The one major negative point as far as lenders are concerned is the increased cost associated with processing the increased number of payments. Some lenders have calculated that it costs $10 to process each payment; however, this may not remain an issue as lenders become more sophisticated with computer processing.

Buy-downs

Buy-downs became popular during the extremely high interest rate period of 1981–82. The concept is designed to address the issue of affordability of housing and not the issue of protecting lenders' relative yields. Although market interest rates cannot be changed (the market dictates what they will be), the effective rate to a home buyer can be changed by "buying-down" the market rate to a rate which will allow a potential home buyer to qualify for a loan. This buy-down happens when a builder, home seller, parent of a buyer, or home buyer prepays a portion of the interest a lender will earn over the life of the loan. This one-time nonrefundable payment is put into an interest-earning account which a lender debits monthly to subsidize the reduced monthly payment.

Through this method, mortgage payments can be bought down for a temporary period, usually one to ten years, or permanently.

The buy-down can be structured in many ways; for example, a reduced monthly payment could remain constant over the life of the loan, increase yearly, or increase only once.

If a buy-down is a permanent one, a home buyer is qualified for the loan on the ability to make the established monthly payment. If the buy-down is only temporary, as most are, the buyer is qualified on ability to make the initial lower payment rather than ability to meet the increased payment. This benefit allows many more families to qualify for a mortgage loan.

Convertible Mortgages

The main attraction of this mortgage, the latest in a series of new types of mortgages, is that it appears to combine the best features of the fixed-rate and the adjustable-rate mortgage. This mortgage, sometimes called a convertible ARM, allows a borrower to start out with the features that make an ARM attractive. Later, if it is to the borrower's benefit, the existing ARM mortgage can be converted to a fixed-rate mortgage.

The attractive features of any ARM include, as we have already discussed, an interest rate which is normally about 200 basis points below the fixed-rate interest rate and yearly and lifetime caps on interest rate increases. As with most standard ARMs, borrowers using this mortgage are qualified at the lower ARM interest rate which, of course, allows for more to qualify.

The one attractive feature to borrowers of a fixed-rate mortgage that is missing with a standard ARM is that the interest rate is not capped at the same level it was at closing. This attractive feature is normally found only in fixed-rate mortgages. Of course, if interest rates should drop, an ARM mortgagor is going to benefit from the drop in rates while the fixed-rate holder would have to refinance to enjoy the interest rate drop.

A convertible mortgage affords the borrower with the opportunity for a period of time to convert the ARM mortgage to a fixed-rate mortgage in the future. The opportunity need only be used if the borrower decides it would be beneficial to convert. At first glance the ability to convert may not appear to be of great value to a borrower. A borrower could always refinance the existing ARM and obtain a new fixed-rate mortgage. The problem with that strategy is the cost of refinancing. It is generally acknowledged that the cost of refinancing is from 2 to 4 percent of the outstanding balance. That can amount to many thousands of dollars.

With the convertible ARM, the borrower can convert and may only have to pay a fixed amount, say $250 to $500. If the loan has been sold into the secondary mortgage market, an additional fee may be charged; for example, Fannie Mae charges one point to convert one of its ARMs to a fixed-rate mortgage.

The time frame within which to convert depends on who owns the mortgage, but most instruments allow the borrower to convert anytime after the thirteenth month until the sixtieth month.

When would a borrower choose this ARM over a normal ARM or a fixed-rate mortgage? Much of that answer depends on whether the borrower can qualify for a fixed-rate mortgage. In addition, a borrower must decide whether the spread between the mortgages makes sense to select one over the other. Generally, a 200 basis points spread should exist between the fixed-rate mortgage and the ARMs.

The convertible ARM generally costs 25 to 50 basis points more than a normal ARM. The convertible ARM makes sense to a borrower if the borrower expects interest rates to drop over the next couple of years. If that occurs, the borrower will have benefitted from the lower ARM interest rate initially, and after converting, the benefit of locking in the fixed-rate rate for the life of the mortgage.

Graduated Payment Mortgage (GPM)

The GPM is an instrument that was specifically designed to provide borrowers with an opportunity to match their expected increasing income with a mortgage payment that is initially low but increases yearly. This instrument is not designed to address the issue of sheltering lenders from interest rate shifts. It does, however, help alleviate the problem of how to qualify more potential home owners for mortgages. Many otherwise qualified potential home owners are unable to qualify for a standard fixed-rate mortgage because their current income is not sufficient; however, if their conservatively estimated future income could be factored in, they could qualify.

With a GPM, the interest rate and the term of the loan are set, as with a standard fixed-rate mortgage. The difference is that the initial monthly payment begins at a lower level than it would with a standard mortgage. The result is monthly payments which are not sufficient to fully amortize the loan. Since the payments do not fully amortize the loan, the borrower, in effect, is borrowing the difference between the payment being made and the interest actually due. The amount of accrued but unpaid interest is added to the outstanding principal amount. Through this negative amortization, the outstanding principal balance actually increases for a period of time, rather than decreasing as with a standard mortgage.

Example: Comparison of fixed-rate mortgage payment to GPM payment. Assume for comparison a $75,000 house, 20 percent down payment, $60,000 loan at 12 percent for 30 years. Add 2½ percent of market value for taxes and insurance = $156 per month.

Standard fixed-rate monthly payment	*Year*	*5-year GPM 7½ increase monthly payment*
$ 617.17	1	$ 474.83
617.17	2	510.45
617.17	3	548.73
617.17	4	589.88
617.17	5	634.12
617.17	6–30	681.68
$162,172.71	Total interest paid	$177,577.04

When the $156 per month for taxes and insurance is added, the necessary family income to qualify for this standard fixed-rate mortgage is $2,750 per month.

With the same $156 for taxes and insurance added, the necessary family income to qualify for this five-year GPM is $2,250 per month.

The following year the monthly payment increases at a predetermined rate, say 7½ percent, with additional increases occurring each year for a set number of years. Depending on the plan selected, as the yearly increases occur, at some point the monthly payments will equal or exceed the payment under a standard mortgage. At that point negative amortization stops but the payment increases will have to continue until they reach a level which will fully amortize the outstanding balance over the remaining years of the loan.

From the example, two important points emerge. First, the amount of family income to qualify for a GPM is substantially less and therefore more families can qualify. Of course, if family income does not increase at the hoped-for rate, the burden of annual 7½ percent mortgage payment increases may result in a default. The second point is that the total amount of interest paid is increased with a GPM. This is the result of the negative amortization during the early years of the mortgage when principal is increasing rather than decreasing as with a fully amortized mortgage.

In addition to conventional GPMs, the Department of Housing and Urban Development has an insured GPM (Section 245) which is basically the same as described above.

Price Level Adjusted Mortgage (PLAM)

A PLAM is one of the more recent alternative mortgage instruments and one which holds much promise, especially if a period of hyperinflation should reappear. The underlying concept of a PLAM is that the "real" mortgage payment remains constant over the life of the mortgage. This means that the rate at which interest is charged to a borrower is guaranteed to provide a lender with a "real" return above inflation.

Under a standard mortgage, the mortgage payment is at a level sufficient to return to the lender the money loaned plus interest, in addition to some additional money to make up for the decrease in the value of the money repaid. This "inflation premium" adds several hundred basis points to a typical standard mortgage payment, possibly more during higher inflation periods. Even with this inflation premium, lenders have lost considerable purchasing power over the past decade because of the difficulty in predicting future inflation. Much of today's affordability crisis stems from lenders charging high initial interest rates in an attempt to receive compensation for the small real value of the final payments.

The PLAM is designed to address this problem of real return and offers a solution that benefits both borrower and lender. A PLAM takes the expensive guesswork out of lending in an inflationary economy. The real return is guaranteed by increasing the monthly mortgage payment at the same rate as the increase in inflation (or stated differently, by the decrease in the value of money) as measured by an appropriate index such as the Consumer Price Index. The outstanding principal balance is also adjusted to constant dollars. The adjustments to both the monthly payments and the outstanding principal are on a yearly basis.

The basic assumption with a PLAM, as with many other alternative mortgage instruments, is that household income will increase at or close to the inflation rate. Therefore, as the mortgage payment increases, the same percentage of monthly income will be used to meet that payment.

Reduction Option Loan

This relatively new alternative mortgage instrument was developed after the convertible mortgage and shares some of the same features. This alternative provides a borrower with the certainty of a fixed-rate mortgage initially but does not lock that rate in unless the borrower so desires. This loan allows the borrower to switch to a lower fixed-rate anytime between the beginning of the second year and the end of the fifth year. This valuable option saves the borrower the hassle and expense of refinancing the loan if interest rates drop.

This loan, developed by Shearson Lehman Mortgage, only costs the borrower $100 plus ¼ of 1 percent of the outstanding balance of the mortgage to switch to a lower fixed-rate mortgage. This amount is a meaningful savings over the typical refinancing cost of 3 to 6 percent of the loan amount.

Reverse Annuity Mortgage (RAM)

The RAM is designed to enable older retired home owners who are probably on fixed income to use the equity in their homes (probably totally paid for) as a source of supplemental income while still retaining that ownership.

RAM works as follows: a lender has the house appraised and then lends a certain percentage of the current value. The loan itself is to be paid to the home owner in the form of a monthly annuity. This annuity is either from the mortgage lender directly or else the proceeds of the loan are used to purchase one from a life insurance company. The annuity provides monthly payments for the life of the loan or the life of the annuitant(s) depending on how the RAM is structured. Throughout the time of the loan, the home owner owns and lives in the house.

A lender's security for a RAM is the same as with a standard mortgage: the home itself. If the home owner (or owners) dies before the term, the estate is liable for the debt. Of course, if the house is sold before death, the debt must be paid off.

If, when the loan comes to term, the home owner (or owners) is still alive, a new RAM can be created, assuming that the property has appreciated. The proceeds from the new RAM first repay the old one and the difference purchases a new annuity for the home owner.

The interest rate on a RAM debt can be either fixed or adjustable but that fact must be disclosed and explained to a borrower. In addition, prepayment must be allowed with no penalty.

Although this mortgage concept has not been used much to date, it may become a necessary part of future mortgage lending as the American public grows older, especially if double-digit inflation returns.

10- or 15-Year Mortgage

The American home owner has become so conditioned to monthly mortgage payments that any other schedule seems quite unusual. However, this attitude has changed over the last couple of years as more home owners see the advantage of paying off their mortgage debt early. This can be accomplished by starting out with a 10- or 15-year mortgage. This term for the mortgage debt has become popular especially since the period of time in 1986–1987 and 1991 when long-term fixed-rate interest rates slipped below 10 percent.

Conclusion

The principal inducement behind the recent rapid growth of alternative mortgage instruments has been the need to ensure that mortgage lending would remain a profitable business venture for those intermediaries involved in it. This goal cannot be reached immediately because of the billions of dollars of low-yielding mortgages still in lenders' portfolios, but the use of alternative mortgage instruments is vital to the process of restructuring lenders' portfolios. If the goal of profitability is met, all parties concerned with mortgage lending will benefit, whether they be saver, borrower, lender, or society in general. Society benefits because the family that buys its own home regards this as a meaningful accomplishment and often continues to invest in its community in a variety of ways beyond payment of real estate taxes.

PROCESSING THE RESIDENTIAL MORTGAGE LOAN   6

INTRODUCTION

The residential mortgage loan processing function includes all actions and procedures that occur from the time a potential borrower asks to file an application through the time the loan is presented to the underwriter for a decision as to whether to grant the loan. The speedy, professional completion of this function is crucial to any mortgage lender and may be the determining factor in whether the residential mortgage lending operation is successful and profitable.

As a general rule, loan processing takes the longest time of all the steps in producing a closed residential mortgage loan. Until recently, this step could take up to forty-five days, but the trend today is toward faster loan processing. Today, some mortgage lenders advertise they will get an answer to the applicant within ten days.

INTERVIEW

The first step in the long process toward a closed mortgage loan is the initial interview. The importance of this initial contact with potential borrowers cannot be overemphasized, and if this contact is handled correctly, it can save both borrower and mortgage lender considerable time and money. The reason is that this contact can establish early on whether a potential borrower is qualified for a mortgage loan. The mortgage lending officer conducting this interview should be careful not to give the impression they are making a credit decision, only that they are explaining the general nature of the financial obligations inherent in a mortgage loan.

Although a lender cannot refuse an application if a potential borrower wants to submit one, most individuals will not apply for a mortgage loan if they realize they will not qualify after having the financial obligations of a mortgage loan explained to them. Therefore, this initial interview should establish whether the

73

basic qualifications are present for an application to be taken. A lender must be careful, though, that they not discourage a potential borrower from applying for a mortgage loan if they so desire. Further, as mentioned, mortgage lenders must be careful that this initial interview not be represented as a credit decision. If a lender, at this stage of the process, tells a potential applicant that based upon income the applicant does not qualify, that is a credit decision requiring a notice of adverse action. (Adverse action will be discussed later in this chapter.)

APPLICATION

The application is the most important document in the residential mortgage lending process. Everything that follows is done to verify information on the application.

At this point it is important to emphasize that all lenders should use the FNMA/FHLMC Uniform Application, even if at the time of origination it is believed the loan will stay in a lender's portfolio. If market conditions reach a point where a lender must sell existing loans out of its portfolio into the secondary mortgage market and it has not used the uniform documentation, that lender may have a difficult time selling those mortgages. Additionally, the use of one's own forms may place a lender in violation of the various consumer protection laws if they are not drafted correctly. The FNMA/FHLMC Uniform Application has been accepted as meeting all consumer protection requirements.

Most applicants, even if they have been mortgage borrowers before, have no idea of the amount of information they will be asked to provide a mortgage lender before that lender can make a decision on whether or not to make a loan. In order to speed up processing, a lender may want to distribute to real estate brokers and/or applicants a list of information which should be brought to the lender at the time of application.

This list should request that the applicant bring information on the following topics:

- Names in which title to the property will be held and how title will be held (e.g., joint tenants)
- Address of property to be purchased—copy of the Contract of Sale should be included to provide legal description
- Birth date and social security number of applicant(s) for use by credit bureau
- Principal residence address for previous two years (if not at present address for two years, previous address)
- Financial information an applicant should bring to interview/application
  —borrower (and co-borrower, if applicable) income
  —any supplemental income
  —if self-employed, signed income tax returns previous two years

Residential Loan Application

MORTGAGE APPLIED FOR	☒ Conventional ⬛ FHA ⬛ VA	Amount $ 62,000	Interest Rate 16¾%	No. of Months 360	Monthly Payment Principal & Interest $ 846.26	Escrow/Impounds (to be collected monthly) ☒Taxes ☒Hazard Ins. ☒ Mtg. Ins.

Prepayment Option
Standard FNMA/FHLMC Option

Subject Property

Property Street Address 7882 Village Drive	City Cincinnati	County Hamilton	State Ohio	Zip 45242	No. Units 1

Legal Description (Attach description if necessary) Lot #145 Township of Sycamore	Year Built 1977

Purpose of Loan ⬛ Purchase ☒Purchase ⬛ Construction-Permanent ⬛ Construction ⬛ Refinance ⬛ Other (Explain)						ENTER TOTAL AS PURCHASE PRICE IN DETAILS OF ⬛ PURCHASE
Complete this line if Construction-Permanent or Construction Loan	Lot Value Data	Orginal Cost	Present Value (a)	Cost of Imps. (b)	Total (a + b)	
	Year Acquired $	$	$	$	$	
Complete this line if a Refinance Loan	Purpose of Refinance		Describe Improvements [ ] made [ ] to be made			
Year Acquired	Original Cost	Amt. Existing Liens				
$	$				Cost: $	

Title Will Be Held In What Name(s) Stuart M. and Sharon D. Lopes	Manner In Which Title Will Be Held Tenancy by the Entirety

Source of Down Payment and Settlement Charges Savings, Equity in Present Home

This application is designed to be completed by the borrower(s) with the lender's assistance. The Co-Borrower Section and all other Co-Borrower questions must be completed and the appropriate box(es) checked if ⬛ another person will be jointly obligated with the Borrower on the loan, or ⬛ the Borrower is relying on income from alimony, child support or separate maintenance or on the income or assets of another person as a basis for repayment of the loan, or ⬛ the Borrower is married and resides, or the property is located, in a community property state.

Borrower			Co—Borrower		
Name Stuart M. Lopes	Age 42	School Yrs 16	Name Sharon D. Lopes	Age 41	School Yrs 15
Present Address No. Years 8 ☒Own Rent			Present Address No. Years 8 ☒Own Rent		
Street 973 Captain Court			Street 973 Captain Court		
City/State/Zip Cincinnati, OH			City/State/Zip Cincinnati, OH		
Former address if less than 2 years at present address			Former address if less than 2 years at present address		
Street			Street		
City/State/Zip			City/State/Zip		
Years at former address Own Rent			Years at former address Own Rent		

Marital Status ☒Married ⬛Separated ⬛Unmarried (incl. single, divorced, widowed)	DEPENDENTS OTHER THAN LISTED BY CO-BORROWER NO. 2 AGES 7-5	Marital Status ☒Married ⬛Separated ⬛Unmarried (incl. single, divorced, widowed)	DEPENDENTS OTHER THAN LISTED BY BORROWER NO. 2 AGES 7-5

Name and Address of Employer Robots Unlimited 279 Vine Street Cincinnati, OH 45241	Years employed in this line of work or profession? 10 years	Name and Address of Employer Bellin Hospital 10233 Montgomery Rd. Cincinnati, OH 45242	Years employed in this line of work or profession? 6 years
	Years on this job 10 Self Employed*		Years on this job 3 Self Employed*

Position/Title Industrial Robot Spec.	Type of Business Machinery	Position/Title Registered Nurse	Type of Business Hospital
Social Security Number*** 123-45-6789	Home Phone 439-4704	Business Phone 984-7623	Social Security Number*** 987-65-4321	Home Phone 439-4704	Business Phone 891-0935

Gross Monthly Income				Monthly Housing Expense**			Details of Purchase	
Item	Borrower	Co-Borrower	Total	Rent	$ Present	Proposed	Do Not Complete If Refinance	
Base Empl. Income	$ 2417	$ 850	$ 3267	First Mortgage (P&I)	356.75	$846.26	a. Purchase Price	$ 70,000
Overtime				Other Financing (P&I)			b. Total Closing Costs (Est.)	2,100
Bonuses				Hazard Insurance	12.00	16.00	c. Prepaid Escrows (Est.)	165
Commissions				Real Estate Taxes	50.00	75.00	d. Total (a + b + c)	$ 72,265
Dividends/Interest				Mortgage Insurance	7.80	12.40	e. Amount This Mortgage	$ 62,000)
Net Rental Income				Homeowner Assn. Dues	75.00	0	f. Other Financing	(0)
Other† (Before completing, see notice under Describe Other Income below.)				Other:			g. Other Equity	(0)
				Total Monthly Pmt.	$ 501.55	$946.66	h. Amount of Cash Deposit	2,000)
				Utilities	110.00	210.00	i. Closing Costs Paid by Seller	(0)
Total	$ 2417	$ 850	$ 3267	Total	$611.55	$1159.66	j. Cash Reqd. For Closing (Est.)	$ 8,265

Describe Other Income		
⬛⬛ B—Borrower C—Co-Borrower	NOTICE:† Alimony, child support, or separate maintenance income need not be revealed if the Borrower or Co-Borrower does not choose to have it considered as a basis for repaying this loan.	Monthly Amount
		$
		$

If Employed In Current Position For Less Than Two Years, Complete the Following						
B/C	Previous Employer/School	City/State	Type of Business	Position/Title	Dates From/To	Monthly Income
						$

These Questions Apply To Both Borrower and Co—Borrower

If a "yes" answer is given to a question in this column, please explain on an attached sheet.	Borrower Yes or No	Co-Borrower Yes or No		Borrower Yes or No	Co-Borrower Yes or No
Are there any outstanding judgments against you?	No	No	Are you a U.S citizen?	Yes	Yes
Have you been declared bankrupt within the past 7 years?	No	No	If "no", are you a resident alien?		
Have you had property foreclosed upon or given title or deed in lieu thereof in the last 7 years?	No	No	If "no", are you a non-resident alien?		
Are you a party to a law suit?	No	No	Explain Other Financing or Other Equity (if any)		
Are you obligated to pay alimony, child support, or separate maintenance?	No	No			
Is any part of the down payment borrowed?	No	No			
Are you a co-maker or endorser on a note?	No	No			

*FHLMC/FNMA require business credit report, signed Federal Income Tax returns for last two years; and, if available, audited Profit and Loss Statement plus balance sheet for same period.
**All Present Monthly Housing Expenses of Borrower and Co-Borrower should be listed on a combined basis.
***Optional for FHLMC

FHLMC 65 Rev. 10/86   43565 SAF Systems and Forms, Inc   Fannie Mae Form 1003 Rev. 10/86

This Statement and any applicable supporting schedules may be completed jointly by both married and unmarried co-borrowers if their assets and liabilities are sufficiently joined so that the Statement can be meaningfully and fairly presented on a combined basis; otherwise separate Statements and Schedules are required (FHLMC 65A/FNMA 1003A). If the co-borrower section was completed about a spouse, this statement and supporting schedules must be completed about that spouse also. ☐ Completed Jointly ☐ Not Completed Jointly

Assets		Liabilities and Pledged Assets				

Indicate by (*) those liabilities or pledged assets which will be satisfied upon sale of real estate owned or upon refinancing of subject property

Description	Cash or Market Value	Creditors' Name, Address and Account Number		Acct. Name if Not Borrower's	Mo. Pmt. and Mos. Left to Pay	Unpaid Balance
Cash Deposit Toward Purchase Held By McNeal, Incorporated	$ 2,000	Installment Debts (Include ''revolving'' charge accounts) Co.	Acct. No.		$ Pmt/mos.	$
Checking and Savings Accounts (Show Names of Institutions (Account Numbers) Bank, S & L or Credit Union		Addr 620 Vine Street City Cincinnati, OH Co. Shillitos	727-385- 392-1 Acct. No.		25 / 8	185
Addr 100 Center St. City Cincinnati, OH 45241 Acct. No. 4578-3	1,500	Addr 741 Fairfield Road City Cincinnati, OH Co. Master Card	2533-300 216-629 Acct. No.		25 / 20	500
First National Bank, S & L or Credit Union		Addr 40 Redcoat Road City Cincinnati, OH Co. Visa	5504-521 216-6297 Acct. No.		25 / 11	275
Addr 11 Fifteenth Street City Cincinnati, OH 45241 Acct. No. 179854	7,000	Addr 28 Fairfield Road City Cincinnati, OH Co. Sears	403-414- 88 Acct. No.		20 / 12	240
Bank, S & L or Credit Union Second National Bank Addr. City Acct. No.		Addr. City Other Debts including Stock Pledges			/	
Stocks and Bonds (No./Description)		Real Estate Loans Co. Second National Bank Addr 11 Fifteenth Street City Cincinnati, OH	Acct. No. 932786]		/	37,000
Life Insurance Net Cash Value Face Amount $ 50,000	1,000	Co. Addr. City	Acct. No.		/	
Subtotal Liquid Assets	11,500					
Real Estate Owned (Enter Market Value from Schedule of Real Estate Owned)	49,500	Automobile Loans Co. First National Bank Addr 100 Center Street City Cincinnati, OH	Acct. No. 796403		/	8,280
Vested Interest in Retirement Fund	2,500					
Net worth of Business Owned (ATTACH FINANCIAL STATEMENT)		Co. Addr. City	Acct. No.		/	
Automobiles Owned (Make and Year) 1986 Buick Regal	10,000					
1983 Chevrolet	3,500	Alimony/Child Support/Separate Maintenance Payments Owed to			/	
Furniture and Personal Property	10,000					
Other Assets (Itemize)		Total Monthly Payments			$ 325	
Total Assets	A $87,000	Net Worth (A minus B) $			Total Liabilities	B $ 46,480

SCHEDULE OF REAL ESTATE OWNED (If Additional Properties Owned Attach Separate Schedule)

Address of Property (Indicate S if Sold, PS, if Pending Sale or R if Rental being held for income)		Type of Property	Present Market Value	Amount of Mortgages & Liens	Gross Rental Income	Mortgage Payments	Taxes, Ins. Maintenance and Misc.	Net Rental Income
973 Captain Court	PS	Condo	$ 49,500	$ 37,000	$	$ 356.75	$ 144.80	$ 0
		TOTALS►	$	$	$	$	$	$

List Previous Credit References

	Creditor's Name and Address		Account Number	Purpose	Highest Balance	Date Paid
B-Borrower C-Co-Borrower						
B-C	Wickes Furniture 10 Main St. Cincinnati		729-4128	Furniture	$ 350	1-81

List any additional names under which credit has previously been received _____

AGREEMENT: The undersigned applies for the loan indicated in this application to be secured by a first mortgage or deed of trust on the property described herein, and represents that the property will not be used for any illegal or restricted purpose, and that all statements made in this application are true and are made for the purpose of obtaining the loan. Verification may be obtained from any source named in this application. The original or a copy of this application will be retained by the lender, even if the loan is not granted. The undersigned ☒ intend or ☐ do not intend to occupy the property as their primary residence.
I/we fully understand that it is a federal crime punishable by fine or imprisonment, or both, to knowingly make any false statements concerning any of the above facts as applicable under the provisions of Title 18, United States Code, Section 1014.

Stuart Y. Lopez	Date 5/22/89	_Sharon D. Lopez_	Date 5/22/89
Borrower's Signature		Co-Borrower's Signature	

Information for Government Monitoring Purposes

The following information is requested by the Federal Government for certain types of loans related to a dwelling, in order to monitor the lender's compliance with equal credit opportunity and fair housing laws. You are not required to furnish this information, but are encouraged to do so. The law provides that a lender may neither discriminate on the basis of this information, nor on whether you choose to furnish it. However, if you choose not to furnish it, under Federal regulations this lender is required to note race and sex on the basis of visual observation or surname. If you do not wish to furnish the above information, please check the box below. [Lender must review the above material to assure that the disclosures satisfy all requirements to which the Lender is subject under applicable state law for the particular type of loan applied for.]

Borrower: ☐ I do not wish to furnish this information	Co-Borrower: ☐ I do not wish to furnish this information
Race/National Origin:	Race/National Origin:
☐ American Indian, Alaskan Native ☐ Asian, Pacific Islander	☐ American Indian, Alaskan Native ☐ Asian, Pacific Islander
☐ Black ☐ Hispanic ☒ White	☐ Black ☐ Hispanic ☒ White
☐ Other (specify): _____	☐ Other (specify): _____
Sex: ☐ Female ☒ Male	Sex: ☒ Female ☐ Male

To Be Completed by Interviewer

This application was taken by: ☒ face to face interview ☐ by mail ☐ by telephone	_C Howell_ Interviewer Cindy Howell 384-9729 Interviewer's Phone Number	Second National Bank Name of Interviewer's Employer 11 Fifteenth Street Cincinnati, OH 45241 Address of Interviewer's Employer

FHLMC FORM 65 Rev. 10/86   **Reverse**   Fannie Mae Form 1003 Rev. 10/86

76

—creditor and account number information: credit cards, revolving charge, past mortgages, etc.

—name(s) and address(es) of current employer(s); if less than two years, previous employers

- List of liquid assets and where held with account numbers (good faith deposit, checking, etc.)

Mailing Out Application Forms

Although it is strongly recommended that all mortgage loan applications be completed in a face-to-face interview, circumstances sometimes require that an application be completed through the mail. These circumstances almost always involve an applicant from out of town who can't return for an interview. When this situation presents itself, a lending institution needs to be as specific as possible in a transmittal letter concerning directions on:

- completing the application
- requesting additional information
- signing the various verifications

The letter to the applicant should provide specific instructions to sign the forms which will thereby authorize banks, employers, and others to provide the desired information to a lender. When the signed verifications are received from the applicant, the lender will mail them out.

After all required information has been received from an applicant, a mortgage lender will send a typed final application form to a borrower for signature. Both this final application and the initial application should be kept in the loan file. Of course, as with a face-to-face applicant, all of the federally mandated consumer protection forms and documents must be provided to an applicant who is using the mail.

CONSUMER PROTECTION

As a result of actual and perceived violations of the rights of consumers during the 1970s the federal government enacted a series of rules and regulations governing how the application and processing of mortgage loans must be handled. These are summarized in the following sections. All mortgage lending personnel are urged to become familiar with all of these regulations.

Equal Credit Opportunity Act (ECOA)

The provisions of ECOA, sometimes referred to as Regulation B, became effective on October 28, 1974 and were initially limited to prohibiting discrimination on the basis of sex or marital status. The prohibited bases of discrimination were broadened in 1976 when the ECOA amendments became law.

The general rule of ECOA is "...A creditor shall not discriminate against an applicant on a prohibited basis regarding any aspect of a credit transaction...." The prohibited bases are:

- race
- color
- religion
- national origin
- sex
- marital status
- age
- The fact that all or part of an applicant's income is derived from any public assistance program
- The fact that an applicant has in good faith exercised any rights under the Consumer Credit Protection Act or any similar state law

These prohibited biases are sometimes referred to as the "nifty nine" and apply to all mortgage lenders. A few states and some regulators (such as NCUA, the credit union regulator) have added additional prohibitions usually dealing with the handicapped and with sexual orientation. As a general rule, most mortgage lenders have had little difficulty in adhering to ECOA. On the other hand, each year some mortgage lender is sued for violation of ECOA. As a result, all mortgage lending personnel must be familiar with the provisions of this act.

Encouraging applications   All mortgage lenders must be careful to encourage potential borrowers to make application for a mortgage loan. This should be interpreted to mean that all inquiries concerning whether a potential borrower would qualify for a mortgage loan should be answered by stating that credit decisions can only be made based on a written application. This should be followed up with an invitation to make application.

It is important that lenders realize that an application does not necessarily have to be in writing. The requirement that an adverse action letter be sent to all who have "applied" for mortgage credit applies equally to oral requests for credit. Lenders can prevent themselves from unintentionally violating the adverse action letter requirement by stating to all who orally request credit decisions that they can only be made based on a written application.

Monitoring information   Loan originators or loan processors who take loan applications should be prepared to answer questions from applicants as to why the FNMA/FHLMC application requests information relating to race, national origin, and sex. Some protected classes may express their uneasiness with these questions. The lender must explain that the information is only for government monitoring purposes and is not considered when determining whether to grant a loan. The applicant must also be told that this information need not be supplied, but if it is not, then the lender must supply this information based on visual observation.

Marital status   The marital status of an applicant or applicants may be requested for a mortgage loan. This information is important to a lender because of the different requirements in some states for establishing a secured interest in real estate depending on whether or not a person is married. However, in establishing the marital status, the only terms that can be used by a lender are whether the applicant is married, unmarried, or separated.

A lender may never ask questions about an applicant's spouse unless:

- the spouse will be contractually liable
- the applicant is relying on the spouse's income to qualify
- the applicant resides in a community property state or the security is in such a state
- the applicant is relying on alimony, child support, or separate maintenance payments from a spouse or former spouse

Notification of adverse action   As previously noted, applicants must be notified within 30 days after receipt of a completed application whether the loan has been approved substantially as requested or if the creditor is taking "adverse action." An application is considered complete when all required information has been received by the lender. If the application is rejected, the lender must state a specific reason for the rejection.

Truth-in-Lending

The Consumer Credit Protection Act of 1968 contains Title I, better known as Truth-in-Lending (or Regulation Z). The purpose of this legislation was to require that all lenders, including mortgage lenders, disclose to borrowers exactly how much obtaining credit was going to cost them. Under these regulations a lender is required to make certain disclosures concerning the extension of credit to a borrower:

- Annual percentage rate (APR)
- finance charges
- right of rescission

Annual percentage rate (APR)   The most meaningful disclosure is of the annual percentage rate (APR). The APR is the annual interest rate the mortgage borrower will actually pay after all other fees and charges associated with the loan are taken into consideration. The APR must be computed and disclosed with accuracy to the nearest 1/8 percent. For example, an exact APR of 10.16 could be stated as exactly that or could properly be rounded to the nearest 1/8 percent, resulting in an APR of 10.25 percent. A mortgage lender may not avoid calculating and disclosing the actual APR by simply stating that the rate does not exceed 11 percent or by quoting a rate that would be meaningfully higher than the actual APR. A lender can compute the APR on the basis of either a 360- or 365-day year. The APR and the finance charge discussed below must be disclosed in a preliminary manner within three business days of application.

Finance charges   In addition to the APR disclosure, a mortgage lender is required to provide within three business days after a written application a good faith estimate of the amount financed. The amount financed includes the principal loan amount, any other amount that is financed by the lender, and the finance charge. The finance charge is "...the dollar amount the credit will cost you." The "good faith estimate of settlement costs" required for those loans subject to RESPA (Real Estate Settlement Procedures Act) may be substituted for this disclosure if it provides all of the required information. Most mortgage lenders use one form for these two disclosures.

The charges which must be disclosed to a borrower include all fees that are required as a condition of the loan, such as the following:

- interest
- loan discount
- origination fees
- mortgage insurance premiums
- principal repayment (amortization schedule)

Typical closing costs (fees paid to a third party) that do not need to be included in the finance charge include:

- appraisal fee
- credit report fee
- title examination fee, title insurance
- lawyer fees
- property survey

When the loan under discussion is a fixed-rate loan, the APR and finance charge disclosures are relatively simple. But, if the loan is a closed-end adjustable-rate mortgage on the borrower's principal dwelling, the disclosures are a bit more complicated. The disclosures become more complicated because the total finance charge cannot be calculated because future changes in the interest rate are unknown.

Most lenders fulfill their truth-in-lending requirements for adjustable-rate mortgages by first disclosing that the interest rate, payment, or term can change. Next, the lender discloses the APR and total finance charges using the initial

NAVY FEDERAL CREDIT UNION

RESPA GOOD FAITH ESTIMATES OF SETTLEMENT COSTS AND FEDERAL TRUTH-IN-LENDING DISCLOSURE

MEMBER'S NAME GEORGE P ANDERSON MARTHA A. ANDERSON	NFCU ACCOUNT NO. SUFFIX 0123456/0123457 001/10	DATE 07/16/92
PROPERTY ADDRESS 3459 EAGLE ROCK COURT, ANNANDALE, VIRGINIA 22030-4151	TYPE OF LOAN VA LOAN	

You have applied to Navy Federal Credit Union for a proposed mortgage loan in the amount of 151,650.00 to be repaid at a simple interest rate of 9.500 % for a term of 360 months. The following RESPA Good Faith Estimates of Settlement Costs include all settlement service charges you must pay, but IT MAY NOT COVER ALL ITEMS YOU HAVE TO PAY IN CASH AT SETTLEMENT — FOR EXAMPLE, DEPOSIT IN ESCROW FOR REAL ESTATE TAXES AND INSURANCE. YOU MAY WANT TO ASK ABOUT THE COST OF ANY ITEMS YOU MUST PAY THAT ARE NOT SHOWN ON THIS FORM. YOU MAY BE REQUIRED TO PAY OTHER ADDITIONAL AMOUNTS AT SETTLEMENT. For further explanation of the charges, consult your booklet entitled "A Homebuyer's Guide to Settlement Costs."

LINE NO. ON HUD-1	SETTLEMENT SERVICE	CHARGES INCLUDED IN AMOUNT FINANCED OR PREPAID FINANCE CHARGES	CHARGES EXCLUDED FROM AMOUNT FINANCED
801	Loan Origination Fee .750	$ 1,137.38 e	$ e
802	Loan Discount 1.000	$ PAID BY SELLER e	$ e
803	Appraisal Fee	$ e	$ e
901	Interest Based on 39.47 per day for 16 days	$ INCLUDED WITH FIRST PAYMENT e	$ e
902	Mortgage Insurance Premium 1.125 VA-FUNDING FEE	$ 1,687.50 e	$ e
1002	Mortgage Insurance ___ months at ___ per mo.	$ N/A e	$ e
1101	Settlement Fee	$ e	$ N/A e
1107	Attorney's Fee (may include 1102 through 1106)	$ e	$ e
1108	Title Insurance	$ e	$ e
1201	Recording Fees	$ e	$ e
1202	City/County Tax Stamps	$ e	$ e
1203	State Tax	$ e	$ e
1301	Survey	$ e	$ e
	TOTALS	(A) 2,824.88 e	

EXPLANATION OF AMOUNT FINANCED
The Loan Amount of 151,650.00 e less the total (column A) of the Prepaid Finance Charges of 2,824.88 equals the Amount Financed of 148,825.12 e.

AMOUNT FINANCED	is 148,825.12 e, the amount of credit provided to you or on your behalf.
FINANCE CHARGE	is 310,854.85 e, the dollar amount the credit will cost you, if you pay as scheduled. This figure includes e 308,029.97 mortgage interest plus 2,824.88 prepaid finance charges and N/A e of mortgage insurance premiums not included in prepaid finance charges.
TOTAL OF PAYMENTS	is 459,679.97 e, the amount you will have paid when you have made all payments as scheduled. This figure includes the FINANCE CHARGE plus the AMOUNT FINANCED.

ANNUAL PERCENTAGE RATE is 9.716 % and is the cost of your credit as a yearly rate. Includes interest adjusted from settlement
YOUR PAYMENT SCHEDULE WILL BE:

Number of Payments	Amount of Payments (principal and interest only)	When Payments Are Due
1 e	$ 1,906.68 * e	09/01/92 e
359	1,275.16	MONTHLY THEREAFTER

☐ Your loan will also include monthly payments of ☐ FHA Mortgage Insurance ☐ Private Mortgage Insurance as follows: NONE

LATE CHARGE: You will be charged 4% of the monthly payment for principal and interest only if a payment is not received within 15 days of the first of the month due date.

INSURANCE: Property hazard insurance is required as a condition of this loan. The required insurance may be purchased from any insurance company of your choice that is acceptable to NFCU. The minimum amount is your loan amount or the replacement cost of the dwelling, whichever is less.

PREPAYMENT: If you pay off early, you will not have to pay a penalty. (In addition, if you pay off early, you may be entitled to a refund.)

ASSUMPTION: If you are obtaining a VA guaranteed or FHA insured mortgage loan, someone buying your home in the future may be allowed, subject to conditions, to assume the remainder of your mortgage on the original terms. NFCU *conventional loans* however, *are not assumable.*

SECURITY: You are giving a security interest in the property being purchased.

See your mortgage documents for any additional information they may contain about nonpayment, default, any required repayment of the obligation in full before the scheduled date and prepayment funds.

e means an estimate

NFCU 294M (2-60)

06011992

_____ _____   _____ _____
      DATE   DATE

81

A PHH GROUP COMPANY

QUESTIONS AND ANSWERS ABOUT "TRUTH-IN-LENDING" STATEMENT

Federal law provides that you receive a "Truth-in-Lending Disclosure Statement." Study it carefully as well as the other information about your loan we gave you. Your loan is an important transaction. Following are some of the most frequently asked questions about the Truth-in-Lending Statement and their answers. Additional information can be obtained from your real estate agent or mortgage loan officer.

Q. What is a Truth-in-Lending Disclosure Statement and Why Do I Receive It?

A. Your Disclosure Statement provides information which Federal law requires us to give you. The purpose of the statement is to give you information about your loan and help you shop for credit.

Q. What is the ANNUAL PERCENTAGE RATE?

A. The Annual Percentage Rate, or A.P.R., is the cost of your credit expressed in terms of an annual rate. Because you may be paying "points" and other closing costs, the A.P.R. disclosed is often higher than the interest rate on your loan. The A.P.R. can be compared to other loans for which you may have applied and give you a fair method of comparing price.

Q. What is the AMOUNT FINANCED?

A. The amount financed is the mortgage amount applied for *minus* prepaid finance charges and any required deposit balance. Prepaid finance charges include items such as loan origination fee, commitment or placement fee (points), adjusted interest, and initial mortgage insurance premium. The Amount Financed represents a *net* figure used to allow you to accurately assess the amount of credit actually provided.

Q. Does this mean I will get a lower mortgage than I applied for?

A. No. If your loan is approved for the amount you applied for, that's how much will be credited toward your home purchase or refinance at settlement.

Q. Why is the ANNUAL PERCENTAGE RATE different from the interest rate for which I applied? Why is the AMOUNT FINANCED different?

A. The Amount Financed is lower than the amount you applied for because it represents a *net* figure. If someone applied for a mortgage of $50,000 and their prepaid finance charges total $2,000, the amount financed would be shown as $48,000, or $50,000 minus $2,000.

The A.P.R. is computed from this *lower* figure, based on what your proposed payments would be. In a $50,000 loan with $2,000 in prepaid finance charges, and an interest rate of 14%, the payments would be $592.44 (principal and interest) on a loan with a thirty year term. Since the A.P.R. is based on the *net* amount financed, rather than on the actual mortgage amount, and since the payment amount remains the same, the A.P.R. is higher than the interest rate. It would be 14.62%. If this applicant's loan were approved he would still receive a $50,000 loan for thirty years with monthly payments @ 14% of $592.44.

Q. How will my payments be affected by the Disclosure Statement?

A. The Disclosure Statement only discloses your estimated payments. The interest rate determines what your monthly principal and interest payment will be.

Q. What is the FINANCE CHARGE?

A. The Finance Charge is the cost of credit. It is the total amount of interest calculated at the interest rate over the life of the loan, plus prepaid finance charges and the total amount of mortgage insurance charged over the life of the loan. This figure is *estimated* on the disclosure statement given with your application.

Q. What is the TOTAL OF PAYMENTS?

A. This figure indicates the total amount you will have paid, including principal, interest, prepaid finance charges, and mortgage insurance if you make the minimum required payments for the entire term of the loan. This figure is *estimated* on the Disclosure Statement and is estimated in any adjustable rate transaction.

Q. My statement says that if I pay the loan off early, I will not be entitled to a refund of part of the finance charge. What does this mean?

A. This means that you will be charged interest for the period of time in which you used the money loaned to you. Your *prepaid* finance charges are not refundable. Neither is any interest which has already been paid. If you pay the loan off early, you should not have to pay the full amount of the "finance charges" shown on the disclosure. This charge represents an estimate of the full amount the loan would cost you if the minimum required payments were made each month through the life of the loan.

Q. Why must I sign the Disclosure Statement?

A. Lenders are required by law to provide the information on this statement to you in a timely manner. Your signature merely indicates that you have received this information, and does not obligate either you or the Lender in any way.

WHITE — Applicant   YELLOW — File

QUESTIONS & ANSWERS ABOUT "T-I-L" STATEMENT
USMC 1013-C 1/86 jtr

interest rate and then using a narrative to explain what future increases in the interest rate will mean to the borrower. This narrative should contain a description of the index and margin which will determine future increases as well as disclose any limits of yearly and lifetime rate increases. Also, the lender must provide an explanation of how the consumer may calculate payments based on a $10,000 example. In addition, a lender must provide a 15-year historical example of how the index-plus-margin would have produced changes in interest rate and payments.

Right of rescision   Truth-in-lending regulations also require that mortgage lenders disclose to borrowers who are refinancing an existing home mortgage or getting a second mortgage (either open- or close-ended) that they have three business days in which to rescind the loan transaction if they so desire. Mortgage processors should understand that this right does not apply to a purchase money mortgage. This right of rescision is intended to provide borrowers with a limited cooling-off period during which they can cancel the whole transaction and get all funds expended back from the lender.

Real Estate Settlement Procedures Act (RESPA)

RESPA became law in 1974 (and was later amended in 1976) and applies to all federally related mortgage loans which means practically all purchase money residential mortgages. The purpose of RESPA is to inform borrowers of the costs that will be associated with the loan and loan closing. This knowledge will give them the opportunity to shop for the best deal for them. The exempt mortgages include:

- loan to finance property of 25 or more acres
- home improvement loan
- loan to refinance an existing mortgage
- loan to finance a vacant lot
- construction loan (unless this loan can convert to a permanent loan)

RESPA requires a lender to deliver or place in the mail, no later than three business days after, and not including the day the application is received, a copy of HUD's current Special Information Booklet. This publication describes and explains the typical settlement costs that are incurred when closing a residential mortgage loan.

Good faith estimate of settlement costs   In addition, RESPA requires a mortgage lender to provide within three business days a "good faith estimate of settlement costs" which a borrower will incur at closing. This estimate does not have to be exactly what the final closing statement will be but must be a good faith estimate.

The items which normally are found in the closing statement include among others:

- appraisal fee
- commitment fee
- credit report
- settlement or closing fee
- title examination fee, title insurance
- survey
- recording fee
- pest inspection

Kickbacks and unearned fees   RESPA contains very broad prohibitions against kickbacks and unearned fees. First, no person can give or accept any fee, kickback, or thing of value pursuant to any oral or written agreement or understanding that business incidental to the settlement of a federally related mortgage loan will be referred to any person. Second, no person can give or accept a portion, split, or percent of any fees charged in connection with the settlement of a federally related mortgage loan, other than for services actually performed.

HUD-1   Finally, RESPA provides a borrower with the right to inspect the Uniform Settlement Statement (HUD-1) on the business day before settlement. This two-page form is completed by the closing agent and lists all the charges paid by both the seller and buyer. Both parties must sign this form and the lender will keep the original in the loan file.

Flood Disaster Protection Act

The purpose of this legislation was to require lenders to inform borrowers whether their property was in a flood hazard area. If the property was in a flood hazard area, borrowers were to be advised that in order to obtain a mortgage they had to be covered by flood insurance. Mortgage lenders have two prescribed notification requirements pursuant to the Flood Disaster Protection Act depending on whether the property is located in a community participating in the National Flood Insurance Program. If the property is located in a special flood hazard area, the lender is required to notify the purchaser of this fact and also whether the flood disaster insurance is available in that community. If this insurance is available, the lender must require the borrower to obtain the insurance. If flood insurance is not available, the lender can make the loan if it sees fit, but usually it will not.

Mortgage lenders need to remember that they are legally responsible for making the determination of whether the property is in a flood disaster area even if they expect the appraiser to so inform them.

NOTICE TO BORROWER OF
SPECIAL FLOOD HAZARD AND
FEDERAL DISASTER ASSISTANCE

Date
Borrowers Name(s)

Mail Address

Property Address

Notice to Borrower of Special Flood Hazard

You are hereby notified that the improved real estate or mobile home described above is or will be located in an area designated by the Secretary of the Department of Housing and Urban Development as a special flood hazard area. This area is delineated

on_____'s Flood Insurance Rate Map (FIRM) or, if the FIRM is unavailable, on the Flood Hazard Boundary Rate Map (FHBM). This area has a 1% chance of being flooded within any given year. The risk of exceeding the 1% chance increases with time periods longer than one year. For example, during the life of a 30 year mortgage, a structure located in a special flood hazard area has a 26% chance of being flooded.

Notice to Borrower About Federal Flood Disaster Assistance
(Lender Check One)

☐ Notice in Participating Communities

The improved real estate or mobile home securing your loan is or will be located in a community which is now participating in the National Flood Insurance Program. In the event your property is damaged by flooding in a Federally declared disaster, Federal disaster relief may be available. However, such relief will be unavailable if your community is not participating in the National Flood Insurance Program at the time such assistance would be approved (assuming your community has been identified as flood-prone for at least one year). This assistance, usually in the form of a loan with a favorable interest rate, may be available for damages incurred in excess of your flood insurance.

☐ Notice in Non-participating Communities

The improved real estate or mobile home securing your loan is or will be located in a community which is not participating in the National Flood Insurance Program. This means that you are not eligible for Federal flood insurance. In the event your property is damaged by flooding in a Federally declared disaster, Federal disaster relief will be unavailable (assuming your community has been identified as flood-prone for at least one year). Federal flood disaster relief will be available only if your community is participating in the National Flood Insurance Program at the time such assistance would be approved.

Acknowledgement by Borrower

Delivery of these notices is hereby acknowledged.

Borrower's Signature: _____ Date_____

41520-8 (2/78) *
Borrowers Flood Hazard and Disaster Relief Notice   **Lenders Copy**   SAF Systems and Forms

Fair Credit Reporting Act

This law regulates the users and use of consumer credit information. The purpose of this law is to insure that accurate credit information is used when credit decisions are made. Mortgage lenders are able to underwrite a mortgage application only when they have complete information. Much of the required information comes from a credit report. This legislation, which mostly impacts credit reporting agencies and how credit information is obtained, also requires lenders to handle this credit correctly. Basically, this requires mortgage lenders to only request credit information on those individuals who have given their permission for their credit to be reviewed. The standardized mortgage application contains this authorization.

If a mortgage lender turns down an applicant because of poor credit as established by the credit report, the lender must notify the applicant of this fact and provide the name, address, and phone number of the reporting credit bureau. This notice should also inform the applicant of the right to discuss or question any information on the credit report with the credit bureau. Under no circumstances should the lender discuss the contents of the credit report with the applicant until the applicant has seen a copy of the credit report. Any discussions about the accuracy of the credit report should be between the applicant and the credit bureau, not with the mortgage lender. Lenders should give applicants the time and chance to cure any problems with their credit reports since credit bureaus do make mistakes and at times will report on the wrong person.

Home Mortgage Disclosure Act

The purpose of this legislation (also known as Regulation C) is to require mortgage lenders to keep a record and report yearly on the disposition of mortgage applications. Mortgage lenders must report the type of real estate loans they make and where they make them so that the federal government can determine if that lender is refusing to make loans in certain urban areas (whether they are "redlining"). This information is contained in the Loan Application Register and it is usually the processor's responsibility to maintain this register. The type of information that it registers includes the following:

1. Application or loan information
   —type of loan
   —purpose of loan
   —occupancy
   —action taken
2. Applicant information
   —race or national origin
   —sex
3. Type of purchaser (of mortgage loan, if sold)
4. Reasons for denial

This record keeping is also important because the federal government can examine these records for consumer protection violations.

QUALIFYING AN APPLICANT

Income

A borrower's income (in some situations combined with that of a co-borrower's) provides the means for the repayment of the mortgage debt and other household and long-term debts in addition to everyday expenses. Not only is the amount of that income important, but the prospect for continuation of that income must be determined.

In determining whether the income is sufficient to fulfill all existing debt and the mortgage applied for, five possible sources of income should be analyzed:

- employment income
- self-employment income
- rental/interest/investment/commission income
- child support/alimony/separate maintenance income
- retirement/pension/disability/welfare income

As will be discussed later, the manner in which a lender can inquire about these sources of income is limited by certain laws, particularly the Equal Credit Opportunity Act.

The income which is most commonly relied upon is employment income. This income should be verified for the past two years. The Request for Verification of Employment (VOE) form requests the following information from an employer:

- date of employment
- amount of current income
- type of income
- present position
- probability of continued employment

The amount of income usually is not an item of controversy, but the type of income may generate controversy. If all income is derived from commissions or bonuses, an obvious problem exists regarding the possibility of lower sales income in a subsequent year, which would not support the continuation of the commission income at the present level. As a rule, if the past two or three years establish the current level as "normal, " the income should be given full consideration. If income derived from overtime or part-time work is necessary to qualify the loan, a lender should establish whether the additional income is expected to continue and whether the amount of that income is reasonable for the additional employment.

FannieMae

Request for Verification of Employment

Instructions:

Lender — Complete items 1 through 7. Have applicant complete item 8. Forward directly to employer named in item 1.
Employer — Please complete either Part II or Part III as applicable. Sign and return directly to lender named in item 2.

Part I — Request

1. To (Name and address of employer)	2. From (Name and address of lender)
Country Estates 24 West Street New York, New York 10000	**STATEN ISLAND SAVINGS BANK** **15 Beach Street** **Staten Island, New York 10304**

3. Signature of Lender	4. Title	5. Date	6. Lender's Number (Optional)
Theresa Tarkagelo	Administrative Assistant	2/27/89	

I have applied for a mortgage loan and stated that I am now or was formerly employed by you. My signature below authorizes verification of this information.

7. Name and Address of Applicant (Include employee or badge number)	8. Signature of Applicant
John Smith 40 Lynn Court, Oceanview, N.Y. 10001	John Smith

Part II — Verification of Present Employment

Employment Data	Pay Data			12C. For Military Personnel Only	
9. Applicant's Date of Employment: February, 1975	12A. Current Base Pay (Enter Amount and Check Period) $ 2,500 — ☐ Annual ☒ Monthly ☐ Weekly ☐ Hourly ☐ Other (Specify)			Pay Grade	
10. Present Position: Vice President	12B. Earnings			Type	Monthly Amount
11. Probability of Continued Employment: Excellent	Type	Year To Date	Past Year	Base Pay	$
13. If Overtime or Bonus is Applicable, Is Its Continuance Likely?	Base Pay	$ 7,500	$ 30,000	Rations	$
	Overtime	$	$	Flight or Hazard	$
Overtime ☐ Yes ☒ No	Commissions	$	$	Clothing	$
Bonus ☒ Yes ☐ No	Bonus	$	$ 3,000	Quarters	$
				Pro Pay	$
				Overseas or Combat	$

14. Remarks (If paid hourly, please indicate average hours worked each week during current and past year)

Annual Bonus of 10% paid for the last three (3) years.

Part III — Verification of Previous Employment

15. Dates of Employment	16. Salary/Wage at Termination Per (Year) (Month) (Week)
	Base ______ Overtime ______ Commissions ______ Bonus ______

17. Reason for Leaving	18. Position Held

19. Signature of Employer	20. Title	21. Date
Albert E. Myers Albert E. Myers	Personnel Officer	March 27, 1989

The confidentiality of the information you have furnished will be preserved except where disclosure of this information is required by applicable law. The form is to be transmitted directly to the lender and is not to be transmitted through the applicant or any other party.

Fannie Mae
Form 1005 Nov. 85

The same VOE form should be used to verify previous employment if the current employment is less than two years.

Self-employment   Even though the self-employed are in the highest risk category for default, they must be treated basically the same as others. The difficulty in verifying the income of the self-employed is obvious. A loan processor must be extremely careful that enough information is made available so that the under-writer will be able to analyze the risk.

A lender should require signed copies of the prior two year's 1040s with all schedules plus a current accountant-prepared profit and loss statement and a balance sheet evidencing a stable or increasing income stream. Self-employment income is considered stable income if the borrower has been self-employed for two or more years during which time the income was stable or increasing.

When computing the income available for the proposed mortgage and other debts in addition to living expenses, the net income from the tax returns is used. Depending on the business a borrower is in, depreciation and other paper losses may be added back to net income to arrive at a figure for available income.

Interest and dividends   Interest and/or dividend income may be used as income if it is properly documented and has been received for the past two years. An average of the past two years' income will be used to qualify the borrower. Copies of brokers' statements or of the interest/dividend checks, photocopies of tax returns, or other account statements may be used to verify this income. A lender should take care to determine if any of these funds will be used for making the down payment or for paying moving expenses.

Rental income   Rental income is often relied upon by borrowers in qualifying for a mortgage loan. This income is easy to verify by obtaining copies of the lease agreement or cancelled checks. In order to allow for maintenance, taxes, and a vacancy factor, many underwriters will allow only 75 percent of rental income to count toward qualifying for the mortgage loan.

Child support, alimony, or separate maintenance   In today's society, more and more borrowers are claiming child support, alimony, or separate maintenance as additional income. This income can be used as long as proof exists that payment has been made in a regular manner and is based on a written agreement or court order. A mortgage lender must be mindful of the ECOA (Equal Credit Opportunity Act) requirements when asking about this type of income. Basically, ECOA requires a lender to inform the applicant that they can use this type of income but they don't have to divulge it if they don't want to.

Pension, retirement, and social security   An applicant can rely on pensions, re-tirement, or social security to qualify for a mortgage loan. As with any type of income, it must be verifiable. This type of income is usually easy to verify by letter

FannieMae

Self-Employed Income Analysis

Borrower Name

Property Address

General Instructions: This form is to be used as a guide in Underwriting the Self-employed borrower. The underwriter has a choice in analyzing the Individual Tax return by either the Schedule Analysis Method or the Adjusted Gross Income (AGI) Method.

The Schedule Analysis Method derives total income by analyzing Schedule C, D, E, and F for stable continuing self-employed income.

Schedule Analysis Method

	19__	19__	19__
A. Individual Tax Return (Form 1040)			
1. Schedule C:			
a. Net Profit or Loss			
b. Depletion	(+)		
c. Depreciation	(+)		
d. Less: 20% Exclusion for Meals and Entertainment	(−)		
2. Schedule D Recurring Capital Gains	(+)		
3. Schedule E Part II: Partnership/S Corporation Income (Loss)**			
4. Schedule F			
a. Net Profit or Loss			
b. Depreciation	(+)		
5. Schedule 2106 Total Expenses	(−)		
6. W-2 income from Corporation	(+)		
7. Total			

**Partnership Income (Loss) = [From IRS Schedule K-1 (Form 1065)]
   Ordinary Income (Loss) (+) Guaranteed Payments
   S Corporation Income (Loss) = [From IRS Schedule K-1 (Form 1120-s)]
   Ordinary Income (Loss) + Other Income (Loss)

B. Corporate Tax Return Form (1120) - Corporate Income to qualify the borrower will be considered only if the borrower can provide evidence of access to the funds

	19__	19__	19__
1. Taxable Income (Tax and Payments Section)	(+)		
2. Total Tax (Tax and Payments Section)	(−)		
3. Depreciation (Deductions Section)	(+)		
4. Depletion (Deductions Section)	(+)		
5. Mortgages, notes, bonds payable in less than one year (Balance Sheets Section)	(−)		
6. Subtotal			
7. Times individual percentage of ownership	X %	X %	X %
8. Subtotal			
9. Dividend Income reflected on borrower's individual income tax returns	(−)		
10. Total Income available to borrower			

C. S Corporation Tax Returns (Form 1120s) or Partnership Tax Returns (Form 1065) - Partnership or S Corporation income to qualify the borrower will be considered only if the borrower can provide evidence of access to the funds.

1. Depreciation (Deductions Section)	(+)		
2. Depletion (Deductions Section)	(+)		
3. Mortgages, notes, bonds payable in less than one year (Balance Sheets Section)	(−)		
4. Subtotal			
5. Times individual percentage of ownership	X %	X %	X %
6. Total income available to borrower			
Total Income Available (add A, B, C)	I	II	III

D. Year-to-Date Profit and Loss
Year-to-date income to qualify the borrower will be considered only if that income is in line with the previous year's earnings or if audited financial statements are provided.

1. Salary/Draws to Individual			$
2. Total Allowable add back	$	X _____ % of individual ownership =	$
3. Total net profit	$	X _____ % of individual ownership =	$
4. Total			$

Combined Total I, II, III, YTD = $_____ divided by _____ months = $_____ Monthly Average

This form is only a reference to help organize information from the tax returns. You must refer to the selling guide for our complete underwriting requirements on the self-employed.

Fannie Mae
Form 1084A   Nov. 89

from the company or organization providing the income, or by a copy of the checks received.

Welfare payments The ECOA states emphatically that all income must be treated equally when an applicant is trying to qualify for a mortgage loan. That includes welfare payments, or aid to dependent children income. The lender should, of course, verify the amount and how long it will last when determining if sufficient income exists to approve the application.

Other assets In addition to verifying the income of a borrower, the assets of that borrower or co-borrower are important to an underwriter in determining whether a loan should be made. These assets, which must be verified, will be used for the down payment, any prepaid items such as credit report, appraisal, closing cost, moving expense, and for those many other expenses associated with moving into a new house. A Request for Verification of Deposit (VOD) form should be used to verify savings and checking accounts.

If any of the funds used by an applicant come from relatives or others, a gift letter must appear in the file. This letter, signed by the donor, states that the funds are truly a gift and need not be repaid. The loan processor should verify that these funds exist and be able to trace where these funds came from.

RESIDENTIAL MORTGAGE CREDIT REPORT

Of great concern to any mortgage lender is how this applicant(s) has handled credit in the past. This is established by a credit report. The credit report must be issued by an independent credit reporting agency and must be less than 90 days old.

The type of credit report used for a loan which is saleable on the secondary mortgage market is a Residential Mortgage Credit Report. This report should be ordered for and become a part of each residential mortgage loan application. This specialized report provides a mortgage lender with additional information that can be found on a simpler factual credit report. The additional information provided by this report includes the following:

- credit information from national repositories of credit
- a check of public records for divorce, liens, judgments, etc.
- verification of current employment and address
- list of credit inquiries within previous 90 days

This report must also contain a certification that it meets the standards of the secondary mortgage market. The information shows how debts have been handled.

STATEN ISLAND SAVINGS BANK

REQUEST FOR VERIFICATION OF DEPOSIT

INSTRUCTIONS:	LENDER · Complete items 1 thru 8. Have applicant(s) complete item 9. Forward directly to depository named in item 1.
	DEPOSITORY · Please complete items 10 thru 15 and return DIRECTLY to lender named in item 2

PART I - REQUEST

1. TO (Name and address of depository)	2. FROM (Name and address of lender)
State Bank 1100 Main Street Oceanview, New York 10001	STATEN ISLAND SAVINGS BANK 15 Beach Street Staten Island, New York 10304

3. SIGNATURE OF LENDER	4. TITLE Administrative Assistant Mortgage Origination Dept.	5. DATE 2/27/89	6. LENDER'S NUMBER (Optional)
Theresa Tarangelo			

7. INFORMATION TO BE VERIFIED

TYPE OF ACCOUNT	ACCOUNT IN NAME OF	ACCOUNT NUMBER	BALANCE
savings	John & Susan Smith	222-00	$ 18,400.00
checking	John & Susan Smith	666-00-33	$ 1,800.00
			$
			$

TO DEPOSITORY: I have applied for a mortgage loan and stated in my financial statement that the balance on deposit with you is as shown above. You are authorized to verify this information and to supply the lender identified above with the information requested in items 10 thru 12. Your response is solely a matter of courtesy for which no responsibility is attached to your institution or any of your officers.

8. NAME AND ADDRESS OF APPLICANT(s)	9. SIGNATURE OF APPLICANT(s)
John & Susan Smith 40 Lynn Court Oceanview, New York 10001	*John Smith* *Susan Smith*

TO BE COMPLETED BY DEPOSITORY

PART II - VERIFICATION OF DEPOSITORY

10. DEPOSIT ACCOUNTS OF APPLICANT(s)

TYPE OF ACCOUNT	ACCOUNT NUMBER	CURRENT BALANCE	AVERAGE BALANCE FOR PREVIOUS TWO MONTHS	DATE OPENED
savings	222-00	$ 18,000.00	$ 18,200.00	3/8/87
checking	666-00-33	$ 1,500.00	$ 1,600.00	3/8/87
		$	$	
		$	$	

11. LOANS OUTSTANDING TO APPLICANT(s)

LOAN NUMBER	DATE OF LOAN	ORIGINAL AMOUNT	CURRENT BALANCE	INSTALLMENTS (Monthly/Quarterly)	SECURED BY	NUMBER OF LATE PAYMENTS
		$	$	$ per		
		$	$	$ per		
		$	$	$ per		

12. ADDITIONAL INFORMATION WHICH MAY BE OF ASSISTANCE IN DETERMINATION OF CREDIT WORTHINESS:
(Please include information on loans paid-in-full as in item 11 above)

13. SIGNATURE OF DEPOSITORY	14. TITLE	15. DATE
Frances Jonason	Branch Manager	March 15, 1989

The confidentiality of the information you have furnished will be preserved except where disclosure of this information is required by applicable law. The form is to be transmitted directly to the lender and is not to be transmitted through the applicant or any other party.

FNMA Form 1006
Rev June 78

This report will list all of the applicant's debts for the past seven years by creditor's name, date account was opened, high credit, current status, required payment, unpaid balance, and payment history. The payment history will be in a "number-of-times-past-due" format.

When a mortgage lender orders a credit report, it should be ordered using the full name of the applicant(s) and the social security number(s). If the applicants are co-borrowers and not married to each other, then separate credit reports must be provided.

If the credit report demonstrates an applicant has difficulty in handling financial obligations, the amount of current income and its relationship to outstanding obligations is most crucial. This is especially true if the debt was a type of installment debt similar to a mortgage loan. In some situations, a mortgage lender may not be able to justify a loan to an applicant regardless of current income because of past credit problems. In all situations, an applicant should be advised that if the loan is turned down because of adverse credit information, they can contact the credit bureau which furnished the information.

Derogatory Items

If any of the derogatory items listed below appears on the credit report, the loan processor should require a letter explaining the reason for the credit problem as if the situation still exists. This information will be critical to the underwriter's determination. These items include:

- derogatory ratings
- bankruptcy
- suits
- judgments
- late payments
- concealed liabilities
- numerous inquiries

Fair Credit Reporting Act

A mortgage lender must be aware of the Fair Credit Reporting Act and the limitations that are placed on credit information gathering. That law, as mentioned earlier, is designed to ensure fair and accurate reporting of information regarding consumer credit. A mortgage lender seeking credit information from a consumer reporting agency must certify the purpose for which the information is sought and use it for no other purpose. This act prohibits investigative reports relating to character, general reputation, mode of living, and other subjective areas which are based on interviews with neighbors and others.

At the time a lender orders a credit report, it should indicate to the credit agency or bureau the type of loan being applied for (i.e., conventional, FHA, or VA). (A lender should be sure that the credit reporting agency is approved by FHA or VA.) The report from a reporting agency should be used as a verification of information supplied on the application. The credit bureau will be relying on its own files, various national repositories of credit information, and from the public record.

When a credit report is received, the lender should check it against the application and look for discrepancies. Some are almost certain to occur since many applicants cannot remember all details exactly, but if major deletions or erroneous information of a serious nature are present, the applicant should be asked to explain. An applicant may not be aware of some of the information contained in a credit report. If upon being made aware of that information, the applicant believes a mistake has been made, the applicant should be advised to discuss the information with the credit bureau. On occasions, wrong information is transmitted and can often be corrected by a discussion between the applicant and the credit bureau.

TITLE INSURANCE

The purpose of title insurance is to protect the mortgage lender against any defects in the title of the mortgagor. Title insurance is required for all residential mortgage loans that will be sold into the secondary mortgage market.

As a general rule, after the loan has been approved, a loan processor will order the preliminary title report. This report will list the current owners and any liens or encumbrances against the property. The final title insurance policy will not be received until after the loan has closed so that it can show the mortgage lender's position. This report will be discussed in Chapter 13.

FINAL CHECK

Before sending a residential mortgage loan file on to an underwriter, a loan processor should review the file to ascertain that all required documents are present and properly prepared. This will include:

- application: both final typed and preliminary application
- completed verification for:
- —employment(s) (and former employment if needed)
- —deposit(s)
- —past mortgages or landlords
- Residential Mortgage Credit Report

TICOR TITLE GUARANTEE   TICOR TITLE INSURANCE

This Certificate of Title has been prepared by TICOR TITLE GUARANTEE COMPANY, a New York Corporation, and TICOR TITLE INSURANCE COMPANY, a California Corporation, together herein called "The Company".

Certificate of Title

Prepared For:

JOHN G. HALL, ESQ.
57 Beach Street
Staten Island, New York 10304

Title No. TAA 87-00450
Appl. File No. 6527/87

Nature of Transaction: Mortgage

Amount of Insurance: $80,000.00

Proposed Insured: Staten Island Savings Bank

Seller or Borrower: JOHN SMITH and SUSAN SMITH, his wife

Seller or Borrower/s Atty: None

Premises (See Schedule "A"): 59 Silver Lane, Staten Island, N.Y. 10315

County: Richmond   Town/City: Inc. Village:

Tax Map Designation: :

Section: 15   Block: 3617   Lot/s: 12

The Certificate of Title has been prepared in accordance with the information and instructions received. If any changes or additions are desired, please notify The Company promptly.

Questions concerning the within certificate should be directed to:

LAND ABSTRACT STATEN ISLAND CORP.
57 Beach Street
Staten Island, N.Y. 10304

TICOR TITLE GUARANTEE COMPANY
and
TICOR TITLE INSURANCE COMPANY

Dated: April 1, 1989

Certified by: LAND ABSTRACT STATEN ISLAND CORP.
_____
Authorized Signature

Redated: _____
Julia M. Hall, Pres.

By: _____
Authorized Signature

701

- **Uniform Residential Appraisal Report**
- **evidence that all federally mandated consumer protection requirements have been followed for:**
—ECOA
—RESPA
—Truth-in-lending

Set Up Date   2/15/89
Reset
Reset

Mellon Financial Services
Processing Check Sheet

Applicant: DAVID PRESTON WALTERS   Co-Applicant: DORIS MITCHELL WALTERS

Property Address: 127 MONET PLACE   Type: VA

KENNER, LOUISIANA 70065   Term/Rate: 30 YEARS/13.50%

Date of Application: 2/15/89   S.P.:   58,500.00

Source: CAROLYN RIVERS   Loan: 58,500.00

X	Requested Items		Date Requested	Date Received	Remarks
X	Appraisal & Application Fees		2/15	2/15	
X	Purchase Agreement		2/15	2/15	
	Plans and Specifications (Proposed)				
X	Titles (Existing)		2/15	2/15	
X	Credit Report		2/15	2/28	
X	Employment	Applicant	2/15	2/25	
X	Verifications	Co-Applicant	2/15	2/25	
	Previous	Applicant			
	Employment	Co-Applicant			
	Verifications				
	Union Verification				
X		1. FIRST BANK	2/15	2/27	
X	Deposit	2. PLANTATION BANK	2/15	2/20	
	Verifications	3.			
		4.			
X	Appraisal – Type VA		2/15	3/10	
	FHA Appraisal Acknowledgement Letter Sent to Applicant				
	Appraisal Sent to Listing and Selling Agent				
	Divorce Decrees/Death Certificate (Where Permitted)				
X	W-2 Forms/1040 Forms		2/15	2/15	
	Financial and P & L Statements				
X	Insurance Preference Letter		2/15	2/15	
X	Good Faith Estimate and Disclosure		2/15	2/15	
X	Certificate of Eligibility		2/15	2/25	
	DD-214/Statement of Service				
X		1. SUN FINANCE	2/15	2/27	
	Mortgage	2.			
	Rating	3.			
	Letters	4.			
	Gift Letter				
X	Loan Approval		3/10	3/11	

P-89
MFS 3176
(2/85)

—Flood insurance
—Others (if applicable)
• money collected for:
—credit report
—appraisal
—other third-party expenditures

When a loan processor has reviewed the file and is satisfied that all relevant information is available for an underwriting decision to be made, the file should be forwarded to an underwriter as expeditiously as possible.

It is not recommended that the same person who processed a loan also be the person who underwrites the loan. The chances for fraud in this situation are too great. If a lending institution is so small that it cannot afford a qualified underwriter, it should use one of the various underwriting services offered by mortgage insurance companies and others.

UNDERWRITING THE RESIDENTIAL MORTGAGE LOAN ════════ 7

The term underwriting is used in many segments of the American economy to describe the process of analyzing information relating to risk and making a decision whether or not to accept that risk. In real estate, underwriting is an integral part of the mortgage lending process, regardless of the type of loan or the type of property securing the mortgage. Although similarities exist in the underwriting of all types of real estate loans, the differences are fundamental and of great importance.

This chapter examines the steps and issues involved in underwriting a residential mortgage loan with the assumption being that the loan could be sold into the secondary mortgage market.

_____ *INTRODUCTION*

All mortgage loans involve the risk of possible financial loss to a mortgage lender or investor. The underwriting involved to determine this risk on a residential mortgage loan requires the gathering and analysis of much information about both the applicant and the real estate which will secure the loan.

Underwriting can involve more than just what is done by a mortgage lender. On any one residential loan, three separate underwriting reviews could occur at various stages of the mortgage lending cycle:

1. A mortgage lender will analyze the risk and determine whether to lend funds to a borrower for a period of time secured by a certain piece of real estate.
2. A mortgage insurer or guarantor will determine if mortgage insurance is to be written, or a guarantee made based on the loan as submitted.
3. A permanent investor will determine if the mortgage or mortgages as submitted will be purchased.

Each of these underwriters will analyze the submission, estimate the risk to the institution being represented, and determine if the benefits are sufficient to balance the risk. Mortgage lending is a risk business and a lender must be willing to take a business risk to earn a fee or make a profit and therefore satisfy the real estate financing needs of the nation. All mortgage lenders have a responsibility to attempt to satisfy any request for a mortgage loan as long as the risk is fully analyzed and acceptable. The duty to make a loan if at all possible must be balanced by a mortgage lender's duty to protect loaned funds, which are the savings of depositors or life insurance policyholders.

UNDERWRITING BY A MORTGAGE LENDER

Of the three stages mentioned, mortgage lenders have the most difficult underwriting task because they face the delinquency problems that can result from improperly underwritten mortgages. A mortgage banker has a unique problem. Unlike other mortgage lenders, a mortgage banker underwrites a loan knowing that the loan must be sold to a permanent investor either directly or through the secondary mortgage market. If a loan is not attractive as made, because of poor underwriting, that loan may not be marketable. This can involve considerable loss to a mortgage banker. Since most mortgage lenders have the option of placing mortgages they originate in their own portfolios, their loss potential for a poorly underwritten mortgage is less than that of a mortgage banker. All lenders, of course, share the danger that a poorly underwritten mortgage may become delinquent.

If a default occurs, the cost of either curing the default or foreclosing could eliminate present or future profit made from either marketing or servicing. For example, loss could result from a poorly underwritten mortgage if the defaulted loan is in a pool of mortgages securing a GNMA mortgage-backed security. In this situation, the originating mortgage lender must pay the monthly accrued principal and interest to the security holder from its own funds. As is evident, the underwriting phase in the mortgage lending cycle can have a lasting effect, obligating the originating mortgage lender to exercise professional expertise in underwriting.

Underwriting Guidelines

Unfortunately, no single uniform set of underwriting guidelines exists for all residential mortgage loans. To a great extent, the underwriting guidelines of both Fannie Mae and Freddie Mac are the standards that most lenders attempt to follow. Even those lenders who don't intend to sell loans to these two secondary mortgage market players should attempt to follow these well conceived underwriting guidelines. In the past, most lenders have had to adopt and follow different underwriting rules, regulations, and formulas depending on whether a residential mortgage loan is to be sold to an investor or kept in a portfolio and whether the loan is conventional, FHA-insured, or VA-guaranteed. Many of these differences are not of major significance in underwriting but instead affect loan processing.

It is important to realize that only guidelines exist—not specific, precise formulas that can be applied to every applicant. Underwriting is an art, not a science, and the successful underwriter is one who can analyze all relevant material and approve a mortgage applicant while protecting the assets of others.

Underwriting and the Federal Government

The 1970s witnessed the federal government becoming very involved in the fairness of certain underwriting guidelines. The government wanted to end all discriminatory lending practices and to ensure that each individual would be treated equally when they applied for a mortgage loan. In essence, the burden shifted from the applicant having to demonstrate that he or she qualified for a mortgage loan to the lender having to establish the fact that the applicant was not qualified. This shift in the underwriting concept makes a mortgage lender liable for civil and/or criminal penalties if the letter and spirit of the various anti-discrimination laws are not followed exactly.

RATIOS

Loan-to-Value Ratios

The loan-to-value ratio (LTV) is probably the most important of all the ratios when underwriting a residential mortgage loan. The lower the LTV the safer the loan is for a lender. The reason is that the lower the LTV, the higher the equity the borrower will have in the property and thus the more that borrower has to lose. The LTV is calculated as follows:

$$\frac{\text{Mortgage amount}}{\text{Lesser of sales price or appraised value}} = \text{LTV}$$

One of the reasons 95 percent of LTV loans have fallen on disfavor with some lenders recently is because a borrower will have no equity in the property if the loan goes bad shortly after having been made. The reason for this, according to Mortgage Guaranty Insurance Corporation, "...is once default occurs, there is a better than 50 percent chance of foreclosure, largely because of the borrower's inability to sell the property at a price high enough to cover the remaining loan balance plus selling costs and delinquent interest."

Various studies have been made which support this position by establishing that a 90 percent LTV loan was twice as likely as an 80 percent LTV loan to default, and a 95 percent LTV loan has nearly three times the default risk as a 90 percent LTV loan. A 97 percent LTV loan, according to these same studies, was nearly six times more risky than a 90 percent LTV loan.

It should be obvious that any loan entered into over 80 percent LTV should be supported by some type of mortgage insurance. Mortgage insurance is discussed in detail in Chapter 8.

Equity

Where can the money for the down payment come from—anywhere? The money for the down payment (or the equity) can come from any cash source. That source could be money in a financial institution, stocks and bonds, or from the sale of real estate. The existence of these funds should be established by a Verification of Deposit (VOD). The major issues with the VOD for the underwriter is when was the account opened and in what name(s) it is held. Deposits in joint accounts and recently opened new accounts can hide loans from family members.

As a general rule, the secondary mortgage market is interested in establishing that the borrower has been able to save some of the down payment for the mortgage loan. If the LTV is below 80 percent, the down payment could be gifted, but if the LTV is over 80 percent, at least 5 percent of the purchase price must have been saved by the borrower. The borrower is expected to be able to establish how that money had been saved.

As mentioned, some or all of the down payment could come from a gift, but it is essential that a true gift has been made and that there is no expectation of that money being repaid. A legally binding gift letter must be signed by the grantor and the source of the funds being given established.

Income Ratios

An underwriter is concerned about both the ability to repay the mortgage debt and the willingness to do so. First, the issue of ability to repay will be considered.

The most important test of whether an applicant can afford a particular mortgage loan is by computing the various income ratios. These ratios, established by either the insuring/guaranteeing entities or the secondary mortgage market, have evolved through the years and after millions of mortgage loans as realistic guidelines for making mortgage loans with a low risk of default. The so-called front-end ratio is arrived at by computing the percent of monthly income necessary to meet the monthly housing expense.

The monthly housing expense is determined in various ways depending on whether a loan is conventional, FHA, or VA. The percentage of income which can be used for these expenses also varies depending on the type of

STATEN ISLAND SAVINGS BANK

EXECUTIVE OFFICES · 15 BEACH STREET   STATEN ISLAND N Y 10304   (718) 447-7900

SOURCE OF FUNDS AFFIDAVIT

I hereby certify that the funds used for the deposit on 59 Silver Lane, S.I.N.Y.
                                                        (property)

in the amount of $ 10,000.00   were paid on February 20, 1989   by
                                                  (date)

check drawn on State Bank   . The Balance
                  (lending institution)

in the account is now $ 1,800.00   .

This money was derived from   checking   and not borrowed in
                                (type of account)

any way.

Further, I wish to certify that the balance due at settlement, approximately

$ 15,500   will be obtained from State Bank   .
                                          (lending institution)

Date: February 27, 1989   _John Smith_____
                                      (Borrowers' signature)

                                      _Susan Smith_____
                                      (Borrowers signature)

The foregoing instrument was
Notorized before me this 27
day of FEBRUARY   , 1989.

_Roberta O'Keen_____

loan. When computing the monthly housing expense on a conventional loan, the following monthly charges or monthly share of annual expenses are added (if applicable):

- principal
- interest
- hazard insurance
- real estate tax
- mortgage insurance premium
- home owners association fee
- ground rents
- any payment on an existing or proposed second mortgage

The secondary mortgage market used to make a distinction based on the loan-to-value ratio or the type of mortgage instrument in determining the amount of gross monthly income that could be used for housing expenses. Today, the ratio is the same for all loans regardless of the LTV or whether the loan is an ARM or FRM. As a result, the total of the applicable items included in the monthly housing expense should not exceed 28 percent of gross monthly income. Gross monthly income means income before any type of deductions.

In some situations, if no long-term debts exist, a lender may be able to justify higher ratios, but care must be taken that the loan still can be sold in the secondary mortgage market.

Long-term Debt Ratio

Individuals often have other contractual debt obligations in addition to mortgage payments to be met each month. The ratio of these debts to gross monthly income must be calculated separately. This ratio is called the back-end, or long-term, debt ratio. For example, mortgage payments, any revolving charges or other payments on installment debts which have more than ten remaining payments, and any alimony or child support payments should not total more than 36 percent of gross monthly income.

Higher ratios may be justified by mitigating factors, such as:

- demonstrated ability of an applicant to allocate a higher percent of gross income to housing expenses
- larger down payment than normal
- demonstrated ability of applicant to accumulate savings and maintain a good credit rating
- a large net worth
- potential for increased earnings because of education or profession

Veterans Administration	**LOAN ANALYSIS**	LOAN NUMBER 06011992

SECTION A – LOAN DATA

1. NAME OF BORROWER GEORGE P. ANDERSON	2. AMOUNT OF LOAN $ 151,650.00	3. CASH DOWN PAYMENT ON PURCHASE PRICE $ 28,350.00

SECTION B – BORROWER'S PERSONAL AND FINANCIAL STATUS

4. APPLICANT'S AGE 45	5. OCCUPATION OF APPLICANT CDR O-5	6. NUMBER OF YEARS AT PRESENT EMPLOYMENT 16 YRS	7. LIQUID ASSETS (Cash, savings, bonds, etc.) $ 20,346.00	8. CURRENT MONTHLY RENTAL OR OTHER HOUSING EXPENSE $ 800.00
9. UTILITIES INCLUDED ☐ YES ☒ NO	10. SPOUSE'S AGE 44	11. OCCUPATION OF SPOUSE COMPUTER SUPERVISOR	12. NUMBER OF YEARS AT PRESENT EMPLOYMENT 4 YRS	13. AGE OF OTHER DEPENDENTS 14, 12

NOTE: ROUND ALL DOLLAR AMOUNTS BELOW TO NEAREST WHOLE DOLLAR.

SECTION C – ESTIMATED MONTHLY SHELTER EXPENSES (This Property)

	ITEMS	AMOUNT
14.	TERM OF LOAN: 30 YEARS	
15.	MORTGAGE (PRINCIPAL AND INTEREST) PAYMENT 9.500%	$1275.16
16.	REALTY TAXES	150.00
17.	HAZARD INSURANCE	35.00
18.	SPECIAL ASSESSMENTS	
19.	MAINTENANCE	80.00
20.	UTILITIES (including heat)	200.00
21.	OTHER (HOA, Condo fees, etc.)	15.00
22.	TOTAL	$ 1755.16

SECTION D – DEBTS AND OBLIGATIONS
(Itemize and indicate by (✓) which debts considered in Section E, Line 41)

	ITEMS	(✓)	MO. PAYMENT	UNPAID BAL.
23.			$	$
24.				
25.				
26.				
27.	SEE ATTACHED			
28.				
29.				
30.	JOB RELATED EXPENSE (e.g., child-care)			
31.	TOTAL		$ 1235.00	$82450.00

SECTION E – MONTHLY INCOME AND DEDUCTIONS

	ITEMS	SPOUSE	BORROWER	TOTAL
32.	GROSS SALARY OR EARNINGS FROM EMPLOYMENT	$ 3014.00	$ 3806.70	$ 6820.70
33.	FEDERAL INCOME TAX	600.00	900.00	
34.	STATE INCOME TAX	200.00	500.00	
35.	DEDUCTIONS RETIREMENT OR SOCIAL SECURITY	100.00	300.00	
36.	OTHER (Specify)			
37.	TOTAL DEDUCTIONS	$ 900.00	$ 1700.00	$ 2600.00
38.	NET TAKE-HOME PAY	2114.00	2106.70	4220.70
39.	PENSION, COMPENSATION OR OTHER NET INCOME (Specify)		1270.00	1270.00
40.	TOTAL (Sum of lines 38 and 39)	$ 2114.00	$ 3376.70	$ 5490.70
41.	LESS THOSE OBLIGATIONS LISTED IN SECTION D WHICH SHOULD BE DEDUCTED FROM INCOME			436.57
42.	TOTAL NET EFFECTIVE INCOME			$ 5054.13
43.	LESS ESTIMATED MONTHLY SHELTER EXPENSE (Line 22)			1755.16
44.	BALANCE AVAILABLE FOR FAMILY SUPPORT			$ 3298.97

45. PAST CREDIT RECORD ☒ SATISFACTORY ☐ UNSATISFACTORY	46. DOES LOAN MEET VA CREDIT STANDARDS? (Give reasons for decision under "Remarks," if necessary, e.g., borderline case) ☒ YES ☐ NO

47. REMARKS (Use reverse, if necessary)

```
                          FAMILY SUPPORT   -    850.00
                                              ---------
                                              2,448.97

                  VA RATIO:        23.628
```

SECTION F – DISPOSITION OF APPLICATION

☒ Recommend that the application be approved since it meets all requirements of Chapter 37, Title 38, U.S. Code and applicable VA Regulations and directives.

☐ Recommend that the application be disapproved for the reasons stated under "Remarks" above.

48. DATE 06/28/92	49. SIGNATURE OF EXAMINER *Mildred H Harvela*
50. FINAL ACTION ☒ APPROVE APPLICATION ☐ REJECT APPLICATION	51. DATE 6-28-92	52. SIGNATURE AND TITLE OF APPROVING OFFICIAL

VA FORM SEP 1983 **26-6393**   EXISTING STOCKS OF VA FORM 26-6393, MAY 1979, WILL BE USED.

266393
NFCU 892M (8-89)

Example: Ed and Jane Smith want to borrow $92,000 in order to purchase a single-family detached house appraised at $115,000. He earns $35,000 a year as a bricklayer and she earns $25,000 as an assistant professor of English. The only long-term debt is a car payment of $400 a month with 25 months remaining.

Calculations

Gross monthly income (borrower)		$2,917
Gross monthly income (co-borrower)		2,083
Substantiated other gross income		-0-
Total monthly income		5,000
28% of gross monthly income	$1,400	
36% of gross monthly income	1,800	
Monthly housing expense		
Principal & interest		
(at 10% for 30 years)	808	
Private mortgage insurance	-0-	
Insurance escrow	30	
Tax escrow	125	
Other	-0-	
Total housing expense	963	
Total of all long-term debts	400	
Total of all monthly payments	1,363	

Federal Housing Administration

When the loan requested is FHA-insured, the income ratios are slightly higher than with a conventional loan. Before 1990, FHA used net income when calculating ratios, but has since decided to adopt the more universal gross income calculations. The new FHA ratios are 29 percent for the mortgage payment ratio and 41 percent for the total debt ratio.

Veterans Administration—VA Mortgage

The VA uses a modified residual method in qualifying a veteran for a mortgage loan, and this result is then double-checked against a total-debt-to-income-ratio of 41 percent. The residual income standards are based on a Department of Labor Consumer Expenditure Survey with regional differences.

Loans with ratios between 41.1 percent and 45 percent would be acceptable provided the residual was at least 20 percent over the appropriate standard. The VA will also accept some deviations if written justifications exist and are acceptable.

EMPLOYMENT

An evaluation must be made of the employment of the applicant and co-applicant and the probability that it will continue. For most applicants, the income which will repay the mortgage loan will be derived from being employed. An underwriter should have a Verification of Employment (VOE) form in the file which should provide all information needed about an employed individual.

The important points for the underwriter to review carefully on the VOE include the following:

- salary/wage correspond with the application
- probability of continued employment acceptable
- overtime/bonus likely to continue
- dates of employment correspond with the application
- signature of employer on form

If the applicant has been employed at the current employer for less than two years, a VOE from the former employer is necessary. For a self-employed person (the highest risk category of any applicant) the accounting forms discussed in Chapter 6 should be used.

An applicant who has demonstrated job stability and is in a line of work which has a promising future should be considered favorably by an underwriter. The education of an applicant or co-applicant and whether they are in a profession which has strong growth potential may actually be enough to make a close underwriting call on a loan a "makable" one.

In today's society, moving from one job to another, especially if the new job is for more pay and is in the same field of endeavor, is a positive point. On the other hand, extensive job changes without advancement or pay increases may be indicative of future financial instability. Gaps in employment are indicators of possible future problems and should be adequately explained.

WILLINGNESS TO REPAY

A key factor in underwriting an application for a mortgage loan is how an applicant has handled credit in the past. Ability to repay has already been discussed; here, we are concerned with willingness to repay. The primary way of establishing willingness to repay is by careful review of the credit report. The credit report that should be used for first mortgages is the Residential Mortgage Credit Report. This credit report was discussed in detail in Chapter 6.

If an underwriter can determine that an applicant has had a credit history of meeting payments according to contract terms, then that application should be considered in a positive manner. If, on the other hand, the credit history shows some credit problems such as slow payment, then an underwriter needs to analyze the credit very carefully. If an applicant has declared bankruptcy, it is incumbent on an underwriter to have complete information in order to make an informed loan decision.

Bankruptcy

The fact that a bankruptcy exists in an applicant's credit history does not in itself lead to a negative response to an application. The reasons for the bankruptcy and the type of filing are important factors for an underwriter to consider. As an example, if the bankruptcy was caused by unemployment, extensive medical bills, or other circumstances beyond the control of the applicant and these facts can be verified, the bankruptcy should not be the reason for a credit denial. As a general rule, if a bankruptcy exists in the credit history, the credit will be acceptable if two years of excellent credit history have been maintained since the discharge.

A form of bankruptcy which has become common is a wage earner's petition. A wage earner's petition under chapter 13 of the Bankruptcy Law provides for partial or full repayment of debts over a period of time, usually two to five years. When all payments have been satisfactorily made, underwriters should consider that accomplishment as reestablishing credit. Occasionally, a mortgage loan will be applied for before full discharge. In such a situation, the approval of the bankruptcy judge may be required. Certain other bankruptcies, such as those over seven years old, should not be considered at all unless the principal was $50,000 or more.

Past Foreclosures or Deed in Lieu

If the applicant has a past foreclosure or has entered into an agreement for a deed in lieu of foreclosure, that applicant has indicated a problem handling credit. The secondary mortgage market requires these applicants to have had three years of excellent credit history since the foreclosure or deed in lieu before they can be considered for a mortgage loan.

PROPERTY GUIDELINES

The next stage in underwriting a residential mortgage loan involves an analysis of the real estate which will secure the mortgage debt. Although it is expected that the income of a borrower will be available to fulfill the mortgage obligation, a mortgage lender must protect both its own position and that of any investor by having adequate security for the debt. The adequacy of the security will be established by an appraisal.

An appraisal is an opinion or estimate of market value made by an appraiser who is either an independent fee appraiser or employed by a mortgage lender. An appraisal not only helps establish the adequacy of the security but also establishes the value of security upon which the loan-to-value ratio will be applied. (See Chapter 12.)

Redlining

An underwriter must underwrite the appraisal as carefully as any other information. But the underwriter must not designate any area or neighborhood as being unacceptable nor allow any appraiser to do so; in other words, a lender will not "redline." (Redlining is defined as the withdrawal of mortgage funds from an area due to perceived risks in that area based on racial, social, or ethnic factors.) Instead, a lender should make a sound supportable judgment as to the market value of a given piece of real estate and whether that value provides sufficient security.

Appraisal Items

The following are some of the items found on the appraisal that should be carefully reviewed by the underwriter:

Location Location is always the most critical of all evaluating factors.

- Land value is not more than 30 percent of total appraised value.
- Adequate sewage and water facilities and other utilities are present.
- Property is readily accessible by an all-weather road.
- No danger is posed to health and safety from immediate surroundings (including environmental hazards).

Physical security The age, equipment, architectural design, quality of construction, floor plan, and site features are considered in establishing the adequacy and future value of the physical security.

- Evidence of compliance with local codes should be in file for underwriter's review.
- Topography, shape, size, and drainage of a lot are equally important.
- View amenities, easements, and other encroachments may have either a positive or negative influence on market value.

Local government.

- The amount of property tax can have a great effect on future marketability.
- Building codes, deed restrictions, and zoning ordinances help to maintain housing standards and promote a high degree of homogeneity.

Comparable sales.   This section is critical for underwriting residential real estate loans.

- Ascertain that the comparables are truly comparable in regard to location, type of real estate, and time of sale.
- Determine if the adjustments are more than 10 percent per category.

In order to permit the sale of the loan into the secondary mortgage market and to satisfy certain regulatory requirements, the Uniform Residential Appraisal Form (URAR) such as FHLMC Form 70 should be used.

Underwriting Systems

Two systems exist for evaluating the creditworthiness of an applicant. Practically all mortgage lenders use the judgmental system which relies on trained underwriters to evaluate each application on a case-by-case basis. This means that the same standards are applied to each application in the same manner. Although exceptions are allowed, the reason for the exception must be clearly demonstrable. For example, if a larger-than-normal down payment is made, then an increased total debt ratio of 40 percent of gross monthly income may be acceptable.

The second system attempts to determine the creditworthiness of an applicant by assigning points to certain attributes and facts. On their face, these systems are not illegal or discriminatory, although ECOA regulations state that these systems must be "…demonstrably and statistically sound and empirically derived." Because of the complexities and potential for unintended discrimination, few, if any, mortgage lenders are currently using this second system.

Underwriting Guidelines and Loan Application Register

The underwriting standards used by a lender should be clearly written, nondiscriminatory, and available for review by the general public. These standards should be periodically reviewed to ensure continuing compliance with evolving legislation and good business practices. All mortgage lenders (excluding credit unions) also need to be concerned about the Community Reinvestment Act (CRA), which establishes guidelines for taking care of the credit needs of the community.

The Home Mortgage Disclosure Act (HMDA) requires all mortgage lenders to maintain a Loan Application Register within which they retain important information on each application for a mortgage loan. The information to be retained must include:

- name(s) of applicant
- amount of loan requested
- zip code and census tract of property
- sex, race, marital status, age of applicant
- interest rate
- terms and fee
- loan-to-value ratio
- year property was built
- disposition of the application

This information will allow both regulators and the public to determine whether lending standards are being applied in a nondiscriminatory manner.

THE UNDERWRITING DECISION

When all information relating to an applicant's financial capabilities, credit characteristics, and physical security is present a decision must be made to accept, reject, or modify the mortgage loan application. This decision must be sent to an applicant within 30 days of the date of application.

If the application is accepted, a mortgage lender should send a commitment letter to the approved applicant and explain the procedures that will be followed next in connection with loan closing.

If the application is modified by any action, such as offering less credit or credit at different terms, and that counteroffer is accepted, the loan proceeds as with a normal loan acceptance.

On the other hand, if an application is rejected, an applicant must be notified of the rejection, provided with the ECOA notice of nondiscrimination, and informed that the reason for rejection will be given if requested. This is usually accomplished by a Statement of Credit Denial.

Although all underwriters should attempt to approve a loan application if at all prudently possible, the approval of a loan that will become delinquent is a disservice to the borrower, the mortgage lender, and those the latter represents.

Quality Control

Quality control has recently resurfaced as the pivotal element in the efforts of residential mortgage lenders to maintain profitability. It has been pushed to the forefront over the past 25 years as those lenders have had to revise methods of

SINGLE FAMILY RESIDENCE

EFFECTIVE INCOME:

	Borrower	Co-Borrower	Total		Payment	
Base	_____	_____	_____		P & I	_____
Overtime	_____	_____	_____		Haz. Ins.	_____
Commission	_____	_____	_____		Taxes	_____
Bonus	_____	_____	_____		PMI	_____
Net Rental	_____	_____	_____		HOA	_____
Other	_____	_____	_____		Other	_____
Total	_____	_____	A_____		F. Total	_____

B. 25% of Income (A)   _____   G. Debt over 10 mos.   _____

C. 4:1 Ratio F/A   H. Total

D. 33% of Income (A)   _____

E. 3:1 Ratio H/A   _____

Questions to be asked when underwriting the loan.

APPLICATION — GENERAL	YES	NO
Do loan amount and term meet requirements?	_____	_____
Is application complete?	_____	_____
Is math accurate?	_____	_____
Is application signed by applicant(s)?	_____	_____
Is application signed by credit union?	_____	_____
Are exhibits less than 90 days old?	_____	_____

CREDIT UNDERWRITING

Credit Report

	YES	NO
Is it the proper type?	_____	_____
Have public records been checked?	_____	_____
Are all accounts verified?	_____	_____
Are all credit ratings acceptable?	_____	_____
Are marginal accounts explained by applicant?	_____	_____

INCOME

	YES	NO
Is employment verified for two years?	_____	_____
Is income on application supported by verifications?	_____	_____
Is income sufficient for housing & expense? (4:1 ratio)	_____	_____
Is income sufficient for total obligations? (3:1 ratio)	_____	_____

DOWNPAYMENT

	YES	NO
Does borrower have sufficient liquid assets for closing?	_____	_____
Are the assets for closing verified?	_____	_____
Are the source of these assets documented?	_____	_____

PROPERTY UNDERWRITING

	YES	NO
Is property a single family residence?	_____	_____
Is property to be owner-occupied?	_____	_____
Is property free of commercial aspect?	_____	_____
Is property either fee simple or leasehold?	_____	_____
Does property abut a publicly dedicated & maintained road?	_____	_____
Is property free of excessive functional obsolesence?	_____	_____
Is property free of excessive economic obsolesence?	_____	_____
Is property readily marketable?	_____	_____
If property is rural, does it meet the requirements?	_____	_____
Is the appraisal acceptable?	_____	_____

112

STATEMENT OF CREDIT DENIAL, TERMINATION, OR CHANGE

Date:

Applicant's Name: __Frank Stavola__   Date __January 1, 1989__

Applicant's Address: __1001 North Street, Missoula, Montana 59801__

Description of Account, Transaction, or __Mortgage Loan__

Requested Credit: __$100,000__

Description of Action Taken: __denial__

PART I. PRINCIPAL REASON(S) FOR CREDIT DENIAL, TERMINATION, OR OTHER ACTION TAKEN CONCERNING CREDIT.

THIS SECTION **MUST BE COMPLETED IN ALL INSTANCES**

- ☐ Credit application incomplete
- ☐ Insufficient number of credit references provided
- ☐ Unacceptable type of credit references provided
- ☐ Unable to verify credit references
- ☐ Temporary or irregular employment
- ☐ Unable to verify employment
- ☐ Length of employment
- ☐ Income insufficient for amount of credit requested
- ☐ Other, Specify: _____
- ☐ Other, specify: _____

- ☒ Excessive obligations in relation to income
- ☐ Unable to verify income
- ☐ Length of residence
- ☐ Temporary residence
- ☐ Unable to verify residence
- ☐ No credit file
- ☐ Limited credit experience
- ☐ Poor credit performance with us
- ☐ Delinquent past or present credit obligations with others

- ☐ Garnishment, attachment, foreclosure, repossession, collection action, or judgment.
- ☐ Bankruptcy
- ☐ Value, or type of collateral not sufficient
- ☐ Inadequate down payment
- ☐ No deposit relationship with us
- ☐ We do not grant credit to any applicant on the terms and conditions you have requested.

PART II. DISCLOSURE OF USE OF INFORMATION OBTAINED FROM AN OUTSIDE SOURCE. This section should be completed if the credit decision was based in whole or in part on information that has been obtained from an outside source.

☐ Our credit decision was based in whole or in part on information obtained from the consumer reporting agency listed below. You have a right under the Fair Credit Reporting Act to know the information contained in your credit file at the consumer reporting agency. The consumer reporting agency played no part in our decision and is unable to supply specific reasons why we have denied credit to you.

__Overall Credit Agency__
Name of Consumer Reporting Agency

__999 South Street__
Street Address

__Missoula, Montana, 59801__
City, State, Zip

__406-243-6700__
Telephone Number

☐ Our credit decision was based in whole or in part on information obtained from an outside source other than a consumer reporting agency. Under the Fair Credit Reporting Act, you have the right to make a written request, no later than 60 days after you receive this notice, for disclosure of the nature of this information

If you have any questions regarding this notice, you should contact:

__North Shore Mortgage Company__
Institution Name

__111 East Street__
Street Address

__Kalispell, Montana__
City, State, Zip

__406-111-2020__
Telephone Number

Notice:

The Federal Equal Credit Opportunity Act prohibits creditors from discriminating against credit applicants on the basis of race, color, religion, national orgin, sex, marital status, age (provided the applicant has the capacity to enter into a binding contract); because all or part of the applicant's income derives from any public assistance program; or because the applicant has in good faith exercised any right under the Consumer Credit Protection Act. The federal agency that administers compliance with this law concerning this creditor is:

operations to cope with economic and regulatory shockwaves sent through the nation's mortgage markets. Given the outlook for this sector of the financial industry, quality control will remain the primary action item for profitable mortgage lenders in the 1990s.

During the past 10 years, quality control has often been virtually ignored by many primary mortgage lenders, much to the chagrin of investors. The popular wisdom of that day was that this was a side effect of increased competition. As more and more competitors entered the mortgage lending field, volume became the key strategy for maintaining profits. Often, this increased volume was achieved at the expense of adequate safeguards, and most of the default and foreclosure problems facing lenders and mortgage insurers alike in the mid-1980s were the result.

The extent of that quality control problem can be measured in a number of ways. The mortgage insurance business was under tremendous earnings pressure during the mid-1980s because of dramatically increasing claims. In 1985, a study conducted by the Mortgage Insurance Companies of America showed that one out of four claims involved fraud or substandard underwriting on the part of mortgage lenders.

It is ironic that these quality control problems have become such an issue recently since investors and insurers have had quality control programs for many years. Both HUD and Fannie Mae have required for years that seller/servicers perform an audit on 10 percent of the loans closed. It is common knowledge that these requirements were often ignored. Even when followed, however, they were not as effective as they should have been. The principal objection to a program of this type is that it can root out problems only after a loan has been closed. To be truly effective, such a program must prevent such loans from reaching the closing stage.

Most mortgage investors and insurers believe that both fraud and sloppy or substandard underwriting are the function of inexperienced, ill-trained, and understaffed originators, processors, and underwriters. To that nearly fatal equation must be added management that does not place the proper emphasis on training its people to do their best.

MORTGAGE INSURANCE $=$ *8*

Insurance of any type is designed to spread the economic risk or loss from a particular hazard over a large group—the insured group. Mortgage insurance is a financial guarantee provided to a mortgage lender in return for a premium paid by a mortgage borrower (normally, there are some exceptions), which insures a lender against all or most of the losses that would be suffered if a borrower defaults on the mortgage obligations. This function is performed by all types of mortgage insurance, whether it be government-sponsored or private.

The various classifications of mortgage insurance are:

- Federal Housing Administration (FHA) insurance
- Veterans Administration (VA) guarantee
- private mortgage insurance

The social benefit derived from mortgage insurance is that it allows for more people to purchase homes. The reason is that lenders are willing to accept smaller down payments than the normal 20 percent down if one of the types of mortgage insurance is present. Since lower down payments are required, more people can save the reduced amount and thus get into a home of their own. In addition, the use of mortgage insurance lessens risk and makes mortgage investments more attractive to mortgage investors. Before examining current government and private mortgage programs, a brief review of the historical development of mortgage insurance will be helpful to an understanding of present practices.

The Beginning

Early title insurance companies began mortgage insurance in the 1890s by insuring the repayment of mortgages in addition to the validity of title. The first statutory law providing for this type of insurance was enacted in New York state in 1904.

The social and demographic changes in the United States that occurred after 1900 (particularly following World War I) propelled mortgage lending into a more important position in the American economy. As mortgage lending became more prevalent and important, mortgage insurance became more accepted and desired. Because of this increased interest, title insurance companies became involved in providing this financial service as a no-cost add-on to title insurance.

The business was practiced differently then from the way it is practiced today. It was customary in the early 1900s for a mortgage company to exchange a new mortgage for a defaulted one or to buy back a troubled loan sold to an investor. As the real estate boom of the 1920s continued, this custom gave way to the actual guaranteeing of principal and interest by a new entity—mortgage guaranty companies. During their peak years (1925–32), as many as fifty of these companies were in operation, located primarily in the state of New York. These companies prospered by originating and selling mortgages with a guarantee as mortgage participation bonds to institutional investors or to individual investors. The units sold to individual investors were usually in $500 or $1,000 denominations. Yield and apparent safety made the units very attractive. A trustee would hold the mortgages and be responsible for foreclosure if any default in payment occurred. The prevailing viewpoint during this period was that real estate values would continue to appreciate, and if any lax underwriting or appraising occurred, the resulting questionable mortgage would be saved by inflation. This optimism affected the investing public. Large portions of accumulated savings were invested in mortgage bonds issued by apparently successful mortgage guaranty companies.

Due to the general optimism about the economy and the laissez-faire attitude of the government, these mortgage guaranty companies were virtually unregulated. Lack of regulation often led to poor underwriting, self-dealing, fraud, and ultimately to a lack of adequate reserves to meet any meaningful emergency.

Before the stock market crash of 1929, the real estate industry was in serious trouble. Real estate values started to drop and foreclosures resulted which further depressed values. It was inevitable that these companies would not survive the bank holiday declared by President Roosevelt in March, 1933. Many billions of dollars were lost by institutional investors with similarly tragic results to private investors because of the failure of these companies. The collapse left such an ugly mark on the real estate finance industry that private mortgage insurance did not reappear for almost 25 years.

GOVERNMENT (FHA) INSURANCE

The years immediately following the stock market crash witnessed much debate on the proper role of the government in the nation's economy. Many in Congress urged action; others were against it. Most, however, agreed that government action would benefit real estate by helping to put a floor under real estate prices. Those in favor of stimulation reasoned that expanding waves from a healthy real estate industry would have a multiplying effect on the remainder of a depressed economy. The National Housing Act (1934) contained provisions to help stimulate the construction industry. The act created the Federal Housing Administration (FHA) to encourage lenders to make real estate mortgages again by providing government-backed mortgage insurance as protection. Title I of this law provided insurance, initially free, to lenders who would loan money for home improvements and repairs.

Title II provided for the establishment of a Mutual Mortgage Insurance Fund to be funded by premiums paid by mortgagors out of which any claims by the protected lenders could be satisfied. Initially, the mortgagor paid an annual insurance premium of .5 percent based on the original amount. This has been changed to the current practice of paying a 4.3 percent and an annual .5 percent of the original loan amount for up to 15 years.

The basic program under this act was section 203(b), designed to provide government insurance to lenders who made loans on one- to four-family houses. (Through the years, most have been single-family.) This program is still successfully helping to meet the national housing needs after helping to provide housing for more than 17 million families.

FHA-INSURED HOME MORTGAGES
(In Millions of Dollars)

Year	Amount
1960	$ 4,601
1965	7,465
1970	8,114
1975	6,165
1980	16,458
1985	23,964
1987	81,881
1989	45,893

Source: Federal Housing Administration

Now a part of the Department of Housing and Urban Development (HUD), FHA has other insurance programs, each designed to meet a specific need. But the Mutual Mortgage Insurance Fund remains the largest and most important.

Early Opposition

Initially, the legislation to establish FHA was faced with opposition from some thrift institutions that believed that the federal government should not get involved in housing. Even after enactment, FHA did not meet with great acceptance among financial centers since many felt that mortgage insurance as a concept was discredited or felt strongly that government should not get involved in what was basically a private enterprise.

History, however, has proven this to be a shortsighted belief, especially in view of the many changes for which FHA has paved the way in real estate finance. As an example, FHA insurance has allowed for the development of a national mortgage market by providing for the transferability, and thus the liquidity, of mortgage instruments. The FHA-insured mortgage was attractive to many investors because it established property and borrower standards with corresponding reduction in risk.

The FHA mortgage insurance program allowed life insurance companies to justify a successful request to purchase loans with higher loan-to-value ratios and with lower down payments to state insurance commissioners. The program also gave insurance companies the opportunity to lend across the nation. With this new authorization, life insurance companies could lend in those areas of the country that desperately needed capital. Subsequently, they could receive a higher yield than what was previously available in the capital-surplus area of New England where most of the major life insurance companies were located. Mortgage companies were the principal intermediaries for moving this capital from capital-surplus areas to capital-deficit areas by originating mortgages with FHA insurance and then selling them to life insurance companies.

Mortgage Lending Benefits Derived from FHA

One of the primary reasons for the increase in home ownership (from about 40 percent of all homes occupied in 1930 to about 63 percent today) is the leadership provided by FHA that led to:

- property and borrower standards
- reintroduction of mortgage insurance
- self-amortizing mortgage loans
- higher loan-to-value ratios
- longer mortgage terms

These factors contributed not only to the higher percentage of home ownership but also to a financial environment conducive to a rebirth of private mortgage insurance.

Mortgage loans to be insured by FHA can be originated by any of the various mortgage intermediaries, although as a practical matter about seventy-five percent of all FHA mortgages have been originated by mortgage bankers. Initially, this high percentage of origination was due to the local lending philosophy of the other mortgage lenders and the correspondent system that developed between mortgage bankers and life insurance companies. Most FHA-insured mortgages are still originated by mortgage bankers.

HUD-FHA MORTGAGE INSURANCE PROGRAMS

203 Mutual Mutual Mortgage Insurance and Improvement Loans
   (b) One- to Four-Family Housing
   (h) One-Family Housing for Disaster Victims
   (i) Outlying Properties; One-Family Non-farm or Farm Housing
   (m) Vacation Homes
207 Multifamily Housing Mortgage Insurance
   Rental Housing of Eight or More Units
   Mobile Home Parks
213 Cooperative Housing Mortgage Insurance
   Dwelling Unit Released from a Cooperative Project-Sales Mortgage
   Management-Type Cooperative Projects of Five or More Units
   Sales-Type Cooperative Projects of Five or More Units
   Investor-Sponsored Cooperative Projects of Five or More Units
220 Urban Renewal Mortgage Insurance and Insured Improvement Loans
   One- to Eleven-Family Housing in Urban Renewal Areas
   Construction of Two or More Units in Approved Urban Renewal Area
221 Low-Cost and Moderate-Income Mortgage Insurance
   (d) (2) One- to Four-Family Housing for Low- and Moderate-Income
       Families and Displaced Families
   (h) Individual Units Released from 222(h) Project Mortgage
   (i) Conversion of 221 (d) (3) Below-Market Interest Rate Rental Project
       into Condominium Plan
   (d) (3) Housing Projects (Below-Market Interest Rate) for Housing
       Moderate-Income Families, Individuals 62 or Older, or
       Handicapped
   (d) (3) Same as Above, but with Market Interest Rate Program and Rent
       Supplement Program
   (d) (4) Housing Projects for Moderate-Income Families. Market Interest
       Rate Program for Profit-motivated Sponsors

(h) Substandard Housing for Subsequent Resale after Rehabilitation

(j) Conversion of 221(d) (3) Rental Project into a Cooperative Project

222 Servicemen's Mortgage Insurance
One-Family Housing for Servicemen

223 Miscellaneous Housing Insurance
Housing and Mortgage Insurance for Housing in Declining Neighborhoods
Insurance for Government-Acquired Properties

231 Housing Mortgage Insurance for the Elderly
Housing Project of Eight or More Units for Occupancy by Elderly or Handicapped

232 Nursing Homes and/or Intermediate Care Facilities Mortgage Insurance
Housing for 20 or More Patients

233 Experimental Housing Mortgage Insurance
Proposed or Rehabilitated Housing Using Advanced Technology
Rental Housing Using Advanced Technology

234 Condominium Housing Mortgage Insurance
(c) Individual Units in Condominium Projects
(d) Condominium Projects with Four or More Units

235 Mortgage Insurance and Assistance Payments
(i) One-Family Unit in Single- or Two-Family Dwelling. Open-End Advances Permitted in Connection with Previously Insured Mortgage
(j) Individual Units Released from 235(j) Rehabilitation Sales Project Mortgage
(k) Housing for Lower-Income Families

236 Mortgage Insurance and Interest Reduction Payments
Rental on Cooperative Housing for Lower-Income Families, Individuals 62 or Over, or Handicapped

273 Special Mortgage Insurance for Low- and Moderate-Income
Special Credit Risks; Single-Family Units

240 Mortgage Insurance on Loans for Title Purchase
Purchase of Fee Simple Title

241 Supplementary Financing for FHA Project Mortgages

242 Mortgage Insurance for Hospitals
Construction or Rehabilitation of Nonprofit and Proprietary Hospitals

244 Mortgage Coinsurance

245 Graduated Payment Mortgage

803/809/810 Armed Services Housing

809 One- to Four-Family Housing for Civilian Employees at or near R & D Installations

810 (h) Individual Units Released from 810(g) Multifamily Mortgage

810 (f) Rental Housing with Eight or More Units for Military or Civilian Personnel

810 (g) Same as above, but for Later Resale as Single-Family Housing

1000 Mortgage Insurance for Land Development
      Purchase of Land for Development of Building Sites for Subdivisions or
      New Communities
1100 Mortgage Insurance for Group Practice Facilities
      Construction of Rehabilitation of Facilities for Dentistry, Medicine or
      Optometry Practice

Note: This chart is intended for quick reference to HUD-FHA insurance programs. Check
for specific details in the appropriate FHA issuances.
Source: Department of Housing and Urban Development.

FHA Insurance Evolves

FHA and its various insurance programs have been in existence for over 50 years
and have assisted approximately 17 million families that might not otherwise have
been able to purchase a home. In 1989, FHA insurance backed better than $43
billion worth of mortgages for almost 700,000 buyers.

During the past 60 years, FHA has often been a leader in innovation and has
helped shape the way residential mortgage lending is done today. These years have
not all been smooth, as witnessed by the dramatic fall-off in loans insured during the
1970s and early 1980s. Some of the reasons for this decline in insured loans were:

- internal reorganization and change of FHA's status within HUD
- fraud, abuse, and influence peddling by some lenders
- excessive government red tape and paperwork delay

These issues were addressed, and the amount of FHA insurance began to increase
again reaching record levels in the second half of the 1980s. But then another problem
developed. By the end of the 1980s, Congress realized that radical changes had to occur
to remedy persistent high default and foreclosure rates. These changes included:

- higher insurance premiums
- underwriting changes (use of gross income)
- elimination of investor loans

FHA in the 1990s

Today, as in prior years, the most important FHA program is section 203(b). The
maximum loan amount permitted and other requirements periodically change, but
the most recent limits for high-cost areas is $124,875.

The low down payment requirement for a FHA mortgage is what makes this
program so popular. The minimum down payment is established as follows: 3
percent of first $25,000 and 5 percent of remainder based on total acquisition cost
or value, whichever is less.

Acquisition cost includes the contract price of the property or appraised value (whichever is lower) plus 57 percent of closing costs for the purchase. FHA allows a borrower to finance the origination fee, survey, appraisal, title insurance, and up to $200 of the home inspection cost. The maximum term is 30 years, and the loan is assumable (with some limitations) with no prepayment penalty to a qualified borrower.

Example: If Mr. and Mrs. G. R. Straight want to purchase a home which has a total acquisition cost (including some closing costs) of $110,000, their down payment would be:

3 percent of $25,000	=	$ 750
5 percent of $85,000	=	4,250
Total down payment	=	$5,000
Loan-to-value	=	95.5 percent

Not only are the down payment requirements for an FHA mortgage attractive to potential mortgage applicants, the underwriting standards are more generous than a conventional mortgage. The percent of gross income that can be used for housing expenses is 29 percent, and the ratio of long-term debt to gross income is up to 41 percent. In addition, FHA permits the use of bonafide gifts for the entire down payment.

FHA Insurance Premium

In 1991, the amount of the mortgage insurance premium was changed to allow for sufficient revenues to the Mutual Insurance Fund, which was suffering increasing

---

U.S. DEPARTMENT OF HOUSING AND URBAN DEVELOPMENT
HOUSING — FEDERAL HOUSING COMMISSIONER

Mortgage Insurance Certificate

FHA Case No.
352:222222-2

Section
703(b)

Mortgagor's Name *(Last Name First)*
Jones, Jon & Linda

Property Address
205 Smith Street

City, State and ZIP Code
Perth Amboy, NJ   08861

Mortgage Amount
$84,078

This Certificate, when endorsed in the block below, is evidence of insurance of the mortgage loan described herein under the indicated Section of the National Housing Act *(12 USC 1701 et seq.)* and Regulations of the Department of Housing and Urban Development Published at 24 CFR 200.1 et seq.

Endorsed for insurance by an Authorized Agent of the Federal Housing Commissioner.

Margaretten & Company, Inc.
271 Maple Street
P.O. Box 3021
Perth Amboy, NJ   08862

MORTGAGEE'S NAME AND ADDRESS

(Signature)   *(Date)*
1/16/89

(REMOVE CERTIFICATE BEFORE SIGNING)   (HB 4045.1)   HUD-59100.1 (12-83)

Previous Edition May Be Used Until Exhausted

VA Application For Home Loan Guaranty	USDA-FmHA Application For FmHA Guaranteed Loan	HUD/FHA Application For Commitment for Insurance Under the National Housing Act	1. AGENCY CASE NUMBER ▲ LH123456DC	2A. LENDER'S CASE NUMBER 06011992	2B. SECTION OF THE ACT (HUD ONLY)

3A. NAME AND PRESENT ADDRESS OF BORROWER (Include)
GEORGE "J". ANDERSON
MARTHA A. ANDERSON
820 FOLLIN LANE
VIENNA, VA 22180

3B. BORROWER'S SOCIAL SECURITY NO.
123-45-6789
987-65-4321

5A. BORROWER: If you do not wish to complete Items 5B or 5C, please initial in the space to the right. — INITIALS

5B. RACE/NATIONAL ORIGIN
▲1 [X] WHITE, NOT HISPANIC   4 ☐ ASIAN OR PACIFIC ISLANDER
2 ☐ BLACK, NOT HISPANIC   5 ☐ HISPANIC
3 ☐ AMERICAN INDIAN OR ALASKAN NATIVE

5C. SEX
▲1 [X] MALE   2 ☐ FEMALE

4A. NAME AND ADDRESS OF LENDER (Include ZIP Code)

• NAVY FEDERAL CREDIT UNION
P.O. BOX 3326
SECURITY PLACE
MERRIFIELD, VA 221193326

ATTN: CHONG SUMNER
(703) 255-7340

6A. COBORROWER: If you do not wish to complete Items 6B or 6C, please initial in space to the right. — INITIALS

6B. RACE/NATIONAL ORIGIN
▲1 ☐ WHITE, NOT HISPANIC   4 ☐ ASIAN OR PACIFIC ISLANDER
2 ☐ BLACK, NOT HISPANIC   5 ☐ HISPANIC
3 ☐ AMERICAN INDIAN OR ALASKAN NATIVE

6C. SEX
▲1 ☐ MALE   2 [X] FEMALE

4B. ORIGINATOR'S I.D. (HUD) OR LENDER I.D. CODE (VA)
15700600007

4C. SPONSOR'S I.D. (HUD Only)

7. PROPERTY ADDRESS INCLUDING NAME OF SUBDIVISION, LOT AND BLOCK NO., AND ZIP CODE 3459 EAGLE ROCK COURT ANNANDALE VA 22030-4151, LOT 10, SEC 3, GREENBRIAR, COUNTY OF FAIRFAX

8A. LOAN AMOUNT $151,650.00
8B. INTEREST RATE 9.50%
8C. PROPOSED MATURITY YRS 30 60 MOS.
8D. DISCOUNT AMT. (Only if borrower permitted to pay) $

VA ONLY: Veteran and lender hereby apply to the Administrator of Veterans Affairs for Guaranty of the loan described here under Section 1810, Chapter 37, Title 38, United States Code, to the full extent permitted by the veteran's entitlement and severally agree that the Regulations promulgated pursuant to Chapter 37, and in effect on the date of the loan shall govern the rights, duties, and liabilities of the parties.

HUD/FHA ONLY: Mortgagee's application for mortgagor approval and commitment for mortgage insurance under the National Housing Act.

SECTION I – PURPOSE, AMOUNT, TERMS OF AND SECURITY FOR PROPOSED LOAN.

9A. PURPOSE OF LOAN - TO:
▲1 [X] PURCHASE EXISTING HOME PREVIOUSLY OCCUPIED
2 ☐ FINANCE IMPROVEMENTS TO EXISTING PROPERTY
3 ☐ REFINANCE
4 ☐ PURCHASE NEW CONDO. UNIT
5 ☐ PURCHASE EXISTING CONDO. UNIT
6 ☐ PURCHASE EXISTING HOME NOT PREVIOUSLY OCCUPIED
7 ☐ CONSTRUCT HOME-PROCEEDS TO BE PAID OUT DURING CONSTRUCTION PURCHASE PERMANENTLY SITED
8 ☐ MANUFACTURED HOME PURCHASE PERMANENTLY SITED
9 ☐ MANUFACTURED HOME AND LOT REFINANCE PERMANENTLY SITED
10 ☐ MANUFACTURED HOME TO BUY LOT REFINANCE PERMANENTLY SITED
11 ☐ MANUFACTURED HOME/LOT LOAN HUD ONLY – FINANCE COOP-
12 ☐ PURCHASE

9B. TYPE OF AMORTIZATION
1 [X] REG. FIXED PAYMENT   6 ☐ ARM
GPM LOAN BAL.
2 ☐ NEVER TO EXCEED REASONABLE VALUE
3 ☐ OTHER GPM   7 ☐ OTHER (Specify)
4 ☐ GEM (GROWING EQUITY MORT.)
☐ TEMPORARY
5 ☐ BUY DOWN

9C. HUD ONLY-BORROWER WILL BE
1 ☐ OCCUPANT   5 ☐ ESCROW COMMITMENT
2 ☐ LANDLORD   6 ☐ FIRST TIME HOME BUYER
3 ☐ BUILDER
4 ☐ OPERATIVE BUILDER

9D. VA ONLY- TITLE WILL BE VESTED IN
☐ VETERAN
[X] VETERAN AND SPOUSE
☐ OTHER (Specify)

11. LIEN:
[X] MORTGAGE   ☐ OTHER (SPECIFY)

12. ESTATE WILL BE:
[X] FEE SIMPLE   ☐ LEASEHOLD (Show expiration date)

13. IS THERE A MANDATORY HOMEOWNERS ASSOCIATION?
☐ YES   ☐ NO (If "Yes," complete Item 14F)

14. ESTIMATED TAXES, INSURANCE AND ASSESSMENTS		15. ESTIMATED MONTHLY PAYMENT	
A. ANNUAL TAXES	$ 1,800.00	A. PRINCIPAL AND INTEREST	$ 1,275.16
B. AMOUNT OF HAZARD INSURANCE ON SECURITY	151,650.00	B. TAXES AND INSURANCE DEPOSITS	185.00
C. ANNUAL HAZARD INSURANCE PREMIUM	420.00	C. OTHER HOME OWNERS ASSOCIATION	15.00
D. ANNUAL SPECIAL ASSESSMENT PAYMENT			
E. UNPAID SPECIAL ASSESSMENT BALANCE			
F. ANNUAL MAINTENANCE ASSESSMENT	180.00	TOTAL	$ 1,475.16

SECTION II – PERSONAL AND FINANCIAL STATUS OF APPLICANT

16. PLEASE CHECK APPROPRIATE BOXES. IF ONE OR MORE ARE CHECKED, ITEMS 18B, 21, 22 AND 23 MUST INCLUDE INFORMATION CONCERNING BORROWER'S SPOUSE (OR FORMER SPOUSE IF BOX "D" IS CHECKED). IF NO BOXES ARE CHECKED, NO INFORMATION CONCERNING THE SPOUSE NEED BE FURNISHED IN ITEMS 18B, 21, 22 AND 23

A. [X] THE SPOUSE WILL BE JOINTLY OBLIGATED WITH THE BORROWER ON THE LOAN
B. ☐ THE BORROWER IS MARRIED AND THE PROPERTY TO SECURE THE LOAN IS LOCATED IN A COMMUNITY PROPERTY STATE
C. [X] THE BORROWER IS RELYING ON THE SPOUSE'S INCOME AS A BASIS FOR REPAYMENT OF THE LOAN
D. ☐ THE BORROWER IS RELYING ON ALIMONY, CHILD SUPPORT, OR SEPARATE MAINTENANCE PAYMENTS FROM A SPOUSE OR FORMER SPOUSE AS A BASIS FOR REPAYMENT OF THE LOAN.

17A. MARITAL STATUS OF BORROWER	17B. MARITAL STATUS OF CO-BORROWER OTHER THAN SPOUSE	17C. MONTHLY CHILD SUPPORT OBLIGATION	17D. MONTHLY ALIMONY OBLIGATION	18A. AGE OF BORROWER	18B. AGE OF SPOUSE OR COBORROWER	18C. AGE(S) OF DEPENDENT(S)
1 [X] MARRIED 3 ☐ UNMARRIED 2 ☐ SEPARATED	1 ☐ MARRIED 3 ☐ UNMARRIED 2 ☐ SEPARATED	$	$	45	44	14,12

19. CURRENT MONTHLY HOUSING EXPENSE	20. UTILITIES INCLUDED?	21. LIABILITIES (Itemize all debts)		
$ 800.00	☐ YES [X] NO	NAME OF CREDITOR	MO. PAYMENT	BALANCE
		SEE ATTACHED	$	$

22. ASSETS	
A. CASH (Including deposit on purchase)	$ 20,346.00
B. SAVINGS BONDS - OTHER SECURITIES	3,734.00
C. REAL ESTATE OWNED	140,000.00
D. AUTO	13,000.00
E. FURNITURE AND HOUSEHOLD GOODS	80,000.00
F. OTHER (Use separate sheet, if necessary)	3,000.00
G. TOTAL	$ 260,080.00

JOB RELATED EXPENSE (Specify)

TOTAL $ 1,235.00 $ 82,450.00

23. INCOME AND OCCUPATIONAL STATUS

ITEM	BORROWER	SPOUSE OR COBORROWER
A. OCCUPATION	CDR O-5	COMPUTER SUPERVISE
B. NAME OF EMPLOYER	U.S. NAVY	APPLE CORPORATION
C. NUMBER OF YEARS EMPLOYED	16	4
D. GROSS PAY	MONTHLY $ 3,806.70 HOURLY $	MONTHLY $ 3,014.00 HOURLY $
E. OTHER INCOME (Disclosure of child support, alimony and separate maintenance income is optional)	MONTHLY ▲ $ 1,270.00	MONTHLY ▲

24. ESTIMATED TOTAL COST

ITEM	AMOUNT
A. PURCHASE EXISTING HOME OR CONSTRUCTION	$ 180,000.00
B. ALTERATIONS, IMPROVEMENTS, REPAIRS	
C. LAND (If acquired separately)	
D. REFINANCE (Attach list of debts to be paid)	
E. PREPAID ITEMS	520.00
F. ESTIMATED CLOSING COSTS	2,432.38
G. HUD MIP OR VA FUNDING FEE PAID IN CASH	37.50
H. DISCOUNT (Only if borrower permitted to pay)	
I. TOTAL COSTS (Add Items 24A through 24H)	182,989.88
J. LESS CASH FROM BORROWER	32,989.88
K. LESS OTHER CREDITS	
L. LOAN AMOUNT EXCLUSIVE OF MIP OR FUNDING FEE FINANCED	150,000.00
M. MIP/FUNDING FEE FINANCED	1,650.00
N. LOAN AMOUNT INCLUDING MIP/FUNDING FEE	151,650.00

NOTE – If land acquired by separate transaction, complete Items 25A and 25B.

25A. DATE ACQUIRED	25B. UNPAID BALANCE

VA FORM 26-1802a, FEB 1988
HUD FORM 92900.1
NFCU 528M (8-89)

SUPERSEDES VA FORM 26-1802A AND HUD FORM 92900
JUN 1985, WHICH WILL NOT BE USED.

Page 1 of 5

123

losses. This fund had been badly depleted in the 1980s as FHA loan defaults per year reached as high as 11 percent. For an FHA loan with less than 10 percent down, the mortgage insurance premium for 1991 and 1992 will be 3.8 percent the first year and 0.5 percent for up to 30 years depending on the amount of the down payment. For 1993–94, the up-front premium drops to 3 percent, and in 1995 and beyond it drops further to 2.25 percent.

VETERANS ADMINISTRATION

As a gesture to returning World War II veterans, Congress enacted the Servicemen's Readjustment Act (1944), which authorized the Veterans Administration (VA) to guarantee loans (among other benefits) made to eligible veterans. The original guarantee was for the first 50 percent of the loan amount or $2,000, whichever was less. This has been increased through the years to the current guarantee limit of $46,000. (The VA guaranty now ranges from 50 percent for mortgages with original loan amounts of $45,000 or less to 25 percent for mortgages with original loan amounts ranging between $144,000 and $184,000 with the guaranty limited to the maximum of $46,000.)

Unlike other loans, the VA appraises the house and then issues a Certificate of Reasonable Value (CRV) that establishes the amount on which the guaranty figures are based. A veteran does not pay a premium for this guarantee, unlike FHA insurance, but does pay a "funding fee." This funding fee is based on the amount of down payment:

- less than 5 percent down=1.875 percent fee
- 5 - 10 percent down=1.375 percent fee
- over 10 percent down=1.125 percent fee
- all refinances=1.250 percent fee

HISTORY OF VA MAXIMUM GUARANTEES

September 16, 1940	$ 4,000.00
April 20, 1950	7,500.00
May 7, 1968	12,500.00
January 1, 1975	17,500.00
January 1, 1978	25,000.00
October 7, 1980	27,500.00
February 1, 1988	36,000.00
January 1, 1990	46,000.00

CERTIFICATE OF REASONABLE VALUE

1. CASE NUMBER
LH123456DC

2. PROPERTY ADDRESS (Include ZIP code and county)
3459 EAGLE ROCK COURT
ANNANDALE , VA
22030-4151
COUNTY OF FAIRFAX

3. LEGAL DESCRIPTION
LOT 10, SEC 3, GREENBRIAR

COUNTY OF FAIRFAX

4. TITLE LIMITATIONS AND RESTRICTIVE COVENANTS:
USUAL UTILITY EASEMENTS
BUILDING RESTRICTION LINE

☐ CONDOMINIUM ☐ PLANNED UNIT DEVELOPMENT

5. NAME AND ADDRESS OF FIRM OR PERSON MAKING REQUEST/APPLICATION (Include ZIP code)

NAVY FEDERAL CREDIT UNION
P.O. BOX 3326
SECURITY PLACE
MERRIFIELD , VA 221193326

ATTN: CHONG SUMNER
(703) 255-7340

6. REMAINING ECONOMIC LIFE OF PROPERTY IS ESTIMATED TO BE NOT LESS THAN (Enter number of years) 40 YEARS

7. ESTIMATED REASONABLE VALUE OF PROPERTY $185,000

8. EXPIRATION DATE 8-1-92

9. ADMINISTRATION OF VETERANS AFFAIRS BY (Signature of authorized agent) P. J. Columbo

10. DATE ISSUED 6-28-92

11. VA OFFICE D.C.

GENERAL CONDITIONS

(NOTE: THE VETERANS ADMINISTRATION DOES NOT ASSUME ANY RESPONSIBILITY FOR THE CONDITION OF THE PROPERTY. THE CORRECTION OF ANY DEFECTS NOW EXISTING OR THAT MAY DEVELOP WILL BE THE RESPONSIBILITY OF THE PURCHASER.)

1. This certificate will remain effective as to any written contract of sale entered into by an eligible veteran within the validity period indicated.
2. This dwelling conforms with the Minimum Property Requirements prescribed by the Administrator of Veterans Affairs.
3. The aggregate of any loan secured by this property plus the amount of any assessment consequent on any special improvements as to which a lien or tight to a lien shall exist against the property, except as provided in Item 13 below, may not exceed the reasonable value in Item 7 above.
4. Proposed construction shall be completed in accordance with the plans and specifications identified below, relating to both onsite and offsite improvements upon which this valuation is based and shall otherwise conform fully to the VA Minimum Property Requirements. Satisfactory completion must be evidenced by either
  A. VA Final Compliance Inspection Report (VA Form 26-1839), or
  B. VA Acceptance of FHA Compliance Inspection Reports or other evidence of completion under FHA supervision applicable to proposed construction.
5. By contracting to sell property, as proposed construction or existing construction not previously occupied, to a veteran purchaser who is to be assisted in the purchase by a loan made, guaranteed, or insured by VA, the builder or other seller agrees to place any downpayment received by the seller or agent of the seller in a special trust account as required by section 1806 of title 38, U.S. Code.
6. The VA guaranty is subject to and conditioned upon the lending institution's compliance, at the time of the making, increasing, extending or reviewing of the proposed loan, with section 102 of P.L. 93-234, "Flood Disaster Protection Act of 1973."

12. PURCHASER'S NAME AND ADDRESS (Complete mailing address. Include ZIP code)

GEORGE P ANDERSON
MARTHA A ANDERSON
820 FOLLIN LANE
VIENNA, VA 22180

13. EXCEPTIONS TO GENERAL CONDITION NUMBER 3 ABOVE

☐ ENERGY CONSERVATION IMPROVEMENTS. The buyer may wish to contract the local utility company or a qualified person or firm for a home energy audit. If energy-related improvements are suggested, your mortgage may be increased to include the following: Thermostats, water heaters, heating/cooling systems, attic insulation, insulation for floors and foundation walls, weather-stripping/caulking, storm windows and storm doors. The mortgage may be increased by (a) up to $2,000 without a separate determination of the value of the energy-related improvements; (b) up to $3,500 if supported by a value determination by a designated appraiser; or (c) more than $3,500 subject to a value determination by VA or HUD, as applicable, and subsequent endorsement of the certificate of reasonable value or HUD conditional commitment.

☐ OTHER (Cite and explain in item 25 below)

SPECIFIC CONDITIONS (Applicable when checked or completed)

14. THE REASONABLE VALUE ESTABLISHED HEREIN FOR THE RELATED PROPERTY IS

☐ BASED UPON OBSERVATION OF THE PROPERTY IN ITS "AS IS" CONDITION
☐ PREDICATED UPON COMPLETION OF PROPOSED CONSTRUCTION (If checked complete Item 15)
☐ PREDICATED UPON COMPLETION OF REPAIRS LISTED IN ITEM 17

15. PROPOSED CONSTRUCTION TO BE COMPLETED (Identify plans, specifications and exhibits)

16. INSPECTIONS REQUIRED

☐ FHA COMPLIANCE INSPECTIONS FOR PROPOSED CONSTRUCTION
☐ VA COMPLIANCE INSPECTIONS ☐ LENDER TO CERTIFY

18. NAME OF COMPLIANCE INSPECTOR

17. REPAIRS TO BE COMPLETED

19. HEALTH AUTHORITY APPROVAL—Execution of VA Form 26-6395 by the Health Authority (or Health Authority form or letter) indicating approval of the individual:

☐ WATER SUPPLY ☐ SEWAGE DISPOSAL SYSTEM

20. ☐ This document is subject to the provisions of Executive Orders 11246 and 11375, and the Rules and Regulations of the Secretary of Labor in effect this date, and 38 CFR 36.4390 through 36.4393, and also the provisions of the certification executed by the builder, sponsor or developer named herein which is on file in this office.

21. WOOD DESTROYING INSECT INFORMATION - EXISTING CONSTRUCTION - The seller shall, at no cost to the veteran-purchaser, prior to settlement, obtain in written statement from a qualified pest control operator reporting wood destroying insect information using VA Form 26-8850 or other form acceptable to VA. The veteran-purchaser will acknowledge receipt of a copy of the statement in Item 14 of VA Form 26-8850. PROPOSED CONSTRUCTION - VA Form 26-8375, Termite Soil Treatment Guarantee, is required.

22. WARRANTY ☐ (If checked, complete Item 23)

23. NAME OF WARRANTOR

24. ☐ Since this property is located in a special Flood Hazard Area as established by FEMA, flood insurance will be required in accordance with 38 CFR 36.4326. (Check if applicable).

25. SAFE DRINKING WATER ACT

☐ Certification required that in construction any solders and flux did not contain more than 0.2 percent lead and any pipes and pipe fittings did not contain more than 8.0 percent lead.

26. OTHER REQUIREMENTS

VA FORM 26-1843, SEP 1987

EXISTING STOCKS OF VA FORM 26-1843, AUG 1986, WILL BE USED.

261805C
NFCU 526M (1-91)

VA *Down Payment*

Originally, this program was designed to allow a veteran to buy a home with no money down. It still operates on that concept although a veteran now must pay some fees, and a down payment might be required if the loan amount exceeds a certain limit. Consequently, a veteran can now buy a home costing up to $184,000 with no down payment, assuming income is sufficient to support the mortgage payment. The $46,000 guarantee (current amount) is the reason no down payment is required. Although a lender makes a $184,000 mortgage, only $138,000 ($184,000 - $46,000 = $138,000), or 75 percent of its value, is made with any risk. If foreclosure is necessary, the real estate should bring at least the $138,000 the lender had at risk. This amount, combined with the $46,000 guarantee, should make the lender whole.

If a veteran wanted to buy a home appraised at more than $184,000, a lender would probably require a down payment equal to 25 percent of the amount in excess of $184,000 to keep the loan within the 75 percent loan-to-value ratio. A lender could opt for private mortgage insurance on the amount over $184,000.

Eligibility

The popularity of the VA-guaranteed mortgage was reaffirmed when the number of loans backed by this program passed the 12 million mark in early 1987.

A veteran is eligible for a VA-guaranteed mortgage if the service record indicates:

- World War II: 90 days active service between 9-16-40 and 7-25-47
- Pre-Korean: 181 days active service between 7-26-46 and 6-26-50

VA-GUARANTEED HOME MORTGAGE LOANS MADE
(In Millions of Dollars)

Year	Number	Amount
1960	145,000	$ 1,985
1965	164,000	2,652
1970	168,000	3,440
1975	299,000	8,884
1980	266,000	14,500
1985	192,000	13,046
1987	451,000	33,312
1989	183,000	14,046

Source: Department of Veterans Affairs

Veterans Administration

Certificate of Eligibility

9829879

FOR LOAN GUARANTY BENEFITS

NAME OF VETERAN *(First, Middle, Last)*		SERVICE SERIAL NUMBER,'SOCIAL SECURITY NUMBER
DAVID PRESTON WALTERS	CANCELLED	123 45 6789

ENTITLEMENT CODE	BRANCH OF SERVICE	DATE OF BIRTH
4	ARMY	1/2/45

IS ELIGIBLE FOR THE BENEFITS OF CHAPTER 37, TITLE 38, U.S. CODE, AND HAS THE AMOUNT OF ENTITLEMENT SHOWN AS AVAILABLE ON THE REVERSE, SUBJECT TO THE STATEMENT BELOW, IF CHECKED.

☐ Valid unless discharged or released subsequent to date of this certificate. A certification of continuous active duty as of date of note required.

ADMINISTRATOR OF VETERANS AFFAIRS

Mary Barbarin

(Signature of Authorized Agent)

Veterans Administration
Regional Office

(Issuing Office)

701 Loyola Avenue

New Orleans, LA 70113

30 JUL 1987

(Date Issued)

- Korean conflict: 90 days active service between 6-27-50 and 1-31-55
- Post-Korean: 181 days active service between 2-1-55 and 8-4-64
- Vietnam era: 90 days active service between 8-5-64 and 5-7-75
- Post-Vietnam: 181 days active service between 5-8-75 and 9-7-80
- Pre-Desert Storm: 24 months of active duty between 9-8-80 and 8-3-90 (tentative date, not declared as yet)
- Desert Storm: (not declared as yet)

Veterans who believe they are eligible for a VA-guaranteed loan must apply to the VA for a Certificate of Eligibility which establishes eligibility and the amount of the guarantee available. The 1974 law which increased the guarantee also provided for restoration of veterans' entitlement.

Restoration of Veterans' Entitlement

Before the law was changed, once a veteran's entitlement was used it could not be restored. A 1974 law provided for partial and, in some situations, full restoration of benefits. This change was partially motivated by Congress' desire to

Form Approved
OMB No. 2900-0045

☒ VA REQUEST FOR DETERMINATION OF REASONABLE VALUE (Real Estate) ☐ HUD APPLICATION FOR PROPERTY APPRAISAL AND COMMITMENT	HUD Section of Act	1. CASE NUMBER LH123456DC

2. PROPERTY ADDRESS (include ZIP code and county)	3. LEGAL DESCRIPTION	4. TITLE LIMITATIONS AND RESTRICTIVE COVENANTS:
3459 EAGLE ROCK COURT ANNANDALE , VA 22030-4151 COUNTY OF FAIRFAX	LOT 10, SEC 3, GREENBRIAR COUNTY OF FAIRFAX	USUAL UTILITY EASEMENTS BUILDING RESTRICTION LINE 1. ☐ CONDOMINIUM 2. ☐ PLANNED UNIT DEVELOPMENT

5. NAME AND ADDRESS OF FIRM OR PERSON MAKING REQUEST/APPLICATION (include ZIP code)

NAVY FEDERAL CREDIT UNION •
P.O. BOX 3326
SECURITY PLACE
MERRIFIELD , VA 221193326

ATTN: CHONG SUMNER
(703) 255-7340

6. LOT DIMENSIONS:			
100 X 200			
1. ☐ IRREGULAR:	SQ/FT 2. ☐ ACRES:		

7. UTILITIES (✓) ▶

	ELEC.	GAS	WATER	SAN. SEWER
1. PUBLIC	X	X	X	X
2. COMMUNITY				
3. INDIVIDUAL				

8. EQUIP.	1. ☒ RANGE/OVEN	4. ☒ CLOTHES WASHER	7. ☒ VENT FAN
	2. ☒ REFRIG.	5. ☒ DRYER	8. ☐ W/W CARPET
	3. ☒ DISH-WASHER	6. ☒ GARBAGE DISP.	9. ☐

9. BUILDING STATUS ▶	10. BUILDING TYPE ▶	11. FACTORY FABRICATED?	12A. NO. OF BUILDINGS	12B. NO. OF LIVING UNITS	13A. STREET ACCESS	13B. STREET MAINT.
1. ☐ PROPOSED 4. ☒ EXISTING 2. ☐ SUBSTANTIAL REHABILITATION 5. ☐ 3. ☐ UNDER CONSTRUCTION ALTERATIONS, IMPROVEMENTS, OR REPAIRS	1. ☒ DETACHED 3. ☐ ROW 2. ☐ SEMI-DETACHED 4. ☐ APT. UNIT	1. ☐ YES 2. ☒ NO	1	1	1. ☐ PRIVATE 2. ☒ PUBLIC	1. ☐ PRIVATE 2. ☒ PUBLIC

14A. CONSTRUCTION WARRANTY INCLUDED? (if "Yes," complete Items 14B and C also.)	14B. NAME OF WARRANTY PROGRAM	14C. EXPIRATION DATE (Month, day, year)	15. CONSTR. COMPLETED (Mo., yr.)
1. ☐ YES 2. ☒ NO			01/85

16. NAME OF OWNER	17. PROPERTY:		18. RENT (if applic.)
LEWIS HODGES	☒ OCCUPIED BY OWNER ☐ NEVER OCCUPIED ☐ VACANT ☐ OCCUPIED BY TENANT (Complete Item 18 also)		$ /MONTH

19. NAME OF OCCUPANT	NAME OF BROKER	DATE AND TIME AVAILABLE FOR INSPECTION
OWNER 703/545-2674	REMAX 703/786-3525	☐ AM ☐ PM

CALL FIRST/OWNER 703/458-7375 703/856-6723	25. ORIGINATOR'S IDENT. NO. 15700600007	26. SPONSOR'S IDENT. NO.	27. INSTITUTION'S CASE NO. 06011992

28. PURCHASER'S NAME AND ADDRESS (Complete mailing address, include ZIP code)

GEORGE P ANDERSON
MARTHA A ANDERSON
820 FOLLIN LANE
VIENNA, VA 22180

EQUAL OPPORTUNITY IN HOUSING

NOTE - Federal laws and regulations prohibit discrimination because of race, color, religion, sex, or national origin in the sale or rental of residential property. Numerous State statutes and local ordinances also prohibit such discrimination. In addition, section 805 of the Civil Rights Act of 1968 prohibits discriminatory practices in connection with the financing of housing.

If HUD/VA finds there is noncompliance with any antidiscrimination laws or regulations, it may discontinue business with the violator.

29. NEW OR PROPOSED CONSTRUCTION - *Complete Items 29A through 29G for new or proposed construction cases only.*

A. COMPLIANCE INSPECTIONS WILL BE OR WERE MADE BY:	B. PLANS (check one)	C. PLANS SUBMITTED PREVIOUSLY UNDER CASE NO.:
☐ FHA ☐ VA ☐ NONE MADE	☐ FIRST SUBMISSION ☐ REPEAT CASE (if checked, complete Item 29C.)	

D. NAME AND ADDRESS OF BUILDER	E. TELEPHONE NO.	F. NAME AND ADDRESS OF WARRANTOR	G. TELEPHONE NO.

30. COMMENTS ON SPECIAL ASSESSMENTS OR HOMEOWNERS ASSOCIATION CHARGES	31. ANNUAL REAL ESTATE TAXES	33. LEASEHOLD CASES (Complete if applicable)	
NONE	$ 1,800.00	LEASE IS: ☐ 99 YEARS ☐ RENEWABLE ☐ HUD/VA APPROVED	EXPIRES (Date) ANNUAL GROUND RENT $
	32. MINERAL RIGHTS RESERVED? ☐ YES (Explain) ☒ NO		

34. SALE PRICE OF PROPERTY	34A. IS BUYER PURCHASING LOT SEPARATELY? (if "Yes," see instruction page under "Sale Price")	35. REFINANCING—AMOUNT OF PROPOSED LOAN	36. PROPOSED SALE CONTRACT ATTACHED	37. CONTRACT NUMBER PREVIOUSLY APPROVED BY VA THAT WILL BE USED
$ 180,000.00	☐ YES ☒ NO	$	☒ YES ☐ NO	

CERTIFICATIONS FOR SUBMISSIONS TO HUD

In submitting this application for a conditional commitment for mortgage insurance, it is agreed and understood by the parties involved in the transaction that if at the time of application for a Firm Commitment the identity of the seller has changed, the application for a Firm Commitment will be rejected and the application for a Conditional Commitment will be reprocessed upon request by the mortgagee.

It is further agreed and understood that in submitting the request for a Firm Commitment for mortgage insurance, the seller, the purchaser and the broker involved in the transaction shall each certify that the terms of the contract for purchase are true to his or her best knowledge and belief, and that any other agreement entered into by any of these parties in connection with this transaction is attached to the sales agreement.

BUILDER/SELLER'S AGREEMENT: All Houses: The undersigned agrees to deliver to the purchaser a statement of appraised value on Form HUD-92800.5B. Proposed Construction: The undersigned agrees, upon sale or conveyance of title within one year from date of initial occupancy, to deliver to the purchaser Form HUD-92544, warranting that the house is constructed in substantial conformity with the plans and specifications on which HUD based its value and to furnish HUD a conformed copy with the purchaser's receipt thereon that the original warranty was delivered to him/her. All Houses: In consideration of the issuance of the commitment requested by this application, I (we) hereby agree that any deposit or down payment made in connection with the purchase of the property described above, whether received by the undersigned or an agent of the undersigned, shall upon receipt be deposited in escrow or in trust or in a special account which is not subject to the claims of my creditors and where it will be maintained until it has been disbursed for the benefit of the purchaser or otherwise disposed of in accordance with the terms of the contract of sale.

Signature of: ☐ Mortgagee ☐ Builder ☐ Seller ☐ Other X	Date	19

MORTGAGEE'S CERTIFICATE: The undersigned mortgagee certifies that to the best of his/her knowledge, all statements made in this application and the supporting documents are true, correct and complete.

Signature and Title of Mortgage Officer: X	Date	19

CERTIFICATIONS FOR SUBMISSIONS TO VA

1. On receipt of "Certificate of Reasonable Value" or advice from the Veterans Administration that a "Certificate of Reasonable Value" will not be issued, we agree to forward to the appraiser the approved fee which we are holding for this purpose.
2. CERTIFICATION REQUIRED ON CONSTRUCTION UNDER FHA SUPERVISION (Strike out inappropriate phrases in parentheses)

I hereby certify that plans and specifications and related exhibits, including acceptable FHA Change Orders, if any, supplied to VA in this case, are identical to those (submitted to)(to be submitted to)(approved by) FHA, and that FHA inspections (have been) (will be) made pursuant to FHA approval for mortgage insurance on the basis of proposed construction under Sec.

38. SIGNATURE OF PERSON AUTHORIZING THIS REQUEST	39. TITLE	40. TELEPHONE NUMBER	41. DATE
C. SUMNER	SUPERVISOR MTG SECTION	(703) 255-7340	06/02/92

42. DATE OF ASSIGNMENT	43. NAME OF APPRAISER	
06/05/92	ROBERT R. PALMER	(703) 657-8775

WARNING Section 1010 of title 18, U.S.C. provides: "Whoever for the purpose of influencing such Administration makes, passes, utters or publishes any statement knowing the same to be false shall be fined not more than $5,000 or imprisoned not more than two years or both."

VA FORM 26-1805, AUG 1986
2618058

SUPERSEDES VA FORM 26-1805/HUD FORM 92800-1, JUN 1984, WHICH WILL NOT BE USED.

NFCU 526M (8-89)

128

stimulate housing during that economic downturn. A veteran's entitlement can be restored if:

- real estate was sold for reasons of health or condemnation
- real estate was sold because of change in employment
- real estate was destroyed by fire or a natural hazard
- loan was paid in full

Eligibility is also restored by the veteran obtaining a release of liability. A veteran's entitlement is restored to the extent it was not used.

Example: A veteran purchased a home in January, 1970 for $25,000. The maximum entitlement at that time was $12,500. This veteran wants to purchase another home today for $75,000 using the remaining entitlement.

$25,000 loan amount on first home
x.60
$15,000 amount of entitlement used

The amount of guaranty used exceeds the amount available, but the amount available is 50 percent of the purchase price, which exceeds the 25 percent required by a lender.

Maximum loan available now is established by subtracting the entitlement used from the current entitlement:

$27,500 current entitlement
–12,500 entitlement used
$15,000 remaining entitlement
x 4
$60,000 maximum loan with no down payment

In this case the veteran will have to put $5,000 down ($80,000 price – $60,000 maximum loan ÷ 25 percent down payment = $20,000 ÷ 25 = $5,000).

PRIVATE MORTGAGE INSURANCE

After a lapse of a quarter of a century, private mortgage insurance companies (MIs) returned as the FHA mortgage insurance programs proved successful. The first of the reborn MIs was Mortgage Guaranty Insurance Corporation (MGIC), organized in 1957 under a Wisconsin state law passed in 1956. For many years MGIC was the largest MI, but today GE Capital Mortgage Insurance Companies has the largest market share and insurance in force.

The return of private mortgage insurance was important for potential home buyers who had difficulty in saving the 20 percent down payment normally required by a mortgage lender. Lenders would approve a mortgage with a smaller down payment if the mortgage were covered by private mortgage insurance.

The reasons for the rebirth of the MIs and their impressive growth since then include:

- secondary mortgage market requirement that all loans over 80 percent LTV must be supported by mortgage insurance
- slow loan processing with government programs
- low loan limits for FHA mortgages
- interest in low down payment conventional loans

Of great importance to the rapid growth of MIs was the Emergency Home Finance Act (1970) which authorized FNMA and FHLMC to purchase conventional mortgages. If these loans had a loan-to-value ratio in excess of 80 percent, mortgage insurance was required to cover the lender's exposure down to 75 percent of value (lower of either sale price or appraisal). These high-ratio conventional mortgages became increasingly popular in the 1970s, and once these mortgages could be traded in the secondary market, most mortgage lenders, in particular savings associations, began to offer them.

Coverage

The coverage used to lower exposure for a lender down to 75 percent is as follows:

80.1–85 LTV	=	12 percent coverage
85.1–90 LTV	=	17 percent coverage
90.1–95 LTV	=	22 percent coverage

In certain situations, lenders may require deeper coverage than the normal 75 percent for certain loan products and in certain geographical areas.

The formula for determining this coverage is explained in the following example.

Example: The following formula determines the amount of mortgage insurance required:

$$\frac{\text{Loan amount} - 75 \text{ percent of value}}{\text{Loan amount}} = \text{Required percentage coverage} \qquad \text{or}$$

If a property is appraised at $100,000 and the borrower wants to put 10 percent down:

$$\frac{\$90,000 - \$75,000 = \$15,000}{\$90,000} = 16.66 \text{ or } 17 \text{ percent}$$

Strength of MIs Today

Strong regulatory control coupled with actuarial sound reserves—missing with the old mortgage insurance business—is now present with the new MIs. All MIs are carefully regulated by the laws of the state in which they are organized as well as the states where they do business. The regulating entity is normally the state insurance commission or department. Rating agencies, such as Moody's and Standard & Poor's, also rate the MIs.

The specific regulations vary among the states but generally provide that an MIC can insure first liens on one- to four-family residences that do not exceed 95 percent of fair market value. Authority has been expanded to include the various alternative mortgage instruments. Before an MI can begin insuring loans, it must meet minimum limits for paid-in capital and surplus. Then its insurance exposure is limited to 25 times the value of its capital, surplus, and contingency reserves.

MIs must maintain three types of reserves:

1. *Unearned premium reserve.* Premiums received but unearned for the term of a policy are placed in this reserve.
2. *Loss reserve.* This reserve is established for losses or potential losses on a case-by-case basis as the company learns of defaults and foreclosures.
3. *Contingency reserve.* This is a special reserve required by law to protect mortgage lenders against the type of catastrophic loss that can occur in severe economic periods. Half of each premium dollar received goes into this reserve and cannot be used by an MI for ten years unless losses in a calendar year

INDUSTRY ASSETS & RESERVES

Total industry	1986	1987	1988	1989
Admitted assets	$3,286,047	$3,506,123	$3,228,591	$3,444,974
Unearned premium reserve	$337,155	$329,924	$412,165	$446,941
Loss reserve	$1,284,674	$1,630,997	$832,712	801,949
Contingency reserve	$1,016,297	$793,502	$719,536	$528,545

Source: MICA

exceed 35 percent of earned premiums and the insurance commissioner of the state where the insurer is domiciled concurs in the withdrawal.

Before a mortgage lender can do business with an MI, the lender must be approved in regard to its capacity to underwrite, appraise, and service (if required) the high-ratio loans to be insured. An approved lender is issued a master policy and can get an insurance commitment within a day or two of submitting an application.

Evolving MI Business

After a third of a century of progress and service, MIs have recently evolved into one of the more innovative members of the real estate finance business. In addition to the function of insuring mortgage loans of all types, MIs are:

- serving as middlemen between sellers of mortgage loans and investors
- extensively involved in private mortgage-backed securities
- operating conduits that pool and sell privately insured mortgage-backed securities
- assisting in the portfolio restructuring of lenders

Many of these added functions are logical extensions of the mortgage insurance business and have assisted in the tremendous growth of MIs over the past 20 years. For example, the bringing together of originators and investors is facilitated by the large number of MI salespeople calling on lenders and the existence of many underwriting offices across the country. This secondary market assistance is provided free or at a reduced fee, but the hope of the MI is that this service and others will be repaid with additional insurance business.

1980s—Difficult Years

The 1980s were difficult years for the MI industry as the number of defaults and foreclosures increased dramatically. The decade ended with the MI industry paying claims to mortgage lenders in the billions of dollars. This sum is very large and is strong evidence of the value of mortgage insurance during periods of economic downturn and deflation in housing values. If these losses had not been absorbed by MIs, then lenders would have had to suffer the losses, with the resulting economic chaos. As it was, the losses were too much for some MIs and they either stopped writing new business or merged with larger, better capitalized MIs.

Claims

Both mortgage lenders and mortgage insurers are very interested in the quality of mortgage loans made. Investors are also interested, but presumably the loans they purchase either will be low loan-to-value loans or will be insured. It is the function

PRE-TAX PROFIT AND LOSS

Total industry	1986	1987	1988	1989
Underwriting income/(loss)	($591,942)	($995,078)	($420,418)	($247,519)
Investment income	291,426	$271,339	$173,333	$261, 168
Other income	$4	($17)	($3,925)	($12,999)
Statutory income (loss)	($300,512)	($723,756)	(251,009)	$650

Sources: 1986 & 1987—Standard & Poor's
1988 & 1989—MICA

of an MI to analyze the risk and charge a premium based on that risk. The MI can then spread that risk over a large number of geographically dispersed loans. Until the early 1980s, this process worked well, and all parties to the transaction—MIs, mortgage lenders, and home buyers—benefitted as a result.

In the 1980s the situation changed, and the MI industry suffered spectacular losses with $5 billion paid out in claims to policyholders. The changes that occurred were the dramatic increases in inflation and interest rates, which resulted in a general slowing of property appreciation. These problems were followed by the collapse of the energy-oriented economies in the Southwest. These problems resulted in many home owners not being able to sell their property and pay off their mortgages to avoid foreclosure. This slowing of property appreciation, combined with the expansion of 95 percent loan-to-value lending, coupled with exotic loan programs, significantly raised the claims incidence for MIs. Many of the MIs discovered, to their financial disappointment, that the level of claims on loans written in the early 1980s were five or six times that of loans written in the 1970s.

One of the results of these staggering losses was the confrontations that sometimes develop between MIs and mortgage lenders over origination and servicing practices. The Mortgage Insurance Companies of America estimates that during this period 5 out of every 1,000 policyholders experienced a denial of claim because of some irregularity.

Because mortgage lending is a risk business, defaults by mortgage borrowers will occur even in the best of times. When a default is not cured, a claim on an MI could result. Claims are settled in one of two ways:

1. The MI will reimburse the lender the percentage of loss specified in the policy.
2. At the MI option, it will pay the lender the entire loan amount and take title to the property and sell the property to mitigate the loss to the MI.

Example: *MI Claims Settlement.* Assume a home appraised at $70,000 is purchased with 10 percent down at 14 percent for 30 years. Default has occurred and a claim against the MI is filed. MI had 22 percent coverage.

Principal balance	$62,500
Accumulated interest from default date at 14 percent	5,000
	$67,500
Attorney fees—3 percent	2,025
Property taxes	500
Hazard insurance	250
Preservation of property	250
Statutory disbursements	100
	$70,625
Escrow funds	(300)
Other funds	( )
Claim total	$70,325
Adjusted claim	$70,325
Percentage w/coverage	x .22
Payoff	$15,471.50

As an alternative approach, MI could pay claim off ($70,325), take title to the property, and sell it. Assuming property sold for $60,000:

Sales price	$60,000
Less 6 percent sales commission	3,600
Less expenses	1,000
Less carrying cost of money	1,500
	$53,900
Payoff to lender	$70,325
Proceed of sale	53,900
Net loss	$16,425

Private Mortgage Insurance Companies

The major private mortgage insurance firms in North America are members of their own trade association, the Mortgage Insurance Companies of America (MICA). The association consists of the following domestic and Canadian private mortgage insurance companies:

- Commonwealth Mortgage Assurance Company—Philadelphia, PA
- GE Capital Mortgage Insurance Companies—Raleigh, NC

- Home Guaranty Insurance Corporation—Richmond, VA
- Mortgage Guaranty Insurance Corporation—Milwaukee, WI
- PMI Mortgage Insurance Co.—San Francisco, CA
- Republic Mortgage Insurance Company—Winston-Salem, NC
- Triad Guaranty Insurance Corporation—Winston-Salem, NC
- United Guaranty Corporation—Greensboro, NC
- U.S. Mortgage Insurance Company—Blue Bell, PA
- Verex Assurance, Inc.—Madison, WI
- The Mortgage Insurance Company of Canada—Toronto, Ontario

MARKETING RESIDENTIAL LOANS === *9*

The marketing function of residential mortgage loans includes selling loans, obtaining investor commitments, managing interest rate risk, and preparing and shipping loan packages. In this day, when most mortgage lenders sell all or some of their loan production, the ability to market successfully is crucial to profitability and market share.

This chapter will examine the process and the various alternatives for marketing residential mortgage loans which have already been closed. It will not discuss the marketing issues of how best to originate mortgage loans; that was discussed in Chapter 4. However, because this chapter is interrelated with Chapters 10 and 11, frequent reference will be made to them.

Development of Marketing

The marketing of residential mortgage loans has become increasingly important for all types of mortgage lenders. The growth of the secondary mortgage market with transactions each year approaching $300 billion is witness to that importance. Before 1961, the only originating lender which needed to be concerned about marketing of loans was the mortgage banker. Practically all other mortgage originators were portfolio lenders.

In 1961, savings and loan institutions were authorized to buy and sell whole loans originated outside their normal lending area, and with that change the marketing of residential loans took on greater importance. The Depository Institutions Deregulation and Monetary Control Act (1980) completed the evolution as it revised federal lending regulations to the extent that any federally chartered

137

financial institution could buy and sell whole loans or participations under the exact terms as if originating such a loan.

Marketing Alternatives

In today's sophisticated mortgage market, all mortgage lenders have various alternatives for placement of their loan production. These alternatives include:

1. Retaining loan production in own portfolio
2. Selling whole loans or participations to government-related secondary mortgage market entities (FNMA/FHLMC)
3. Selling whole loans or participations to private secondary market entities
4. Directly issuing mortgage-backed securities (MBS)
5. Selling loans to conduits for packaging into MBS

These alternatives are available to all mortgage lenders, but some will opt not to use one or more for various reasons. A mortgage banker, for example, will never retain production in its portfolio. Some thrifts, on the other hand, may opt for this alternative most of the time. Credit unions are also examples of lenders who basically keep all of their production in their own portfolios. Except in those situations where a lender will not consider one or more alternatives (e.g., a mortgage banker and portfolio lending), a mortgage lender should consider all alternatives before selecting the most advantageous.

Retaining production in portfolio   For many years this was the only option available to thrifts and commercial banks, and it served them well. In the early 1960s, a few thrifts began selling some of their loan production, but until the late 1970s most thrifts were primarily portfolio lenders. In fact, one type of thrift, mutual savings banks which are located primarily in the capital-surplus Northeast, could not generate enough loan production and as a result had to balance savings deposits with mortgages purchased from mortgage bankers. Savings banks as a result had their mortgage portfolios made up of their own production supplemented by that of mortgage bankers.

In a highly volatile interest rate environment as has existed since 1978, portfolio lending has obvious dangers. The number of thrifts that have closed or merged since 1980 illustrates vividly the result of those dangers. They failed, among other reasons, because their portfolio yield could not keep pace with their cost of funds. The spread between cost of funds and portfolio yields needs to be between 200 and 300 basis points for profitable lending. For the period 1981–83 the spread for most thrifts was negative, resulting in financial failure for the weakest and shrinking net worth for the remainder. If these thrifts had sold the mortgage originated before this period, they would not have faced this interest rate risk.

Even though the trend is clearly toward selling some or all of current production, it is expected that some mortgage lenders in the 1990s will continue to portfolio loans. Some of them, such as credit unions, have valid reasons for keeping some mortgages in their portfolio. Credit unions are having a problem putting all of the share deposits to work, so they keep many of their mortgages in portfolio to put that excess liquidity to work. Other lenders have similar problems or see similar investment opportunities in their own mortgages. (Of course, these mortgages should still be saleable so that if a need ever develops, these lenders will be able to sell.)

In the more sophisticated mortgage market of the 1990s, those institutions that opt to be portfolio lenders have some ways to protect themselves. As mentioned earlier, the principal dangers to a portfolio lender are increasing interest rates which increase the cost of funds and a portfolio of fixed-rate mortgages which does not respond to changed market conditions. These dangers can be minimized by better asset/liability management. By that is meant lengthening the maturity of liabilities (deposits), shortening the maturity of assets (mortgages), or indexing the interest rates on those assets. This is achieved by longer terms for certificates of deposit and the use of adjustable rate mortgages or similar instruments. These suggested changes will help all lenders but especially those mortgage lenders which opt for portfolio lending.

Selling production to FNMA/FHLMC   All mortgage originators are now authorized to sell to both of these government-related agencies. Both will buy whole loans or participations and fixed-rate or adjustable-rate mortgages. An extensive review of the programs, fees, and commitment requirements for both FNMA and FHLMC is covered in Chapter 10.

The attractiveness to a mortgage lender of selling loans to either of these entities is based on the following factors:

- no portfolio risk from changing interest rates
- increased ability to meet local housing demand
- instant liquidity
- increased servicing volume and income
- potential for marketing profit
- participation leverage

As previously discussed, mortgage bankers must sell their loan production to some investor. Although they can choose from many investors, they usually sell that production which does not go into GNMA mortgage-backed securities to these two government-related agencies. Other lenders, on the other hand, can sell to either of these agencies, other investors, or retain loan production in their portfolios. The deciding factors include price, servicing fees, underwriting requirements, and commitments outstanding.

Direct sales to private secondary mortgage market entities   The direct sale by mortgage bankers to private investors of loans originated in one part of the country and sold in another was the only alternative to portfolio lending until the start of FNMA in 1938. Mortgage companies in the late 1890s were originating farm mortgages in the Ohio Valley and selling those loans to wealthy individuals or life insurance companies located in the northeastern states. This activity started the loan correspondent system and produced the first use of commitments in mortgage lending. The use and the various types of commitments will be discussed in a later section.

Oftentimes, when the term *secondary mortgage market* is used, mortgage lenders automatically think of FNMA or FHLMC, but there also exists a thriving private secondary mortgage market. Although FNMA and FHLMC account for about 65 percent of secondary mortgage market activity, the remaining 35 percent involves the following players:

- commercial banks
- savings banks
- savings and loan institutions
- life insurance companies
- pension funds
- private conduits

Mortgage bankers, at times, also purchase mortgages originated by other lenders, but never for their own portfolio. This purchase activity is always to fill an outstanding commitment or to issue GNMA MBS. All mortgage lenders, including mortgage bankers, will periodically purchase mortgages from other lenders with servicing released. These mortgages in turn are sold to the government-related agencies with the servicing rights retained. In this way, mortgage lenders are able to build their servicing portfolio without the expense of origination. Other mortgage lenders are purchasing mortgages from other lenders because they have a permanent or temporary imbalance of deposits and loan production.

Details of sale   The direct sale to private secondary mortgage market players can be either on a continuous basis supported by outstanding commitments or on a case-by-case negotiated basis.

Example: Whether a direct sale is the result of a continuing relationship or of a negotiated transaction, the details of the sale will include the following items:

1. Type of mortgage loans to be delivered
   a. FHA/VA or conventional
   b. whole loan or participation
2. Total dollar amount of this sale

3. Yield (net) to the investor
4. Servicing requirements and fees
    a. servicing fee
    b. whether released or retained
5. Commitment fees (if any) charged to seller
    a. how much
    b. refundable or not
6. Delivery requirements to purchaser
    a. immediate delivery
    b. future delivery and when
7. Underwriting standards to be used
    a. FNMA/FHLMC standards
    b. other standards (whose)
8. Type of loan documentation to be used
9. Recourse to seller
    a. whether for mortgage default
    b. whether for breach of warranties
10. Method of monthly remittance to investor
11. Loan characteristics of mortgages to be delivered
    a. type of properties
        —single family detached
        —1–4 family
        —condominiums
        —cooperatives
        —second homes
    b. location (geographically)
    c. maximum loan amounts per mortgage loan
    d. coupon rates of loans
    e. loan-to-value maximums
    f. mortgage insurance required
12. Other requirements to be negotiated

As a general rule, these private secondary market purchasers use the same underwriting and documentation requirements as FNMA and FHLMC. At times, though, they may vary these requirements slightly, such as increasing ratios by a percent or two, to make themselves more competitive with FNMA/FHLMC.

The principal advantage to a mortgage lender of these direct transactions with private investors is that those mortgage loans which cannot be sold to FNMA or FHLMC because the loan is nonconforming (above the statutory loan limit) or has other unique features, can still be sold. In addition, the marketing profit to an originating lender may be greater in a direct sale on a negotiated basis than in the more competitive environment of dealing with FNMA or FHLMC.

Directly issuing mortgage-backed securities   Until 1977, the mortgage-backed securities field was the exclusive turf of government and government-related agencies. This changed in 1977 when the Bank of America issued the first private MBS. Since then many other private concerns, including many different types of mortgage lenders, have issued MBS. This entire subject of mortgage-backed securities is covered extensively in Chapter 11.

Even though mortgage bankers do not have the problem of securing existing portfolios, they have been very active in direct-issue MBS. Practically all of the GNMA MBS that have been issued to date are backed by FHA/VA loans originated or purchased from other lenders by mortgage bankers. To date all types of mortgage lenders, with the possible exception of credit unions, have directly issued mortgage-backed securities. Those that have not are usually those who are not sophisticated enough to do it themselves, and as a result have used conduits instead.

Selling loan production to conduits for packaging into MBS   The number of conduits in the marketplace that will buy loans from mortgage lenders and then package those mortgages with other mortgages from other lenders is growing every year. One example, CUNA Mortgage Corporation, buys mortgages only from credit unions and in turns sells those mortgages to FNMA or FHLMC which then issues MBS. Wall Street and mortgage insurance companies have also been active in purchasing mortgages from many lenders and then directly issuing MBS themselves.

MORTGAGE LOAN COMMITMENTS

Commitments are critical to successful mortgage lending in the 1990s for those lenders that sell mortgages. A commitment is an undertaking by either a mortgage lender to make a loan or an investor to buy a loan. A commitment is legally binding as a contract if it agrees completely with the loan application or the offer to sell. If a commitment varies the terms of an application or offer, then it becomes a counteroffer and must be accepted by the borrower or seller before a binding contract can result.

Commitments from investors to buy mortgage production are essential for successful marketing. During the early 1970s, a few mortgage lenders would originate mortgages without a commitment from a permanent investor to purchase those loans. Because interest rates moved so slowly during that period, the interest rate exposure of an originator was limited. But, practices changed in 1974.

During the early part of that year, rates dropped meaningfully from where they were at the end of 1973. As a result, a few mortgage bankers decided to save on fees and not get any commitments from investors since they assumed rates would continue to drop or at least stay even. By the middle of that year, rates were headed up and stayed up for the rest of the year. A similar situation developed in 1987, to the dismay of a few unprepared mortgage lenders. As a result, those originators with uncovered or only partially covered loan production were forced to discount mortgages in the pipeline in order to sell them or, if they could, put them into their own portfolios. For all practical purposes, that was the end of the practice of not covering loan originations by either a firm (mandatory) or stand-by commitment. Of course, those mortgage lenders who are not originating loans for sale (for their own portfolio instead) still continue to do so without the need of, or protection of, commitments to sell.

A firm commitment assures the mortgage borrower or seller of loans that the loan or sale will occur if certain conditions as set in the commitment are met. A further discussion of mortgage loan commitments to borrowers appears in Chapter 3.

A stand-by commitment obligates the issuer to purchase mortgages at a certain yield for a certain period of time, but it does not obligate the originator to whom it is issued to deliver any loans. Both parties recognize the likelihood that the mortgage loans may not be delivered and that the stand-by is a type of insurance for the mortgage originator. This process is valuable to an issuer because it is a fee generator. The fees required for both types of commitments are, as a general rule, established by the marketplace. Stand-by fees are usually twice as much as those required for mandatory delivery. This is because an investor must be compensated for holding funds at the ready to purchase loans which may or may not be delivered.

WHAT IS YIELD?

Mortgage loans are sold to investors based on the yield of the loan package. The establishment of yield is, regrettably, neither an easy nor an exact task. Yields are impacted by defaults, foreclosures, repayments, and prepayments. When investors have a large enough package, they can establish *to a degree* the impact of these events. Often MBS are marketed based on certain assumptions regarding these events.

Yield is determined by dividing the annualized income by the money invested, e.g.,

$$\frac{\$120,000 \text{ annualized income}}{\$1,000,000 \text{ invested}} = 12 \text{ percent yield}$$

As a general rule, when yield to an investor is being negotiated it refers to a net yield to that investor. Therefore, if a mortgage lender originates a package of mortgages at 13 percent and wants to retain 3/8 servicing, the yield to an investor would be 12.625 percent. From this figure, any commitment fees must be subtracted. Yield conversion tables are required to arrive at an exact yield, but as a general rule, a 1 percent commitment fee equals 14 basis points.

Weighted Average Yield

Seldom does the mortgage market rate remain constant long enough for a lender to originate a package of loans with the same interest rate. If a lender has mortgages with varying interest rates, the yield to an investor will be calculated on a weighted average basis.

For example, assume a lender has an outstanding commitment requiring delivery of $10 million in mortgages with a net yield to the investor of 12.625 percent. The following calculations will occur:

1. Lender determines which loans in the pipeline will be used to fulfill commitment. Assume:

$$\begin{array}{l} \$ \ 5 \text{ million at } 13 \quad \text{percent} \\ \ \ \ \ 3 \text{ million at } 12\frac{1}{2} \text{ percent} \\ \underline{\ \ \ \ 2 \text{ million at } 12\frac{3}{4} \text{ percent}} \\ \$10 \text{ million} \end{array}$$

2. Yields are then converted into annualized income:

$$\begin{array}{l} \$ \ 5 \text{ million} \times 13 \quad \text{percent} = \$ \ 650,00 \\ \$ \ 3 \text{ million} \times 12\frac{1}{2} \text{ percent} = \$ \ 375,000 \\ \underline{\$ \ 2 \text{ million} \times 12\frac{3}{4} \text{ percent} = \$ \ 247,500} \\ \$1,272,500 \text{ annualized income} \end{array}$$

3. Divide annualized income by loan package to establish weighted average yield:

$$\frac{\$ \ 1,272,500}{\$10,000,000} = .12725$$

In this example the weighted average yield of .12725 exceeds the commitment of .12625 net—lender can either increase the price to the investor to reflect the yield or lower the weighted average yield by substituting a few more 12⅜ percent mortgages for a few 13 percents.

Price for a Package

Once a package of loans has been put together, the yield is adjusted by the price for the package. Assume a $10 million package has been put together with a net yield of 12⅝ percent. If, at the time the package is ready for delivery, the market requires a 12⅞ yield, the package must be discounted to produce the market yield.

$1,262,500 annualized income ÷ .98 percent = $1,288,265 or .1288 or 12⅞

Occasionally, a loan will sell at a premium, thus reducing the yield:

$1,262,500 annualized income ÷ 1.01 = 12½ percent

THE SECONDARY
MORTGAGE MARKET === *10*

This chapter will examine the government and government-related agencies that make up the organized secondary mortgage market. This chapter will also review the development and players in the so-called unorganized or private secondary mortgage market.

Marketing of residential mortgages and the activity of the secondary mortgage market have taken on new importance since the near disaster faced by thrifts in the early 1980s. The size of the secondary mortgage market is now nearly as large as that of the primary market. In the later half of the 1980s, for example, for every four mortgages originated in the primary market, three mortgages were sold into the various secondary mortgage market outlets. Total secondary mortgage market transactions for 1990 were just under $300 billion, a figure higher than originations for any year before 1986.

Selling Mortgage Loans

Today, all loan production should be capable of being traded in the secondary mortgage market even though the intent at origination is for that production to be placed in a lender's portfolio. Any institution which originates mortgages not suitable for the secondary mortgage market faces the possibility of disaster if interest rates shoot up again (as they probably will) or liquidity is needed for whatever reason. Some lenders believe that since all loans can ultimately be sold to some investor, why worry if the loans don't meet the requirements of the secondary market? That belief is true; all mortgage loans can be sold to someone, but the price these loans get may be such that a sale isn't really an option at all.

Sound, modern asset management dictates that all institutions involved in residential lending should also be engaged in what is generically called mortgage

SECONDARY MARKET ACTIVITY
SALES/ORIGINATIONS

Source: MBA

banking. This prudent approach should be followed even if current economic conditions and investment philosophy dictate retaining some or all mortgage loan production in portfolio. The term mortgage banking refers to the process of originating mortgages which are capable of being sold (even if not actually sold) into the secondary mortgage market.

Growth of Residential Mortgage Lending and the Secondary Mortgage Market

One of the most important reasons for the sharp increase in real estate lending activity since the end of World War II has been the demand for and the supply of mortgage money at reasonable rates. The demand resulted from both the pent-up housing market of the Depression and war years, and the movement to and population growth in the Sunbelt states. These areas did not have sufficient capital to meet demand; therefore, availability of capital was essential to continued growth. This availability, although sporadic at times, has been largely the result of the development of a secondary market for mortgages. During periods of tight money or credit restraints such as existed in 1969–70, 1974, and 1979–81, the activity of the secondary market accounted for a large portion of the residential lending that did occur.

Today, the activity of the secondary market is greater than ever and provides the foundation for all mortgage lending in this country. As the need for more and cheaper credit for housing grows in the 1990s, it is estimated that 80 percent of this credit will be funded by the secondary market. In particular, the use of mortgage-backed securities will allow for a direct path from the mortgage markets to the capital markets.

Primary Markets versus Secondary Markets

The distinction between what are known as the primary and secondary mortgage markets is not always clear, especially today with so many originations being

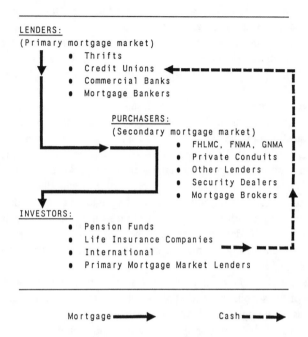

SECONDARY MORTGAGE MARKET
AND
TRADING MORTGAGES FOR CASH

LENDERS:
(Primary mortgage market)
- Thrifts
- Credit Unions
- Commercial Banks
- Mortgage Bankers

PURCHASERS:
(Secondary mortgage market)
- FHLMC, FNMA, GNMA
- Private Conduits
- Other Lenders
- Security Dealers
- Mortgage Brokers

INVESTORS:
- Pension Funds
- Life Insurance Companies
- International
- Primary Mortgage Market Lenders

Mortgage ⟶   Cash ▬ ▬ ➤

funded from sources other than deposits at financial intermediaries. However, most authorities agree that a primary market exists when a lender extends funds directly to a borrower. This process includes origination, processing, underwriting, servicing, and market of the loan. This process occurs, of course, whether a lender is originating the mortgage for its own portfolio, for direct sale to an investor, or for sale into the secondary mortgage market.

The secondary market exists when primary lenders and permanent investors buy and sell existing mortgages. This activity could occur as part of the normal course of business for the mortgage lender or be utilized only during periods of credit restraints. Thus, the primary market involves an extension of credit to borrower and the secondary market a sale of the credit instrument.

ECONOMIC FUNCTIONS OF THE SECONDARY MORTGAGE MARKET

In order to provide the needed economic assistance to mortgage lending, the secondary mortgage market performs these four important economic functions:

1. *Provide liquidity.* Provided the mortgages are of sufficient quality, any originator, portfolio lender, or investor can sell its mortgages in the market at any time. This ability allows an institution to meet immediate needs for capital such as deposit withdrawals, policy loans, or other demands. Many investors who have not traditionally invested in mortgages (such as pension funds, trust accounts, and others) are now beginning to invest because the required liquidity is present. These investors, attracted by higher yields available with mortgages, realize that a ready market exists if they are forced to liquidate their holdings.

2. *Moderate the cyclical flow of mortgage capital.* During periods of general capital shortage, the funds available for mortgages are usually very scarce (e.g., 1969–1970, 1974, and 1979–1981) and real estate activity slows down. Institutions operating in the secondary market during these periods purchase existing mortgages from primary mortgage lenders, and in this way provide funds for additional mortgages to be originated. This availability of capital for mortgages helps to lessen the counter-cyclical nature of real estate. Today, the secondary mortgage market also serves as a link between the mortgage market and the capital market by the sale of mortgage-backed securities.

3. *Assist the flow of capital from surplus areas to deficit areas.* The operations of the secondary market allow an investor in a capital-surplus area, such as New England, to invest in mortgages originated in a capital-deficit area such as the South or West, thus providing capital for needed mortgage activity. Capital-surplus areas are the older, slower-growing areas of the country which have a surplus of capital exceeding the demand of home buyers. Capital-deficit areas are those where the demand for housing credit exceeds the supply of capital created by the savings of individuals.

4. *Lessen the geographical spread in interest rates and allow for portfolio diversification.* The mobility of capital allows for a moderation of the geographical differences in mortgage interest rates since capital will flow to areas of high interest, thus pressuring rates downward. In addition, regional risk (e.g., a large industry closing) is spread to more investors, thus lessening its effect.

FEDERAL NATIONAL MORTGAGE ASSOCIATION (FNMA)

Any discussion of secondary markets must start with the Federal National Mortgage Association, also known as "Fannie Mae." FNMA is the most active participant historically and currently is also the nation's largest holder of residential mortgage debt.

The importance of an effective secondary market has been recognized since

1924, when a bill was introduced in Congress to establish a system of national home loan banks which could purchase first mortgages. The legislation failed to become law. The first federal attempt to establish and assist a national mortgage market was the Reconstruction Finance Corporation (RFC), created in 1935 and followed in 1938 by a wholly-owned subsidiary, the National Mortgage Association of Washington, soon renamed the Federal National Mortgage Association.

From its beginning until 1970, FNMA only purchased FHA/VA mortgages that were originated predominantly by mortgage bankers. In 1970, Congress—in the same bill which created the Federal Home Loan Mortgage Corporation—authorized FNMA to purchase conventional mortgages. Today, FNMA purchases more conventional mortgages than any other type.

In 1950, FNMA was transferred to the Department of Housing and Urban Development (HUD), and was later partitioned into two separate corporations by amendments to the Housing and Urban Development Act of 1968. This was done to permit the new FNMA to more actively support the mortgage market outside the federal budget.

The new entity, named the Government National Mortgage Association (GNMA or "Ginnie Mae") remained in HUD and retained the special assistance and loan liquidation functions of the old FNMA. GNMA will be discussed in greater detail in a later section.

The new FNMA corporation was to be basically private, though some regulatory control remained with HUD. In addition, FNMA retained a $2.25 billion line of credit with the U.S. Treasury. It retained the Federal National Mortgage Association's name, as well as the assets and responsibilities for secondary market operations.

Today, the corporation is run by a 15-member board of directors, consisting of ten selected by the stockholders and five appointed by the President of the United States. Approximately 60 million shares are currently outstanding and traded regularly on the New York Stock Exchange.

Financing Mortgage Purchases

FNMA finances its secondary market operations by tapping the private capital markets using both short- and long-term obligations. The short-term obligations (less than a year) are discount notes, which, as the term implies, are sold to investors at a price less than the face amount paid at maturity. The long-term obligations are called debentures and are generally issued with maturities ranging from one to 25 years. In 1990, the split of debt instruments was about two-thirds long term and about one-third short term.

FNMA Earnings

Fannie Mae produces earnings from two sources, fee income and the spread between its borrowing costs and the yield on its mortgage investment. Fannie Mae started the 1990s with record earnings in 1990 of $1,173 million. This continued the record earnings of recent years which have resulted in a substantial improvement over 1982 when FNMA lost a total (net) of $105 million and had a negative spread of $506 million.

The recent success of FNMA can be traced directly to efforts to manage and minimize the interest rate risk which is inherent in the mortgage lending business. FNMA's current strategy is:

- Expand the mortgage-backed securities business which provides FNMA with fee-based income. This income flows from the fees FNMA charges for its guaranty of timely payment of principal and interest.
- Manage loan portfolio better by matching the maturity of the assets and liabilities more closely.
- Lessen interest rate risk by selling old, low-yielding mortgages.

Secondary Market Operations

FNMA, like other institutions in the secondary mortgage market, has made extensive changes in its programs and in the way it operates in an attempt to adapt to changing economic conditions. These changes occur often, even monthly; therefore, any discussion of FNMA's current programs runs the risk of being dated quickly. Recognizing that risk, a text without at least an overview of current practices and programs of FNMA would diminish the importance of FNMA in the secondary mortgage market.

FNMA purchases mortgages only from approved seller/servicers that have obtained delivery commitments. To become an FNMA-approved seller/servicer, a lender must have a minimum net worth of $250,000. FNMA requires an appropriate level of experience on a lender's part and will review the volume of originations and serviced loans. FNMA wants assurances that a lender's quality control system contains written procedures, identifies discrepancies, and takes corrective action.

Commitments are obtained from FNMA by telephoning special numbers (depending on the program in which the lender is interested) to establish the commitment yield quoted on a net basis, which does not include servicing. The servicing fee, which FNMA requires a lender to collect, ranges from 25 to 50 basis points depending on the type of mortgage and the volume and experience of the mortgage lender.

Mortgage Characteristics

FNMA offers standard purchase and negotiated purchase programs for many different types of mortgage loans, including both fixed-rate and adjustable-rate loans. The mortgages that FNMA will buy include:

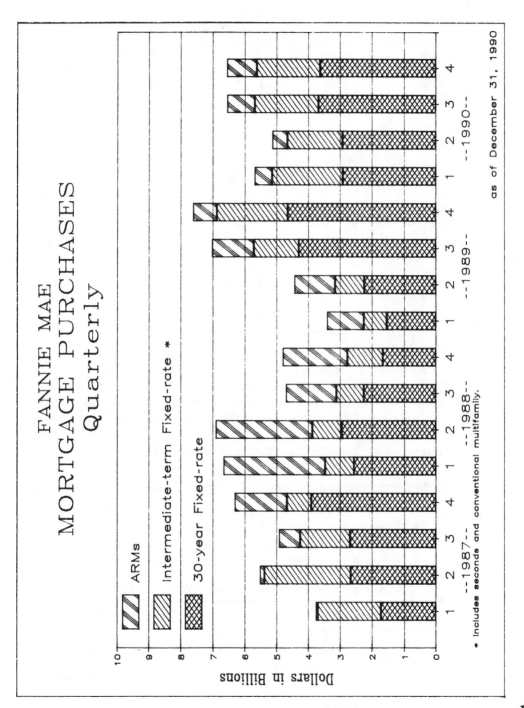

FANNIE MAE
MORTGAGE PURCHASES
Quarterly

ARMs

Intermediate-term Fixed-rate *

30-year Fixed-rate

Dollars in Billions

10 9 8 7 6 5 4 3 2 1 0

1 2 3 4 1 2 3 4 1 4 3 1 1 2 3 4 1 2 3 4
--1987--   --1988--   --1989--   --1990--

* Includes seconds and conventional multifamily.

as of December 31, 1990

153

FNMA ACTIVITY
(In Millions of Dollars)

Year	Purchases	Sales	Year-end portfolio	MBS
1960	$ 980	$ 42	$ 2,903	-
1965	757	46	2,520	-
1970	5,078	-	15,502	-
1975	4,263	2	31,824	-
1980	8,099	-	57,327	-
1985	21,510	1,301	98,282	23,649
1986	30,826	10,868	97,895	60,566
1987	20,531	5,214	93,470	63,229
1988	23,110	5,047	99,867	54,878
1989	22,518	3,036	107,756	69,764
1990	23,959	5,800	113,875	96,700

Source: FNMA

- conventional and government-backed first mortgages on 1- to 4-family units
- conventional second mortgages on 1- to 4-family units
- conventional multi-family mortgages on 5 or more units

FNMA purchases conventional whole loans and participation interests in 5 percent increments between 50 and 95 percent. Eligible properties include first mortgages on owner-occupied principal residences, second homes, and investment properties. First mortgages can be secured by units in condominiums, cooperatives, and planned unit developments (and manufactured housing in some cases).

Maximum Loan-to-Value Ratios for Standard Purchases

The following maximum loan-to-value ratios apply to FNMA's standard purchases:

- 95 percent for fixed-rate mortgages if owner-occupied principal residence
- 90 percent for adjustable-rate if owner-occupied principal residence
- 90 percent for fixed- and adjustable-rate on owner-occupied refinances
- 80 percent for investment properties and second homes

FANNIE MAE 1990 RESIDENTIAL MORTGAGE PORTFOLIO

Conventional, 30 year fixed-rate:	43 percent
Conventional, intermediate term, fixed-rate:	22 percent
Adjustable-rate:	20 percent
FHA/VA:	15 percent
	100 percent

Source: 1990 FNMA Annual Report

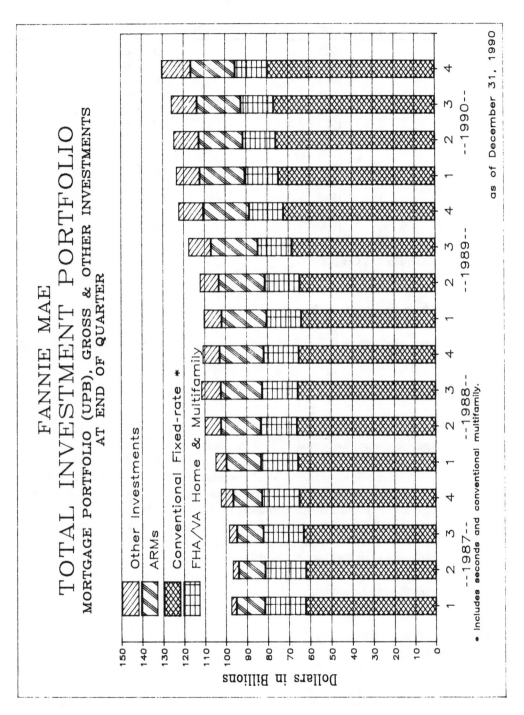

FANNIE MAE
TOTAL INVESTMENT PORTFOLIO
MORTGAGE PORTFOLIO (UPB), GROSS & OTHER INVESTMENTS
AT END OF QUARTER

Other Investments
ARMs
Conventional Fixed-rate *
FHA/VA Home & Multifamily

Dollars in Billions

--1987-- --1988-- --1989-- --1990--

* Includes seconds and conventional multifamily.

as of December 31, 1990

155

CONFORMING LOAN LIMITS FOR FANNIE MAE AND FREDDIE MAC

1975	$55,000*
1977	75,000*
1980	93,750*
1981	98,500
1982	107,000
1983	108,300
1984	114,000
1985	115,300
1986	133,250
1987	153,100
1988	168,700
1989	187,600
1990	187,450
1991	191,250

*Determined by Congress
Source: Fannie Mae

Mortgage Insurance Requirements

Mortgage insurance is required on conventional first mortgage loans if the loan-to-value ratio at the time of FNMA's purchase is greater than 80 percent.

Delivery Requirements

During much of FNMA's history most of its programs were optional delivery. These contracts amounted to FNMA's being on the receiving end of a "put" contract and as a result were not always beneficial to FNMA's financial position.

Practically all of Fannie Mae's programs now require mandatory delivery of at least 95 percent of the commitment amount. On occasion a mortgage lender may be unable to fulfill a commitment. In that situation the lender can "buy back" the commitment by paying a fee which compensates Fannie Mae for the lost yield. On the other hand, if an outstanding commitment has at least one additional dollar outstanding, another loan can be delivered under that commitment.

As mentioned earlier, most of the standard purchases no longer require the lender to pay a commitment fee.

FEDERAL HOME LOAN MORTGAGE CORPORATION (FHLMC)

The Emergency Home Finance Act of 1970, in addition to giving FNMA the power to purchase conventional mortgages, authorized the establishment of the Federal

Home Loan Mortgage Corporation, also known as "Freddie Mac." It was originally intended to provide secondary market facilities for members of the Federal Home Loan Bank System, which meant savings and loan associations, but its charter has been modified to include all mortgage lenders today.

The corporation's initial capital was from the sale of $100 million of nonvoting common shares to the 12 district Federal Home Loan Banks (FHLB). Today, Freddie Mac is a publicly traded corporation just like Fannie Mae with 60 million shares outstanding and listed on the New York Stock Exchange.

A part of the enabling legislation authorized FHLMC to request that the FHLB guarantee FHLMC debts or help it raise funds. This authorization has not been used to date. Although FHLMC is not formally a part of the federal government, its ties to the FHLB and its tax-exempt status have led investors to classify it as a quasi-governmental agency. As a result, its debt offerings, like FNMA, sell at governmental or near-governmental rates.

Largest Purchaser of Conventional Loans

Since its beginning, Freddie Mac has been the largest purchaser of conventional loans with total purchases and mortgage-backed securities issued exceeding $500 billion by year-end 1990. In 1990, Freddie Mac purchased approximately $75 billion worth of mortgages from various lenders. These loans were purchased from the over 5,000 lenders approved to do business with Freddie Mac. Fulfilling its secondary mortgage market function in addition to its purchases, Freddie Mac issued nearly $75 billion in original issue mortgage securities and another $50 billion in derivative securities.

Freddie Mac offers two basic ways for lenders to participate in the secondary mortgage market. Lenders can sell mortgages either under the Cash Program or swap them for securities under the Guarantor Program. In either case, the lender keeps the origination fees and earns servicing income while the loans are outstanding. As with Fannie Mae, a generous float period exists whereby a lender can earn substantial interest on mortgage payments before the funds are to pass to Freddie Mac.

Secondary Market Operations

Similar to Fannie Mae, before a lender sells loans to Freddie Mac it must become an approved seller/servicer. The major difference between the two is that Freddie Mac requires a high net worth before granting approval to deal with a lender. By January 1, 1993 a lender must have a net worth of at least $1 million. Lenders telephone special numbers to receive current quotes on yield requirements. If a lender decides to obtain a commitment, it gives its identification number and tells the operator the type and amount of loans(s) the lender wants to sell and the delivery period desired. The operator confirms the commitment over the phone and

FEDERAL HOME LOAN MORTGAGE CORPORATION
(In Millions of Dollars)

Year	Purchases	Sales	Portfolio
1970	$ 325	$ —	$ 325
1975	1,713	1,521	4,987
1980	3,723	2,526	5,056
1985	44,012	38,658	14,022
1986	103,474	100,198	12,159
1987	76,840	75,018	12,258
1988	44,075	39,777	16,815
1989	78,589	75,562	21,329

Source: FHLMC 1989 Annual Report

mails two copies of the written contract to the lender. When received, the lender signs and returns the contract within 24 hours. The yield to Freddie Mac is a net yield: that is, it does not include the lender's servicing fee.

Mortgage Characteristics

FHLMC, under either the Cash Program or the Guarantor Program, offers to purchase from approved sellers the following mortgages:

- Fixed-rate mortgages
  —15-year conventional
  —30-year conventional
- Adjustable-rate mortgages
  —2 percent annual rate-capped, Treasury-indexed
  —1 percent annual rate-capped, Treasury-indexed
  —Cost of funds-indexed
- Fixed-rate graduated payment
  —15- and 30-year with 7.5 percent annual payment increase
  —15- and 30-year with 5 percent annual payment increase
- FHA/VA under the Guarantor Swap Program only
- Fixed-rate seconds secured by owner-occupied
- Multi-family loans secured by 5 or more units

Financing Mortgage Purchases

Freddie Mac finances its secondary mortgage market operations somewhat differently than Fannie Mae. Rather than finance its purchases with debt securities in the capital market, as does Fannie Mae, Freddie Mac issues mortgage-backed securities. One of the early successes was the Guarantor Program, under which a mortgage lender sold mortgages to Freddie Mac and, in turn, Freddie Mac sold back to the lender an MBS secured by those same mortgages. For this action, Freddie Mac earned a guarantee fee.

In effect, Freddie Mac finances its mortgage purchases with capital generated from the sale of either whole mortgages (rarely) or participations (generally) in groups of mortgages. It effectively buys and sells mortgages on a constant basis. Some capital is generated by the sale of debt securities.

The practical result of this activity is the sale of so-called Participation Certificates (PC) which are sold to thrift institutions, pension funds, and others. PCs are mortgage-backed securities which have the timely payment of principal and interest guaranteed by Freddie Mac. These PCs give the investor an undivided interest in the pooled mortgages. See Chapter 11 for a complete discussion on mortgage-backed securities.

Recourse

Mortgage lenders that sell mortgage loans to either Fannie Mae or Freddie Mac have a decision to make on the issue of whether the loans sold will have recourse. Recourse is defined as the obligation a seller/servicer has to repurchase a mortgage loan from an investor if a default and foreclosure occurs. Two types of recourse exist:

1. Repurchase, for whatever reason, if loan becomes delinquent.
2. Repurchase after delinquency, but only if seller did not process or underwrite the loan according to the investor's requirements.

Most loans sold into the secondary mortgage market are with recourse, but only if the requirements of the investor were not followed. It is possible for a seller to sell loans without recourse, but the yield is less to the seller since the investor has a higher risk.

Delivery Requirements

Freddie Mac, similar to Fannie Mae, expects a mortgage lender to deliver the dollar amount of mortgages they contracted to deliver when they obtained a commitment. Though their requirements are slightly different, both secondary mortgage market investors will allow a slight variance up or down from the commitment amount.

Documents to be Delivered

After agreeing to purchase a mortgage, neither Freddie Mac nor Fannie Mae want to keep all the documents a mortgage lender finds necessary to have when

STATE OF LOUISIANA
PARISH OF JEFFERSON

ASSIGNMENT OF NOTE AND MORTGAGE

     BE IT KNOWN, That on this ___21ST___ day of the month of ___MARCH___, 19_89_, before me, a Notary Public duly commissioned and qualified, in and for the Parish and State aforesaid, and therein residing, personally came and appeared ___DONNA J. PILLARD___, who declared unto me, Notary, that he/she is ___VICE PRESIDENT___ of Mellon Financial Services Corporation #7 and who, acting in said capacity and duly authorized hereunto, declared that, for value received, the said Mellon Financial Services Corporation #7 does herein and hereby assign, transfer, sell and deliver to

GOVERNMENT NATIONAL MORTGAGE ASSOCIATION

without recourse, one certain mortgage note made and subscribed by
_____DAVID PRESTON WALTERS AND_____
_____DORIS MITCHELL WALTERS_____
dated ___MARCH 16, 1989___, in the original principal sum of $___58,500.00___, payable to the order of ___BEARER___
Paraphed Ne Varietur by ___JANE DOE___
_____, Notary Public and the said Mellon Financial Services Corporation #7 does hereby assign, transfer and deliver to

GOVERNMENT NATIONAL MORTGAGE ASSOCIATION

    Real estate located in the Parish of ___JEFFERSON___
_____, State of Louisiana, and being:

LOT #12, SQUARE #3, CHATEAU ESTATES SUBDIVISION, PARISH OF JEFFERSON, STATE OF LOUISIANA

the mortgage, passed before ___JANE DOE___,
Notary Public, by which the aforesaid note is secured, recorded in ___JEFFERSON___ Parish, Louisiana, on the _16TH_ day of ___MARCH___, 19_89_, in ___M.O.B. 267 FOLIO 38___,
and the said Mellon Financial Services Corporation #7 does hereby warrant that the principal remaining unpaid on the aforesaid note as of this date is the sum of $_58,500.00_, that Mellon Financial Services Corporation #7 has full power and authority to assign, transfer and deliver same; that it has executed no prior assignment thereof; that it has executed no release, discharge satisfaction or cancellation of said note or mortgage and that it has not released any portion of the security or released the liability of the maker or makers thereof.

    To fully accomplish, effectuate and evidence said assignment and transfer, the Mellon Financial Services Corporation #7, through its proper officer, endorsed and hereinabove described note, without recourse, to the order of

GOVERNMENT NATIONAL MORTGAGE ASSOCIATION

whereupon I, Notary, did paraph said note for identification herewith.

    THUS DONE AND PASSED IN D U P L I C A T E ORIGINALS IN MY OFFICE IN THE CITY OF METAIRIE, STATE OF LOUISIANA, on the day and in the month and year first hereinabove written in the presence of the undersigned competent witnesses who have affixed their signatures hereto with said appearer and me, Notary, after due reading of the whole.

WITNESSES:

Pamela M. Edwards

Janice Myes

Mellon Financial Services Corporation #7

By: _Donna Pillard_
    DONNA J. PILLARD, VICE-PRESIDENT

Jane Doe
    NOTARY PUBLIC JANE DOE

My commission expires at death

SH-2 (2/85)
MFS 5050

160

processing a mortgage loan. As a general rule, they only want the mortgage, note, assignment of the mortgage, and a loan schedule whereby the characteristics of the mortgage(s) sold are listed. The mortgage lender, on the other hand, must keep these documents either in their original form or record on microfilm. These documents must be available at all times if an investor wants to perform its own quality control audit, or if the loan becomes delinquent.

GOVERNMENT NATIONAL MORTGAGE ASSOCIATION (GNMA)

The Government National Mortgage Association, known as Ginnie Mae, was organized within HUD under the authority of the Housing and Urban Development Act of 1968 which split the old FNMA into two separate entities—FNMA and GNMA.

GNMA was given authority to operate in the following three areas, the first two of which were inherited from the old FNMA:

1. The special assistance function (SAF). Under this function, GNMA was authorized to make available below-market interest rate loans to low-income families who normally could not obtain loans through private means. An example would be one of the Tandem Plans through which GNMA purchases below-market interest rate mortgages for sale to FNMA at market yield, with GNMA absorbing any loss.
2. The management and liquidation of previously originated (old FNMA) mortgages.
3. The mortgage-backed security (MBS) program. Under this new program, GNMA will guarantee the timely payment of principal and interest on mortgage-backed securities (composed of FHA-insured, VA-guaranteed, or Farmers Home Administration mortgages) issued by a GNMA-approved mortgagee and sold to an investor.

It is in this last area that GNMA has had its greatest effect on mortgage lending and the secondary markets.

The primary purpose behind the rebirth of a mortgage-backed security was to attract more funds into the housing market by providing a liquid instrument with a governmental guarantee to nontraditional mortgage investors. For an extensive discussion of how a GNMA MBS is structured and an examination of other MBS, see Chapter 11.

PRIVATE SECONDARY MORTGAGE MARKET

In addition to the government and government-related agencies, private companies have recently become quite active as well as important in the secondary mortgage market. Reasons for the emergence of the private secondary mortgage market include the following:

- Deregulation and a shift in political sentiment to less government.
- Government-related agencies borrowing in the capital markets at the same time as excessive federal deficits drive up interest rates and thus crowd some other borrowers out.
- Perception of unfair competition, since government-related agencies borrow more cheaply than private companies.
- Growth of primary and secondary mortgage markets provide profit opportunities for private entities.

Much of the activity by these private entities is with those mortgage loans classified as nonconforming. These loans are so classified because they exceed the set statutory limit above which FNMA and FHLMC cannot purchase mortgages. The private companies cannot compete with FNMA and FHLMC on loans below that limit because government-related agencies have a substantial advantage with their lower cost of funds.

UNIFORM DOCUMENTATION

In order for mortgages to be readily saleable in the secondary market, a degree of uniformity must exist. Before FHLMC joined FNMA in the secondary market the required uniformity existed because all mortgages sold in the secondary market were either FHA-insured or VA-guaranteed. After 1970, conventional mortgages could also be bought and sold in the secondary market and a need developed for uniform documentation.

Both FNMA and FHLMC have worked diligently to produce the state-by-state uniform documents that all mortgage lenders should use for all originations. GNMA has also adopted these forms, which include among others:

- mortgage note
- deed of trust
- mortgage
- loan application
- appraisal form
- verification documents

These forms can also be used for VA-guaranteed mortgages if a VA-guaranteed loan rider is added to the mortgage or deed of trust to make the mortgage instrument conform to special VA requirements. These forms regrettably cannot be used for FHA-insured loans; FHA-approved forms must be used. This may change in the future.

These uniform forms may contain some minor variations to comply with different state laws.

MORTGAGE-BACKED SECURITIES

11

Demographics for the 1990s point to a steady demand for housing and therefore mortgage lending. Projections are for mortgage originations to become $400–500 billion annually in the 1990s. Even in an economic environment without excessive federal deficits and their resulting demands on credit, this projected growth cannot be met by traditional sources or capital. Mortgage-backed securities (MBS) provide one of the few ways to meet this demand. In the 1980s, this type of financing became important to mortgage lenders that deal in the secondary mortgage market because of the increased amount of housing that can thus be financed. At the end of 1990, more than $ 1 trillion in agency MBS were held by investors. This chapter provides an introduction to mortgage-backed securities and a review of the recent developments of this important fixed-income security.

Concept of MBS

The basic concept behind MBS is simple: to provide a way for more capital to flow into housing. Disintermediation among the traditional mortgage lenders in the late 1960s resulted in a shortage of capital for housing and focused attention on the need to develop additional sources of finance. These additional sources were the so-called nontraditional mortgage lenders (i.e., those institutions which traditionally had not invested in mortgages) such as pension funds, retirement systems, some insurance companies, and trusts among others.

   This critical need for more capital was addressed by reviving an old idea— the use of a capital market instrument backed by a pool of mortgages. This concept had been used in the 1920s by some large mortgage insurance companies which sold participation bonds to the general public. Neither these mortgage insurance companies nor the bonds they guaranteed survived the Great Depression.

Among the many reasons why nontraditional mortgage investors were not previously interested in mortgages are the following more basic ones:

- diverse state real estate laws (e.g., foreclosure, redemption)
- lack of liquidity (ability to sell quickly) of mortgages
- lack of day-to-day evaluation of mortgages
- monthly cash flow of principal and interest that required monthly reinvestment decisions

What was needed was a way to make mortgage debt a more attractive investment to more investors. The tool used was an instrument investors were already familiar with—a capital market security. That's the whole key to MBS: a capital market instrument that is understood and readily traded in capital markets.

How successful have MBS been since they were introduced? To understand how successful, a look at the residential mortgage market before the first MBS was issued is required. In 1970, the so-called traditional investors were savings and loans, mutual savings banks, commercial banks, and life insurance companies. They held 78 percent of the outstanding residential mortgage debt. In contrast, at the end of 1986 these same investors held only 49 percent of the outstanding debt. Much of the difference was now in the form of MBS with over 35 percent of outstanding residential mortgage debt in that form. MBS now constitute the largest classification of holders of residential debt, with over $833 billion outstanding at the end of 1989.

Types of MBS

If all of the various mortgage-backed securities are considered, all represent either an equity or a creditor position for an investor. That is to say, MBS either provide an investor with an undivided ownership interest in a pool of mortgages, or the pool of mortgages secures a debt.

Pass-through   In the first type, an equity position, the investor has a fractional undivided ownership in a pool of mortgages represented by an investment trust. (The trust does not actually manage the mortgages; therefore, no federal income taxes are due from the trust.) The monthly principal, interest, and any prepayments from the mortgagors are passed through the security issuer to the investors. The security issuer or pool sponsor is usually one of the traditional originators of mortgages. Mortgage bankers have issued more MBS than any other, but recently savings and loans, commercial banks, and sponsors of conduits have increased their activity.

The pass-through payments can be made in one of three ways depending on the type of security. The simplest type is the straight pass-through which is used primarily in private placements. With this instrument, principal and interest are paid to an investor when collected, but if a default by a mortgagor occurs, the investor's cash flow is reduced by that amount.

Some of the early GNMA (Government National Mortgage Association) MBS were of the second type, the partially modified pass-through. With this type, the monthly principal and interest due an investor is paid as collected, but if a default occurs, an issuer is only obligated to pass through a predetermined percentage of what is owed.

Neither of these first two were very attractive to investors since they required greater certainty of cash flow in order for mortgages to be considered as investments. The third form, the modified pass-through, became the instrument accepted in the marketplace and is the one used almost exclusively today.

The modified pass-through is the MBS which best meets the needs of investors since it offers near certainty of monthly cash flow. This certainty is an absolute guarantee in some situations; witness the full faith and credit of the federal government backing the monthly payment for GNMAs. With this instrument, the issuer of a certificate is required to pass through to investors principal and interest even if not collected. If the investor is unable to pass through this amount, then GNMA will make the payment. This makes the instrument very attractive to investors since monthly cash flow is ensured. Many nontraditional mortgage investors, including pension funds (the most sought after), invested heavily in GNMAs, making them the most popular pass-through to date.

Mortgage bonds   In contrast with the equity position an investor takes with a pass-through, a mortgage bond puts an investor in a creditor position with a pool of mortgages serving as collateral. Since the issuer is in a debtor position, mortgage bonds are carried on the balance sheet as a liability. Two types of bonds have been used: the pay-through or cash flow bond and the straight or traditional bond. The Collateralized Mortgage Obligation is a type of bond, but is unique enough that it will be discussed separately.

Pay-through bond   The primary difference between the two mortgage bonds is how the mortgages are given value. With the pay-through bond, the mortgages serve as the source of cash flow to pay off the bond. The monthly principal and interest collected from the mortgagor—the cash flow—is used to make the bond interest payment. That payment can be monthly, quarterly, or every six months.

Pay-through bonds have the ability to stand on their own since the cash flow necessary to make the bond interest payment comes from the mortgages that are serving as the security.

Example: XYZ Savings and Loan has $100 million in "below water" mortgage loans. Assume they are 7 percent mortgages—way below today's market. The S&L needs additional capital to make more loans and therefore increase its portfolio yield. But it doesn't want to sell mortgages at a loss and take an immediate hit to the bottom line. Instead of selling these mortgages, it could use them as security for a bond. Assume a $50 million bond and that the market requires a yield of 15 5/8. The cash flow from the $100 million at 7 percent generates $665,000. The bond interest obligation is $662,000. The bond therefore stands completely on its own. The S&L is using $100 million of low-yielding loans to get more money to lend out at a higher rate. It did not have to sell the mortgages, but instead had the opportunity to use them for liquidity.

The cash flow generated by the underlying mortgages will be put in the hands of a fiduciary—a trustee. This action removes the possibility that the funds could be seized by creditors of the issuer if the issuer gets into financial difficulty. Therefore, with the cash flow going to a trustee the money will be able to flow through to investors.

Straight Bond

Generally, whenever any debt instrument is issued investors will require some security. The security for a pay-through bond is the cash flow from a pool of mortgages. Contrast that type with the so-called straight bond, which also puts the investor in a creditor position. The straight bond investor has in effect loaned money to the issuer. This debt obligation is very similar to a corporate bond, but the security is the market value of a pool of mortgages.

For example, if a $50 million bond is issued, the issuer will put as many mortgages into the pool as necessary to produce a market value of $50 million. This could require $100 million at 7 percent if the market rate is 14 percent.

Obviously, with this type of bond there is an underlying risk that the market can change quickly. In the early 1980s, mortgage yields in the marketplace could change 100 basis points in a month. In that situation, an investor who owned this type of bond would see the value of the security plummet. In order to protect investors, issuers were required to keep in the pool a sufficient number of mortgages with a market value equal to the issue outstanding. If the value of the mortgages in the pool drops because the market yield is increasing, the issuer is obligated to put more mortgages into the pool. In early issues the trustee would in effect "mark to market" the mortgages in the pool every six months. The current practice is to evaluate the mortgages in the pool quarterly with the issuer obligated to put more mortgages into the pool if the market value has decreased.

GOVERNMENT NATIONAL MORTGAGE ASSOCIATION (GNMA) _____

To understand MBS more fully, one must start with the Government National Mortgage Association (GNMA), or, as it's called, Ginnie Mae. As mentioned,

GNMA was not the first to use mortgage-backed securities. The first MBS was issued in the 1920s. Because many financial institutions and individual investors lost considerable money with these instruments, the return of MBS might not have been so successful if the federal government were not involved as a guarantor.

The way a GNMA MBS works is as follows. First, an issuer, most often a mortgage banker, will seek a commitment from GNMA to guarantee a pool of acceptable FHA, Farmers Home Administration (FmHA), or VA mortgages. A nonrefundable fee of $500 for the first $1.5 million, and $200 for each additional million, must accompany the request. After receiving the guarantee, a security is issued, backed by a pool of FHA, FmHA, or VA mortgages that have either been originated for this purpose, or taken out of portfolio, or purchased on the secondary market. This MBS is sold through a securities dealer to an investor based on the guarantee that the issuer will pay all principal and interest due even if not collected. This guarantee of the issuer is backed by GNMA, which, in return, is backed by the full faith and credit of the federal government.

The face rate of a GNMA is 50 basis points less than the mortgage contract rate. That means the face value of the security is ½ percent less than the mortgages in it. Until recently, all GNMA MBS issued required that all of the mortgages in the pool have the same interest rate. (The new GNMA II MBS allow a 1 percent spread.) If all of the mortgages in a pool carry a contract rate of 14 percent, then the face rate of the GNMA will be 50 basis points less, or 13½. The extra 50 basis points are split, with 44 basis points going to the servicer and six basis points to GNMA.

The GNMA fee is for its guarantee. The 44 basis points paid the security issuer is more than the 38 basis points a servicer typically gets for servicing FHA or VA mortgages. The additional fee is to compensate the issuer for any payments later required to be made to investors that were not collected from mortgagors.

The first GNMA MBS was sold by the Associated Mortgage Company to the State of New Jersey Pension Fund in 1970. That is of interest not only from a historical viewpoint, but also because the parties represent the two financial institutions most heavily involved in MBS.

By the end of 1990, when more than $1 trillion of agency MBS were held by investors, GNMA securities accounted for nearly 40 percent of the total. In 1990, GNMA issuance was $64.3 billion.

CONVENTIONAL MBS

The 1930s produced many improvements in housing finance, including fully amortized long-term loans, government mortgage insurance, and the beginning of a secondary mortgage market. Although the secondary mortgage market was developing, the traditional pattern of housing finance, until the 1970s, was for whole mortgage loans to remain in the portfolio of lenders until borrowers repaid. The exception to this pattern was the origination and secondary mortgage market activity of mortgage bankers.

Since the late 1970s, housing finance has been evolving rapidly due to the changes brought about by deregulation of financial institutions and the ravages of inflation. Portfolio lending is no longer the advisable strategy. After the financial battering thrifts took in 1981–82, their revised lending activities emphasized originations for sale into the secondary mortgage market and the securitizing of portfolios. To accomplish this task, more and more thrifts turned to conventional MBS. Conventional MBS has allowed mortgage originators to tap the capital markets as a source of funds for housing—a source substantially larger than thrift institution deposits.

A conventional MBS is one which contains conventional mortgages and not mortgages insured by FHA or guaranteed by VA. The underlying conventional mortgages may or may not have private mortgage insurance.

A conventional MBS issuer typically remits principal, interest, and any principal repayments to investors on the 25th day of each month. Since mortgagors typically pay their mortgages on or about the first, this delay in payment results in a slight decrease in yield to an investor. On the other hand, the monthly cash flow increases the bond equivalent yield since a bond typically has interest paid semi-annually.

Example: A pool of 15 percent mortgages (30-year fully amortized) with a 25-day delay in first payment will deliver a mortgage yield of 14.82 percent. This assumes that the pool is priced at par and prepayment is 12 years. If compared with a 15 percent corporate bond paying interest semi-annually, the yield would be 15.29 percent.

Mortgage Insurance

An investor in a conventional MBS has at least four layers of protection for its monthly cash flow. The most important protection comes from the *pool insurance* covering the initial aggregate principal balance of all mortgages in the pool. For example, if an investor requires a prime pool rated AAA, a rating agency will require a 7 percent coverage. This policy would protect investors against loss caused by a default on any mortgage loan or loans up to 7 percent of initial balance. The total dollar amount of coverage remains the same throughout the pool's life minus any claims paid.

In addition, investors are protected by a special hazard insurance policy which typically is 1 percent of initial aggregate principal balance. This protects against certain risks not covered in individual hazard insurance policies.

Each individual loan, especially if it has a loan-to-value ratio in excess of 80 percent, will probably be covered by an individual mortgage insurance policy which protects the lender against default. It has become common for the originating lender also to become the security issuer; thus, this protection will help protect an MBS investor.

Finally, the home owner equity provides some degree of protection to investors.

When all of these factors are combined with the contractual obligation of the security issuer to pay the monthly principal, interest, and principal prepayments to an investor, conventional MBS investors have a very secure investment.

Credit Rating

The rating a private conventional MBS receives from a rating agency is very important since that rating helps establish the yield requirements of investors. Ratings depend on three major items:

- type of mortgages in the pool
- experience of the servicer
- pool mortgage insurance

The so-called prime pool, which gets the highest rating, will consist of mortgages that fit within the parameters established by Standard and Poors in the table below. Other types of properties can be in a pool, but the required amount of pool insurance will be higher since the perceived risk is higher.

Since a conventional MBS is a pass-through, an investor is ensured its monthly cash flow from the servicer. If the servicer does not collect it from the mortgagors, the servicer pays it out of its own pocket. Thus the financial strength of the servicer is also of concern to the rating agency.

CHARACTERISTICS OF PRIME MORTGAGE COLLATERAL POOL

Mortgage security:	first lien on single-family (one unit) detached properties
Mortgage payments:	fixed-rate level payment, fully amortizing loans
Mortgagor status:	secured properties are mortgagor's primary residences
Location of properties:	well-dispersed throughout an area having a strong diversified economic base
Mortgage size:	less than FHLMC/FNMA limit
Loan-to-value:	80 percent or less
Mortgage documentation:	FHLMC/FNMA

MORTGAGE INSURANCE _____

The most important of the three items reviewed by a rating agency is the amount of pool insurance and the financial strength of the mortgage insurance company providing it.

Although various exotic techniques have been used to provide the desired pool protection in order to obtain a particular credit rating, normally this protection has come from pool insurance issued by a private mortgage insurance company. Because an investor may have to look to this insurance, the financial strength of the mortgage insurance company will be examined by the rating agency.

The amount of insurance depends on the level of creditworthiness desired by an issuer. Since an investment grade rating requires 100% repayment of principal with interest, the rating agency must determine the frequency of expected foreclosure and the severity of loss based on experience. The frequency of expected foreclosure is assumed from a "worst case" situation similar to that which existed in the Great Depression. The severity of loss is derived from actual loss experience assuming a 25 percent cash outlay for foreclosure-related expenses.

Example: For a AAA credit rating, S&P assumes a 15 percent frequency of foreclosure and a 47 percent severity of loss. Thus, 15% x 47% = .07% coverage required. That means that the amount of pool insurance required for an S&P AAA rating is .07 percent of the initial aggregate mortgage principal of the pool.

For a AA credit rating, a 10 percent frequency and a 40 percent loss is assumed. Thus, 10% x 40 = .04% coverage required for a AA credit rating.

Note that a higher credit rating requires more insurance to cover the assumption of greater risk.

Issuers of Conventional MBS

Federal Home Loan Mortgage Corporation (FHLMC)   Freddie Mac, as it is normally called, was the first issuer of conventional MBS in 1971 when it sold Participation Certificates (PC) backed by conventional loans purchased from savings and loan associations. Today, mortgage bankers, credit unions, commercial bankers, as well as thrifts, can do business with Freddie Mac.

The guarantee on the PCs issued by Freddie Mac is its own and not that of the federal government. Although this guarantee of Freddie Mac may create a "moral obligation" in the federal government since the guarantee is not unqualified like the one for GNMA, there has always been a spread in the yield to investors.

In 1989 (latest year available), Freddie Mac issued over $73 billion in original issue securities and had sold, since its inception, $412 billion of PCs. Of the nearly $1 trillion in outstanding MBS, about 31 percent were issued by Freddie Mac.

Federal National Mortgage Association (FNMA)   Fannie Mae, as it is normally called, was a decade behind Freddie Mac when it issued its first MBS in October, 1981 but now has caught up to a great extent with about 29 percent of the total. In 1990, Fannie Mae issued a staggering $97 billion of MBS.

Both Fannie Mae and Freddie Mac can only issue MBS backed by mortgages with a principal balance below their conforming loan limit ($191,250 in 1991). This limitation did not hinder their activity much in the 1980s, but may in the 1990s.

Critics of Fannie Mae and Freddie Mac state that these government-related agencies have an unfair advantage over private competitors in the MBS area in particular and the secondary mortgage market in general. The advantages the government-related agencies have are:

1. Access to capital markets at government or near-government rates
2. Exemptions from many securities laws

Recently, the federal government has supported the growth of a private secondary mortgage market and MBS in the 1990s by introducing legislation to remove some of the advantages these government-related agencies have had.

Private issuers of MBS   Many private MBS are sponsored by or affiliated with private mortgage insurance companies that use the conduit concept. A conduit works by channeling the originations of a number of traditional mortgage originators into a single security. This is attractive to investors because it provides them with greater economic and geographical diversity in the mortgage pools. Mortgage insurance companies are interested in sponsoring these conduits because both primary mortgage insurance and pool insurance are normally required. The mortgage insurance companies hope this insurance is purchased from them.

Prepayment Considerations

Normally, when evaluating capital market securities the yield to maturity is the most important consideration. But with MBS a prepayment factor seriously impacts all yield calculations. Prepayments occur because people move and sell their homes, refinance, or have other reasons for not letting a mortgage run the full 30 years. Although many sophisticated models exist today, many prepayment assumptions are derived from FHA experience. If all FHA mortgages that were originated in 1960 are examined, the propensity for prepayment can be established, since all have now been paid off. Some of these mortgages were paid off only months after being originated, others paid off after 1, 10, or 20 years, and some were not paid off until the full 30 years had expired. If all are examined, 30-year FHA mortgages show a propensity to be repaid in 12 years. Therefore, a pool of mortgages backed by FHA and VA mortgages is going to show the same propensity as the mortgages in the pool. Based on such studies, it is assumed that a GNMA MBS will prepay in 12 years and the yield is calculated on that assumption.

This assumption actually will vary with the type of mortgage and the maturity. Conventional mortgages have a different propensity, and that experience is stated as a percentage of FHA experience. For example, a 200 percent experience means the pool will prepay twice as fast as a pool of FHA mortgages. The assumption will also vary based upon when the mortgage was originated. The propensity to prepay mortgages originated in 1982 at a rate of 17 percent is probably at the end of a year. The reason is that many of these high interest rate mortgages have been refinanced in the lower interest rate environment of 1983 or later.

CONCEPTUAL PROBLEMS WITH MBS

Mortgage-backed securities have accomplished what they were designed to do. They have allowed more dollars to flow into housing. But they are not a perfect invention. There are still some very basic conceptual problems with MBS. Probably the most important is the irregular cash flow. This refers not to the monthly cash flow but to prepayments. The biggest problem with prepayments is that they usually come at the wrong time. Mortgagors tend to start prepaying when interest rates are falling and an investor wants to be able to lock in a yield. On the other hand, when interest rates are going up and an investor would like to get some of the money back so it can be reinvested at a higher yield, prepayments fall off.

Call protection is another problem overhanging MBS. The issue of call protection is also tied into monthly cash flow of principal and interest for some investors. Many investors would like to have an issuer reinvest the cash flow rather than having it flow through. In other words, if an investor puts money out at 13 percent and then interest rates drop, the investor will get the monthly payment of principal and interest, but it probably cannot reinvest it at 13 percent. In this situation, an investor would like some protection on its yield. The problem is that providing active management of an investment trust for mortgages in order to protect yield would incur some tax liabilities.

There are five items to keep in mind when discussing conceptual problems with MBS. Already discussed are the reinvestment and prepayment risks. There are three others:

1. The market price could change, although that's a risk with any type of commodity subject to market price.

2. Credit risk can also impact liquidity and price of MBS. Although this risk is not as strong now, in 1981–82 questions surfaced about some of the security issuers. The credit risk concerns the ability of a servicer to make required payments if mortgagors default.
3. A liquidity risk exists, which concerns the ability to resell a security. There is no liquidity risk with GNMA, FNMA, or FHLMC because of their real or perceived link with the federal government, but as more financial and nonfinancial institutions issue MBS there may be some initial liquidity risk until the marketplace has fully accepted the integrity of the issuer.

COLLATERALIZED MORTGAGE OBLIGATION (CMO)

As has been mentioned, the lack of any call protection has been a major impediment preventing nontraditional mortgage investors and others from becoming extensive purchasers of MBS. This problem has been addressed to a degree by CMOs, which were introduced by FHLMC in 1983.

These debt instruments have been described as serial pay-through bonds which allow for any nonscheduled payments (prepayments) to be distributed first to one of the various classes of holders.

As an example, the first FHLMC CMO has three classes of holders with different maturities:

Class I   3.2 years maturity
Class II   8.6 years maturity
Class III 20.4 years maturity

Through semi-annual sinking fund payments, Class I bonds will be fully retired before any principal reduction occurs in Class II or III. In other words, all principal payments go to one class until it is fully retired and then to the next. The maturity of each class is derived from the scheduled mortgage cash flow and the prepayment assumptions based on the characteristics of the mortgages in the pool. Through this vehicle, investors have some degree of assurance that their investment will earn the stated yield and not be "called" before maturity. This has been a successful answer to the call issue, and many other issuers have joined FHLMC in issuing CMOs.

Problems with CMOs

The desired result with CMOs was to provide call protection to investors while avoiding "active management" which would trigger taxation. The Internal Revenue Service challenged the sought-after tax status in the so-called "Sears Regula-tion" which resulted in a Sear's CMO offering being denied trust tax status. In order for CMOs to get the desired tax status, the offering had to resemble a debt obligation, but this form created certain accounting problems for some issuers. The problem was that debt usually has to be carried on the balance sheet of the issuer, and this was difficult for issuers with capital problems.

REAL ESTATE MORTGAGE INVESTMENT TRUSTS (REMIC)

The 1986 Tax Reform Act provides that any issuer that meets the requirements of the law may be treated as a trust for taxation purposes. The primary purpose of the REMIC legislation was to provide more efficient and flexible financing arrange-ments than those that existed for CMOs under the prior tax law. The provisions of this law became effective January 1, 1987 and provided that CMOs may continue to be used until January 1, 1992, after which only REMIC may be used. The requirements which issuers had to meet related to the type of mortgages which qualified for REMICs and the trust status and how the cash not yet distributed to security holders could be invested.

Issuers of REMIC are allowed to treat these securities as the sale of assets and not as a debt obligation which might create capital inadequacy issues. The law did provide, though, for REMIC transactions to be treated as debt for accounting purposes while reporting it as a sale of assets for tax purposes. These new provisions result in taxation only on the security holders.

Another important provision of the Tax Reform Act was that thrifts who purchase REMICs could include these securities in the classification of qualified real estate investments for thrifts. This allows for thrifts to qualify for the bad debt deduction tax benefit.

The Tax Reform Act also changed the existing law which stipulated that foreign purchasers of pass-through securities were subject to a 30 percent with-holding tax. By the removal of this withholding tax, REMICs are much more attractive to foreign purchasers.

SELLING MBS TO INVESTORS

To date, three ways of offering MBS to investors have been used. A private placement is an offering of a security usually to only one investor, although more than one could be involved. Terms are negotiated up front directly between the issuer and the investor. The negotiations establish the type of security, type of coupon, yield, geographic diversity, and discount. Because terms are negotiated up front, the mortgages which will be in the pool may not have been originated; thus, delivery will be sometime in the future, possibly not for six to nine months. Since it's a private placement and not an offering to the public, there is no requirement for SEC registration. This fact can save money and time, although many investors may still require SEC registration since they may want to market these securities in the future. Also, there is no requirement for a bond rating with a private placement, but if an investor wants to sell these bonds later a rating would be important. The underwriting fee is fairly modest: 25-100 basis points. Usually the first time a new type of MBS is issued, it is sold in a private placement. Later, once there is some experience with the new MBS and market acceptances, the new types of MBS can become a public issue.

A public-institutional offering is one made to a fairly large number of financial institutions. In this situation, the terms are negotiated between the issuer and the underwriter. After terms are established the underwriter sells these terms to interested institutions. Since the mortgages have probably already been originated, delivery can be almost immediate. This is a public issue; therefore, an SEC requirement exists along with a bond rating for marketability. The underwriting fee for this offering is still a fairly modest 50-100 basis points.

Finally, there is the public-retail offering. This has not been as popular recently, but could be an area for future expansion. These MBS are sold both to insitutions and individual investors. Some of the bonds offered in the late 1970s were public-retail, but now about the only public-retail offerings are revenue bonds. Since this is a public offering, SEC registration is required, as well as a bond rating. Underwriters have been taking 250-500 basis points as a fee in public-retail offerings, and this has drastically cut the yield to the individual and thus their acceptance.

RESIDENTIAL REAL ESTATE APPRAISAL === *12*

Throughout the economic activity of man, no meaningful business decision is made nor does any significant investment of any type occur without an appraisal first being made. The purpose of all appraisals is to establish an estimate of value. As will be discussed later, there are many types of appraisals for many different reasons.

The objective of this chapter is to provide an overview of the fundamentals of residential real estate appraisal, define the standard terminology used, and explain the common methods of estimating value. Because of important recent developments in this field, new students of residential mortgage lending are encouraged to do additional reading or take course work in appraisal. Care should be exercised in realizing that what is sought in a residential appraisal is an estimate of value given by a well-trained professional.

Value

Value is normally defined as the relationship between an object desired and the person desiring it. It is the ability of one commodity to command another commodity, usually money, in exchange. Tying value to price, one can say that value, stated as a price, is that point where supply and demand coincide or intersect.

Purpose of Appraisals

In order to properly underwrite a residential mortgage loan application, an appraisal is required. The primary purpose of an appraisal to a mortgage lender is to estimate the value of the real estate that it is considering using as security for a mortgage loan. Not only is this a requirement of state and federal laws and regulations but is a requirement to sell these loans in the secondary mortgage market.

UNIFORM RESIDENTIAL APPRAISAL REPORT

Appraisers and the appraisal process were under intense scrutiny in the mid-1980s because of the extremely high residential delinquency rates and resulting losses to the private mortgage insurance industry and to mortgage investors. Some important players in residential mortgage lending blamed the high delinquency rates on inflated and poorly prepared appraisals. The Federal National Mortgage Association and the private mortgage insurance companies were among the more vocal in the criticism. As a result of this criticism and a desire to improve the appraisal profession, the various appraisal organizations worked with the five government agencies involved in residential real estate to develop a single form acceptable by all agencies.

In the fall of 1986 a new appraisal form, known as the Uniform Residential Appraisal Report (URAR), was agreed to by all interested parties. This new appraisal form is accepted by the Federal National Mortgage Association, the Federal Home Loan Mortgage Corporation, the Federal Housing Authority, the Veterans Administration, and the Farmers Home Administration. Use of the new form became required for all single-family appraisals dated after April 30, 1987.

In 1986, these organizations also developed a series of professional practice standards that will assist appraisers in preparing the new Uniform Residential Appraisal Report. These standards represent an important step forward for the profession since they are the first uniform standards ever to be adopted by the various appraisal organizations.

Attesting to the increased use of personal computers in real estate, the new report is designed to be used with computers with a programmable format. This new URAR appears to have resolved much of the criticism leveled at the appraisal profession, and most appraisers have praised the totality of the new form.

Uniform Standards of Professional Appraisal Practice

Financial Institution Reform, Recovery, and Enforcement Act (FIRREA) legislation also addressed the issue of appraisals and as a result of this legislation and other developments in the appraisal field, Uniform Standards of Professional Appraisal Practices were established. These standards were developed by the appraisal industry through the private nonprofit body known as the Appraisal Foundation. The FIRREA legislation also required that beginning July 1, 1991 all real estate transactions needing an appraisal must include one performed by either a state licensed or certified appraiser. A licensed appraiser is one who possesses basic

Property Description & Analysis   **UNIFORM RESIDENTIAL APPRAISAL REPORT**   File No.

SUBJECT

Property Address	1846 American Way	Census Tract 02134
City Ogden	County Weber	State Ut	Zip Code 84405
Legal Description	Lot 1, Block 10, Sunnyside Subdivision	
Owner/Occupant Ima Seller		Map Reference 45
Sale Price $ 70,000	Date of Sale 5-22-86	PROPERTY RIGHTS APPRAISED
Loan charges/concessions to be paid by seller $ .00		[x] Fee Simple
R.E. Taxes $ 900.00	Tax Year 1986 HOA $/Mo. .00	[ ] Leasehold
		[ ] Condominium (HUD/VA)
Lender/Client Brace Mortgage Corporation		[ ] De Minimis PUD
50 North Main Street, Layton, Ut		

LENDER DISCRETIONARY USE

Sale Price	$ 70,000
Date	05-22-86
Mortgage Amount	$ 62,000
Mortgage Type	Conv.
Discount Points and Other Concessions	
Paid by Seller	$ .00
Source	

NEIGHBORHOOD

LOCATION			
	[ ] Urban	[x] Suburban	[ ] Rural
BUILT UP	[ ] Over 75%	[x] 25-75%	[ ] Under 25%
GROWTH RATE	[ ] Rapid	[x] Stable	[ ] Slow
PROPERTY VALUES	[ ] Increasing	[x] Stable	[ ] Declining
DEMAND/SUPPLY	[ ] Shortage	[x] In Balance	[ ] Over Supply
MARKETING TIME	[ ] Under 3 Mos.	[x] 3-6 Mos.	[ ] Over 6 Mos.

PRESENT LAND USE	%	LAND USE CHANGE	PREDOMINANT
Single Family	85	Not Likely [x]	OCCUPANCY
2-4 Family		Likely [ ]	Owner [x]
Multi-family		In process [ ]	Tenant [ ]
Commercial		To:	Vacant (0-5%) [ ]
Industrial			Vacant (over 5%) [ ]
Vacant			

SINGLE FAMILY HOUSING

PRICE $ (000)	AGE (yrs)
60K Low	10
125K High	1
72K Predominant	--

NEIGHBORHOOD ANALYSIS	Good	Avg	Fair	Poor
Employment Stability		x		
Convenience to Employment	x			
Convenience to Shopping	x			
Convenience to Schools	x			
Adequacy of Public Transportation				
Recreation Facilities			x	
Adequacy of Utilities	x			
Property Compatibility	x			
Protection from Detrimental Cond			x	
Police & Fire Protection			x	
General Appearance of Properties	x			
Appeal to Market	x			

Note: Race or the racial composition of the neighborhood are not considered reliable appraisal factors.

COMMENTS: No detrimental factors in neighborhood other than there is no public transportation in this subdivision

SITE

Dimensions 50 x 125			Topography	Level
Site Area Desireable			Size	Average
Zoning Classification R 4 Single Family	Zoning Compliance Yes		Shape	Rectangular
HIGHEST & BEST USE: Present Use Present Use	Other Use		Drainage	Average
			View	Good

Corner Lot No

UTILITIES	Public	Other	SITE IMPROVEMENTS	Type	Public	Private
Electricity	x		Street	Paved	x	
Gas	x		Curb/Gutter	Cement	x	
Water	x		Sidewalk	Cement	x	
Sanitary Sewer	x		Street Lights	Arc	x	
Storm Sewer	x		Alley	N/A		

Landscaping	Average
Driveway	Fair
Apparent Easements	Electric
FEMA Flood Hazard Yes*	No xx
FEMA* Map/Zone	

COMMENTS (Apparent adverse easements, encroachments, special assessments, slide areas, etc.):
None noted

IMPROVEMENTS

GENERAL DESCRIPTION		EXTERIOR DESCRIPTION		FOUNDATION		BASEMENT		INSULATION	
Units	1	Foundation	Ave	Slab	N/A	Area Sq. Ft.	0	Roof	x
Stories	1	Exterior Walls	Wood	Crawl Space	Yes	% Finished	0	Ceiling	x
Type (Det./Att.)	Det	Roof Surface	Tile	Basement	No	Ceiling	drywall	Walls	x
Design (Style)	Ramb.	Gutters & Dwnspts.	Yes	Sump Pump	No	Walls	drywall	Floor	
Existing	Yes	Window Type	Sash	Dampness	None	Floor	pressbd	None	
Proposed	No	Storm Sash	Yes	Settlement	None Note	Outside Entry	no	Adequacy	
Under Construction	No	Screens	Yes	Infestation	None Note			Energy Efficient Items:	
Age (Yrs.)	5	Manufactured House							
Effective Age (Yrs.)	3								

ROOM LIST

ROOMS	Foyer	Living	Dining	Kitchen	Den	Family Rm.	Rec. Rm.	Bedrooms	# Baths	Laundry	Other	Area Sq. Ft.
Basement												
Level 1	x	x	x	x				3	1 ½	x		1525
Level 2												

Finished area above grade contains: 6 Rooms; 3 Bedroom(s); 1 ½ Bath(s); 1525 Square Feet of Gross Living Area

INTERIOR

SURFACES	Materials/Condition
Floors	Hardwood
Walls	Drywall
Trim/Finish	Good
Bath Floor	Tile
Bath Wainscot	Yes
Doors	Holow core

HEATING	
Type	Gas FA
Fuel	Gas
Condition	Ave
Adequacy	Ave
COOLING	
Central	Yes
Other	
Condition	Good
Adequacy	Good

Fireplace(s) 0 #

KITCHEN EQUIP.	
Refrigerator	
Range/Oven	x
Disposal	x
Dishwasher	x
Fan/Hood	x
Compactor	n/a
Washer/Dryer	n/a
Microwave	x
Intercom	n/a

ATTIC	
None	x
Stairs	n/a
Drop Stair	n/a
Scuttle	n/a
Floor	
Heated	
Finished	

IMPROVEMENT ANALYSIS	Good	Avg	Fair	Poor
Quality of Construction		x		
Condition of Improvements		x		
Room Sizes/Layout	x			
Closets and Storage		x		
Energy Efficiency		x		
Plumbing-Adequacy & Condition	x			
Electrical-Adequacy & Condition		x		
Kitchen Cabinets-Adequacy & Cond.		x		
Compatibility to Neighborhood	x			
Appeal & Marketability	x			

AUTOS

CAR STORAGE		
Garage	x	Attached	x
No. Cars 2 Carport		Detached	
Condition Good None		Built-In	x

Adequate	x
Inadequate	
Electric Door	x
House Entry	x
Outside Entry	x
Basement Entry	

Estimated Remaining Economic Life 40 Yrs.
Estimated Remaining Physical Life 40 Yrs.

Additional features: 10' x 12' Patio off living room

COMMENTS

Depreciation (Physical, functional and external inadequacies, repairs needed, modernization, etc.):
None Noted - property in good repair

General market conditions and prevalence and impact in subject/market area regarding loan discounts, interest buydowns and concessions:
Market is 30-60 days no concessions at the present time

Freddie Mac Form 70 10/86   CERTIFIED PRINTERS, INC. • 1-800-FORMS LA • (213) 464-1212   10 CH Fannie Mae Form 1004 10/86

UNIFORM RESIDENTIAL APPRAISAL REPORT   File No.

Purpose of Appraisal is to estimate Market Value as defined in the Certification & Statement of Limiting Conditions.

COST APPROACH

BUILDING SKETCH (SHOW GROSS LIVING AREA ABOVE GRADE)

If for Freddie Mac or Fannie Mae, show only square foot calculations and cost approach comments in this space

Measure	No. Stories	Sq. Ft.
25 x 61	1	1525
25 x 20	Garage	500
10 x 12	Patio	120
Total Gross Living Area		1525

ESTIMATED REPRODUCTION COST - NEW - OF IMPROVEMENTS:

Dwelling 1525 Sq. Ft. @ $ 45.00	= $	68,625
Sq. Ft. @ $	=	
Extras	=	
Special Energy Efficient Items	=	
Porches, Patios, etc. 120 sq ft @12	=	1,440
Garage/Carport 500 Sq. Ft. @ $ 15.00	=	7,500
Total Estimated Cost New	= $	77,565

	Physical	Functional	External
Less Depreciation 13,950			= $ 13,950

Depreciated Value of Improvements .... = $ 63,615
Site Imp. "as is" (driveway, landscaping, etc.) = $
ESTIMATED SITE VALUE .... = $ 12,000
(If leasehold, show only leasehold value.)
INDICATED VALUE BY COST APPROACH = $ 75,615

(Not Required by Freddie Mac and Fannie Mae)
Does property conform to applicable HUD/VA property standards? [x] Yes [ ] No
If No, explain:

Construction Warranty [ ] Yes [x] No
Name of Warranty Program
Warranty Coverage Expires

SALES COMPARISON ANALYSIS

The undersigned has recited three recent sales of properties most similar and proximate to subject and has considered these in the market analysis. The description includes a dollar adjustment, reflecting market reaction to those items of significant variation between the subject and comparable properties. If a significant item in the comparable property is superior to, or more favorable than, the subject property, a minus (−) adjustment is made, thus reducing the indicated value of subject. If a significant item in the comparable is inferior to, or less favorable than, the subject property, a plus (+) adjustment is made, thus increasing the indicated value of the subject.

ITEM	SUBJECT	COMPARABLE NO. 1		COMPARABLE NO. 2		COMPARABLE NO. 3	
Address	1846 American Wy	2045 Constitution		2160 Constitution		2408 American Way	
Proximity to Subject		2 blocks		3 blocks		6 blocks	
Sales Price	$ 70,000		$ 75,000		$ 66,000		$ 72,000
Price/Gross Liv. Area	$ 45.90 ☑	$ 47.62 ☑		$ 44.00 ☑		$ 47.21 ☑	
Data Source	Contract						
VALUE ADJUSTMENTS	DESCRIPTION	DESCRIPTION	+ (−) $ Adjustment	DESCRIPTION	+ (−) $ Adjustment	DESCRIPTION	+ (−) $ Adjustment
Sales or Financing Concessions							
Date of Sale/Time	Same Time	2-86		11-85		1-86	
Location	Average	Average		Average		Average	
Site/View	Average	Average		Average		Average	
Design and Appeal	Ranch	Ranch		Ranch		Ranch	
Quality of Construction	5 yrs	6 yrs		5 yrs		5 yrs	
Age	Average	Average		Average		Average	
Condition							
Above Grade Room Count	Total Bdrms Baths 6 3 1.5	Total Bdrms Baths 7 3 1.5		Total Bdrms Baths 6 3 1.5		Total Bdrms Baths 6 3 1.5	
Gross Living Area	1525 Sq. Ft.	1575 Sq. Ft.	-2381	1500 Sq. Ft.	+1000	1525 Sq. Ft.	
Basement & Finished Rooms Below Grade	Full	Full		Full		Full	
Functional Utility	Average	Average		Average		Average	
Heating/Cooling	Central	Central		Central		Central	
Garage/Carport	2 car	2 car		1 car	+3000	2 car	
Porches, Patio, Pools, etc.	Patio slab	Patio slab		None	+1440	Patio slab	
Special Energy Efficient Items	---	---		---		---	
Fireplace(s)	---	---		---		Fireplace	-1200
Other (e.g. kitchen equip., remodeling)	Equipped Kitchen	Equipped Kitchen		Equipped Kitchen		Equipped Kitchen	
Net Adj. (total)		[ ] + [xx] − $ 2,381		[xx] + [ ] − $ 5,440		[ ] + [xx] − $ 1,200	
Indicated Value of Subject		$72,619		$71,440		$70,800	

Comments on Sales Comparison: Sales are recent and in subject area

RECONCILIATION

INDICATED VALUE BY SALES COMPARISON APPROACH $ 71,300
INDICATED VALUE BY INCOME APPROACH (If Applicable) Estimated Market Rent $ /Mo. x Gross Rent Multiplier = $
This appraisal is made [xx] "as is" [ ] subject to the repairs, alterations, inspections or conditions listed below [ ] completion per plans and specifications.
Comments and Conditions of Appraisal:

Final Reconciliation: Heaviest emphasis based upon Market approach. Since all comparisons are approximately same age, income approach not applicable.

This appraisal is based upon the above requirements, the certification, contingent and limiting conditions, and Market Value definition that are stated in
[ ] FmHA, HUD &/or VA instructions.
[ ] Freddie Mac Form 439 (Rev. 7/86)/Fannie Mae Form 1004B (Rev. 7/86) filed with client May 24 19 86 [x] attached.
I (WE) ESTIMATE THE MARKET VALUE, AS DEFINED, OF THE SUBJECT PROPERTY AS OF May 24 19 86 to be $ 71,000
I (We) certify: that to the best of my (our) knowledge and belief the facts and data used herein are true and correct; that I (we) personally inspected the subject property, both inside and out, and have made an exterior inspection of all comparable sales cited in this report; and that I (we) have no undisclosed interest, present or prospective therein.

Appraiser(s) SIGNATURE _Joe Smith_
NAME
Review Appraiser SIGNATURE n/a
(if applicable) NAME
[x] Did [ ] Did Not
Inspect Property

Freddie Mac Form 70 10/86   Fannie Mae Form 1004 10/86

skills in real estate appraisal sufficient to prepare a noncomplex residential assignment. A residential certified appraiser is one whose qualifications are such that they are qualified to handle all residential properties, particularly those deemed to be complex or those above a certain level, currently $1 million.

PRINCIPLES OF REAL ESTATE VALUE

An appraisal may be required to provide an estimate of value at almost any stage of a real estate transaction or activity. For example, at any given moment an appraisal of real estate may be needed to estimate:

- market value for mortgage loan purposes
- assessed value for taxation purposes
- insurance value
- market value for sale or exchange purposes
- compensation in condemnation proceedings
- rental value

The value determined for the same piece of real estate can vary according to the purpose of the appraisal; the estimated value for insurance purposes could be much different from the value estimated for condemnation purposes. In this discussion the value to be estimated will be market value since most mortgage lenders are required by law or regulation to lend only a certain percentage of market value.

Market Value

Market value is defined by the Uniform Standards of Professional Appraisal Practice as "...the most probable price which a property should bring in a competitive and open market under all conditions requisite to a fair sale, the buyer and seller, each acting prudently and knowledgeably, and assuming the price is not affected by undue stimulus." Implicit in this definition is the consummation of sale as of a specific date and the passing of title from seller to buyer under conditions whereby:

1. buyer and seller are typically motivated;
2. both parties are well informed and well advised, and acting in what they consider their best interests;
3. a reasonable time is allowed for exposure in the open market;
4. payment is made in terms of cash in United States dollars or in terms of financial arrangements comparable thereto; and

5. the price represents the normal consideration for the property sold unaffected by special or creative financing or sales concessions granted by anyone associated with the sale."

Market Price

The market price is that price for which the real estate actually sells. In theory, market value and price should be the same, but they rarely are. For example, a seller may decide to accept less (market price) than asked (presumed market value) in order to facilitate the sale if the seller believes time is more valuable than the difference in money.

Changes to Value

Value of a given piece of real estate does not remain the same. Nor does it constantly go up as mortgage lenders in the Southwest and Northeast learned in the 1980s. For example, during 1986–87 it was not uncommon in some areas in Texas, notably Houston, for real estate values to drop 30 or 40 percent a year. In general, the value of a piece of real estate can be changed by:

- population growth or decline
- economic developments
  —micro or local changes
  —macro or national developments
- financial factors such as
  —rates of inflation
  —cost of financing
  —type of financing available
- shifts in social standards
- governmental regulations affecting
  —zoning
  —building codes
  —taxation
- shifts in traffic patterns or public transportation
- physical forces such as
  —water supply
  —soil contamination
  —location on an earthquake fault

If these factors remain constant, the market value of a given piece of real estate may still change as a result of the other more basic value determinants. The most basic is supply and demand. Real estate is similar to all other marketable commodities in that its value is increased or decreased by the supply of that commodity and the demand for it. Supply conditions are impacted by the number of units on the market, the number being constructed, the number of building permits issued, and the size of existing units. The demand depends on the level of employment, income, prices, family size, age of head of household, bank deposits, retail sales, and other factors of this type.

Market value of real estate is influenced to a great extent by whether the real estate is being put to its highest and best use. This use is defined as the use which creates the highest present value. The Uniform Standards state, "Two separate highest and best uses exist for each site: one for the site as though vacant and one for the site as though improved. The first looks through the building as though it did not exist and estimates the best use of the site as though it were vacant. The second estimates the best use of the site and building(s) with all improvements together."

The principle of diminishing returns recognizes that continuing additions to the whole will not continue to increase the value of the whole by the value of the additions after a certain point.

Finally, the principle of substitution perceives that the upper limit of the value of a piece of real estate tends to be established by the cost of acquiring an equally desirable substitute property, or the cost of building a like structure.

THE APPRAISAL PROCESS

The first step in the appraisal process is to plan the appraisal. Since the appraisal is intended to solve a problem, that is to estimate value, it must be clearly stated as to what type of value is sought. The process required to provide this estimate of value necessitates identification of the following:

- the real estate to be appraised
- type of value sought
- effective date of the appraisal
- character of the property
- property rights
- character of market in which the property is located

The next step in the appraisal process is to identify the data that the appraiser will need. The data required by the appraiser can be found in the public record, from mortgage lenders, other appraisers, or possibly most important, from real estate agents. Other sources could include the local chamber of commerce, planning and zoning authorities, and even providers of building supplies and equipment. Finally, the appraiser has the professional twin responsibilities of keeping this data current and relying only on timely data.

THE APPRAISAL PROCESS

Definition of the Problem

Identify real estate	Identify rights	Date of value	Objective of appraisal	Definition of value

↓

Preliminary Survey and Appraisal Plan

Data needed	Data sources	Personnel needed	Time schedule	Completion flow chart

↓

Data Collection and Analysis

General data		*Specific data*	
Locational	*Economic*	*Subject property*	*Comparative*
Region	Market	Title	Costs
City	Analysis	Site	Sales
Neighborhood	Financial	Physical	Rentals
etc.	Economic base	Highest and best use	Expenses
	Trends		

↓

Application of the Three Approaches

Cost	Market data	Income

↓

Reconciliation of Value Indications

↓

Final Estimate of Defined Value

ALTERNATIVE APPROACHES TO VALUE

In developing a real estate appraisal, an appraiser is required to use an appropriate appraisal method or technique. There are various methods or techniques which can be used and the selection of the correct one depends on the professional decision of the appraiser. The most common one used for residential loan appraisal is the Direct Sales Comparison or Market Data Approach.

Direct Sales Comparison Approach

This approach relies on the concept or principle that an informed purchaser will pay no more for property than the price or cost of a substitute with the same characteristics and utility. As a result, this approach works on the ability to locate similar or comparable properties which have recently sold in that locale. Recognizing that no two properties are the same, through an appropriate adjustment process the two homes can be compared and an adjusted price can be developed. The principal of substitution is evident with this approach since the value of a property similar to the subject property should closely approximate the value of the subject property. The market value for the comparable is best substantiated by the actual recent sales price.

An appraiser will use as many recent sales of similar or comparable property as possible; the more used, the better will be the estimate. The URAR calls for the use of three comparables. The market price will be adjusted for whatever physical differences exist between the comparable and the subject property. On the other hand, features in the subject property not present in the comparable are added to the value of the comparable to adjust the value. The basic formula is as follows:

Value of comparable property + or – adjustments = Value of subject property

---

Example: If house A with a finished basement worth $15,000 currently sells for $115,000 and is otherwise comparable to house B except for the finished basement, then the estimate of value for house B would be $100,000: the house A value of $115,000 – $15,000 for finished basement = house B value of $100,000.

Financing concession   A complicating factor in using this approach is that the sales price of comparable properties may have been established because of certain financing concessions. For example, the seller paid a part or all of the closing costs, or the down payment is lower than typical, or the interest rate is lower, or some other concession which could increase the sales price. The opposite of these items could lower the sales price of a comparable. The appraiser must take these items into consideration when preparing the appraisal relying on comparables with these characteristics. To assist an appraiser with possible financing concessions, a mortgage lender is required to provide an appraiser with as much information on the sale as is possible. That includes providing a copy of the sales contract and the purchase price.

Cost Approach

This approach is the second most important for estimating value of residential real estate. It involves an estimate of the current cost of production which is defined as the reproduction cost or that cost to build an exact replica of the improvements. This approach can be stated as cost less accrued depreciation, plus the value of the land. When figuring costs, both direct costs (such as supplies, labor, and profits) and indirect costs (such as fees, taxes, and financing costs) are taken into consideration. In addition, an appraiser will consider that the subject property will not be the same as a reproduced structure because of depreciation or loss in value of the subject property. Therefore, adjustments must be made to the reproduction cost reflecting existing depreciation. Depreciation includes:

- *Physical deterioration.* A loss in value from the cost of a new structure is made equal to the loss of economic life in the subject property caused by wear and tear. This physical deterioration may or may not be curable.
- *Functional obsolescence.* A loss in value resulting from structural components such as bathrooms and kitchens or in the overall layout that are outmoded or inefficient as judged by current trends or standards.
- *Economic obsolescence.* A loss in value resulting from changes external to the property such as changes in zoning classifications, sharp increases in property taxes, or other negative influences.

The cost approach can be explained simply:

$$\text{Cost of reproduction} - \text{depreciation} + \text{land value} =$$
$$\text{Value of subject property}$$

Example: Assume the problem is to estimate the value of a 100 year old Victorian which has depreciated 50 percent. The cost of building a comparable building is $350,000. The estimate of value is made in this way: cost of reproduction is $350,000 - $175,000 = $175,000 + land value = value of subject property.

Income Approach

This approach to estimating value uses the net operating income of the property. Although the other two approaches can be used for residences and other types of property, this approach is normally used to arrive at an estimate of value for income-producing real estate such as office buildings, apartments, and other commercial establishments. The concept is that an ascertainable relationship exists between the income a property earns and the price, or value, someone would be willing to pay for that property.

Obviously, this approach can be used only for those properties that have or will have income, but a special technique called the gross rent multiplier (GRM) can be used either to estimate value for a single-family residence or to serve as a check against the other approaches. The theory behind GRM is that the same market will influence both the sales price and the rental price and, therefore, both tend to move up or down in tandem. This relationship can be expressed as a ratio:

$$\frac{\text{Sale price}}{\text{Gross income}} = \text{GRM}$$

Example: If a house recently sold for $95,000 and rented for $700 a month, the GRM would be:

$$\frac{\$95,000}{\$700} = 135.71, \text{ say } 136$$

Thus, if the appraisal assignment is to estimate the value of a rental unit comparable to another property being rented at $650, the result would be:

$650 x 136 = $88,400 (value of subject house using the income approach)

Reconciliation and Final Value Estimate

Although most appraisal problems call for a single final estimate of value, many appraisers will use more than one approach to arrive at this final estimate. In fact, many appraisers will use all three approaches—direct sales or market data, cost, and income—in estimating value to provide as valid an estimate as possible.

In most situations, the estimates of value using all three approaches should be fairly similar. If the estimates are widely divergent, the data-gathering method and analysis for each approach must be carefully reviewed. If the estimates remain far apart, the appraiser must consider the purpose of the appraisal. If the appraisal is to estimate value for a condemnation suit, the market data is most important. For insurance purposes, the replacement cost is most important. If, on the other hand, the subject property is a residential rental, then the income approach using the gross rent multiplier will be most important.

It is in the correlation of value that an appraiser's skill comes to the forefront and the problem of estimating value answered.

This reconciliation and final value estimate is not a simple arithmetical process. It is, however, an exercise of judgment, analysis, and reason which will result in a professional estimate of value.

Required Forms

The residential appraisal must be submitted on the current appraisal forms. These include:

- single family—URAR (FNMA form 1004)
- 2-4 family—Small Residential Income Property Form (FNMA form 1025)
- Condos, PUDs, Cooperatives—Condo/PUD form (FNMA form 1073)

The following attachments must be a part of each appraisal report:

- 2 sets of original 35 mm photos (front, rear, and street scene)
- location map showing comparables
- exterior sketch of dwelling with measurements
- floor plan showing rooms with doorways

Age of Appraisal

The appraisal report must be dated within 120 days of the date the mortgage loan is approved. If an appraisal is older than that (up to 180 days), it can be updated by the original appraiser certifying that the value has not declined since the original appraisal was prepared. If older than 180 days, a new appraisal is required.

CLOSING THE
RESIDENTIAL LOAN ══ *13*

After a decision (either by an individual underwriter or loan committee) to grant a mortgage loan is made, the mortgage lending process proceeds to loan closing. The term *loan closing* as used in residential mortgage lending refers to the process of formulating, executing, and delivering all documents required by a permanent investor, the disbursing of the mortgage funds, and the protecting of the investor's security. A clear distinction should be drawn between this type of closing and a real estate sales closing in which a different set of documents would be required, such as a purchase agreement, sales contract, and a closing statement, among others. Of course, as is typical, when the sale also involves financing, both sets of documents or a combination of the two are often required.

Process of Loan Closing

The process of loan closing really begins with the taking of the mortgage application and the issuance of a commitment letter and concludes in the exchange of documents and funds and the recording of all pertinent instruments. It is important to realize that a loan closing is not the end of the mortgage lending cycle, which continues through servicing until the loan is finally repaid or refinanced.

Essential documents that should be contained in a complete residential mortgage file vary by state as well as by the type of loan—conventional or FHA/VA. A lender's peculiar requirements can also add or subtract from the list. As in any discussion involving legal documents, a review of the requirements of each state's law is required. When establishing a loan closing process, competent counsel should be consulted on state law concerning any of the documents discussed.

The handling of loan closing   Loan closing, depending on the law or custom in the jurisdiction, can be handled by any of the following:

- outside attorney
- escrow agent
- title insurance company
- staff of the mortgage lender

In some situations an insured closing may be required. An insured closing agent can be anyone, such as an attorney, who has been approved and accepted by a title company. The title company is, in effect, insuring that the loan was closed according to the lender's directions as well as the title company's requirements and that they are insuring against any fraud or dishonesty on the part of the loan closer. At one time, most closings were handled by an outside attorney, and many still are, but more and more mortgage lenders have staff members who are qualified loan closers. They have the competency to prepare and analyze all necessary closing documents and, as a general rule, can do it cheaper than an outside attorney. Care must be taken, though, to ascertain whether state law requires a licensed attorney to close a loan.

Whichever method is used, the purpose of loan closing is to ensure that the loan is closed according to all laws of that state. The expected result, of course, is to provide the mortgage lender with a first lien on the property.

There are many types of loan closings including the closing of construction loans, loans to be warehoused, and loans with permanent investors. This chapter is concerned primarily with the closing of a permanent residential mortgage loan.

Steps in Closing a Residential Mortgage Loan

When the underwriter has indicated that the loan application is acceptable, certain steps should be taken to close the loan. These steps include the following:

1. Advise applicant of loan acceptance by a commitment letter (and, if applicable, set rate, terms, etc.)
2. Order final title report (and survey if separate) and any other documents or verifications still outstanding
3. Schedule closing and prepare closing documents
4. Conduct closing, obtain all required signatures, disburse funds
5. Return all closing documents to mortgage lender for inclusion in loan file
6. Record mortgage

DOCUMENTS REQUIRED

The following documents are discussed relative to the closing of a residential mortgage loan. The process of gathering, producing, and preparing the necessary

The following information is provided to members who are applying for mortgage financing from NFCU and is intended to assist you in understanding what is required to complete processing of your loan. Your loan processor will notify you of any additional requirements applicable to your mortgage transaction.

Selection of Settlement Agent: You may select your own settlement agent to close your loan transaction or one recommended by NFCU. All settlement agents must meet NFCU requirements; if the one you select has not previously been approved by NFCU, the agent must provide NFCU with a Standard Closing Protection Letter at least one week prior to settlement, issued by the title insurance company which will insure the title to the property you are purchasing.

Title Insurance: You will be obligated to purchase a lender's title insurance policy, protecting NFCU's interest as mortgagee in the property, with coverage for at least the amount of your loan. Your settlement agent normally will obtain this insurance in your behalf.

Survey: The survey shows the location and dimensions of the property you are purchasing (land and structure) including all easements, rights of way, encroachments, and flood zone certification. The settlement agent will normally assist you in obtaining a current survey.

Hazard Insurance: This provides insurance protection to a dwelling and its contents in the case of fire or wind damage, theft, liability for property damage, and personal liability. You will be required to obtain a hazard insurance policy with the mortgagee clause reading as follows:

Navy Federal Credit Union, its successors and assigns
Security Place
P. O. Box 3303
Merrifield, VA 22119-3303

This policy must provide coverage for the amount of your loan or the replacement cost of the dwelling, whichever is less with a deductible amount not exceeding $500. The original policy (an insurance binder is acceptable for this requirement for properties in the state of Maryland) and a paid receipt for the first year's premium must be in NFCU's possession five days prior to settlement.

Escrow Account: NFCU requires that an escrow account be established for the payment of hazard insurance premiums; private mortgage and/or flood insurance premiums, if applicable; property taxes; special assessments and ground rent, if any. Your settlement agent will notify you of the initial deposits required to establish your escrow account. Dividends will be paid on this acocunt at the same rate and conditions as share savings accounts.

Termite/Soil Treatment Guarantee: A termite certificate from a licensed termite/pest exterminator guaranteeing that the property is free of infestation must be submitted to NFCU prior to settlement. If the property is new construction, a 5 year soil treatment guarantee is required in lieu of a termite guarantee.

Well/Septic Inspection: If the property you are purchasing has a well and/or septic sewer system, written evidence must be provided showing that the system(s) has/have been inspected and approved within the past 60 days by the local health authority.

Property Inspection: If a final inspection of the property is required to verify that construction or repairs are complete, NFCU must receive a satisfactory final inspection report *prior to settlement*. In the case of a VA or FHA loan, the final inspection must be countersigned by the local VA/FHA office.

Residential Use or Use and Occupancy Permit: (Required for newly constructed residences only.) This permit, issued by the applicable local government authority, certifies that all required preliminary inspections have been completed and approved and that the residence is habitable.

Residency Requirement: NFCU is legally prohibited from funding a mortgage loan if the secured property will not be occupied as your principal residence (unless your loan is classified as a future principal residence). You must occupy the premises as your principal residence (as opposed to rental or vacation property) within 90 days after settlement.

Membership Requirement: All mortgage loan applicants must be members of NFCU. If a borrower or co-borrower is not currently a member but is eligible for membership, we will gladly send a membership application upon receipt of your mortgage loan application.

Please acknowledge receipt of this Mortgage Loan Requirements Form by signing below and returning a copy in the stamped, self-addressed envelope provided. Give the second copy to your sales agent in this transaction.

Signature of Member

Date   6-28-92

06011992

NFCU 851M (8-88)

documents and the careful checking of all forms is often referred to as a preclosing procedure. This list of documents contains those normally required, but some states may require additional ones. These documents usually need not appear in any particular order in a loan file. However, some secondary mortgage market transactions may require the documents in a specified order.

Lenders may want to have printed on the inside cover of their loan file the documents that should be in that file. In that way, lenders can double-check that all required documents are in the file.

The documents below are listed in alphabetical order with a discussion of the reason for the required document. A few examples of these documents are found as exhibits in this chapter; others are found in the case study in Chapter 17.

Adjustable rate rider   If the mortgage is an adjustable-rate mortgage, a statement signed by the borrower acknowledging that he or she understands that the interest rate could increase should be in the loan file.

Application   Both the original and the typed final application are required for a closed loan. Be sure all lines are completed and all required signatures appear.

Appraisal   An appraisal is required for all real estate loans. If the loan is a single-family detached conventional mortgage, the Uniform Residential Appraisal Report should be used. If another type of residential real estate, care should be exercised that the correct appraisal form is used.

Assignment of mortgage   If the mortgage is being purchased from a mortgage lender who originated it for later sale, an instrument assigning the mortgage to a permanent investor and an estoppel certificate should be included in the loan file.

Building restrictions   Any local building restrictions that affect the mortgaged premises should be contained in the loan file with a statement as to whether this property meets local building restrictions. This may be contained in a lawyer's opinion.

Cancelled mortgage   If the loan being closed is for the purpose of refinancing a previous loan, the original mortgage and note should appear in the file and be cancelled with the satisfaction of that mortgage recorded.

Certificate of occupancy   In all new construction and refurbishing that requires it, a certificate issued by the local authorities should appear declaring that the building is habitable.

Chattel lien   If personal property is serving as a security in addition to the real estate, a financing statement or other document creating the lien is required.

Closing instruction   These instructions to the closing agent informing him of what to do, and how, should be retained to help establish whether the closing was held correctly.

Closing statement   The closing statement for a mortgage closing (like a closing statement for a real estate sale) will determine how the proceeds are to be apportioned to the parties. A receipt signed by the mortgagor is required, indicating that loan proceeds have been disbursed according to instructions.

Commitment letter   A commitment letter should be examined closely since it establishes the contractual rights and obligations between the lender and the borrower. Comparison should be made between this commitment letter and the application for the loan to determine if the applicant is receiving everything

MORTGAGE LOAN COMMITMENT

EQUAL HOUSING LENDER

Staten Island Savings Bank
15 Beach Street, Staten Island, N.Y. 10304
(718) 447-7900

L E N D E R

TO: John Smith and Susan Smith
40 Lynn Court
Oceanview, New York 10001

DATE: April 1, 1989
PREMISES: 59 Silver Lane
Staten Island, New York 10315

It is a pleasure to notify you that your application for a first/second mortgage loan has been approved subject to the following matters set forth below and on the reverse side hereof.

AMOUNT, TERMS AND FEES

Amount of Loan ....$	80,000.00	Contract Interest Rate.........	10.50 %
* Loan Origination Fee ....$	800.00	Annual Percentage Rate	10.7727 %
Loan Discount Fee ....$	n/a	Appraisal Fee ....$	225.00 Pd.
Lenders Inspection Fee ......$	n/a	Credit Report Fee ....$	37.00 Pd.
PMI Initial Premium ....$	n/a	Non-Refundable Stand-by Fee..$	800.00
Application Fee ....$	100.00 Pd.		(Please Remit)
............................$		Total amount to be paid: $1,600.00	

*Non-refundable fee

REPAYMENT TERMS

☒ Standard Fixed Payment Mortgage Purchase - 30 Year Fixed Rate

To be repaid in __360__ equal monthly installments of $ __731.80__ (principal and interest) with the first monthly installment due approximately 30 days after of settlement, plus 1/12th of the annual tax and water and/or sewer charges, hazard and mortgage insurance premiums. All payments will be due on the first of each month.

☐ Adjustable Rate Mortgage

To be repaid in equal monthly installments of $_____ (principal and interest) for the initial adjustment period of _____ year(s), plus 1/12th of the annual tax and water and/or sewer charges, hazard and mortgage insurance premiums. All payments will be due on the first of each month. The above stated Contract Interest Rate shall be considered the "Initial Interest Rate" only, and can increase or decrease subject to the limitations in the Disclosure you received following application date.

EVIDENCE OF TITLE

Counsel for the Lender will order and examine title and prepare the note and mortgage and all related documents. The costs of these services together with disbursements are to be paid by you at the time of closing or upon demand. Title shall be subject to the approval of Lender's Counsel.

ADDITIONAL REQUIRED ITEMS OR CONDITIONS

All Items Checked ☒ Below Apply:
☐ Signed Sales Contract — required
☐ Plat of survey, acceptable to Lender, showing the improvements to be properly within the lot lines and no encroachments on other properties — required.
☐ Copy of present Evidence of Title showing Legal Description needed.
☐ The attached list of repairs is to be completed prior to settlement or an escrow in the amount of $_____ will be held until the work is satisfactorily completed.
☐ We will pay out on the Loan upon completion of the building, subject to a satisfactory Compliance Inspection Report by our Appraiser and a Certificate of Occupancy from the Governing Municipality.
☐ A Contractors Statement and Supporting Waivers of Lien are to be provided.
☐ Flood Insurance Mandatory, see reverse
☐ Notice of Recission, see attached
☒ Fire Insurance required in the amount of $ __80,000.00__, see reverse
☐ Private Mortgage Insurance is required. A certified or bank check in the amount of $_____ made payable to _____ must be presented at closing..
☐ _____

SEE REVERSE

The Continuation of Commitment Conditions is on the reverse and is made a part of this Commitment.

INSTRUCTIONS

This commitment will not become effective until the signed Disclosure Statement (if applicable) is received by the Lender together with your signed acceptance and your check to our order in the amount of $ __1,600.00__. This offer will be withdrawn unless accepted by you within TEN (10) DAYS, and further, the mortgage loan must close on or before __May 31, 1989__ or the commitment will be cancelled.

I (WE) hereby accept the terms and
Conditions of this Commitment.

Borrower _John Smith_   Date _4/6/89_

Borrower _Susan Smith_   Date _4/6/89_

Borrower _____   Date _____

Borrower _____   Date _____

"LENDER FILE COPY"

COMMITMENT ISSUED BY: tmt

Barry W. Pite
Authorized Signature

required. If the mortgage is to be insured, guaranteed, or sold to a third party, those commitment letters should also appear.

Contract of sale   If a loan is requested for the purchase of an existing property, the contract of sale should be in the loan file to verify an actual sale and to assist later in verifying the appraisal of the property.

Credit report   A credit report on the borrower is required on all mortgage loans. The correct credit report for a mortgage loan is a Residential Mortgage Credit Report provided by a local credit bureau with a tie-in to a national repository of credit information.

Deed   If a loan is to purchase real estate or refinance an existing mortgage, a copy of the deed should be included in the loan file along with instructions to record.

Disbursement papers   Instructions are required on how funds are to be delivered to the mortgagor or other involved parties.

Escrow   If the transaction involved has been closed in escrow, a copy of the escrow agreement should be in the loan file, and when the term *escrow*, or *impounded*, is used to describe the way monthly payments of taxes and insurance are made, this agreement should also be in the loan file.

FHA/VA   All documents required by an FHA-insured or VA-guaranteed loan (e.g., credit report, verification of employment, building certificate, certificate of occupancy, flood insurance, etc.) should be in the loan file.

Flood insurance   A statement that the property is or is not in a flood area is required and, if in a flood area, whether flood insurance is available and provided.

Good faith estimate of closing costs   Lender must provide a loan applicant with a written estimate of charges payable at settlement within 3 business days of application. Receipt of this Good Faith Estimate should be in the file. This estimate may also be combined with the truth-in-lending loan cost and APR disclosure.

Home owners association agreement   If the property is a condominium, the association agreement binding all home owners is required in the file.

Insurance (hazard) policies   In a residential file the required insurance policy (probably a home owners) covering losses for fire, liability, and any other hazard should exist with a mortgagee loss payable clause.

Mortgage or deed of trust   A mortgage or a deed of trust creating the security interest must appear in the loan file. Any chattel liens on personal property or any financing statement should also appear. Recording instructions are required to protect all parties.

Mortgagor's affidavit   A mortgagor should be required to sign certain affidavits attesting to any current position regarding divorce proceedings, judgments, or liens or any recent improvement on the real estate or other pertinent facts that would affect the mortgage loan.

Agreement
To Purchase
Or Sell

Agreement
To Purchase
Or Sell

JESSIE MATHERS _____ Agent   ~~BUY~~   New Orleans, La.   FEBRUARY 1,   19 89

1.   __WE__ ____offer and agree to purchase ____127 MONET PLACE, KENNER, LOUISIANA 70065
2. HOUSE, LOT AND ALL IMPROVEMENTS. CENTRAL HEAT AND ALL APPLIANCES TO BE IN WORKING ORDER
3. AT AOS. CLEAR TERMITE CERTIFICATE TO BE FURNISHED BY SELLER AT AOS.

4. On grounds measuring about____60' x 110'
5. for the sum of____FIFTY EIGHT THOUSAND, FIVE HUNDRED ____or as per title, and subject to title restrictions if any, AND NO/100____ ($ 58,500.00 ____) Dollars, on the terms of
6. ____NO____ Cash BALANCE SECURED BY VA LOAN
7.
8. SELLER WILL PAY DISCOUNT POINTS NOT TO EXCEED 2.50%

9.   This sale is conditioned upon the ability of the purchaser to borrow upon this property as security the sum of $ 58,500.00
10. by a mortgage loan or loans at a rate of interest not to exceed $13\frac{1}{4}$ % per annum, interest and principal payable in equal
11. MONTHLY ____; installments, over a period of____30____years.
12. (monthly) (quarterly) (semi-annual) (annual)
13.   Should the loan stipulated above be unobtainable by the purchaser, seller or agent within 45 days from date of accept-
14. ance hereof, this contract shall then become null and void, and the agent is hereby authorized to return the purchaser's deposit
15. in full.
    Property sold subject to the following lease or leases:
16. Tenant____n/a____ Rental____n/a____ Expiration____n/a____ Options____n/a
17.
18.   Occupancy__AT ACT OF SALE
19.   Paving charges bearing against the property, if any, to be paid by____SELLER
20.   Real Estate Taxes and rentals (if any) to be prorated to date of Act of Sale.
21.   All proper and necessary certificates and revenue stamps to be paid by seller.
22.   Cost of survey by__PURCHASER
23.
24.
25.
26.   Act of Sale to be passed before____LENDER'S____Notary, on or prior to__MARCH 16,____19 89
27. at expense of purchaser.
28.   If this offer is accepted, purchaser must deposit with seller's agent immediately in ~~cash~~ n/a % of purchase price
29. amounting to $__1000.00 CASH AND BALANCE IN DEMAND NOTE
30.   This deposit is to be non-interest bearing and may be placed in any bank in the City of New Orleans, without
31. responsibility on the part of the agent in case of failure or suspension of such bank.
32.   The seller shall deliver to purchaser a merchantable title.
33.   In the event the purchaser fails to comply with this agreement within the time specified, the seller shall have the
34. right to declare the deposit, ipso facto, forfeited, without formality beyond tender of title to purchaser; or the seller may de-
35. mand specific performance.
36.   In the event the seller does not comply with this agreement within the time specified, the purchaser shall have the
37. right either to demand the return of his deposit in full plus an equal amount to be paid as penalty by the seller; or the
38. purchaser may demand specific performance, at his option.
39.   In the event the deposit is forfeited, the commission shall be paid out of this deposit, reserving to the seller the right
40. to proceed against the purchaser for the recovery of the amount of the commission.
41.   If this offer is accepted, seller agrees to pay the agent's commission of____6%____which commission is earned by
42. agent when this agreement is signed by both parties and when the mortgage loan, if any, has been secured.
43.
44.   Either party hereto who fails to comply with the terms of this offer, if accepted, is obligated and agrees to pay the
45. agent's commission and all fees and costs incurred in enforcing collection and damages.
46.   This offer remains binding and irrevocable through____FEBRUARY 2, 1989
47.   Submitted to__CAROLYN RIVERS____ (Signed) _David Preston Walters_
           (Listing Agent) (Owner)

48.   By__JESSIE MATHERS____   New Orleans, La.____FEBRUARY 1, ____19 89
           Selling Agent

    I/We accept the above in all its terms and conditions.

MSF 3052   (Signed) _Carolyn Rivers_

GOOD FAITH ESTIMATE OF BORROWER'S SETTLEMENT COSTS

Listed below is the Good Faith Estimate of Settlement Charges made pursuant to the requirements of the Real Estate Settlement Procedures Act (RESPA). These figures are only **ESTIMATES** and the actual charges due at settlement may be different. **This form does not cover all items you will be required to pay in cash at settlement and you may wish to inquire as to the amounts of any such other charges.** Please refer to the settlement costs booklet for full explanations.

Applicant(s): Jon & Linda Jones   Type of Loan: FHA
Property Address: 205 Smith St. Perth Amboy, NJ 08861
Estimated Settlement Date: 6/15/89

		MONTHLY PAYMENT ESTIMATE	
Loan (without MIP/Funding Fee):	81,000	Principal and Interest	741.15
Loan (with MIP/Funding Fee):	84,078	Taxes/Insurance (Haz.-Flood)	115.00
Interest Rate	10.50%	PMI/FHA Mtg. Ins.	
Loan Term:	30 years	Ground Rent	
		TOTAL	856.15

801.	Loan Origination Fee	1 %	$ 810.00	1101.	Closing or Escrow Fee	$	–
802.	Loan Discount Fee	3 %	$ 2522.34	1102.	Abstract or Title Search	$	–
803.	Appraisal Fee		$ 125.00	1103.	Title Examination	$	–
804.	Credit Report		$ 35.00	1104.	Title Insurance Binder	$	–
805.	Lender's Inspection Fee		$ 50.00	1106.	Notary Fee	$	–
806.	Mortgage Insurance		$ –	1107.	Attorney Fees	$	–
	Application Fee		$ –	1108.	Title Insurance	$	475.00
807.	Application Fee		$ –	1109.	Lender's Coverage	$	490.00
808.	Tax Service Contract Fee		$ 59.00	1110.	Owner's Coverage	$	–
809.	Commitment Fee		$ –	1111.		$	–
810.	Document Preparation Fee		$ –	1201.	Recording Fees:	$	
811.	Condominium Document		–		Deed: $ 20.00 ;		20.00
	Review Fee		$		Mortgage: $ 25.00 ;		25.00
812.			$		Release: $		
*901.	Interest From 6/15/89			1202.	City/County Tax/Stamps:	$	
	to 6/30 /Day @ 24.19		$ 387.04		Deed: $;		
902.	Mortgage Insurance Premium		$ 3078.00		Mortgage: $;		
903.	Hazard Insurance Premium (1yr)		$ 324.00		Release: $		
904.	Flood Insurance Premium (1yr)		$ .75 per $1000	1203.	State Tax/Stamps:	$	
905.	FHA MIP/VA Funding Fee		$		Deed: $;		
1001.	Hazard Insurance				Mortgage: $;		
	2 months @ 27 month		$ 54.00	1204.		$	
1002.	Mortgage Insurance			1205.	Recording Notice		
	months @ month		$		of Commencement	$	15.00
1003.	City Property Taxes			1301.	Survey	$	250.00
	months @ month		$	1302.	Pest Inspection	$	50.00
1004.	Property Taxes			1303.	Reconveyance Fee	$	–
	2 months @ 100 month		$ 200.00	1304.	Buydown Fee	$	–
1005.	Flood Insurance IF REQUIRED						
	2 months @ 10.50 month		$ 10.50				
1006.	School Tax/Ground Rent						
	months @ month		$				

Estimated summary of your purchase:

A.	Purchase Price	$	125,000.00
B.	Prepaids (section 900)		3789.04
C.	Escrows (section 1000)		254.00
D.	Closing Costs (all other sections)		4926.34
E.	Total	$	134,005.38

MINUS

Cash Deposit	($ 12,500)	
Amount Paid Margaretten	($ 160)	
Mortgage Amount	($ 81,000)	
Cash required for settlement	$	40,345.38

I/We acknowledge I/we have received a copy of the booklet "You and Settlement Costs," and I/we fully understand the amounts indicated above are **ESTIMATES ONLY** and may vary from the actual settlement charges at closing. Further, I/we fully understand that the loan origination fee, interest rate, loan term, and monthly payment indicated above are based on my/our application and may be subject to change. If for any reason the loan for which I/we have applied does not close, I/we agree to reimburse the Margaretten & Company, Inc. for any and all costs incurred to process my/our application including but not limited to appraisal, and Condominium Document review (if applicable).

APPLICANT _Jon Jones_
DATE 4-11-89

APPLICANT _Linda Jones_
DATE 4-11-89

Date of this Estimate: _____

BY: _Joe Black_
MARGARETTEN & COMPANY, INC.

*This interest calculation represents the greatest amount of interest you could be required to pay at settlement. The actual amount will be determined by the day of the month on which your settlement is conducted. To determine the amount you will have to pay, multiply the number of days remaining in the month in which you settle by $_____, which is the daily interest charge for your loan.

REGION 1 GOOD FAITH ESTIMATE OF BORROWER'S SETTLEMENT COSTS
MAR-101 (3/87)

Note It is essential to include a properly executed promissory note. The note creates the obligation to repay the debt which is secured by the mortgage; it should state the amount of the loan, the term, the interest rate, and any other pertinent conditions.

Perc test   If the property has or will need a septic tank, a perc test must have the result in the loan file.

Photographs   Photographs of good, clear quality are required of the front, rear, and street scene for the appraisal to adequately show the mortgaged real estate.

Private mortgage insurance documents   All documents required by a mortgage insurance company to issue their insurance, as well as a copy of their commitment, should appear in the loan file.

Right to cancel notice   If the mortgage is to refinance an existing mortgage, the notice of a 3 day right of rescision is required.

Survey   Since the real estate is the loan security, it is in the mortgagee's interest that a survey be made to identify the property correctly and determine if any encroachments exist. In some states a separate survey will not be required since the title insurance will cover this area also.

Tax, real estate   In some states a form showing that all past due taxes have been paid is required. In other states this form is used to establish adequate reserve for taxes.

Termite certificate   Many lenders require a certificate stating that the property has no termites.

Title insurance or examination   In all cases, it is essential that title be examined or that an approved American Land Title Association (ALTA) title insurance policy or binder be included. This requirement establishes who has right to the real estate and, therefore, who must execute the mortgage to encumber it. The title examination should also disclose any prior encumbrances, tax liens, or other interests.

Truth-in-lending   The loan file must contain a Loan Cost Disclosure Statement which will disclose both the annual percentage rate (APR) and the total finance charge. This may be combined with the Good Faith Estimate of Closing Costs.

Uniform Settlement Statement (HUD-1)   This statement is required at loan closings by the Real Estate Settlement Procedures Act of 1974 (RESPA). The statement offers the borrower and seller a full disclosure of known or estimated settlement costs.

Verification reports   The mortgage lender should verify all relevant statements made on the loan application by obtaining verifying documentation. The most commonly used verification forms are those for employment and deposits.

OMB No. 2502-0265 (Exp. 12-31-86)

A.	B.	TYPE OF LOAN
		1. ☒FHA 2. ☐FmHA 3. ☐CONV. UNINS.
U. S. DEPARTMENT OF HOUSING AND URBAN DEVELOPMENT		4. ☐VA 5. ☐CONV. INS.
	6. FILE NUMBER	7. LOAN NUMBER 10100398
SETTLEMENT STATEMENT		
	8. MORTGAGE INSURANCE CASE NUMBER:	

C. NOTE: *This form is furnished to give you a statement of actual settlement costs. Amounts paid to and by the settlement agent are shown. Items marked "(p.o.c.)" were paid outside the closing; they are shown here for informational purposes and are not included in the totals.*

D. NAME OF BORROWER:	E. NAME OF SELLER:
JON JONES	BRIAN JOHNSON
LINDA JONES	

F. NAME OF LENDER:	G. PROPERTY LOCATION:
MARGARETTEN & COMPANY INC	
205 SMITH ST PO BOX 3021	205 SMITH STREET
PERTH AMBOY NJ08861	PERTH AMBOY NJ08861

H. SETTLEMENT AGENT:	PLACE OF SETTLEMENT	I. SETTLEMENT DATE 05/15/89
STEVEN E SMITH		
210 GOODRIDGE AVE		FUNDING DATE:
WOODBRIDGE NJ 07095		05/15/89

J. SUMMARY OF BORROWER'S TRANSACTION		K. SUMMARY OF SELLER'S TRANSACTION	
100 GROSS AMOUNT DUE FROM BORROWER		**400 GROSS AMOUNT DUE TO SELLER**	
101. Contract sales price	125,000.00	401. Contract sales price	125,000.00
102. Personal property INCLUDED IN 101	---------	402. Personal property INCLUDED IN 401	---------
103. Settlement charges to borrower *(line 1400)*		403.	
104.		404.	
105.		405.	
Adjustments for items paid by seller in advance		*Adjustments for items paid by seller in advance*	
106. City/town taxes to		406. City/town taxes to	
107. County taxes INCLUDED IN 106	---------	407. County taxes INCLUDED IN 406	---------
108. Assessments to		408. Assessments to	
109.		409.	
110.		410.	
120. GROSS AMOUNT DUE FROM BORROWER		**420. GROSS AMOUNT DUE TO SELLER**	
200 AMOUNTS PAID BY OR IN BEHALF OF BORROWER		**500 REDUCTIONS IN AMOUNT DUE TO SELLER**	
201. Deposit or earnest money		501. Excess deposit *(see instructions)*	
202. Principal amount of new loan(s)	84,078.00	502. Settlement charges to seller *(line 1400)*	
203. Existing loan(s) taken subject to		503. Existing loan(s) taken subject to	
204. Second mortgage loan		504. Payoff of first mortgage loan	
		Principal Balance $	
		Interest Adjustment $	
		Reserves ( ) Credit ( ) Deficit $	
205.		505. Payoff of second mortgage loan	
		Principal Balance $	
		Interest Adjustment $	
206.		506. Second mortgage loan to Borrower	
207.		507.	
208.		508.	
209.		509.	
Adjustments for items unpaid by seller		*Adjustments for items unpaid by seller*	
210. City/town taxes to		510. City/town taxes to	
211. County taxes INCLUDED IN 210	---------	511. County taxes INCLUDED IN 510	---------
212. Assessments to		512. Assessments to	
213.		513.	
214.		514.	
215.		515.	
216.		516.	
217.		517.	
220. TOTAL PAID BY/FOR BORROWER		**520. TOTAL REDUCTION AMOUNT DUE SELLER**	
300 CASH AT SETTLEMENT FROM/TO BORROWER		**600 CASH AT SETTLEMENT TO/FROM SELLER**	
301. Gross amount due from borrower *(line 120)*		601. Gross amount due to seller *(line 420)*	
302. Less amounts paid by/for borrower *(line 220)*	( )	602. Less reductions in amount due seller *(line 520)*	( )
303. CASH (☐FROM) (☐TO) BORROWER		**603. CASH (☐TO) (☐FROM) SELLER**	

HUD-1 (3-86)
RESPA, HB 4305.2
MC 0047 F

201

L. SETTLEMENT CHARGES

700. TOTAL SALES BROKER'S COMMISSION				PAID FROM BORROWER'S FUNDS AT SETTLEMENT	PAID FROM SELLER'S FUNDS AT SETTLEMENT
based on price $		@	% =		
Division of Commission (line 700) as follows:					
701. $	to				
702. $	to				
703. Commission paid at Settlement					
704.					

800. ITEMS PAYABLE IN CONNECTION WITH LOAN					
801. Loan Origination Fee	1.000	%		810.00	
802. Loan Discount	2.000	%		1,681.56	
803. Appraisal Fee	to	B —POC	160.00		
804. Credit Report	to	B —POC	35.00		
805. Lender's Inspection Fee					
806.					
807.	APPLICATION FEE				
808. Tax Service Contract					
809.					
810.					
811.					
812.					
813.					

900. ITEMS REQUIRED BY LENDER TO BE PAID IN ADVANCE					
901. Interest from 05/15/89 to 5/31/89 @$ 24.19 /day				411.23	
902. Mortgage Insurance Premium for months to ONE TIME MIP FEE				3,078.00	
903. Hazard Insurance Premium for years to					
904. Flood Ins. Premium years to					
905.					

1000. RESERVES DEPOSITED WITH LENDER					
1001. Hazard Insurance	2	months @ $	22.00 per month	44.00	
1002. Mortgage Insurance		months @ $	per month		
1003. City property taxes	2	months @ $	98.00 per month	196.00	
1004. County property taxes		months @ $	per month		
1005. Annual Assessments ***********months @ $			per month		
1006. Flood Insurance		months @ $	per month		
1007.		months @ $	per month		
1008.		months @ $	per month		

1100. TITLE CHARGES				
1101. Settlement or closing fee	to			
1102. Abstract or title search	to			
1103. Title examination	to			
1104. Title insurance binder	to			
1105. Document preparation	to			
1106. Notary fees	to			
1107. Attorney's fees	to			
(includes above items numbers;				
1108. Title insurance	to			
(includes above items numbers;				
1109. Lender's coverage	$	AMOUNT OF PREMIUM		
1110. Owner's coverage	$	AMOUNT OF PREMIUM		
1111.				
1112.				
1113.				

1200. GOVERNMENT RECORDING AND TRANSFER CHARGES				
1201. Recording fees: Deed $	; Mortgage $	; Release $		
1202. City/county tax/stamps: Deed $	; Mortgage $			
1203. State tax/stamps: Deed $	; Mortgage $			
1204.				
1205.				

1300. ADDITIONAL SETTLEMENT CHARGES			
1301. Survey to			
1302. Pest inspection to			
1303.			
1304.			
1305. ALL TAXES PAID THRU 3RD QUARTER OF 1989			

1400. TOTAL SETTLEMENT CHARGES (enter on lines 103, Section J and 502, Section K)

Brian Johnson
BRIAN JOHNSON

CLOSING AGENT

Jon Jones
JON JONES

Linda Jones
LINDA JONES

HUD-1 (3-86)
MC 0048 F

MORTGAGE LOAN ADMINISTRATION   14

After the closing of the mortgage loan, the next step in the mortgage lending process involves the loan administration, or as it is sometimes known, the servicing department. This step or function can be the most difficult of all the steps in the residential lending process to perform for any mortgage lender; on the other hand, it can be the most profitable of all of the steps. The difficulty in performing this function stems from the myriad of problems that can develop when dealing with computers, systems, people, and their problems. These problems will be discussed in greater detail in the following sections. If these problems are handled correctly and sufficient servicing volume exists, this function can produce a profit for a mortgage lender which may be needed to offset other lending-related losses.

Importance of Loan Administration

For some mortgage lenders, such as mortgage bankers, servicing profits are the primary reason for being engaged in mortgage lending. Other mortgage lenders who were almost exclusively portfolio lenders in the past (such as thrifts or credit unions) are now selling a major portion of their originations and, as a result, are placing a greater emphasis on loan administration. This shift in emphasis is a result of the servicing requirements of the secondary market and because these institutions now recognize the profit potential of loan administration.

Servicing has also played a major role in the recent emergence of the so-called nontraditional mortgage lenders. Many of these players, such as General Motors Acceptance Corporation (GMAC) and Metropolitan Life, have entered the residential mortgage lending competition by buying large servicing portfolios. These large servicing portfolios give these new entrants immediate economies of scale and thus enhance profit potential. GMAC entered residential mortgage lending by buying from two mortgage bankers their servicing portfolios totaling nearly $19 billion. Overnight, this servicing portfolio made GMAC one of the largest servicers of mortgage debt in the world.

Loan Administration Defined

Residential loan administration can be defined as the total effort required to perform both the day-to-day management of the entire servicing portfolio and the individual servicing of a residential loan. Thus, if performed correctly, loan administration should result in the following items occurring:

- rendering of all required services to the mortgagor
- protecting the security interest of the mortgagee (or an investor)
- producing a profit for the servicer

The Federal Home Loan Mortgage Corporation (Freddie Mac) defines servicing as "...the performance of applicable obligations described in the purchase documents, including tasks necessary to maintain mortgages sold to Freddie Mac in a manner that protects Freddie Mac's interest." Freddie Mac defines a servicer as "...an institution approved to service mortgages purchased by Freddie Mac. Any institution that fits a description applicable to a Seller...may become an approved Freddie Mac Servicer by satisfying the Servicer eligibility requirements...." Other secondary market players have similar definitions.

Requirement of All Mortgage Lenders

Mortgage loan administration is a required function for all mortgage lenders whether all or some of the mortgages originated are sold to other investors. Some mortgage lenders who are only involved in the origination phase of mortgage lending, such as mortgage brokers, transfer the responsibility for servicing the mortgages they originated to mortgage investors. In most situations, but not all, the broker will earn a fee from the investor to whom they have transferred servicing. This fee, called a servicing release fee, is in recognition of the fact that something of value is being transferred. Depending on a number of variables, for instance the

LARGEST SERVICERS OF RESIDENTIAL MORTGAGE DEBT IN 1990
(In Billions of Dollars)

1. Citicorp	$66.09
2. Ahmanson (parent of Home Savings)	$59.14
3. Fleet/Norstar	$52.30

Source: *Real Estate Finance Today*, February 25, 1991

type of loan and the volume of loans transferred, the broker could receive as much as 100 to 150 basis points from the investor for the servicing transferred. If the volume of loans is very low, the broker may receive less or nothing at all. This servicing strategy is discussed in greater detail later in this chapter.

SERVICING INCOME

In addition to interest rate spread, origination fees, possible warehousing and marketing profits, the fee a mortgage lender receives from an investor for servicing a mortgage provides practically all of the revenue a mortgage lender receives. The amount of the servicing fee has changed over the years, but today it ranges from ¼ to ½ of 1 percent of the outstanding balance of the loan. The amount varies depending on volume of loans serviced and also by the type of mortgage (e.g., an ARM could require a servicing fee as high as .50 basis). The average for all residential mortgage loans is about ⅜ of 1 percent.

In the current mortgage market, many mortgage lenders are unable to generate a profit from the origination function, especially if a large percentage of their total originations are VA loans. This is because the origination fee for VA mortgages is limited by law to only one percent of the loan amount. These mortgage lenders must look to servicing income to offset origination losses, and sometimes marketing losses, to produce a net profit from mortgage lending.

The early 1980s experienced a period of such high inflation that the tradition of servicing profitability came into serious question. This question is centered around the fact that while the servicing income from a mortgage loan continues to decrease each year over the life of the loan (because the servicing fee is based on the outstanding balance of the loan), servicing expenses can be expected to increase each year.

Servicing income is generated by a servicer retaining a previously agreed upon fraction of one percent of the outstanding principal balance collected monthly. The servicing fee is earned only if the payment is collected. After receiving the monthly payment of principal and interest, a servicer forwards that amount less the servicing fee to the investor.

On loans serviced for others, the servicing function also provides an opportunity for the lender to benefit from float. This float exists because of the unequal timing between loan payment collections and disbursements to the investors. This float can be for as much as four weeks and involve millions of dollars. The float depends upon the date a payment is received by a mortgage lender. For example, in FHLMC yield accounting, a payment due on the first of one month is not required to be remitted to FHLMC until the first Tuesday of the following month.

Other Income

Often overlooked by institutions just getting into servicing is the extent of other income that can be generated by the loan administration department. These fees include, among others:

- late charges
- processing an assumption
- preparation of discharge and release
- reinstatement after default (if different from late fees)
- substitution of hazard insurance policies other than on the renewal or annual premium rate
- insurance commissions from accident, health, mortgage, life, and other casualty policies
- prepayment penalty fees
- bad check fees and other miscellaneous fees

Escrows

Another important function which positively impacts mortgage lending profitability is the value of funds which have been escrowed for the payment of real estate taxes and hazard insurance. Many, but not all, mortgage lenders require that their mortgagors escrow 1/12 of the annual real estate taxes and hazard insurance each month while paying their mortgage principal and interest. This action is justifiable for a lender because if real estate taxes are not paid, the local government could have a superior claim or position in the real estate which is securing the mortgage debt. If the taxes remain unpaid, the local government could sell the real estate for the back taxes. It is for this reason that some lenders will advance funds not yet collected from the mortgagor for payment of real estate taxes when due. This amount will be recovered by increasing the escrow payments for the next year or by adding that amount on to the principal. This same risk exists if the federal government places a tax lien for failure to pay income or other taxes. In the same vein, if the insurance premium is not paid and a loss occurs, the lender could suffer because its security is not worth as much. For this reason, mortgage investors, such as Fannie Mae and Freddie Mac, require that loans sold to them carry hazard insurance.

Many lenders believe that escrows actually help lower the number of delinquencies and foreclosures because when funds are due for taxes and insurance they are already collected.

Use of escrow funds   These escrows are also important to many mortgage lenders because they serve as the compensating balance required for a line of credit from a commercial bank. The existence of these funds not only allows for this line of credit but also keeps the interest rate on that line lower than it would have been without the compensating balances. Mortgagors benefit from this by the lender being able to offer lower mortgage rates. In addition to the use of these funds for compensating balances, mortgage lenders benefit from these funds because they are collected monthly but are only disbursed semi-annually or annually. As a result, the mortgage lender can use these funds during the interim for its own purposes. This can be a meaningful source of low or no cost funds the benefit of which can be passed on to borrowers by lower rates on their mortgages.

During the 1980s many states passed laws requiring lenders to pay interest on escrows. The amount of interest that must be paid varies from state to state. The minimum rates generally fall between 2 percent and 4 percent per annum while others require interest as high as 5½ percent. Even when lenders must pay interest on escrow, these funds are still low cost funds and can have a positive impact on profitability. A few lenders, usually thrifts, have decided not to escrow funds for taxes and insurance because they do not believe they benefit enough from these funds when the cost of collecting and disbursing the funds is calculated. This would appear to be the case only when the servicing volume is low.

When viewed from the mortgagor's side, many prefer the convenience of budgeting these expenses on a monthly basis. The additional income, like any income, received from the interest paid on escrows is nice but generally is not all that important especially since mortgagors must pay income taxes on the interest paid on escrows.

Servicing Responsibilities

Organization of a loan administration department   The organization of the loan administration department can vary from mortgage lender to mortgage lender. Most departments are organized using either the function system or the unit system. If the function system is used, each employee is assigned a specific servicing function such as real estate taxes or assumptions. This system allows for specialization and, if done correctly, speed of operation. The main drawback is if that person becomes sick or leaves the organization, that function will not get performed for a period of time. The unit system utilizes small teams of employees to perform all of the tasks related to a group of loans. The benefit is all employees have the capability to perform all of the functions and can cover for each other during vacations or sick leave. Of course, this also means no one person will be an expert on any one function.

It appears that most large servicers of residential loans use the function system because speed and accuracy are critical to their economies of scale. Smaller lenders are more apt to use the unit system so as to have more coverage of all functions at all times.

First step   The first task in loan administration is to establish a servicing file. Some lenders are using this task as a type of quality control. As the servicing file is being set up, the list of required documents is compared with the list of documents actually in the loan file. If any documents or signatures are missing, this is probably the last convenient time a lender will have to cure any defects.

The next task is to mail notification of first payment to the borrower. The method of payment varies according to the lender, but the most common are:

- *Coupons.* Coupons are provided in one-year supply; mortgagor submits one with each payment. The coupon will have on it the loan number, due date, and payment amount.
- *Monthly billing.* A bill is mailed to the borrower each month. The main advantage is that it is a good reminder that the payment is due, but the cost of mailing is a drawback. This drawback can be offset by including advertising for other services or bills for other services rendered.
- *Pre-authorized automatic payment.* Mortgage payment is automatically deducted from the mortgagor's checking, share draft, or NOW account. This method assures prompt payment on the due date. This is a requirement for bi-weekly mortgages.

The notification of first payment should be the last time correspondence with a mortgagor is required unless a notice of increased monthly payment is necessary because of a change in an index or an increase in taxes or insurance. Of course, if a borrower is late in making a mortgage payment, prompt notice of this fact should be communicated to the mortgagor.

Servicing contract   If the mortgages to be serviced have been sold to another lender or mortgage investor such as Fannie Mae or Freddie Mac, the servicing relationship is established by a servicing contract. This contractual relationship should continue for the life of the mortgage loans sold to that investor, but it can be terminated. Termination can be either for cause (some failure to perform on the part of the servicer) or, in some cases, without cause. If servicing is withdrawn without cause, then it is common for an investor to pay a fee as compensation, typically 1 or 2 percent of the amount serviced.

The responsibilities of a servicer are usually described in detail in the servicing contract or in a servicing manual supplied by an investor. These responsibilities typically include:

- monthly collection and allocation of principal and interest
- disbursement of funds to the investor
- collection and periodic payment of real estate taxes and insurance premiums
- handling of assumption, partial release, and modification of lien requests
- annual review of loans involving, among other tasks, adjustable-rate mortgage interest rates, current insurance policy, taxes paid, and escrow analysis

- any other activity necessary to protect the investor's security interest including, if necessary, collection activity and foreclosure proceedings

Servicing functions   To fulfill these responsibilities successfully, a servicer of a mortgage loan will need either trained people or separate departments to perform five essential functions.

The first is the Cashier Department, which is responsible for receiving payments, depositing these payments, and transmitting this information to loan accounting.

The Loan Accounting Department is responsible for notifying investors that a deposit has been made to their account and for drawing a check (payable to the investor) which distributes principal and interest less the servicing fee. Some investors also require that excess reserves be deposited with them and not in the custodial account.

The Collection Department's function is to collect those payments that are past due. In many ways, this is the most difficult function but it is also the most essential for a successful servicing operation. Those involved in this function must be familiar with the Fair Debt Collection Practices Act, which prohibits certain collection practices. If collection is impossible, then this department is also responsible for initiating foreclosure proceedings.

The Insurance Department will ensure the protection of the investor's security interest by determining that adequate hazard insurance exists and is current with a mortgagee-payable clause. This department also has the responsibility of inspecting repaired property (if the claim was large and affects the actual structure of the security) before releasing the insurance claim payment to the mortgagor.

The Real Estate Taxes Department will protect an investor's security interest by ensuring that the real estate taxes are collected and paid to the local government.

Other departments that may be required depending on the size of the servicing portfolio are: a Real Estate Owned (REO) Department to handle foreclosed property and a Customer Services Department to handle inquires relating to assumptions, payoffs, modifications, etc.

Servicing Portfolios

As the servicing portfolio of a mortgage lender increases, economies of scale probably will also develop. For example, the average annual cost of servicing a residential mortgage loan in a portfolio of $100 million is about $150. That average annual cost can drop to approximately $100 when the portfolio reaches $500 million and may get as low as $75 when the portfolio reaches $1 billion. Because of this evident economy of scale, certain lenders will purchase servicing from other lenders. Many large servicers exist today; in fact, the 100th largest had a servicing portfolio in excess of $2 billion in 1990.

At certain points in the economic cycle, the purchase of servicing is a cheaper way to build up the servicing portfolio than increasing servicing by originations. During these periods of time, those lenders who are active in the servicing of residential loans will attempt to buy servicing from other mortgage lenders. These other lenders may be brokers or other servicers. The price paid for servicing varies, but recently it has ranged from 150 to 250 basis points of the amount serviced. Thus, if one servicer desires to purchase $100 million of servicing from another, the price, depending on the market, could be in the $1.5 to 2.5 million range.

The price one servicer would pay for servicing purchased from another servicer can be better calculated by equating the purchase price to the actual cash flow being generated by the portfolio. For example, all other aspects being equal, a servicer would pay less for a cash flow generated by a .375 percent servicing fee than one generated by a .50 percent fee. In determining the price that a servicer will pay for another's servicing portfolio, the following items will be reviewed:

- average loan balance
- weighted average servicing fee
- weighted average remaining maturity
- weighted average coupon rate
- type of loan
  —fixed rate or adjustable
  —bi-weekly
  —terms and caps of adjustable
- average escrow amounts
- interest to be paid on reserves
- delinquency and foreclosure experience
- geographic make-up
- investors (determines float)
- assumption and prepayment provisions
- remaining life expectations
- ancillary income and other miscellaneous items

Establishing Cost of Servicing

It has been estimated by the Mortgage Bankers Association of America that as much as $150 billion in mortgage servicing changes hands yearly. This number is higher some years than others, but servicing is today often viewed as a marketable asset by many mortgage lenders. One of the key determinants as to whether to buy another's servicing portfolio is your own cost of servicing.

When a mortgage lender calculates its cost of loan servicing, the items it should include are:

- personnel (including fringe benefits)
- occupancy
- electronic data processing

- other direct operating expenses
  - —equipment rentals
  - —postage
  - —telephone
  - —office supplies
  - —travel and entertainment
  - —automobiles
  - —advertising
  - —legal and auditing fees
  - —other operating expenses
- provision for loan losses

ALTERNATIVES TO SERVICING RESIDENTIAL MORTGAGE LOANS

For various reasons that usually involve the issue of whether a lender can service profitably, many mortgage lenders decide not to service the loans they originate. Other lenders realize that they simply don't have the talent to do servicing well. For these mortgage lenders, alternative strategies exist. They include selling the mortgage loans servicing released or entering into a sub-servicing arrangement.

Servicing Released

As has been mentioned, servicing loans sold to another have value to some large servicers. The reason servicing has value is because these servicers can service the loan for less money than they receive as a service fee. For that reason, some of these servicers will pay other lenders for the right to service loans they originated. They acquire the servicing rights by purchasing the mortgage loan for a premium, and then they sell the mortgage loan into the secondary mortgage market, retaining the servicing. The amount of servicing released premium they pay depends on a number of factors including the volume of mortgages sold, where interest rates are, prepayment assumptions, etc. For example, if one lender can sell $5 million of mortgages a month, the acquiring lender may pay as much as 100 basis points as a premium for the servicing. The acquiring lender/servicer is simply buying the right to the future stream of income associated with servicing that loan for a number of years. If the loan prepays early, that lender loss.

Sub-servicing

In order to make residential mortgage lending profitable as soon as possible, some new mortgage lenders such as credit unions have opted not to establish a servicing department for the mortgages they have sold into the secondary mortgage market. As a general rule, they make this decision because they don't have sufficient volume to perform the function profitably or don't have a staff that is qualified. In addition, there are some mortgage lenders who don't want to sell loans servicing released (as described above) because they don't want another financial institution in contact with their customers. Instead, these mortgage lenders contract with another mortgage lender or servicing company to conduct all of the servicing responsibilities for them. These lenders will pay the sub-servicer a servicing fee (usually between $100–125 per loan) based on the total dollars serviced. The originating lender is still responsible to investors for the loans being serviced properly but by using another qualified servicer, the originating lender can have the servicing function performed profitably. For example, if one of these lenders sells a $100,000 mortgage to Fannie Mae and receives a 3/8 of 1 percent servicing fee ($380 a year), it can contract with a sub-servicer to service the loan for, say, $125. The difference between the two fees is profit to the originating lender.

Many of these originating lenders will put into the servicing contract with the sub-servicer the right to pull servicing when sufficient volume is reached to make the function profitable.

FUNDAMENTALS OF REALESTATE LAW ⟹ 15

This chapter provides reference material for the other chapters of the book, as well as a fundamental review of the basic principles of American real estate law.

Possibly no other segment of the U.S. social-economic system is more involved with law than real estate. Whether as a home owner, a developer, or a financier, those involved with real estate must understand the legal framework upon which real estate is defined and the interests therein protected.

Law and real estate have been inseparable since the early days of the development of Anglo-American jurisprudence. This close relationship continues because of custom and the perception that real estate is normally its owner's most precious possession. However, this also has hindered the changes in real estate concepts needed in an evolving society.

A fundamental review of how this relationship between law and real estate developed and a discussion of the interests a person can have in real estate appear in the following sections. Nonlegal terminology is used where the meaning or concept is not altered or affected in any way.

In light of broad differences in state law, this review covers only the general principles of real estate law with no discussion of the unique features of any one state's law. In those situations where there is a basic conflict in the general principles, the majority position is reviewed. Nevertheless, the laws of individual jurisdictions should be carefully determined. This is best accomplished by consulting a competent local attorney.

ENGLISH COMMON LAW

Real estate law throughout the United States, with few exceptions, is based almost entirely on the English common law as it existed at the time of the American

Revolutionary War. This common background has been modified as each jurisdiction legislated changes or as courts interpreted the law differently. Developments in real estate finance since 1776 have required new indigenous laws, but the fact still remains that most of our real estate law is derived from the common law. As a result, the chief problem facing contemporary American real estate law is the existence of 50 jurisdictions with separate real estate laws based on an archaic system of law. This problem is compounded by the fact that this archaic system uses language hundreds of years old and is based on a socio-economic environment entirely different from that of modern-day America. A short review of the development of the common law is vital to an understanding of current real estate law.

Before the Norman invasion of England in 1066, there was no well-developed system of land ownership in England. Land was owned by the family unit rather than the individual, and when the head of the household died, the new head of the household would represent the ownership of the family in a particular piece of land. In 1066, when William the Conquerer invaded England, he imposed a European concept of land ownership upon the English called the feudal system of land tenure, an economic, military, and political system of government which held that the King exclusively owned all land. The most valuable and important commodity in such a society was land. Land represented wealth, and all wealth came from the land. Money hardly existed and barter was the means of exchange. Since the King owned all land, he had complete control over the country and the economy.

A King, of course, needed arms for protection of the realm. For this he depended on the loyalty, fidelity, and allegiance of the lords. In return for their allegiance and military service, the King allowed the lords to use the land, although no ownership was being conveyed. The lords, in turn, allowed lesser lords to use a portion of this land in return for a share of the profits and for swearing allegiance to them. Finally, these lesser lords allowed serfs, who were nothing more than slaves indentured to the land, to use the land in return for a promise of military service. In this pyramid of military allegiance, the serfs owed military service to the lesser lords, who in turn owed service to the lords, who swore allegiance to the King.

The right to own land didn't exist for many years, but one of the incidents of ownership, the ability to pass the use of land to heirs, produced a confrontation with King John in 1215. The result was the Magna Carta, which provided greater rights for the lords, including the right to pass the use of the land on to their sons. Land was passed on to sons only as a result of the doctrine of primogeniture, which dictated that the oldest male child had the right to inherit the land. This was desirable at the time, since it prevented estates from being broken up into smaller tracts and allowed for the development of a landed gentry, which eventually developed the English society. Out of this society evolved the common law and, eventually, English real estate law. Although modified over the years, the feudal system survived until 1660 when it was abolished by law.

As contrasted with the feudal system, the allodial system recognizes that an owner of real estate has title irrespective of the sovereign and thus owes no duty, such as rent or the rendering of military service, to the sovereign. This system developed throughout the world with the exception of Western Europe and certain other areas where the feudal system remained.

The feudal system was an early part of the American land-ownership system in a few locations such as New York and Maryland. With those exceptions, the allodial system was paramount in America based on either conquest, discovery, or purchase.

PRINCIPLES OF REAL ESTATE LAW

The first step in understanding the principles of real estate law is to define terms. Real property is land and everything permanently attached to it. Under the common law, and as a general rule today, this included ownership from the center of the earth, the surface, and up to the heavens. All other property is personal property. Real estate denotes both real property and the business of real estate, including financing.

Property can change from one classification to another fairly rapidly. For example, a tree standing in a forest is real property. When it is felled, it becomes personal property and, finally, after being made into lumber and becoming part of a house, it is real property again. The term "fixture" is used to describe a piece of personal property that has been attached in such a manner that it is now considered real property. This distinction is important, since title to real property is normally transferred by a deed, while personal property is transferred by a bill of sale.

Estate

Today, when people talk about their ownership of land, they are legally talking about the type of estate they have in real estate. This is as true in America as it was in England 500 years ago. An estate is defined as an interest in real property which is measured by its potential duration. There are two recognized classifications of estate in real property: freehold and leasehold, sometimes referred to as non-freehold. The classification freehold estate is the highest form of interest possible in real property, as it involves all the rights in real property including use, passing the property to one's heirs, or selecting who is going to take it in a transfer. It is an estate of infinite duration, in that the chain of title could theoretically last forever. An example of a freehold estate would be a fee simple absolute.

On the other hand, the classification leasehold estate is an inferior interest in real property, because the owner of a leasehold interest only has the right of possession for a period of time. The owner of this interest does not have seisin, which is defined as the ability to pass title to one's heirs or assigns. An example of a leasehold estate would be a tenant's interest in leased property.

Fee Simple Absolute

There has never been nor will there ever be complete ownership of land. Examples of the restraints or limitations on ownership of land include, among others, eminent domain, adverse possession, and easements.

The greatest interest a person can have in real property is known as a fee simple absolute. Any owner of real property, whether it be a large corporation or John Doe, has a fee simple absolute if all possible rights to that piece of real property are possessed.

In order to explain a fee simple absolute, legal pedagogues use the bundle of rights concept. For example, assume that all rights (such as the right to sell, mortgage, and build on a piece of real property) are represented by "sticks," and are contained in this bundle of rights. If all of the "sticks" are present and the owner has all possible rights to the real property, then the bundle of rights is complete and is called a fee simple absolute. If a "stick" is missing, such as the right to use the property the way one wants, then the interest is less than a fee simple absolute.

Defeasible or Conditional Fee

A freehold estate, which is similar to a fee simple absolute but minus a "stick" (or a right) from the bundle of rights, is the defeasible fee simple. This is a freehold estate that could but will not necessarily last forever. An example of a defeasible fee simple occurs when conditions are placed on how the property may be used.

Grantors of land may put any restrictions they desire on how the land is to be used after it has been conveyed. There are, of course, a few exceptions, such as those that are racially oriented. Grantors can always give less than the full interests they own in conveying land, but never more. They can give possession for any desired period of time, or for any specific use—only as a church, for example. If so conveyed, a defeasible fee simple is created that could last forever, but it could also be terminated.

An example of a defeasible fee simple that would automatically end if a certain event occurs is when A grants land to B church on condition that the premises are used only for church purposes. The church has a defeasible fee simple that could last forever but will automatically end if the property ceases to be used for church purposes. When that happens, the title automatically reverts to A or A's heirs. This interest is classified as a fee simple since it could last forever if the property is always used for church purposes.

A distinction is made legally between two types of defeasible fee simple. They are a fee simple subject to a condition subsequent, and a fee simple determinable. The typical person involved in real estate does not need to know the distinction, but counsel for that person should. An example of a fee simple subject to a condition subsequent would occur when A conveys property to B as long as liquor is never sold on the premises. In this situation, the grantee B (the person to whom the land has been conveyed) has a fee simple, but it is subject to a condition subsequent in that if liquor is ever sold on the premises the land will revert to the grantor (the one making the conveyances). The grantor must make an affirmative action for the property to revert, that is, reenter the property and sue to terminate the estate.

The fee simple determinable has been described. Most courts lump these together as being basically the same. If forced to distinguish, courts attempt to find a fee on a condition subsequent in order that the grantor must reenter to terminate rather than have the estate terminate automatically.

Fee Tail

This type of estate came into being from a desire in feudal England to keep land in whole parcels within the family. A fee tail is an estate of potentially infinite duration, but is inheritable only by the grantee's lineal descendants, such as children or grandchildren. For a fee tail to be created under the common law it was necessary to state in the conveyance that the land was being transferred to A and "the heirs of his body." This differed from the wording of any other common law transfer, which required only "and his heirs" to be used.

There were various types of the fee tail. The fee tail general meant the property was inheritable by the issue of the grantee. A fee tail special meant the land was inheritable only by the issue of the grantee and a specifically named spouse. (A conveyance to A and the heirs of body, by his wife, Mary, would be an example.) A fee tail general could specify whether the issue need be male or female, and there also was the possibility of a fee tail special, male or female. Although the fee tail is still allowed in some New England states, the practical effect of it has been abolished in all states today.

Life Estates

A life estate is a freehold estate like the fee simple absolute and others already mentioned, but it is not inheritable. Life estates can be either conventional (created by the grantor) or legal (created by operation of law). The creation of a life estate is a tool often used in estate planning and is a fairly common interest in real estate. By the creation of a life estate the life tenant (the one granted the right) has the use of real estate for a period of time measured by a human life. The human life used to measure the duration of the life estate may be that of another human life, but is most commonly measured by the life of the life tenant. An example is: A conveys a life estate to B for life, and as long as B is alive, B has the right to use the real estate, with certain exceptions, as if he owned it. The only incident of ownership that B lacks is the power to pass a fee simple absolute. The right to sell or mortgage the interest is not expressly given, but a person could acquire only that which B had, which was the use of the land for a period measured by a life.

When A created this life estate, only a part of the complete interest was transferred. In other words, someone else was allowed to use the land for a period of time. However, at the expiration of that period of time, the remaining rights to the real estate are with the grantor. In the example given, where A conveyed land to B for the duration of B's life, the land will revert to A (the grantor) or A's heirs upon the death of B (the life tenant) since no other conveyance was made.

When A created the life estate in B, the remainder could have been transferred in this way: A to B for life, and then to C. In this situation, C is the vested remainderman, because the grantor has transferred the remaining interest to C. The rights of C are vested irrespective of whether C survives the life tenant or not. If a vested remainderman does die before a life tenant, then the vested remainderman's heirs would inherit the fee interest.

On the other hand, a life estate could be created this way: A to B for B's life, and then to C if C is alive, in which case C must survive B to acquire any rights to the land. If C dies before B, the land reverts to the original owner. If it is impossible to determine at the time of the creation of the life estate who definitely will take the fee simple after the death of the life tenant, the remainderman is referred to as a contingent remainderman.

Another common example of this situation would be: A to B for life, and then to B's children. B may not have any children; therefore, their interest is contingent upon their being born. To complicate it even further, the conveyance could read A to B for B's life, and then to B's surviving children. The children, if any, must survive B before they can acquire any interest.

In summary, a conventional life estate is an interest which an individual has in real estate providing most of the incidences of ownership, with the exception of the ability to pass a fee simple absolute. The person who takes possession after the life tenant dies could be either the grantor, if the grantor did not convey the remainder, or it could be a third person who would be classified as either a contingent or a vested remainderman, depending on whether the identity can be determined precisely at the time of the creation of the life estate.

In contrast with the conventional life estate, created intentionally by the grantor, a legal life estate is created by operation of the law. An example of a legal life estate is the right of dower. Dower was originally conceived to prevent a widow from being penniless during a period of English history when life insurance, welfare, and social security were unknown. Dower is a common law right of a widow still present in many jurisdictions. The equivalent right of the husband is *curtesy,* which has either been abolished or merged with dower in nearly all states.

Basically, the right of dower gives a wife, at her husband's death, a life estate in one-third of the real estate owned by her husband during marriage. Generally, the widow has a choice of which real estate will be subject to her dower right, and this right is applicable to all real estate owned by the husband during the marriage, even if he had transferred it before death. In those states where this right exists, a wife's potential dower interest is extinguished if she executes a deed with her husband transferring the land to another.

Currently, in some states, the right of dower has been abolished as unnecessary. This is probably because the need for a right such as dower has been eliminated in most states by the creation of a statutory right of each spouse to a minimum one-third share of the decedent's estate, and because of life insurance, social security, and other benefits.

LEASEHOLDS ESTATES (NON-FREEHOLD ESTATES)

As mentioned earlier, this estate gives the owner the right to possession of real estate for a period of time. The actual duration may or may not be ascertainable at the beginning, but it does not carry with it the ability to pass title to the real estate. The owner of the land (the fee) has given up possession for a period of time, but retains the legal title to the real estate, and the owner (or heirs or assigns) will eventually retake possession. The legal term to describe the missing element in a leasehold estate is seisin.

Although the use of leases can be traced to the beginning of written history, the leasehold estate in England was originally used to circumvent the prohibition against lending money for interest since any interest was usury under early church law. The person borrowing money would allow the lender to use some or all of the land for a period of time in lieu of interest. Therefore, under the common law, a leasehold was considered personal property, but now is considered an estate in real estate. A lease, which creates the leasehold estate, is a peculiar instrument in that it is both a conveyance giving the tenant possession for a period of time, and a contract establishing rights and duties for the parties. The essential elements for a lease are:

- name of landlord and tenant
- agreement to lease
- description of leased property
- duration of lease
- rental agreement
- rights and duties of the parties
- signature

A lease for a year or less may be verbal or in writing, but one for more than a year must be in writing. For the safety of both the landlord and tenant, all leases should be in writing. Most states have a 99-year limitation on a lease, although the vast majority of leases are for less than 10 years. The degree of complexity in leases increases from the relatively simple residential lease to the very complex shopping center lease. The type of tenancy acquired from a lease depends on whether or not the term is renewable and whether notice to terminate must be given by either party.

Additional Interests in Real Estate

In addition to the freehold and leasehold estates in real estate, there are certain other limited interests or rights to real estate. These include easements, profits, and covenants. The effect of these interests is to create a limited right to the real estate of another, although the fact that a piece of real property is subject to an easement, for instance, does not prevent it from being owned in fee simple absolute.

Easements   An easement is a non-possessory interest in the real estate of another, giving the holder the right to a limited use of real estate. An example is the right to drive across the real estate of another to reach a highway. An easement is either in gross (a personal right) or appurtenant (belonging to whoever owns the benefitted real estate). Although most easements are expressed in writing, they can be simply implied. The right of a gas company to install a gas line on a back property line is an example of an expressed easement appurtenant.

Profit   A profit resembles an easement because the holder has an interest in the real estate of another. However, a profit creates the right to enter the property of another and take a portion of the property, such as the soil, or the product of the property, such as trees or oil.

Covenant   Like the previous interests discussed, this interest is in the real estate of another. The difference between a covenant or a promise to do or not to do something and other interests is that the former restricts or limits how the owner can use the real estate. An example of a covenant is the requirement a farmer may put on the part of a farm being sold that the grantee use the real estate only for residential purposes. This interest is of benefit to the grantor because it allows control of the use of the real estate. Therefore, it is an interest in the real estate of another. This interest can be either in gross or appurtenant, although the term often used with covenants is running with the land. This interest should not be confused with a defeasible fee simple since title cannot be lost if a covenant is breached— only damages or an injunction can be sought.

JOINT OR CONCURRENT OWNERSHIP

Joint Tenancy

Ownership in land can be and usually is held by more than one person. The most common type of joint or concurrent ownership is joint tenancy, which can exist between any two or more persons. Although joint tenants share a single title to the real estate, each owns an equal share of the whole. Joint tenancies are quite common, but a few states have abolished or limited them for reasons that will be discussed later. Most states will allow the creation of a joint tenancy by simply referring to A and B as joint tenants. But other jurisdictions require reference to A and B as joint tenants with the right of survivorship. This interest can be created only by affirmative action of the grantor, not by operation of law.

The right of survivorship is the key concept of a joint tenancy. Upon the death of one of the joint tenants, all the deceased's interests in the real property terminate and the ownership in the land is retained by the surviving joint tenant or tenants. In other words, a joint tenancy is not an inheritable estate. Therefore, it does not pass through the estate of the decedent and does not pass to the heirs. Instead, it passes to or is possessed automatically by the surviving joint tenants. For this reason, some states have abolished joint tenancy, and most courts disfavor joint tenancy because it automatically prevents property from flowing through the estate of an individual to the heirs. Therefore, if one wishes to create a joint tenancy, it is mandatory to follow the strict statutory requirements of the respective state. To avoid the possibility that a court could misunderstand a grantor's intention, a joint tenancy should be created by using this phrase: to A and B, as joint tenants with right of survivorship and not as tenants in common.

During the time a joint tenancy is in existence, the portion of the whole belonging to any one of the joint tenants usually may be attached to satisfy that individual's legal debts. But the portion belonging to the other joint tenant(s) may not. Some states have laws that modify this approach if the joint tenants are man and wife and the property in question is their home.

Although any joint tenant may sell or mortgage their interest (with some exceptions for married joint tenants), the effect is a termination of the joint tenancy by either a voluntary or involuntary transfer. It is also terminated by the death of one of two joint tenants, but not by the death of one of more than two. The survivors in that case still have a joint tenancy among themselves.

Under the common law, if both parties did not acquire ownership to real estate at the same time, a joint tenancy could not exist. Consequently, a husband owning property before marriage could not create a joint tenancy with his wife. One method devised to circumvent this requirement was the usage of a "straw man." For instance, the husband would convey title to his real estate to a friend or relative (the so-called "straw man") who would then transfer the title back to the husband and wife as joint tenants, and the unit of time requirement would be satisfied.

Tenancy by the Entirety

A form of concurrent ownership much like joint tenancy is tenancy by the entirety, which is allowed in about 20 states. The reason for its existence is because of a vestige from the common law of some technical requirement for a joint tenancy, such as the unity of time, or because the state had abolished joint tenancy. The primary difference between this form of ownership and the joint tenancy is that a tenancy by the entirety can exist only between a legally married husband and wife, while a joint tenancy can exist between any two or more persons.

Another important feature of a tenancy by the entirety is that the interest of one of the parties cannot be attached for the legal debts of that person. Only if the debts are of both parties can an attachment be made. For this reason, both a husband and wife in some states will be asked to sign the mortgage note if the form of ownership of the real estate is to be as tenants by the entirety, even if only one has income. Many states allowing tenancy by the entirety presume that a conveyance to a husband and wife, silent as to the type of ownership, will be a tenancy by the entirety.

The surviving tenant becomes the sole owner like the surviving joint tenant, but this survivorship right stems from the concept that the husband and wife were one, so ownership was already with the survivor. Divorce or annulment will terminate this tenancy.

Tenants in Common

Tenancy in common is a concurrent estate with no right of survivorship. Therefore, when a person dies, the interest held in the real property passes through the estate. This interest can exist between any two or more individuals and, in effect, jointly gives them the rights and duties of a sole owner. Each of the co-tenants is considered an owner of an undivided interest (not necessarily equal) in the whole property, and each has separate legal title, unlike joint tenants who share a single title. Courts of law look with favor on a tenancy in common, because a co-tenant's share of ownership passes upon death to the heirs and is not forfeited. As contrasted with a joint tenancy or a tenancy by the entirety, a tenancy in common can arise by operation of law; for example, when a person dies intestate (without a will), heirs automatically inherit as tenants in common.

Any tenant in common can sell his interest, mortgage it, or have it attached for debts without destroying the joint interest. A grantee of a tenancy in common acquires only the percentage of the whole owned by the grantor. A tenancy in common is terminated by agreement between the parties or upon a petition to a court.

Community Property

Another form of concurrent ownership is community property, which is the law primarily in those states located in the western part of the United States. Basically, the concept is that half of all property, personal and real, created during marriage belongs to each spouse. The underlying theory of this concept is that both have contributed to the creation of the family's wealth, even though only one was gainfully employed. There are three exceptions to this rule:

1. Property acquired from separate funds, such as a trust account.
2. Property acquired individually before the marriage.
3. Property inherited from another's estate.

With these exceptions, if the necessity of terminating the marriage occurs each should receive a one-half share. Since each has equal interests, both must sign a mortgage note and security agreement.

Tenancy in Partnership

The last form of concurrent ownership is tenancy in partnership. Under the common law, a partnership could not own real estate in its partnership name. Therefore, one of the partners had to own the real estate in his or her own name. This presented the possibility of fraud. The Uniform Partnership Act, as adopted by many states, provides that a partnership can own real property in its firm's name. Upon the death of a partner in a partnership, the surviving partners are vested with the share of the decedent or a percentage ownership of all property owned by the partnership. One partner's share of ownership may not necessarily be equal to that of another. It is quite common for partnerships to provide for a means of compensation for a deceased partner's estate, usually by insurance or a buy-sell agreement.

TRANSFER OF LAND

All title to real estate in America can be traced to one of three origins: conquest, discovery, or purchase. Today, title to real property can be transferred either voluntarily or involuntarily.

Voluntary Transfers

Most transfers of land are voluntary in that a grantor usually intends to transfer title to land to a grantee by the use of a deed or possibly a will. A deed is a legal instrument that purports to transfer a grantor's interest. If a grantor had no actual interest in a particular piece of real estate, an executed deed would transfer nothing. In addition, a properly executed deed from a grantor who did have title but lacked legal capacity (the grantor was legally insane, for example) would also transfer nothing. The validity of the title of the grantor can be determined by abstracting or checking the chain of title for defects.

All states have a law known as a statute of frauds requiring written transfers of real estate. Today, technical words are not needed in a deed, since any words that clearly show the grantor's intention to transfer are sufficient.

There are eight essential elements of a modern deed:

1. Grantor's name
2. Grantee's name

3. Description of real estate to be conveyed
4. Consideration (does not have to be actual amount paid)
5. Words of conveyance
6. Signature of grantor
7. Delivery and acceptances
8. Proper execution

Three basic types of deeds are used, each having a specific purpose and function to perform. The least complicated is a quit claim deed which is used to clear title to real estate. A person signing this deed makes no title guarantee. Instead, a grantor is simply transferring whatever interest is owned, if any. This deed can be used to clear a cloud on the title caused by a widow having a potential right of dower. She would be requested to execute the deed, possibly for a fee, whereby she transferred whatever interest she had (in this case dower), thus clearing the title.

A general warranty deed is the most common deed used to transfer interest in real estate. With this deed a grantor guarantees to a grantee that the title transferred is good against the whole world. This guarantee extends past the grantor to those in the chain of title. If a grantor refuses to use this deed, it may be an indication that the title is defective.

The special warranty deed is a relatively rare deed used in situations where a grantor wants to limit the guarantee. This instrument would be used by an executor of an estate to convey real estate to those specified in a will. By this deed the grantor only guarantees that nothing was done to interfere with the title to the real estate while under the grantor's control and makes no guarantee about a decedent's claim to the real estate.

Real estate that passes according to a will is also a voluntary conveyance, since it passes as the testator or the one making the will intended.

Involuntary Transfers

An involuntary conveyance occurs when a legal owner of real estate loses title contrary to the owner's intention. An example of this would be eminent domain. Any sovereign in the United States (federal, state, city, or county) and some quasi-public entities (such as the telephone company or gas line company) can exercise the right of eminent domain. This right is inherent in a sovereign and is not granted by a constitution, although it is limited by it. The key elements are that it must be exercised for a valid public purpose or use, and that it requires compensation to be paid the legal owner.

Another example of involuntary transfer of title is adverse possession. The public policy behind the doctrine of adverse possession is the encouragement of the usage of land, in addition to settling old claims to real property. Normally, a person possessing the real property of another holds that real estate for the legal owner's benefit. But if certain requirements are satisfied, the one occupying the real property could acquire legal title.

To claim title to real property by adverse possession, the one occupying the real property must prove:

- actual possession
- hostile intent
- notorious and open possession
- exclusive and continuous possession
- possession for a statutory period (which ranges from 5 to 20 years)

Some states also require that the party claiming title by adverse possession base the claim on some written instrument—even if the instrument is not valid. Other states require the claimant to pay real estate taxes for the statutory period.

Other examples of the possibility of involuntary transfer would include foreclosure and subsequent sale if an owner of real estate does not pay the mortgage, real estate tax, or other encumbrances.

When a person dies intestate the title to real property along with the personal property passes, not according to the dictates of the owner, but according to the statutes of that particular state. If the individual had no discernible heirs, the property would escheat (pass) to the state.

Recording

Any time an interest in real estate is being created, transferred, or encumbered, that transaction should be recorded. As in England centuries ago, the reason for recording is to prevent fraud. For example, situations existed where the owner of land would sell, possibly inadvertently, the same real estate to two or more innocent purchasers. Therefore, it was necessary to develop a system by which fraudulent transactions could be prevented. This was accomplished by devising a system of recording transactions affecting real estate. In order to protect a buyer's interest, recording statutes require purchasers of real estate to record the instrument by which they acquired the interest. If recorded, any subsequent purchaser will have either actual knowledge of the prior interest (because he checked the record), or constructive notice (because if he did check he would have discovered the interest).

If the party (the prior purchaser, for instance) who could have prevented a subsequent fraud by recording does not record, then that party will suffer the loss. An individual who wants to purchase real property has an obligation to check the record, usually in a county courthouse, to determine if there have been any transactions involving that particular real estate. Recording gives constructive notice to the whole world that a party has acquired an interest in a particular real property. Therefore, any subsequent purchaser could not acquire the same interest.

If no transaction appears, an innocent purchaser acquiring an interest will be protected against the whole world, even against a prior purchaser.

In summary, a prior purchaser is protected if a record is made, whether a subsequent purchaser checks the record or not. The same is true if there is actual notice. If A sold land to B, and B failed to record, and C, knowing of that transaction, buys the same land and records, B will be protected since C had actual notice of the transaction between A and B. If C did not have actual notice and recorded before B, C would be protected in any dispute between B and C.

All states have a "race statute" which dictates that the first of two innocent parties to record will be protected.

SECURITY INSTRUMENTS AND THEIR FUNCTION ══════ *16*

In all segments of our economy a lender will normally require some security or collateral to protect itself against nonperformance of a borrower. This protection may take the form of a conditional sales contract, an installment sales contract, or some other form. In real estate transactions it takes the form of either a mortgage or a deed of trust.

A mortgage and a deed of trust (sometimes called a trust deed or trust indenture) are alternate forms of real estate finance security instruments used throughout the United States. The purpose of each is to provide an instrument whereby a mortgage lender can obtain a security interest in the real estate which is securing a debt.

As used in the United States today, the mortgage is unique in many features, but its fundamentals are based on the common law as it has developed in England over the past 900 years.

HISTORICAL DEVELOPMENT

The classic common law mortgage, which developed in England after the Norman invasion in 1066, was well developed and established by 1400. Basically it was an actual conveyance—a title transfer—of real estate serving as security for a debt. For a conveyance to be effective under the common law, possession of that real estate actually had to pass, putting the mortgagee in possession of the real estate.

The instrument conveying the real estate title to the mortgagee contained a defeasance clause whereby the mortgagee's title was defeated if payment was made on the due date, called the law day. Originally, when title and possession were in the hands of the mortgagee, all rents and profits generated by the land could be retained by the mortgagee. This practice was established because a mortgagee could not charge interest on a loan; any interest was usury, which was illegal at this time. After this law changed and interest could be charged, the mortgagee was forced to credit all rents and profits to the mortgagor.

Early common law mortgages did not require any action on behalf of mortgagees to protect their rights if a mortgagor failed to perform. Since a conveyance had already been made, the mortgagee had title and possession and thus the only effect of the mortgagor's nonperformance was the termination of the possibility of reversion through the defeasance clause.

The harsh result of a mortgagor not performing after the due date, even when not personally at fault, led mortgagors to petition the King for redress from an inequitable practice. Eventually, the courts of equity gave relief to mortgagors by allowing them to redeem their real estate through payment with interest of past due debts. This was called the equity of redemption. By 1625, this practice had become so widespread that mortgagees were reluctant to lend money with real estate as security since they never knew when a mortgagor might elect to redeem the real estate. Mortgagees attempted to change this by inserting a clause in mortgages whereby the mortgagor agreed not to seek this redress. But courts of equity refused to allow the practice and would not enforce the clause. In order to restore an equitable balance, the courts began to decree that a mortgagor had a certain amount of time after default, usually six months, in which to redeem the real estate. If this were not done, the mortgagor's equity of redemption would be cancelled or foreclosed. This action soon became known as a foreclosure suit and is still used in some states today.

AMERICAN MORTGAGE LAW

In American law, the most important change in the common law that has occurred relates to the concept of who actually owns the real estate that is serving as security for the performance of an obligation. The common law held that the mortgagee was the legal owner of the real estate while it served as security. This was called the title theory; the mortgagee held title. Shortly after the Revolutionary War, a New Jersey court held that a mortgagor did not lose title to real estate serving as security. The court's reasoning was that since the law already recognized the right of a mortgagor to redeem the real estate after default, the law had to accept a continuing ownership interest in the mortgagor. The court held that a mortgage created only a security interest for the mortgagee and that title should therefore remain with the mortgagor. This is the law in 28 states today and is called the lien theory. Although 23 states still classify themselves as either intermediate or title theory states, all states recognize the mortgagor as the legal owner of the real estate. The principal difference between these two theories is in the manner of foreclosure. Currently, mortgagors are able to do as they please with mortgaged real estate as long as the activity does not interfere with the security interest of a mortgagee.

According to current law, any interest in real estate that can be sold can be mortgaged, including a fee simple, a life estate, or a lease. The determining factor is whether a mortgagee can be found willing to lend money with that particular interest as security.

THE SECURITY INTEREST

The Note: Mortgage Debt

The debt secured by a mortgage is evidenced by either a promissory note or a bond. The note is the promise to pay. Normally, the mortgage and the note are separate documents, but in some jurisdictions they are combined. The note should be negotiable so that the originating mortgagee can assign it. This is the normal practice today for most mortgage lenders. Both Fannie Mae and Freddie Mac use the same uniform notes which meet all legal requirements for each of the states. These uniform notes are the ones that all mortgage lenders should use since they contain well-conceived and tested language which protects the rights of both the borrower and lender.

The mortgage instrument, discussed below, must in one way or another acknowledge and identify the debt it secures. When the entire debt is paid (satisfied), the note and the mortgage which secures the debt lose their effectiveness and no longer create a valid lien. A notice of satisfaction, or notice of full payment of a note and mortgage, should be recorded when the debt is paid. This recording is done to clear the cloud on the title created by the mortgage.

As mentioned, the uniform note provides protection for the various parties and also establishes important provisions such as what the interest rate is, how repayment will be made, etc. For example, the note should state that the first payment is due on the first of the month following a full month after closing (if a loan closed on May 15, the first payment would be due on July 1st). Other items that are important include the following:

- Need original signatures.
- All blanks must be filled and any corrections must be initialed (no whiteouts).
- Interest rate, payment schedule, and due dates must be clear.
- Date of note and mortgage must match.
- Use appropriate uniform note for loan type.

The Mortgage Instrument

The mortgage instrument which creates the security interest in the real estate for the lender does not have to appear in any particular form. There are no set requirements except that a mortgage instrument be in writing. Any wording that

NOTE

.......May 3,............................, 19 89...   ....Staten Island.................., ...New York..........
                                                                   [City]   [State]

59 Silver Lane...   Staten Island, New York 103 __15__
                                                     [Property Address]

1. BORROWER'S PROMISE TO PAY

In return for a loan that I have received, I promise to pay U.S. $ __80,000.00__...................... (this amount is called "principal"), plus interest, to the order of the Lender. The Lender is ....Staten Island Savings Bank,.......................
81 Water Street, Staten Island, New York 10304.....................
.... I understand that the Lender may transfer this Note. The Lender or anyone who takes this Note by transfer and who is entitled to receive payments under this Note is called the "Note Holder."

2. INTEREST

Interest will be charged on unpaid principal until the full amount of principal has been paid. I will pay interest at a yearly rate of ...10.50......%.

The interest rate required by this Section 2 is the rate I will pay both before and after any default described in Section 6(B) of this Note.

3. PAYMENTS

(A) Time and Place of Payments

I will pay principal and interest by making payments every month.

I will make my monthly payments on the ....1st.... day of each month beginning on ....July 1,.............................., 19...89.... I will make these payments every month until I have paid all of the principal and interest and any other charges described below that I may owe under this Note. My monthly payments will be applied to interest before principal. If, on June 1, 2019..................., ..., I still owe amounts under this Note, I will pay those amounts in full on that date, which is called the "maturity date."

I will make my monthly payments at ....81 Water Street, Staten Island..................
New York 10304.. or at a different place if required by the Note Holder.

(B) Amount of Monthly Payments

My monthly payment will be in the amount of U.S. $..731.80................................

4. BORROWER'S RIGHT TO PREPAY

I have the right to make payments of principal at any time before they are due. A payment of principal only is known as a "prepayment." When I make a prepayment, I will tell the Note Holder in writing that I am doing so.

I may make a full prepayment or partial prepayments without paying any prepayment charge. The Note Holder will use all of my prepayments to reduce the amount of principal that I owe under this Note. If I make a partial prepayment, there will be no changes in the due date or in the amount of my monthly payment unless the Note Holder agrees in writing to those changes.

5. LOAN CHARGES

If a law, which applies to this loan and which sets maximum loan charges, is finally interpreted so that the interest or other loan charges collected or to be collected in connection with this loan exceed the permitted limits, then: (i) any such loan charge shall be reduced by the amount necessary to reduce the charge to the permitted limit; and (ii) any sums already collected from me which exceeded permitted limits will be refunded to me. The Note Holder may choose to make this refund by reducing the principal I owe under this Note or by making a direct payment to me. If a refund reduces principal, the reduction will be treated as a partial prepayment.

6. BORROWER'S FAILURE TO PAY AS REQUIRED

(A) Late Charge for Overdue Payments

If the Note Holder has not received the full amount of any monthly payment by the end of ....15......... calendar days after the date it is due, I will pay a late charge to the Note Holder. The amount of the charge will be ......2.....% of my overdue payment of principal and interest. I will pay this late charge promptly but only once on each late payment.

(B) Default

If I do not pay the full amount of each monthly payment on the date it is due, I will be in default.

(C) Notice of Default

If I am in default, the Note Holder may send me a written notice telling me that if I do not pay the overdue amount by a certain date, the Note Holder may require me to pay immediately the full amount of principal which has not been paid and all the interest that I owe on that amount. That date must be at least 30 days after the date on which the notice is delivered or mailed to me.

(D) No Waiver By Note Holder

Even if, at a time when I am in default, the Note Holder does not require me to pay immediately in full as described above, the Note Holder will still have the right to do so if I am in default at a later time.

(E) Payment of Note Holder's Costs and Expenses

If the Note Holder has required me to pay immediately in full as described above, the Note Holder will have the right to be paid back by me for all of its costs and expenses in enforcing this Note to the extent not prohibited by applicable law. Those expenses include, for example, reasonable attorneys' fees.

7. GIVING OF NOTICES

Unless applicable law requires a different method, any notice that must be given to me under this Note will be given by delivering it or by mailing it by first class mail to me at the Property Address above or at a different address if I give the Note Holder a notice of my different address.

Any notice that must be given to the Note Holder under this Note will be given by mailing it by first class mail to the Note Holder at the address stated in Section 3(A) above or at a different address if I am given a notice of that different address.

MULTISTATE FIXED RATE NOTE—Single Family—FNMA/FHLMC UNIFORM INSTRUMENT   Form 3200 12/83

230

8. OBLIGATIONS OF PERSONS UNDER THIS NOTE

If more than one person signs this Note, each person is fully and personally obligated to keep all of the promises made in this Note, including the promise to pay the full amount owed. Any person who is a guarantor, surety or endorser of this Note is also obligated to do these things. Any person who takes over these obligations, including the obligations of a guarantor, surety or endorser of this Note, is also obligated to keep all of the promises made in this Note. The Note Holder may enforce its rights under this Note against each person individually or against all of us together. This means that any one of us may be required to pay all of the amounts owed under this Note.

9. WAIVERS

I and any other person who has obligations under this Note waive the rights of presentment and notice of dishonor. "Presentment" means the right to require the Note Holder to demand payment of amounts due. "Notice of dishonor" means the right to require the Note Holder to give notice to other persons that amounts due have not been paid.

10. UNIFORM SECURED NOTE

This Note is a uniform instrument with limited variations in some jurisdictions. In addition to the protections given to the Note Holder under this Note, a Mortgage, Deed of Trust or Security Deed (the "Security Instrument"), dated the same date as this Note, protects the Note Holder from possible losses which might result if I do not keep the promises which I make in this Note. That Security Instrument describes how and under what conditions I may be required to make immediate payment in full of all amounts I owe under this Note. Some of those conditions are described as follows:

Transfer of the Property or a Beneficial Interest in Borrower. If all or any part of the Property or any interest in it is sold or transferred (or if a beneficial interest in Borrower is sold or transferred and Borrower is not a natural person) without Lender's prior written consent, Lender may, at its option, require immediate payment in full of all sums secured by this Security Instrument. However, this option shall not be exercised by Lender if exercise is prohibited by federal law as of the date of this Security Instrument.

If Lender exercises this option, Lender shall give Borrower notice of acceleration. The notice shall provide a period of not less than 30 days from the date the notice is delivered or mailed within which Borrower must pay all sums secured by this Security Instrument. If Borrower fails to pay these sums prior to the expiration of this period, Lender may invoke any remedies permitted by this Security Instrument without further notice or demand on Borrower.

WITNESS THE HAND(S) AND SEAL(S) OF THE UNDERSIGNED.

....(Seal)
John Smith   -Borrower

....(Seal)
Susan Smith   -Borrower

WITNESS:

....(Seal)
Maria Puglia   -Borrower

[Sign Original Only]

clearly indicates that purpose of the instrument, which is to create a security interest in described real estate for the benefit of a mortgagee, is sufficient. Today, most mortgage lenders have adopted the Fannie Mae and Freddie Mac uniform mortgage instrument used in their particular state.

What Is and Isn't a Mortgage

If a conveyance is made to a mortgagee that appears to be a deed absolute but is actually intended to be a conveyance as security for a debt, all state courts have uniformly held that transaction to be a mortgage even if the defeasance clause is missing. On the other hand, if the parties agree in writing that money will be advanced, with the debt for those funds secured by a later mortgage, and a mortgage is not executed, the law holds that a creditor has a security interest in the real estate. This interest is called an equitable mortgage.

A valid mortgage instrument should include:

- names of the mortgagor and mortgagee
- words of conveyance or a mortgaging clause

- amount of the debt
- interest rate and terms of payment
- a repeat of the provisions of the promissory note or bond in some jurisdictions
- description of the real estate securing the debt
- clauses to protect the rights of the parties
- date (same date as note)
- signature of the mortgagor (and notarized, if required)
- any requirements particular to that jurisdiction

Clauses to Protect the Rights of the Parties

The aforementioned elements are the framework upon which a complete mortgage instrument is built. A mortgage instrument, such as the Fannie Mae and Freddie Mac uniform mortgage or deed of trust, will contain clauses to solve all foreseeable problems. Of course there are many types of mortgage clauses, but the most typical and important ones are the acceleration clause, the prepayment clause, and the payment clause.

Acceleration clause   The acceleration clause is the most important clause in the entire mortgage for the protection of the mortgagee. This clause is generally found in both the mortgage and the instrument that evidences the debt. It states that the entire amount of the debt can be accelerated at the mortgagee's election if the mortgagor defaults or breaches any stated covenant. (In some states, automatic acceleration clauses are allowed, but these should be avoided if possible because other options for curing defaults or breaches are available to the mortgagee and may be more beneficial.)

The most common defaults or breaches of covenants by a mortgagor that could trigger acceleration are:

- failure to pay principal and interest when due
- failure to pay taxes or insurance when due
- failure to maintain the property
- committing waste (destructive use of property)

Recently, some mortgagees have inserted clauses providing for acceleration if a mortgagor either further mortgages the secured real estate or sells the real estate with the mortgage still attached. This clause ostensibly protects the mortgagee from a change in risk.

Prepayment clause   A mortgagee, especially an institutional investor, lends money with the expectation that it will be repaid over a period of time at a certain, usually fixed, rate as stipulated in the mortgage. The mortgagee relies on this

——————————————————— [Space Above This Line For Recording Data] ———————————————————

DEED OF TRUST

THIS DEED OF TRUST ("Security Instrument") is made on ....,
19........... The grantor is ....
.... ("Borrower"). The trustee is ....
.... ("Trustee"). The beneficiary is ....
...., which is organized and existing
under the laws of ...., and whose address is ....
.... ("Lender").
Borrower owes Lender the principal sum of ....
.... Dollars (U.S.$..). This debt is
evidenced by Borrower's note dated the same date as this Security Instrument ("Note"), which provides for monthly
payments, with the full debt, if not paid earlier, due and payable on ....
This Security Instrument secures to Lender: (a) the repayment of the debt evidenced by the Note, with interest, and all
renewals, extensions and modifications; (b) the payment of all other sums, with interest, advanced under paragraph 7 to
protect the security of this Security Instrument; and (c) the performance of Borrower's covenants and agreements under
this Security Instrument and the Note. For this purpose, Borrower irrevocably grants and conveys to Trustee, in trust,
with power of sale, the following described property located in .... County, Montana:

which has the address of ...., ...,
                                                          [Street]   [City]
Montana .... ("Property Address");
              [Zip Code]

TOGETHER WITH all the improvements now or hereafter erected on the property, and all easements, rights,
appurtenances, rents, royalties, mineral, oil and gas rights and profits, water rights and stock and all fixtures now or
hereafter a part of the property. All replacements and additions shall also be covered by this Security Instrument. All of the
foregoing is referred to in this Security Instrument as the "Property."

BORROWER COVENANTS that Borrower is lawfully seised of the estate hereby conveyed and has the right to grant
and convey the Property and that the Property is unencumbered, except for encumbrances of record. Borrower warrants
and will defend generally the title to the Property against all claims and demands, subject to any encumbrances of record.

THIS SECURITY INSTRUMENT combines uniform covenants for national use and non-uniform covenants with
limited variations by jurisdiction to constitute a uniform security instrument covering real property.

MONTANA—Single Family—**FNMA/FHLMC UNIFORM INSTRUMENT**   Form 3027 12/83

schedule of repayment to determine future financial strategy, and could be at an
economic disadvantage if forced to accept early payments. This disadvantage
would be the result of either having to give up a high interest rate or having to
reinvest the funds immediately.

As a general rule, a mortgagee does not have to accept early payment unless
so obligated in the mortgage itself or by state law. If a mortgagor desires the option

of early payment, the provision should be negotiated before the mortgage is executed and should be included in the mortgage. Many mortgagees will stipulate in the mortgage that prepayment can be made if a penalty is paid—usually a certain percentage of the outstanding debt. Mortgagees may waive this penalty if they want to remove low-yielding mortgages from their portfolios, but a mortgagor would normally have no desire to prepay a mortgage with a low interest rate. Since 1979, mortgages sold to FNMA or FHLMC may not include a prepayment penalty. Most alternative mortgage instruments do give a mortgagor the privilege of prepaying.

Payment clause   The most obvious clause in a mortgage is the one by which a mortgagor agrees to pay the obligation in an agreed-upon manner. Reference usually is made to the note or bond whereby a mortgagor was obligated to pay a certain amount of money. A separate clause may stipulate a covenant to pay taxes and hazard insurance (with a mortgage-payable clause) as they become due. However, this often is a part of the payment clause. A mortgagee may require taxes and insurance to be placed in escrow and collected monthly as part of the mortgage payment.

Deeds of Trust

Before deeds of trust can be used in any state, special enabling legislation must be enacted. This is required since the deed of trust was not known in the common law. One of the basic legal differences between a mortgage and a deed of trust is that a mortgage is a two-party instrument between a mortgagor and a mortgagee, while a deed of trust is a three-party instrument between a borrower, a lender, and a third party, called a trustee. If a deed of trust is used, a borrower conveys title to a trustee who holds it until the obligation is satisfied, at which time title is conveyed back to the borrower. The title is held for the benefit of the lender.

Another theoretical difference is the necessity of a mortgagee foreclosing on a mortgage if there has been a default. On the other hand, in most states there is no requirement for a foreclosure, with its time-consuming court proceedings, if a deed of trust is used. Instead, the trustee has the power of sale to satisfy the debt. Some states, however, require a foreclosure even if the financing vehicle is a deed of trust. Regardless of the situation, there is always a requirement for a public notice of sale.

In using a deed of trust there is generally no statutory right of redemption, as there is with a mortgage. This is one of the more important reasons why a mortgagee would use a deed of trust rather than a mortgage. In many jurisdictions, a mortgagor has a period of time to redeem the property after default and foreclosure. If the right to redeem exists, this period varies from six months to two years, depending on state law. To a mortgagor, the advantage of a deed of trust is that a mortgagee does not have the right to a deficiency judgment. A deficiency judgment is the result of a lawsuit to make up the difference between the amount obtained at a foreclosure sale and the mortgage obligation.

TRANSFERS OF MORTGAGED REAL ESTATE

In all jurisdictions, whether the title or lien theory is followed, the mortgagor has the ability to transfer real estate that is serving as security for a debt and has options on the method of transfer.

Free and clear   The grantor (the one transferring) could transfer the land free and clear. This would occur if a mortgagor satisfied the obligation secured by the real estate and presumes that the mortgage could be prepaid. In such an event, a prepayment penalty might be required. Much mortgaged real estate sold today is transferred in this manner, with the new owner obtaining new financing. The reason for this is inflation, which has produced increased equity in real estate. The value of this equity is more than a purchaser would want to buy for cash. Therefore, a new purchaser normally would rather finance the purchase price than assume the mortgage and pay cash for the equity. During periods of exceedingly high interest rates, as occurred in 1979-81, purchasers may desire to assume an existing lower interest rate mortgage and pay cash or use another financing technique for the equity.

Subject to the mortgage   The grantor could transfer the real estate subject to the mortgage, with the grantee (the one to whom the property is transferred) paying the grantor for any equity. If this occurs, the original mortgage remains effective and the personal liability of the original mortgagor to pay the mortgage continues, although the mortgage payment will probably be made by the grantee from that point on. The grantee becomes the legal owner of the real estate after the sale, although it continues to serve as security for the original mortgage. The grantee assumes no personal liability for the original mortgage payment and could decide to abandon the real estate with no danger of contingent liability. If the grantee stops the mortgage payment and the mortgagee forecloses, the grantee loses only equity in the real estate while the original mortgagor is liable for any amount of the obligation not satisfied by the sale of the mortgaged real estate.

Assumption of the mortgage   The real estate could be transferred to the grantee, who would buy the grantor's equity and assume the mortgage. This is the most common manner in which real estate is transferred in those cases where the existing mortgage remains intact. In this situation, the grantee assumes personal liability for satisfying the mortgage debt, while the original mortgagor retains only secondary liability.

Recently, some mortgagees have inserted clauses into conventional mortgages to either prohibit the transfer of the mortgage or make the transfer conditional on the approval of the mortgagee. Other mortgagees, especially savings and loan institutions, have inserted due-on-sale clauses in conventional mortgages, which accelerate the entire debt if the real estate is sold with the mortgage still intact. The stated rationale for such a clause is to protect the mortgagee's security interest by forcing the new mortgagor to meet the mortgagee's underwriting requirements. Often, however, the real reason is to force the grantee to assume an increase in the interest rate from the rate on the assumed mortgage to the higher current rate. The validity of these clauses evolved to the point where many courts enforced the mortgagee's right to accelerate. In 1982, a provision of the Garn–St. Germain bill preempted state laws and limited the enforceability of due-on-sale clauses until October 1985. After that date, states may allow enforcement again.

Many mortgagors, after selling the real estate to the grantee who assumes the mortgage, have requested that the mortgagee sign a novation contract which would end any secondary liability on the part of the original mortgagor. Many mortgagees have agreed to sign, but normally they require that the assuming grantee agree to an increase in the interest rate to the level of the prevailing rate.

Assignment of Mortgages

Many originators of mortgage loans, such as mortgage bankers, originate loans for sale to other investors. Any mortgage lender has the right to assign a mortgage even if the mortgagor is unaware of the assignment.

The instrument by which mortgages are assigned should be in writing and the assignment should be recorded immediately to protect the investor from another assignment. At the time of assignment, the mortgagor may be required to sign an estoppel certificate. This is a statement by a mortgagor that there is a binding obligation not yet satisfied, and that the mortgagor has no defenses against the mortgagee. An assigned mortgage has full effect and the mortgage payments may be made directly to the assignee or through the original mortgagee.

DEFAULT

A mortgagor who breaches any of the covenants in a mortgage is considered to be in default. A default is normally caused by a nonpayment of principal and interest, but also could result from a failure to pay taxes, provide hazard insurance, or maintain the premises. A mortgage instrument is usually worded in such a manner that the mortgagee has certain options in the event of a default. Even if automatic acceleration is required in a mortgage, it may not be the best choice for a mortgagee and is certainly not the best alternative for a mortgagor.

There are many reasons why a mortgagor defaults on mortgage obligations. The more common reasons for residential mortgage defaults read like a list of personal tragedies, and usually are:

- loss of employment
- strike
- death of a wage earner
- credit over-extension or bankruptcy
- illness of a wage earner or mounting family medical expenses
- marital problems

In practically all situations, a mortgagee does not want to foreclose if it can be prevented. Although the average consumer may not believe it, mortgagees not only dislike foreclosure, but generally lose money if they must foreclose. After all, most mortgagees are in the business of lending money, not owning or managing real property.

Typically, a loan is delinquent 30 days before a mortgagee or its agent (e.g., a mortgage banker) takes any action. This delay is primarily because of the awareness that people may occasionally miss a payment because of vacation, forgetfulness, or some other logical reason. Although most mortgages provide for acceleration 30 days after the due date for a payment, few are immediately accelerated.

After 30 days, a mortgagee or its agent will attempt to contact the mortgagor to determine why a required payment has not been received. This initial inquiry may enable a mortgagee to resolve whatever problem exists and, after charging a late fee to partially offset additional expenses, allow the mortgage to continue. If the mortgage is FHA-insured, however, the mortgagee may not be able to accelerate if the mortgagor has submitted at least 50 percent of past due amounts.

If the mortgagee does not charge a late fee or accelerate the debt, but instead reinstates the mortgage, it still retains all options, including the right to accelerate for future defaults. Together, a mortgagee and mortgagor are normally able to handle any personal problems that may have led to the delinquency. For example, in a case where a borrower is sick and cannot work for six months, a mortgagee may choose to:

- collect just a portion of the past due amount immediately.
- make a second mortgage to bring the loan current.

- extend the term.
- look to other solutions tailored to the needs of both parties that will rectify the problem.

The percentage of single-family loans that are delinquent 30 days or more changes with swings in the economy and employment. Another important fact is that the inflationary periods of the 1970s have given most home owners enough equity in their homes to encourage them to sell (thus keeping their equity) if they have problems making the mortgage payment rather than let a home be sold at foreclosure.

FORECLOSURE

After all attempts to cure a default fail, a mortgagee must move to foreclose and protect its investment. It is important for all to realize that when a mortgagee or its agent forecloses a defaulted mortgage, it is only fulfilling its fiduciary responsibility to protect the funds loaned, which are actually the savings of the public's money, whether in the form of passbook savings or life insurance.

There are various forms of foreclosure, depending on state law. Any time before a foreclosure sale or other disposition, a mortgagor or anyone claiming through the mortgagor, such as a spouse or junior lienholders, may exercise the equitable right of redemption. This right is exercised by paying the mortgagee the outstanding balance plus interest and costs.

As mentioned previously, the first judicial method of cutting off a mortgagor's equity of redemption was known as strict foreclosure. If not redeemed within a set time, a court decree transferred the mortgagor's interest in the real estate to the mortgagee irrespective of any equity of the mortgagor in the property. This result was grossly unfair to the mortgagor. Therefore, a more balanced approach followed which provided for selling the property to secure the debt. The proceeds of the sale went first to satisfy the mortgagee, then to other lienholders, and then to the mortgagor.

The four modern methods of foreclosure, depending on the law of a state, are:

- judicial proceeding
- power of sale
- strict foreclosure
- entry and possession

Judicial Proceeding

Most states provide for mortgage foreclosure through a court proceeding. This method best protects the interests of the various parties. The action is much like any other civil suit in that the case must be brought in a court with jurisdiction, either a circuit or district court of the state, where the real estate is located. The procedure requires a complaint naming the borrower, who now is the defendant, alleging that a mortgage was executed by the defendant using specifically described real estate as security for a loan and that a default has occurred whereby the mortgagee has had to accelerate. The complaint will request foreclosure.

The defendant always has an opportunity to answer the allegations with any defenses available. For example, the defendant may attempt to prove that:

- No mortgage existed.
- The mortgage was satisfied.
- No default occurred.
- The interest rate was usurious.

If the decision of the court is in favor of a mortgagee, the decree of foreclosure terminates the equitable right of redemption at the time of sale, and a mortgagor loses all rights to the real property except the right to any excess proceeds from the sale after secured parties are paid. The exception is if a state has a statutory right of redemption. The court decree will order a sale and the manner for its execution. Many courts will include an upset price in the decree which is the acceptable minimum bid at the sale. The court usually specifies the officer, such as a sheriff or referee, who will conduct the sale after giving the statutory notice of the sale. To encourage purchasers, a successful bidder acquires title to the property unencumbered by any interest except that of the mortgagor's statutory right of redemption, if allowed.

With one possible exception, anyone who can contract can purchase property at a foreclosure sale. Some states prevent a defaulting mortgagor from purchasing since the unencumbered title would cut off the rights of junior lienholders. Probably the best laws are those that allow a mortgagor to repurchase at a foreclosure sale where all liens on the real estate prior to foreclosure reattach.

The key element in this form of foreclosure is that the sale must be accepted or confirmed by the court retaining jurisdiction. This requirement is for the protection of both the mortgagor and junior lienholders since a court will not approve a price which is unconscionably low.

Power of Sale

This method is sometimes called foreclosure by advertisement, since the clause creating a power of sale calls for an advertisement to give notice of the sale. This method is used primarily with deeds of trust, but it can be used with mortgages. The power to use this method rather than the more cumbersome judicial proceeding comes from a clause that is part of the securing instrument. The clause specifically explains how the sale will be carried out. This forclosure method does not preclude a mortgagor's statutory right of redemption if it exists. Some states do not allow the right of redemption if the instrument is a deed of trust.

Foreclosure by advertisement requires procedures which vary among the states. Therefore, extreme care should be taken to ensure that proper notice is given and that other requirements are fulfilled. The proceeds from the sale are distributed in the same way as those in a judicial proceeding.

Strict Foreclosure

As mentioned earlier, this was the original method of foreclosure. It is still used in some states which classify themselves as title theory states. The action involves a court of equity and requests a decree giving a mortgagor a period of time to exercise the equitable right of redemption or lose all rights to the property, with title vesting irrevocably in the mortgagee. When requesting this type of relief, a mortgagee must be able to prove all allegations just as it must in judicial proceedings.

Entry and Possession

Entry and possession is used only in Maine, Massachusetts, New Hampshire, and Rhode Island. After default, a mortgagee gives the mortgagor notice that possession will be taken. If the mortgagor does not agree peacefully to relinquish possession, the mortgagee will have to use a judicial method. This "peaceful possession" needs to be witnessed and recorded. If the mortgagor does not redeem in the statutory period, title vests with the mortgagee.

DEED IN LIEU

An alternative to foreclosure which can be of benefit to both the mortgagor and mortgagee would be the execution of a deed transferring the secured real estate to the mortgagee in lieu of foreclosure. The benefits to a mortgagor would include not being subject to the embarrassment of a foreclosure suit or possibly being liable for a deficiency judgment. A mortgagee would benefit by immediately acquiring title to the real estate for a quick sale.

For a deed in lieu to be effective in transferring title, the existing mortgage liability of the mortgagor must be extinguished. If not, the transaction and deed will be considered as nothing more than a new security agreement.

The mortgagee must carefully consider the consequences of this alternative before it is used. If a mortgagee decides to take a deed in lieu of foreclosure, the rights of junior lienholders will not be extinguished. On the other hand, if a mortgagee forecloses, junior lienholders' rights are extinguished if not satisfied by the proceeds of the sale, but the mortgagor has the right of redemption, which can be of serious consequence to a mortgagee.

REDEMPTION

In addition to the equity of redemption already discussed, 26 states provide another form of redemption right which begins to accrue to a mortgagor (or those claiming through the mortgagor) after foreclosure and sale. This is called the statutory right of redemption because it only exists if created by statute. This redemption period ranges from six months to two years depending on the state.

There are two reasons for a statutory right of redemption: (a) to provide a mortgagor with a chance to keep the real estate, and (b) to encourage bidders at foreclosure sales to bid the market value. The first is more important in agricultural states where a bad growing season can be followed by bumper crops. This right would provide a method for a mortgagor to keep the farm. This same reasoning applies in some income-property situations, but rarely in a residential case. The second reason is equally important for all types of real estate since a bidder at a forced sale would more likely bid the true market value rather than chance later divestiture by the mortgagor.

The right of redemption currently has a limited impact on single-family transactions since most of these transactions are a trust deed rather than a mortgage. This makes a difference because many states do not allow the statutory right of redemption with a trust deed based on the concept that a grantor had conveyed all interest to the trustee at the creation of the transaction and consequently had nothing on which to base the redemption. Other states allow it, regardless of what the transaction is called, because if real estate secures a debt, then the transaction is a mortgage and all rights attach. Even if the redemption right exists for a mortgagor, it is seldom exercised by single-family mortgagors, who are more likely to sell their property before foreclosure if there is equity to protect.

OTHER CONSIDERATIONS

In some states, a mortgagee could elect to sue rather than foreclose, based on the promissory note the mortgagor signed. If allowed, the decision might be based on

STATE-BY-STATE COMPARISON OF SELECTED ASPECTS OF FORECLOSURE

State	Nature of mortgage	Customary security instrument	Predominant method of foreclosure	Redemption period (months)	Possession during redemption (if customary security instrument used)	Deficiency judgment allowed?
Alabama	Title	Mortgage	Power of Sale	12	Purchaser	Yes
Alaska	Lien	Trust Deed	Power of Sale	None	—	No
Arizona	Lien	Trust Deed	Judicial	None	—	Yes
Arkansas	Intermediate	Mortgage	Power of Sale	12	Purchaser	Yes
California	Lien	Trust Deed	Power of Sale	None	—	No
Colorado	Lien	Trust Deed	Power of Sale	2½	Mortgagor	Yes
Connecticut	Intermediate	Mortgage	Strict Foreclosure	None	—	No
Delaware	Intermediate	Mortgage	Judicial	None	—	No
Dist. of Columbia	Intermediate	Trust Deed	Power of Sale	None	—	Yes
Florida	Lien	Mortgage	Judicial	None	—	Yes
Georgia	Title	Security Deed	Power of Sale	None	—	Yes
Hawaii	Title	Trust Deed	Power of Sale	None	—	Yes
Idaho	Lien	Trust Deed	Power of Sale	None	—	Yes
Illinois	Intermediate	Mortgage	Judicial	12	Mortgagor	No
Indiana	Lien	Mortgage	Judicial	3	Mortgagor	Yes
Iowa	Lien	Mortgage	Judicial	6	Mortgagor	No
Kansas	Lien	Mortgage	Judicial	12	Mortgagor	Yes
Kentucky	Lien	Mortgage	Judicial	None	—	Yes

242

State	Nature of mortgage	Customary security instrument	Predominant method of foreclosure	Redemption period (months) (if customary security instrument used)	Possession during redemption	Deficiency judgment allowed?
Kentucky	Lien	Mortgage	Judicial	None	—	Yes
Louisiana	Lien	Mortgage	Judicial	None	—	Yes
Maine	Title	Mortgage	Entry and Possession	12	Mortgagor	Yes
Maryland	Title	Trust Deed	Power of Sale	None	—	Yes
Massachusetts	Intermediate	Mortgage	Power of Sale	None	—	Yes
Michigan	Lien	Mortgage	Power of Sale	6	Mortgagor	Yes
Minnesota	Lien	Mortgage	Power of Sale	12	Mortgagor	Yes
Mississippi	Intermediate	Trust Deed	Power of Sale	None	—	Yes
Missouri	Intermediate	Trust Deed	Power of Sale	12	Mortgagor	Yes
Montana	Lien	Mortgage	Judicial	12	Mortgagor	Yes
Nebraska	Lien	Mortgage	Judicial	None	—	No
Nevada	Lien	Mortgage	Power of Sale	None	—	Yes
New Hampshire	Title	Mortgage	Power of Sale	None	—	Yes
New Jersey	Intermediate	Mortgage	Judicial	None	—	No
New Mexico	Lien	Mortgage	Judicial	1	Purchaser	Yes
New York	Lien	Mortgage	Judicial	None	—	Yes
North Carolina	Intermediate	Trust Deed	Power of Sale	None	—	No

STATE-BY-STATE COMPARISON OF SELECTED ASPECTS
OF FORECLOSURE (continued)

State	Nature of mortgage	Customary security instrument	Predominant method of foreclosure	Redemption period (months) (if customary security instrument used)	Possession during redemption (if customary security instrument used)	Deficiency judgment allowed?
North Dakota	Lien	Mortgage	Judicial	12	Mortgagor	Yes
Ohio	Intermediate	Mortgage	Judicial	None	—	Yes
Oklahoma	Lien	Mortgage	Judicial	None	—	Yes
Oregon	Lien	Trust Deed	Power of Sale	None	—	Yes
Pennsylvania	Title	Mortgage	Judicial	None	—	Yes
Rhode Island	Title	Mortgage	Power of Sale	None	—	No
South Carolina	Lien	Mortgage	Judicial	None	—	Yes
South Dakota	Lien	Mortgage	Power of Sale	12	Mortgagor	Yes
Tennessee	Title	Trust Deed	Power of Sale	None	—	No
Texas	Lien	Trust Deed	Power of Sale	None	—	Yes
Utah	Lien	Mortgage	Judicial	6	Mortgagor	Yes
Vermont	Intermediate	Mortgage	Strict Foreclosure	6	Mortgagor	Yes
Virginia	Intermediate	Trust Deed	Power of Sale	None	—	Yes
Washington	Lien	Mortgage	Judicial	12	Purchaser	Yes
West Virginia	Intermediate	Trust Deed	Power of Sale	None	—	Yes
Wisconsin	Lien	Mortgage	Power of Sale	None	—	Yes
Wyoming	Lien	Mortgage	Power of Sale	6	Mortgagor	Yes

CAVEAT This chart only lists the customary form of security instrument used in each state and not all the forms that could be used. Therefore, the method of foreclosure and period of redemption (if allowed) will be listed only for the customary form and not for all possible security instruments. The reader is further cautioned that many states have extensive qualifications and limitations on the period of redemption and for obtaining a delinquency judgment. *Consult a local attorney for details.*

the fact that a mortgagee does not believe a forced sale would yield sufficient compensation, but a judgment based on the note could attach to all the debtor's property, and yield full compensation. Some states allow a mortgagee to sue on the mortgage and force a sale and, if not fully compensated, also sue on the note and get a deficiency judgment.

RESIDENTIAL MORTGAGE LOAN CASE STUDY

17

Both the practitioner and the student of residential mortgage lending should be aware of and fully understand the essential loan documents in a mortgage loan file. This chapter contains the essential documents for a conventional residential mortgage loan that requires private mortgage insurance. The mortgage lender intends to sell this loan in the secondary mortgage market.

In previous editions, an FHA and a VA case were also displayed, but at the time this book was being readied for production, both FHA and VA were making substantive changes in their programs which could result in drastic changes in their documentation. For that reason, I decided not to display either loan file. I expect that in future editions, these will be added again.

Residential Loan Application

Compliments of
General Electric Mortgage Insurance Corporation

MORTGAGE APPLIED FOR	Amount	Interest Rate	No. of Months	Monthly Payment Principal & Interest	Escrow/Impounds (to be collected monthly)
☒ Conventional ☐ FHA ☐ VA ☐	$ 171,000	9.375 %	360	$ 1,422.29	☒ Taxes ☐ Hazard Ins. ☒ Mtg. Ins.

Prepayment Option
None

Subject Property

Property Street Address	City	County	State	Zip	No. Units
4463 Loveday Street	Silver Spring	Mont.	MD	20902	1

Legal Description (Attach description if necessary)	Year Built
Lot 16 Block 31 Hemp Hill Estates	1960

Purpose of Loan: ☒ Purchase ☐ Construction-Permanent ☐ Construction ☐ Refinance ☐ Other (Explain)

Complete this line if Construction-Permanent or Construction Loan ☛	Lot Value Data	Original Cost	Present Value (a)	Cost of Imps. (b)	Total (a + b)	ENTER TOTAL AS PURCHASE PRICE IN DETAILS OF PURCHASE.
Year Acquired	$	$	$	$		

Complete this line if a Refinance Loan				
Year Acquired	Original Cost	Amt. Existing Liens	Purpose of Refinance	Describe Improvements [ ] made [ ] to be made
$	$	$		Cost: $

Title Will Be Held In What Name(s)	Manner In Which Title Will Be Held
Theodore A. and Vicki L. Miller	Joint tenants with rights of survivorship

Source of Down Payment and Settlement Charges

This application is designed to be completed by the borrower(s) with the lender's assistance. The Co-Borrower Section and all other Co-Borrower questions must be completed and the appropriate box(es) checked if ☒ another person will be jointly obligated with the Borrower on the loan, or ☐ the Borrower is relying on income from alimony, child support or separate maintenance or on the income or assets of another person as a basis for repayment of the loan, or ☐ the Borrower is married and resides, or the property is located, in a community property state.

Borrower			Co-Borrower		
Name	Age	School	Name	Age	School
Theodore A. Miller	29	Yrs 21	Vicki L. Miller	29	Yrs 16
Present Address No. Years 18mos ☐ Own ☒ Rent			Present Address No. Years ☐ Own ☐ Rent		
Street 2024 Georgian Woods Place #3			Street		
City/State/Zip Wheaton, MD 20902			City/State/Zip same		
Former address if less than 2 years at present address			Former address if less than 2 years at present address		
Street 2101 S. Sipley Street			Street		
City/State/Zip Alexandria, VA			City/State/Zip		
Years at former address 2 yrs. ☐ Own ☒ Rent			Years at former address ☐ Own ☐ Rent		
Marital Status ☒ Married ☐ Separated ☐ Unmarried (incl. single, divorced, widowed)	DEPENDENTS OTHER THAN LISTED BY CO-BORROWER / AGES None		Marital Status ☒ Married ☐ Separated ☐ Unmarried (incl. single, divorced, widowed)	DEPENDENTS OTHER THAN LISTED BY BORROWER / AGES None	
Name and Address of Employer	Years employed in this line of work or profession?		Name and Address of Employer	Years employed in this line of work or profession?	
U.S. Naval Research Lab Code 1010 Washington DC 20735	3 years		NIH 9000 Rockville Pike Bethesda, MD 20892	4 years	
	Years on this job 1+* ☐ Self Employed*			Years on this job 4 ☐ Self Employed*	
Position/Title Research Physicist	Type of Business Government		Position/Title Chemist	Type of Business Government	
Social Security Number 081-60-4823	Home Phone 946-2634	Business Phone 767-9413	Social Security Number 075-54-6256	Home Phone same	Business Phone 402-8723

Gross Monthly Income				Monthly Housing Expense**			Details of Purchase	
Item	Borrower	Co-Borrower	Total		Present	Proposed	Do Not Complete If Refinance	
Base Empl. Income	$3936.42	$2214.50	$6150.92	Rent	$735.00		a. Purchase Price	$ 190000.00
Overtime				First Mortgage (P&I)		$1422.29	b. Total Closing Costs (Est.)	9967.00
Bonuses				Other Financing (P&I)			c. Prepaid Escrows (Est.)	2148.00
Commissions				Hazard Insurance		25.00	d. Total (a + b + c)	$202155.00
Dividends/Interest				Real Estate Taxes		128.00	e. Amount This Mortgage	(171000.00)
Net Rental Income				Mortgage Insurance		48.00	f. Other Financing	( )
Other† (Before completing, see notice under Describe Other Income below.)				Homeowner Assn. Dues			g. Other Equity	( )
				Other:			h. Amount of Cash Deposit	(9000.00)
				Total Monthly Pmt.	$735.00	$1575.29	i. Closing Costs Paid by Seller	(5602.00)
				Utilities			j. Cash Reqd. For Closing (Est.)	$16513.00
Total	$3936.42	$2214.50	$6150.00	Total	$735.00	$1575.29		

Describe Other Income

NOTICE: † Alimony, child support, or separate maintenance income need not be revealed if the Borrower or Co-Borrower does not choose to have it considered as a basis for repaying this loan.

☞ B–Borrower C–Co-Borrower		Monthly Amount
		$

If Employed In Current Position For Less Than Two Years, Complete the Following

B/C	Previous Employer/School	City/State	Type of Business	Position/Title	Dates From/To	Monthly Income
B.	*Fellowship with Naval Research				8/89 to 11/91	$

These Questions Apply To Both Borrower and Co-Borrower

If a "yes" answer is given to a question in this column, please explain on an attached sheet.

	Borrower Yes or No	Co-Borrower Yes or No
Are there any outstanding judgments against you?	No	No
Have you been declared bankrupt within the past 7 years?	No	No
Have you had property foreclosed upon or given title or deed in lieu thereof in the last 7 years?	No	No
Are you a party to a law suit?	No	No
Are you obligated to pay alimony, child support, or separate maintenance?	No	No
Is any part of the down payment borrowed?	No	No
Are you a co-maker or endorser on a note?	No	No

	Borrower Yes or No	Co-Borrower Yes or No
Are you a U.S. citizen?	Yes	Yes
If "no," are you a resident alien?		
If "no," are you a non-resident alien?		

Explain Other Financing or Other Equity (if any): _____

*FHLMC/FNMA require business credit report, signed Federal Income Tax returns for last two years; and, if available, audited Profit and Loss Statement plus balance sheet for same period.
**All Present Monthly Housing Expenses of Borrower and Co-Borrower should be listed on a combined basis.
***Optional for FHLMC
FHLMC 65 Rev. 10/86

Fannie Mae Form 1003 Rev. 10/86

248

This Statement and any applicable supporting schedules may be completed jointly by both married and unmarried co-borrowers if their assets and liabilities are sufficiently joined so that the Statement can be meaningfully and fairly presented on a combined basis; otherwise separate Statements and Schedules are required (FHLMC 65A/FNMA 1003A). If the co-borrower section was completed about a spouse, this statement and supporting schedules must be completed about that spouse also. ☒ Completed Jointly   ☐ Not Completed Jointly

Assets / Liabilities and Pledged Assets

Indicate by (*) those liabilities or pledged assets which will be satisfied upon sale of real estate owned or upon refinancing of subject property

Description	Cash or Market Value	Creditors' Name, Address and Account Number	Acct. Name if Not Borrower's	Mo. Pmt. and Mos. Left to Pay	Unpaid Balance
Cash Deposit Toward Purchase Held By Long and Foster	$ 9000.00	Installment Debts (Include "revolving" charge accounts) Co. Bankeast 5413826554321 Acct. No.		$ 10/19 Pmt/Mos	$ 192.00
Checking and Savings Accounts (Show Names of Institutions (Account Numbers)) Bank, S & L or Credit Union NRL Fed. C/U		Addr. Citibank 412201159872		20/5	87.00
Addr. 2025836	161.13	City Discover Card 60110846603		20/5|	78.00
City 2425402	10251.97	Co. State University of NY Acct. No.		30/39	1151.72
Acct. No. 2429947	21029.19	City		/	
Bank, S & L or Credit Union Sovran Bank		Addr.			
Addr. 62896872	875.56	City		/	
City 93265269	3244.60	Co. Acct. No.			
Acct. No. 98889370	8170.08	Addr.			
Bank, S & L or Credit Union		City			
Addr.		Co. Acct. No.			
City		Addr.			
Acct. No.		City Other Debts including Stock Pledges			
Stocks and Bonds (No./Description)				/	
		Real Estate Loans Co. Acct. No.			
		Addr.			
		City			
Life Insurance Net Cash Value Face Amount $		Co. Acct. No.			
Subtotal Liquid Assets	53732.53	Addr. City			
Real Estate Owned (Enter Market Value from Schedule of Real Estate Owned)		Automobile Loans Co. NRL Fed. C/U 242568-B Acct. No.		164.91/25	4092.02
Vested Interest in Retirement Fund	2500.00	Addr.			
Net worth of Business Owned (ATTACH FINANCIAL STATEMENT)		City Co. Acct. No.			
Automobiles Owned (Make and Year) 89 Mazda	9000.00	City		/	
86 Cavalier	5000.00				
Furniture and Personal Property	10000.00	Alimony/Child Support/Separate Maintenance Payments Owed to			
Other Assets (Itemize)					
		Total Monthly Payments		$ 244.91	
Total Assets	A $ 70232.53	Net Worth (A minus B) $ 64631.79		Total Liabilities	B $ 5600.74

SCHEDULE OF REAL ESTATE OWNED (If Additional Properties Owned Attach Separate Schedule)

Address of Property (Indicate S if Sold, PS if Pending Sale or R if Rental being held for income)	Type of Property	Present Market Value	Amount of Mortgages & Liens	Gross Rental Income	Mortgage Payments	Taxes, Ins. Maintenance and Misc.	Net Rental Income
None		$	$	$	$	$	$
TOTALS →		$	$	$	$	$	$

List Previous Credit References

◇ B—Borrower C—Co-Borrower	Creditor's Name and Address	Account Number	Purpose	Highest Balance	Date Paid
	See credit report			$	

List any additional names under which credit has previously been received _____

AGREEMENT The undersigned applies for the loan indicated in this application to be secured by a first mortgage or deed of trust on the property described herein, and represents that the property will not be used for any illegal or restricted purpose, and that all statements made in this application are true and are made for the purpose of obtaining the loan. Verification may be obtained from any source named in this application. The original or a copy of this application will be retained by the lender, even if the loan is not granted. The undersigned ☒ intend or ☐ do not intend to occupy the property as their primary residence.

I/we fully understand that it is a federal crime punishable by fine or imprisonment, or both, to knowingly make any false statements concerning any of the above facts as applicable under the provisions of Title 18, United States Code, Section 1014.

Borrower's Signature _____ Date 10/20/92   Co-Borrower's Signature _____ Date _____

Information for Government Monitoring Purposes

The following information is requested by the Federal Government for certain types of loans related to a dwelling, in order to monitor the lender's compliance with equal credit opportunity and fair housing laws. You are not required to furnish this information, but are encouraged to do so. The law provides that a lender may neither discriminate on the basis of this information, nor on whether you choose to furnish it. However, if you choose not to furnish it, under Federal regulations this lender is required to note race and sex on the basis of visual observation or surname. If you do not wish to furnish the above information, please check the box below. (Lender must review the above material to assure that the disclosures satisfy all requirements to which the Lender is subject under applicable state law for the particular type of loan applied for.)

Borrower: ☐ I do not wish to furnish this information   Co-Borrower: ☐ I do not wish to furnish this information
Race/National Origin: Race/National Origin:
American Indian, Alaskan Native Asian, Pacific Islander   American Indian, Alaskan Native Asian, Pacific Islander
Black Hispanic X White   Black Hispanic X White
Other (specify):   Other (specify):
Sex: Female X Male   Sex: X Female Male

To Be Completed by Interviewer

This application was taken by:
☒ face to face interview   Chuck Meade   Dominion Bankshares Mortgage Cor_
☐ by mail   Interviewer   Name of Interviewer's Employer
☐ by telephone   12300 Twinbrook Parkway
                               301 827-6654   Rockville, MD 20852
                        Interviewer's Phone Number   Address of Interviewer's Employer

FHLMC Form 65 Rev. 10/86   **REVERSE**   Fannie Mae Form 1003 Rev 10/86

RESALE CONTRACT FOR SINGLE FAMILY HOUSE

THIS CONTRACT OF SALE, made this _____12th_____ day of _____December_____, 199_2_, by and
between the undersigned Seller(s) (hereinafter referred to as Seller) and _Theodore A. and Vicki L. Miller_
_____ (hereinafter referred to as Purchaser).

1. Deposit has been received from Purchaser with this Contract in the form of _____check_____, in the
amount of _Nine thousand and no/100-----------------------------dollars ($_9,000.00_).
**THE ENTIRE DEPOSIT, RECEIPT OF WHICH IS ACKNOWLEDGED BY AGENT, SHALL BE HELD BY THE AGENT AND
DEPOSITED IN AN ESCROW ACCOUNT IN ACCORDANCE WITH THE MARYLAND REAL ESTATE LICENSE LAW (OR
WITH THE APPROPRIATE JURISDICTIONAL LAW) UPON RATIFICATION OF THIS CONTRACT BY BOTH PURCHASER
AND SELLER.**
WITNESSETH, that for and in consideration of the mutual covenants herein, Seller agrees to sell and Purchaser agrees
to buy the property legally described as Lot ___16___, Block ___31___, Subdivision _Hemp Hill Estates_,
located in ___Montgomery___ County, Maryland, with improvements thereon, including built-in heating plant and
air conditioning system, all plumbing and lighting fixtures, kitchen equipment including range, oven, refrigerator, built-in
dishwasher and disposal, wall-to-wall carpeting, cornices, curtain rods and drapery rods, awnings, screens, storm doors
and windows, blinds, shades and indoor shutters, trees, shrubs and plants, all as now installed on the property known
as (address)_4463 Loveday Street, Silver Spring_ _20902_
upon the following terms of sale: (street)   (city)   (zip)
IF THIS CONTRACT IS FOR PROPERTY LOCATED OUTSIDE OF MONTGOMERY COUNTY, **A JURISDICTIONAL CLAUSE
ADDENDUM** SHALL BE ATTACHED, IF APPLICABLE.
Jurisdictional Clause Addendum attached   [ ] Yes   [ ] No
TOTAL PRICE OF PROPERTY IS_One hundred ninety thousand and no/100 -------------------dollars
($_190,000.00_). PURCHASER AGREES TO PAY _____$ Nineteen thousand -------------------
dollars ($_19,000.00_) at settlement (by cash or certified, treasurer's or cashier's check) OF WHICH SUM
THE DEPOSIT SHALL BE A PART. If the deposit exceeds the down payment, any excess of the deposit shall apply first
to settlement costs and the balance shall be refunded to Purchaser at settlement.
2. **FINANCING. a) FIRST TRUST (To be placed or assumed).** Purchaser is to _____place_____ a
conventional first deed of trust in lender's usual form secured by said property of
_One hundred seventy one dollars and no/100------------------dollars ($_171,000.00_)
not due in _____thirty_____ (___30___) years and bearing interest at the rate of _____market_____ percent
to exceed 1%) per annum, or the maximum rate prevailing at the time of settlement, payable at approximately _____
according to lenders schedule dollars ($ _____-_____) per month,
PLUS one-twelfth (1/12) of annual taxes, fire insurance and mortgage insurance, if required by the lender.
b) SECOND TRUST OR SELLER TAKE BACK. If secondary or Seller financing is applicable, **MCAR Addendum Form #1331
is attached. [ ] Yes [ ] No** _n/a_
c) FINANCING APPLICATION. Purchaser placing financing (regardless of type) agrees to make application therefor within
ten (10) calendar days of the final ratification of this Contract and agrees to promptly file any supplemental information
or papers later requested by the lender and agrees that failure to comply with the terms of this provision shall give Seller
the right to declare the deposit forfeited or avail himself of any legal or equitable rights as provided in the paragraph labeled "FORFEITURE OF DEPOSIT/LEGAL REMEDIES."
3. **CONVENTIONAL LOAN.** This Contract is contingent on the ability of Purchaser to secure or receive a firm, written commitment for the herein described conventional financing or lender's approval of assumption, if required, and furnish evidence of commitment or approval to the listing and selling Agents within _____forty-five_____
(___45___) calendar days from the date of final ratification of this Contract, which commitment or approval
Purchaser agrees to pursue diligently (see Paragraph 2c hereof). Purchaser reserves the right to increase the cash down
payment and/or accept a modified commitment for financing and shall so notify Seller and Agent(s) in writing within the
term of this contingency. In the event Purchaser does not obtain the specified financing or increase the cash down payment and/or accept a modified commitment for financing within the specified time period, then this Contract shall be
null and void and Purchaser's deposit shall be refunded pursuant to Paragraph 7b of this Contract. By accepting a loan
commitment which bears an interest rate or loan amount other than the rate or loan amount designated in Paragraph
2 above, the financing contingency contained herein shall be deemed satisfied, and Purchaser hereby waives any rights
which Purchaser may have to declare this Contract null and void for failure to obtain acceptable financing.
TIME IS OF THE ESSENCE WITH REGARD TO THIS PARAGRAPH.
4. **LOAN FEES. a) Conventional Loan fee.** If a new loan is to be placed pursuant to this Contract, Purchaser agrees to pay
a loan origination and/or discount fee of ___market___ percent (_____%)
of the principal sum of ANY CONVENTIONAL LOAN. Seller agrees to pay a loan origination and/or discount fee of
_____none_____ percent (___0___ %) of the principal sum of said loan. Lender's fees
shall be paid by Purchaser including Mortgage Insurance Premiums as required by lender. Purchaser further agrees to
accept any reasonable increase or decrease in said loan origination and/or discount fees where applicable.

b) Assumption. If the existing loan is to be assumed, Purchaser agrees to pay any loan assumption fees, charges or expenses required by lender.
5. **EXAMINATION OF TITLE AND COSTS.** Property is to be conveyed in the name of _same as above_.
**PURCHASER HAS THE RIGHT TO SELECT THE TITLE INSURANCE COMPANY, SETTLEMENT OR ESCROW COMPA-
NY, OR TITLE ATTORNEY.** Purchaser hereby authorizes the undersigned Agent to order the examination of title and the
preparation of all necessary conveyancing papers through _to be designated by purchasers_
and agrees to pay the settlement charges in connection therewith, tax certificate, conveyancing, notary fees, survey where
required, lender's fees and recording charges except those incident to clearing existing encumbrances. Seller hereby
agrees to pay any above-mentioned costs incurred if upon examination the title should be found defective and it is not
remedied as herein stated. Seller also agrees to pay a reasonable closing fee for services rendered to him. SECTION 14-104
OF THE REAL PROPERTY ARTICLE OF THE ANNOTATED CODE OF MARYLAND PROVIDES THAT, UNLESS OTHER-
WISE NEGOTIATED IN THE CONTRACT OR PROVIDED BY LOCAL LAW, THE COST OF ANY RECORDATION TAX OR
ANY STATE OR LOCAL TRANSFER TAX SHALL BE SHARED EQUALLY BETWEEN THE BUYER AND THE SELLER.
Transfer and recordation taxes shall be paid by_____sellers_____.

MCAR FORM #1301   10/89

26. Master Plan.
Purchaser has the right to examine, prior to signing this Contract, the applicable master plan and any municipal land use plan for the area in which the property is located and any adopted amendment to either plan, and approved official maps showing planned land uses, roads and highways, parks and other public facilities affecting the property contained in the Plan.

By signing this provision below, Purchaser acknowledges the following:
1. Seller has offered the Purchaser the opportunity to review the applicable Master Plan and municipal land use plan and any adopted amendment;
2. Seller has informed Purchaser that amendments affecting the plan may be pending before the Planning Board or the County Council or a municipal planning body;
3. Purchaser has reviewed each plan and adopted amendment or does hereby waive the right to review each plan and adopted amendment; and
4. Purchaser understands that to stay informed of future changes in County and municipal land use plans, the Purchaser should consult the Planning Board and the appropriate municipal planning body.

Purchaser _____   Purchaser _____

27. SETTLEMENT. Seller and Purchaser are required and agree to make full settlement in accordance with the terms hereof on or before the ___31st___ day of ___January___ , 19 93 , or as soon thereafter as a report of the title and a survey, if required, can be secured if promptly ordered, and/or an FHA or VA loan, if applicable, can be processed, if applied for immediately.

28. ADDITIONAL PROVISIONS. SPECIAL PROVISIONS IN THE ATTACHED ADDENDA, BEARING THE SIGNATURES OF ALL PARTIES CONCERNED, ARE HEREBY MADE A PART OF THIS CONTRACT. **ADDENDA ATTACHED** ☐ **Yes** ☐ **No.** FHA OR VA ADDENDUM MUST BE ATTACHED IN THE EVENT FHA OR VA FINANCING IS INVOLVED. Front Foot Benefit and water and sewer House Connection charges to be assumed are ___unknown___
_____ dollars ($_____) per year as shown on the county tax bill. Seller advises that the cost of deferred transportation related facility charges, if any, are estimated to be _____n/a_____ dollars ($_____) and are to be paid by Seller at settlement.
___Sellers___ agree to pay Two Thousand dollars ($2,000) toward purchasers closing costs
_____
_____
_____
_____
_____

29. AGENCY. Seller recognizes ___Long and Foster 3%___ as the Agent(s) negotiating this Contract and agrees to pay such Agent(s) a brokerage fee for services rendered as specified in a separate Listing Contract. If not previously paid by Seller, the party making settlement is hereby irrevocably authorized and directed to deduct and pay the aforesaid brokerage fee from the proceeds of the sale. However, should settlement fail to occur within the time herein set forth, the Agent(s) shall still be entitled to the brokerage fee herein provided.

Sales Associate (Signature)		Broker or Salesmanager	
David Smith		421kj	301-555-3283
Sales Associate (Print or type)	**(MCAR#)**	Broker Code	Office Phone Number

30. AGREEMENT OF PRINCIPALS. We, the undersigned, hereby ratify, accept and agree to this Contract and acknowledge receipt of a copy hereof. The principals to this Contract mutually agree that it shall be binding upon them, their heirs, executors, administrators, personal representatives, successors and assigns; that the provisions hereof shall survive the execution and delivery of the deed herein stated and shall not be merged therein. This Contract contains the final and entire agreement between the parties hereto, and neither they nor their Agent(s) shall be bound by any terms, conditions, statements, warranties, or representations, oral or written, not herein contained. This Contract, any modification, amendment or addenda hereto, shall be null, void and unenforceable until Seller and Purchaser have (a) signed or, where appropriate, initialled this Contract and any modification, amendment or addenda, and/or (b) transmitted assent through a wired or electronic medium which produces a tangible record of the transmission (such as a telegram, mailgram, datagram or telecopier "fax"), and (c) provided to the other party, in accordance with the paragraph labeled "NOTICES", the signed or, where appropriate, initialled Contract, modification, amendment or addenda and/or the transmitted assent.

Seller _____   Purchaser _____

Seller _____   Purchaser _____

Date of Signature(s) _____   Date of Signature(s) _____

Phone: _____   Address of Purchaser _____
    Residence   Office

Seller (Print) _____   _____
                       City   State   Zip

Seller (Print) _____   Phone: _____
                              Residence   Office

SELLER OR PURCHASER, WHOEVER PROVIDES FINAL RATIFICATION, IS REQUESTED TO COMPLETE THE FOLLOWING:

Date of Final Ratification: _____   Time of Final Ratification: _____ By _____
                                                             Initials Only

MCAR FORM #1301

10/89

Federal National Mortgage Association

REQUEST FOR VERIFICATION OF EMPLOYMENT

INSTRUCTIONS: LENDER - Complete items 1 thru 7. Have applicant complete item 8. Forward directly to employer named in item 1.
EMPLOYER - Please complete either Part II or Part III as applicable. Sign and return directly to lender named in item 2.

PART I—REQUEST

1. TO (*Name and address of employer*)	2. FROM (*Name and address of lender*)
Naval Research Lab. Code 1010 Washington, DC 20735	Dominion Bankshares Mortgage Corp. 12300 Twinbrook Parkway Rockville, MD 20852

3. SIGNATURE OF LENDER	4. TITLE	5. DATE	6. LENDER'S NUMBER *(optional)*
Julie Donohor	Processor	12/18/92	

I have applied for a mortgage loan and stated that I am now or was formerly employed by you. My signature below authorizes verification of this information.

7. NAME AND ADDRESS OF APPLICANT (*Include employee or badge number*)	8. SIGNATURE OF APPLICANT
Theodore A. Miller 2024 Georgian Park Place #3 Wheaton, MD 20902	*Theodore A. Miller*

PART II—VERIFICATION OF PRESENT EMPLOYMENT

EMPLOYMENT DATA		PAY DATA		
9. APPLICANT'S DATE OF EMPLOYMENT 11/13/91 *See below	**12A. CURRENT BASE PAY** (Enter Amount and Check Period) ☒ ANNUAL ☐ HOURLY ☐ MONTHLY ☐ OTHER ☐ WEEKLY (*Specify*) $47,237		**12C. FOR MILITARY PERSONNEL ONLY**	
10. PRESENT POSITION Research Physicist			PAY GRADE	
	12B. EARNINGS		TYPE	MONTHLY AMOUNT
11. PROBABILITY OF CONTINUED EMPLOYMENT Excellent	TYPE	YEAR TO DATE	PAST YEAR	BASE PAY $	
13. IF OVERTIME OR BONUS IS APPLICABLE, IS ITS CONTINUANCE LIKELY?	BASE PAY $	$	RATIONS $	
			FLIGHT OR HAZARD $	
	OVERTIME $	$	CLOTHING $	
OVERTIME ☐ YES ☒ NO	COMMISSIONS $	$	QUARTERS $	
			PRO PAY $	
BONUS ☐ YES ☒ NO	BONUS $	$	OVER SEAS OR COMBAT $	

14. REMARKS (*if paid hourly, indicate average hours worked each week during current and past year*)

* Dr. Miller has been a federal employee for about one year, but held a postdoctoral fellowship for two years previous to this (8-89) in code 1010 Naval Research Lab performing the same job.

PART III—VERIFICATION OF PREVIOUS EMPLOYMENT

15. DATES OF EMPLOYMENT	16. SALARY/WAGE AT TERMINATION PER (Year) (Month) (Week)
	BASE _____ OVERTIME _____ COMMISSIONS _____ BONUS _____

17. REASON FOR LEAVING	18. POSITION HELD

19. SIGNATURE OF EMPLOYER	20. TITLE	21. DATE
Paul Harmburg	Unit Manager	12/21/92

The confidentiality of the information you have furnished will be preserved except where disclosure of this information is required by applicable law. The form is to be transmitted directly to the lender and is not to be transmitted through the applicant or any other party.

PREVIOUS EDITION WILL BE USED UNTIL STOCK IS EXHAUSTED

FNMA Form 1005
Rev. June 78

Federal National Mortgage Association

REQUEST FOR VERIFICATION OF EMPLOYMENT

INSTRUCTIONS: LENDER - Complete items 1 thru 7. Have applicant complete item 8. Forward directly to employer named in item 1
EMPLOYER - Please complete either Part II or Part III as applicable. Sign and return directly to lender named in item 2

PART I—REQUEST

1. TO (*Name and address of employer*)	2. FROM (*Name and address of lender*)
National Heart, Lung and Blood Inst. NIH Bldg. A 9000 Rockville Pike Bethesda, MD 20892	Dominion Bankshares Mortgage Corp. 12300 Twinbrook Pkwy. Rockville, MD 20852

3. SIGNATURE OF LENDER	4. TITLE	5. DATE	6. LENDER'S NUMBER (*optional*)
Julie Danlio	Processor	12/18/92	

I have applied for a mortgage loan and stated that I am now or was formerly employed by you. My signature below authorizes verification of this information.

7. NAME AND ADDRESS OF APPLICANT (*Include employee or badge number*)	8. SIGNATURE OF APPLICANT
Vicki L. Miller, 2024 Georgian Park Place, Wheaton, MD 20902	*Vicki L. Miller*

PART II—VERIFICATION OF PRESENT EMPLOYMENT

EMPLOYMENT DATA

PAY DATA		

9. APPLICANT'S DATE OF EMPLOYMENT 07/05/88	12A. CURRENT BASE PAY (Enter Amount and Check Period) ☒ ANNUAL ☐ HOURLY ☐ MONTHLY ☐ OTHER $ 25,529 ☐ WEEKLY (*Specify*)	12C. FOR MILITARY PERSONNEL ONLY	

10. PRESENT POSITION Chemist		PAY GRADE	

	12B. EARNINGS	TYPE	MONTHLY AMOUNT
11. PROBABILITY OF CONTINUED EMPLOYMENT Yes	TYPE	YEAR TO DATE	PAST YEAR	BASE PAY	$
13. IF OVERTIME OR BONUS IS APPLICABLE, IS ITS CONTINUANCE LIKELY?	BASE PAY	$ 12/15 24,593	$ 19,565	RATIONS	$
	OVERTIME	$	$	FLIGHT OR HAZARD	$
OVERTIME ☐ YES ☒ NO	COMMISSIONS	$	$	CLOTHING	$
				QUARTERS	$
BONUS ☒ YES ☐ NO	BONUS	$ 325	$ 350	PRO PAY	$
				OVER SEAS OR COMBAT	$

14. REMARKS (*if paid hourly, indicate average hours worked each week during current and past year*)

Next pay increase 1/13/93 $1,045 annual

PART III—VERIFICATION OF PREVIOUS EMPLOYMENT

15. DATES OF EMPLOYMENT	16. SALARY/WAGE AT TERMINATION PER (Year) (Month) (Week)
	BASE _____ OVERTIME _____ COMMISSIONS _____ BONUS _____

17. REASON FOR LEAVING	18. POSITION HELD

19. SIGNATURE OF EMPLOYER	20. TITLE	21. DATE
Janis Quate	Personnel Asst. NHLBI	12/12/92

The confidentiality of the information you have furnished will be preserved except where disclosure of this information is required by applicable law. The form is to be transmitted directly to the lender and is not to be transmitted through the applicant or any other party.

PREVIOUS EDITION WILL BE USED UNTIL STOCK IS EXHAUSTED

FNMA Form 1005
Rev. June 78

REQUEST FOR VERIFICATION OF DEPOSIT

INSTRUCTIONS: LENDER - Complete Items 1 thru 8. Have applicant(s) complete Item 9. Forward directly to depository named in Item 1.

DEPOSITORY - Please complete Items 10 thru 15 and return DIRECTLY to lender named in Item 2.

PART I - REQUEST

1. TO (Name and address of depository)	2. FROM (Name and address of lender)
NRL Federal Credit Union P.O. Box 1026 Oxon Hill, MD 20750	Dominion Bankshares Mortgage Corp. 12300 Twinbrook Parkway Rockville, MD 20852

3. SIGNATURE OF LENDER	4. TITLE	5. DATE	6. LENDER'S NUMBER (Optional)
Julie Davidson	Processor	12/18/92	

7. INFORMATION TO BE VERIFIED

TYPE OF ACCOUNT	ACCOUNT IN NAME OF	ACCOUNT NUMBER	BALANCE
	Theodore A. Miller	2025836	$ current
	same as above	2425402	$ current
	same as above	2429947	$ current
			$

TO DEPOSITORY: I have applied for a mortgage loan and stated in my financial statement that the balance on deposit with you is as shown above. You are authorized to verify this information and to supply the lender identified above with the information requested in Items 10 thru 12. Your response is solely a matter of courtesy for which no responsibility is attached to your institution or any of your officers.

8. NAME AND ADDRESS OF APPLICANT(s)	9. SIGNATURE OF APPLICANT(s)
Theodore A. Miller 2024 Georgian Park Place #3 Wheaton, MD 20902	*Theodore A. Miller*

TO BE COMPLETED BY DEPOSITORY

PART II - VERIFICATION OF DEPOSITORY

10. DEPOSIT ACCOUNTS OF APPLICANT(s)

TYPE OF ACCOUNT	ACCOUNT NUMBER	CURRENT BALANCE	AVERAGE BALANCE FOR PREVIOUS TWO MONTHS	DATE OPENED
Savings	2025836	$ 161.13	$ 161.13	04May88
Checking	2425402	$ 10,251.91	$ 786.81	04May88
Money Makers SV	2429947	$ 21,029.19	$ 24,378.86	04May88
		$	$	

11. LOANS OUTSTANDING TO APPLICANT(s)

LOAN NUMBER	DATE OF LOAN	ORIGINAL AMOUNT	CURRENT BALANCE	INSTALLMENTS (Monthly/Quarterly)	SECURED BY	NUMBER OF LATE PAYMENTS
242568-B	12Apr91	$ 6,531.43	$ 4,092.02	$ 169.9 per mo	Auto. Title	-0-
		$	$	$ per		
		$	$	$ per		

12. ADDITIONAL INFORMATION WHICH MAY BE OF ASSISTANCE IN DETERMINATION OF CREDIT WORTHINESS:
(Please include information on loans paid-in-full as in Item 11 above)

N/A

13. SIGNATURE OF DEPOSITORY	14. TITLE	15. DATE
Suzanne Bear	Loan Processor	21 Dec 92

The confidentiality of the information you have furnished will be preserved except where disclosure of this information is required by applicable law. The form is to be transmitted directly to the lender and is not to be transmitted through the applicant or any other party.

PREVIOUS EDITION WILL BE USED UNTIL STOCK IS EXHAUSTED

FNMA Form 1006
Rev. June 7

REQUEST FOR VERIFICATION OF DEPOSIT

INSTRUCTIONS: LENDER - Complete items 1 thru 8. Have applicant(s) complete item 9. Forward directly to depository named in item 1.

DEPOSITORY - Please complete items 10 thru 15 and return DIRECTLY to lender named in item 2.

PART I - REQUEST

1. TO (Name and address of depository)	2. FROM (Name and address of lender)
Sovran Bank 6610 Rockledge Dr. Bethesda, MD 20817	Dominion Bankshares Mortgage Corp. 12300 Twinbrook Parkway Rockville, MD 20852

3. SIGNATURE OF LENDER	4. TITLE	5. DATE	6. LENDER'S NUMBER (Optional)
Julie Donaldson	Processor	12/18/92	

7. INFORMATION TO BE VERIFIED

TYPE OF ACCOUNT	ACCOUNT IN NAME OF	ACCOUNT NUMBER	BALANCE
Checking	Vicki L. Miller	962896372	$ current
Savings	same as above	93265369	$ current
Money Market	same as above	098889370	$ current
			$

TO DEPOSITORY: I have applied for a mortgage loan and stated in my financial statement that the balance on deposit with you is as shown above. You are authorized to verify this information and to supply the lender identified above with the information requested in items 10 thru 12. Your response is solely a matter of courtesy for which no responsibility is attached to your institution or any of your officers.

8. NAME AND ADDRESS OF APPLICANT(s)	9. SIGNATURE OF APPLICANT(s)
Vicki L. Miller # 075-54-6256 2024 Georgian Park Place #3 Wheaton, MD 20902	*Vicki L. Miller*

TO BE COMPLETED BY DEPOSITORY

PART II - VERIFICATION OF DEPOSITORY

10. DEPOSIT ACCOUNTS OF APPLICANT(s)

TYPE OF ACCOUNT	ACCOUNT NUMBER	CURRENT BALANCE	AVERAGE BALANCE FOR PREVIOUS TWO MONTHS	DATE OPENED
Checking	962896372	$ 875.56	$ High 3	5-90
Savings	93265369	$ 3,244.60	$ Mod 4	5-90
MM Savings	098889370	$ 8,170.08	$ High 4	7-90
		$	$	

11. LOANS OUTSTANDING TO APPLICANT(s)

LOAN NUMBER	DATE OF LOAN	ORIGINAL AMOUNT	CURRENT BALANCE	INSTALLMENTS (Monthly/Quarterly)	SECURED BY	NUMBER OF LATE PAYMENTS
N O N E		$	$	$ per		
		$	$	$ per		
		$	$	$ per		

12. ADDITIONAL INFORMATION WHICH MAY BE OF ASSISTANCE IN DETERMINATION OF CREDIT WORTHINESS.
(Please include information on loans paid-in-full as in Item 11 above)

13. SIGNATURE OF DEPOSITORY	14. TITLE	15. DATE
signature	Customer Service Specialist	12/21/92

The confidentiality of the information you have furnished will be preserved except where disclosure of this information is required by applicable law. The form is to be transmitted directly to the lender and is not to be transmitted through the applicant or any other party.

PREVIOUS EDITION WILL BE USED UNTIL STOCK IS EXHAUSTED

FNMA Form 1006
Rev. June 7

ACCOUNT NO. BBQ 352123230498
ACCOUNT NAME Dominion Bankshares
REPORT ORDERED BY Janis Williams
DATE ORDERED 12/14/92
DATE MAILED 12/18/92
INDIVIDUAL OR JOINT REPORT Joint
TYPE REPORT (CASE OR FILE NO.) Residential
SOURCE CBI/CSC, TRW
REPORT PREPARED BY Lorie Jamison
PRICE (plus applicable sales tax) $43.86

RESIDENTIAL MORTGAGE CREDIT REPORT PREPARED FOR

Dominion Bankshares Mortgage Corporation
12300 Twinbrook Pkwy.
Rockville, MD

GENERAL INFORMATION

1.	APPLICANT'S NAME AND AGE / SPOUSE'S NAME AND AGE	MILLER, Theodore A. - 29 yrs./Vicki L. - 29 yrs.
2.	CURRENT ADDRESS	2024 Georgian Park Pl., Wheaton, MD
3.	LENGTH OF TIME AT PRESENT ADDRESS / OWN?	1½ years/rent
4.	PREVIOUS ADDRESS	2101 S. Sipley St., Alexandria, VA
5.	APPLICANT'S SS # / SPOUSE'S SS #	081-60-4823 / 075-54-6256
6.	MARITAL STATUS / DEPENDENTS	Married / None

APPLICANT'S EMPLOYMENT

7.	NAME OF EMPLOYER / ADDRESS	U.S. Naval Research Lab. Wash. D.C. 20735
8.	POSITION HELD / LENGTH OF EMPLOYMENT	Res. Physicist - 3 years
9.	SOURCE AND DATE OF VERIFICATION / INCOME	Personnel - 12-15-92 / $4,000 p/m
10.	PREVIOUS EMPLOYMENT	n/a

SPOUSE'S EMPLOYMENT

11.	NAME OF EMPLOYER / ADDRESS	N.I.H. 9000 Rockville Pike, Bethesda, MD 20892
12.	POSITION HELD / LENGTH OF EMPLOYMENT	Chemist - 4 years
13.	SOURCE AND DATE OF VERIFICATION / INCOME	Cheri Roundtree / 12/15/92 - $24.71 hr.
14.	PREVIOUS EMPLOYMENT	n/a

CREDIT HISTORY

CREDIT GRANTOR	DATE OPENED	LAST DATE REPORTED	HIGHEST CREDIT	BALANCE OWING	PAST DUE AMOUNT	CURRENT RATING	TERMS	30 DAYS	60 DAYS	90 DAYS	DATE LAST PAST DUE
NRL Fed. Credit Union 242568-B	04-91	10-92	6531	4092	0	I-1	164	0	0	0	–
State University of NY	NOT VERIFIED, REQUIRES WRITTEN AUTHORIZATION										
Bankeast 5413826554321	01-90	11-92	1500	192	0	R-1	10	0	0	0	–
Georgian & Woods (Landlord)	07-91	12-92	735	0	0	O-1	735	0	0	0	–
Crestar Bank 9238199532	10-89	09-92	832	0	0	R-1	0	0	0	0	–

Accounts under co-borrower:

CREDIT GRANTOR	DATE OPENED	LAST DATE REPORTED	HIGHEST CREDIT	BALANCE OWING	PAST DUE AMOUNT	CURRENT RATING	TERMS	30 DAYS	60 DAYS	90 DAYS	DATE LAST PAST DUE
Citibank VISA 412201159872	01-88	11-92	5600	87	0	R-1	20	0	0	0	–
Discover Card 60110846603	10-88	11-92	2300	78	0	R-1	20	0	0	0	–
Baybank 28492734998563892	09-88	06-91	500	0	0	R-1	0	0	0	0	–
Filenes 3722943234799	05-89	10-92	54	0	0	R-1	0	0	0	0	–

Inquiries made in the last 90 days: None

Previous residence:
2101 S. Sipley Street, Alexandria, VA - 2 years

Public Records: NONE FOUND

Prepared by: Equifax - Real Estate Services
854 East Wiggins Ave. Schaumburg, IL 60234 (800-555-1234)

** END OF REPORT **

* Please Wait, initializing *
* Testing phone line *

UNIFORM RESIDENTIAL APPRAISAL REPORT

Property Description & Analysis   File No.

SUBJECT

Property Address 4463 Loveday Street	Census Tract 7032	LENDER DISCRETIONARY USE
City Silver Spring County Montgomery State MD Zip Code 20902		Sale Price $
Legal Description Lot 16, Block 31 Hemp Hill Estates		Date
Owner/Occupant Miller, T.A. & V.L.	Map Reference 33 J 7	Mortgage Amount $
Sale Price $ 190,000 Date of Sale 12/12/92 CD	PROPERTY RIGHTS APPRAISED	Mortgage Type
Loan charges/concessions to be paid by seller $ 2,000 closing costs	[x] Fee Simple	Discount Points and Other Concessions
R.E. Taxes $ 1,534.67 Tax Year 91-92 HOA $/Mo. N/A	[ ] Leasehold	Paid by Seller $
Lender/Client Dominion Bankshares Mortgage	[ ] Condominium (HUD/VA)	
Dark & Associates	[ ] De Minimis PUD	Source

NEIGHBORHOOD

LOCATION			NEIGHBORHOOD ANALYSIS	Good	Avg	Fair	Poor
LOCATION	[ ] Urban	[x] Suburban	[ ] Rural	Employment Stability		x		
BUILT UP	[ ] Over 75%	[x] 25-75%	[ ] Under 25%	Convenience to Employment	x			
GROWTH RATE	[ ] Rapid	[x] Stable	[ ] Slow	Convenience to Shopping	x			
PROPERTY VALUES	[ ] Increasing	[x] Stable	[ ] Declining	Convenience to Schools	x			
DEMAND/SUPPLY	[ ] Shortage	[x] In Balance	[ ] Over Supply	Adequacy of Public Transportation		x		
MARKETING TIME	[ ] Under 3 Mos.	[x] 3-6 Mos.	[ ] Over 6 Mos.	Recreation Facilities	x			

PRESENT LAND USE	%	LAND USE CHANGE	PREDOMINANT OCCUPANCY	SINGLE FAMILY HOUSING					
Single Family	75	Not Likely [x]	[ ] Owner [x]	PRICE $(000)	AGE (yrs)	Adequacy of Utilities		x	
2-4 Family		Likely [ ]	[ ] Tenant			Property Compatibility		x	
Multi-family		In process [ ]	[ ] Vacant (0-5%)	150 Low 10		Protection from Detrimental Cond.		x	
Commercial		To:	[ ] Vacant (over 5%)	299 High 10		Police & Fire Protection		x	
Industrial				190 Predominant 25		General Appearance of Properties		x	
Vacant	25					Appeal to Market		x	

Note: Race or the racial composition of the neighborhood are not considered reliable appraisal factors.The subject is located east of
COMMENTS: Georgia Avenue and north of University Blvd. The neighborhood is characterized by detached homes of average to good quality and appeal. All essential suburban services are close by including: Wheaton Regional Park, Kemp Mill Elementary School, and the Kemp Hill Shopping Center. No adverse neighborhood conditions were noted.

SITE

Dimensions See attached plat		Topography	Slopes up to rear
Site Area 11,697 S.f.	Corner Lot Yes	Size	Average for area
Zoning Classification R-60, Residential	Zoning Compliance In Compl.	Shape	Irregular
HIGHEST & BEST USE: Present Use Yes	Other Use N/A	Drainage	Adequate

UTILITIES	Public	Other	SITE IMPROVEMENTS	Type	Public	Private		
Electricity	x		Street	Macadam	x		View	Typical for area
Gas	x		Curb/Gutter	Concrete		x	Landscaping	Typical
Water	x		Sidewalk	Concrete		x	Driveway	Concrete
Sanitary Sewer	x		Street Lights	Above grd. Elec.	x		Apparent Easements	See comments below
Storm Sewer	x		Alley	No			FEMA Flood Hazard	Yes* No X
							FEMA* Map/Zone	240049 0200 B 8-84

COMMENTS (Apparent adverse easements, encroachments, special assessments, slide areas, etc.)The site contains a concrete driveway leading to a one car carport and a concrete walkway leading to the front entry. Typical suburban utility easements are not adverse factors.

IMPROVEMENTS

GENERAL DESCRIPTION		EXTERIOR DESCRIPTION		FOUNDATION		BASEMENT		INSULATION	
Units	One	Foundation	Conc. Block	Slab	54%	Area Sq. Ft. 540		Roof	
Stories	One	Exterior Walls	Brick/Sid	Crawl Space		% Finished 90%		Ceiling	x
Type (Det./Att.)	Detached	Roof Surface	Asphalt	Basement	46%	Ceiling	Drywall	Walls	x
Design (Style)	Sp. Level	Gutters & Dwnspts	Aluminum	Sump Pump	No	Walls	Panel	Floor	
Existing	Yes	Window Type	Alum. Slid	Dampness	None Noted	Floor	Carpet	None	
Proposed		Storm Sash	Storms	Settlement	None Noted	Outside Entry	No, the	Adequacy Adeq.	x
Under Construction		Screens	Combo	Infestation	None Noted	subject has a		Energy Efficient Items	
Age (Yrs.)	31	Manufactured House	No	No termites, damp-		partial inground		Storm Windows	
Effective Age (Yrs.)	8-10			ness or settlement		basement			

ROOM LIST

ROOMS	Foyer	Living	Dining	Kitchen	Den	Family Rm.	Rec. Rm.	Bedrooms	# Baths	Laundry	Other	Area Sq. Ft.
Basement							X/FP					540
Level 1			X	X/TS					.5	X		625
Level 2	X	X/FP			X							540
Level 3								3	2			625

Finished area above grade contains: 7 Rooms; 3 Bedroom(s); 2.5 Bath(s); 1,790 Square Feet of Gross Living Area

INTERIOR

SURFACES	Materials/Condition	HEATING		KITCHEN EQUIP.		ATTIC		IMPROVEMENT ANALYSIS	Good	Avg	Fair	Poor
Floors	Resil/Cpt/Hdwd	Type	FWA	Refrigerator	x	None		Quality of Construction		x		
Walls	Dry/Panel	Fuel	Gas	Range/Oven	x	Stairs		Condition of Improvements		x		
Trim/Finish	Average	Condition	Good	Disposal	x	Drop Stair		Room Sizes/Layout		x		
Bath Floor	Ceramic	Adequacy	Adeq.	Dishwasher	x	Scuttle	x	Closets and Storage		x		
Bath Wainscot	Ceramic	COOLING		Fan/Hood	x	Floor		Energy Efficiency		x		
Doors	Wood	Central	CAC	Compactor		Heated		Plumbing-Adequacy & Condition		x		
All surfaces are in		Other		Washer/Dryer	x	Finished		Electrical-Adequacy & Condition		x		
average condition		Condition	Avg.	Microwave		Unfin	x	Kitchen Cabinets-Adequacy & Cond		x		
Fireplace(s) RR/LR	#2	Adequacy	Adeq.	Intercom		Storage	x	Compatibility to Neighborhood		x		

AUTOS

CAR STORAGE	Garage		Attached	x	Adequate	x	House Entry	x	Appeal & Marketability		x		
No. Cars 1	Carport	x	Detached		Inadequate		Outside Entry		Estimated Remaining Economic Life 50-52				Yrs.
Condition Average	None		Built-In		Electric Door		Basement Entry		Estimated Remaining Physical Life 52				Yrs.

Additional features: The subject has a rear fenced in yard, a back and front porch, a patio, a shed, and cathedral ceilings. Insulation was not observed but was assumed to be present and adequate.

COMMENTS

Depreciation (Physical, functional and external inadequacies, repairs needed, modernization, etc.) The subject has a three year old roof, a three year old furnace, three year old siding, a two year old hot water heater, four year old kitchen appliances and has been freshly painted on the interior and new carpeting. These improvements have reduced the effective age below the actual age.

General market conditions and prevalence and impact in subject/market area regarding loan discounts, interest buydowns and concessions: Market rates for conventional transactions are typically 7.5% to 12% with loan origination fees usually split between buyer and seller. Sales concessions are generally minimal and do not significantly affect the value.

Freddie Mac Form 70 10/86   Fannie Mae Form 1004 10/86

UNIFORM RESIDENTIAL APPRAISAL REPORT   File No. 903688

Purpose of Appraisal is to estimate Market Value as defined in the Certification & Statement of Limiting Conditions.

COST APPROACH

BUILDING SKETCH (SHOW GROSS LIVING AREA ABOVE GRADE)
If for Freddie Mac or Fannie Mae, show only square foot calculations and cost approach comments in this space

	Measurements		No. Stories	Sq. Ft.
15.1	x	41.4	1	= 625.14
22.6	x	23.9	1	= 540.14
15.1	x	41.4	1	= 625.14
	x			=
	x			=
	x			=
	Total Gross Living Area			1,790

No functional or external obsolescence was noted.

ESTIMATED REPRODUCTION COST – NEW – OF IMPROVEMENTS:

Dwelling 1,790 Sq. Ft. @ $ 75.00 = $	134,250
Esmt 540 Sq. Ft. @ $ 30.00 =	16,200
Extras Incld. in dwelling cost =	0
2/fireplaces	10,000
Special Energy Efficient Items Incld. dwell =	0
Porches, Patios, etc. 2Pchs. Pto.Fenc.S=	8,000
Garage/Carport 317 Sq. Ft. @ $ 7.00 =	2,219
Total Estimated Cost New .... = $	170,669

	Physical	Functional	External	
Less	13%	0	0	
Depreciation	22,190	0	0 = $	22,190

Depreciated Value of Improvements .... = $	148,479
Site Imp. "as is" (driveway, landscaping, etc.) = $	5,000
ESTIMATED SITE VALUE .... = $	50,000
(If leasehold, show only leasehold value.)	
INDICATED VALUE BY COST APPROACH Rounded $	203,500

(Not Required by Freddie Mac and Fannie Mae)
Does property conform to applicable HUD/VA property standards? ☐ Yes ☐ No
If No, explain: N/A

Construction Warranty ☐ Yes ☒ No
Name of Warranty Program
Warranty Coverage Expires

SALES COMPARISON ANALYSIS

The undersigned has recited three recent sales of properties most similar and proximate to subject and has considered these in the market analysis. The description includes a dollar adjustment, reflecting market reaction to those items of significant variation between the subject and comparable properties. If a significant item in the comparable property is superior to, or more favorable than, the subject property, a minus (–) adjustment is made, thus reducing the indicated value of subject. If a significant item in the comparable is inferior to, or less favorable than, the subject property, a plus (+) adjustment is made, thus increasing the indicated value of the subject.

ITEM	SUBJECT	COMPARABLE NO. 1		COMPARABLE NO. 2		COMPARABLE NO. 3	
Address	4463 Loveday St.	703 Hillsboro Drive Hemp Hill Estates		714 N. Belgrade Ct. Kemp Hill Estates		11209 Bybee Street Hemp Hill Estates	
Proximity to Subject		1 Block Southwest		2 Blocks Southwest		6 Blocks Southwest	
Sales Price	$ 190,000	$ 187,500		$ 200,000		$194,500	
Price/Gross Liv. Area	$ 106.15 ☑	$ 104.75 ☑		$08.11 ☑		$ 105.14 ☑	
Data Source	Inspection	Visual/MLS/Lusk		Visual/MLS/Lusk		Visual/MLS/Lusk	
VALUE ADJUSTMENTS	DESCRIPTION	DESCRIPTION	+ (–)$ Adjustment	DESCRIPTION	+ (–)$ Adjustment	DESCRIPTION	+ (–)$ Adjustment
Sales or Financing Concessions		Cash-No adj. Required		Conventional		Conventional	
Date of Sale/Time	12-12-92 CD	8-92 SE		7-92 SE		8-92 SE	
Location	Average	Average		Average		Average	
Site/View	11,697Sf/Typ	11,031Sf/Typ		9,391Sf/Typ		8,027Sf/Typ	
Design and Appeal	Sp. Level/Avg	Sp.Level/Sim		Sp.Level/Sim		Split Lvl/Sm	
Quality of Construction	Average	Average		Average		Average	
Age	31 years	32 Years		27 years		31 years	
Condition	Average	Average		Average		Average	
Above Grade Room Count	Total / Bdrms / Baths 7 / 3 / 2.5	Total / Bdrms / Baths 7 / 3 / 2.5		Total / Bdrms / Baths 7 / 3 / 2.5		Total / Bdrms / Baths 7 / 3 / 2.5	
Gross Living Area	1,790 Sq. Ft.	1,790 Sq. Ft.		1,850 Sq. Ft.		1,850 Sq. Ft.	
Basement & Finished Rooms Below Grade	Partial Rec Room	Partial Rec Room		Partial Rec Room		Partial Rec Room	
Functional Utility	Average	Average		Average		Average	
Heating/Cooling	FWA/CAC	FWA/CAC		FWA/CAC		FWA/CAC	
Garage/Carport	1/Carport	1/Carport		1/Carport		1/Carport	
Porches, Patio, Pools, etc.	2Porches and Patio	Patio	+2,000	Porch	+1,500	Patio	+2,000
Special Energy Efficient Items	Storm Windows	None	+500	None	+500	Insulated Windows	
Fireplace(s)	2/Fireplaces	2/Fireplaces		1/Fireplace	+2,500	None	+ 5,000
Other (e.g. kitchen equip., remodeling)				New Kitchen	–10,000	New Kitchen	–10,000
Net Adj. (total)		☒ + ☐ –$ 2,500		☐ + ☒ –$ –5,500		☐ + ☒ –$ –3,000	
Indicated Value of Subject		$		$		$ 191,500	

Comments on Sales Comparison: Most consideration was placed on comparable 1 which is the same model as the subject. Comparables 2 and 3 provide good supporting data for the sale of split level homes in Kemp Mill Estates.

INDICATED VALUE BY SALES COMPARISON APPROACH .... $ 190,000
INDICATED VALUE BY INCOME APPROACH (If Applicable) Estimated Market Rent $ N/A /Mo x Gross Rent Multiplier N/A = $ N/A
This appraisal is made ☒ "as is" ☐ subject to the repairs, alterations, inspections or conditions listed below ☐ completion per plans and specifications.
Comments and Conditions of Appraisal: No requirements. See attached addendum.

RECONCILIATION

Final Reconciliation: Most consideration is placed on the Market Data Approach which is closely supported by the Cost Approach. The Income Approach was not used due to a lack of recent, verifiable sales/rental data for the market area.

This appraisal is based upon the above requirements, the certification, contingent and limiting conditions, and Market Value definition that are stated in

☐ FmHA, HUD &/or VA instructions.
☐ Freddie Mac Form 439 (Rev. 7/86)/Fannie Mae Form 1004B (Rev. 7/86) filed with client December 21, 19 92 ☒ attached.
I (WE) ESTIMATE THE MARKET VALUE, AS DEFINED, OF THE SUBJECT PROPERTY AS OF December 21, 19 92 to be $ 190,000
I (We) certify: that to the best of my (our) knowledge and belief the facts and data used herein are true and correct; that I (we) personally inspected the subject property, both inside and out, and have made an exterior inspection of all comparable sales cited in this report; and that I (we) have no undisclosed interest, present or prospective therein.

Appraiser(s) SIGNATURE _____
NAME

Review Appraiser SIGNATURE _____
(if applicable) NAME
☐ Did ☒ Did Not Inspect Property

Freddie Mac Form 70 10/86

Fannie Mae Form 1004 10/86

258

ALL NUMERICAL DISCLOSURES EXCEPT THE LATE PAYMENT DISCLOSURE ARE ESTIMATES. NOTICE TO BORROWER(S) REQUIRED BY FEDERAL LAW AND FEDERAL RESERVE BOARD.

REAL PROPERTY TRANSACTION SECURED BY A FIRST LIEN ON DWELLING.

LOAN:
LENDER:
DOMINION BANKSHARES MORTGAGE CORP.
6110 Executive Boulvard
Rockville, MD 20852

DATE: 121792
TYPE: CONVENTIONAL
BORROWER: Theodore A. Miller
CO-BORROWER: Vicki L. Miller
ADDRESS: 2024 GEORGIAN PARK PL., #3
CITY STATE/ZIP: WHEATON, MD 20902
PROPERTY: 4463 LOVEDAY STREET
CITY STATE/ZIP: SILVER SPRING, MD 20902
EST SETTLEMENT DATE: 010192

ANNAUL PERCENTAGE RATE The cost of your credit as a yearly rate.	FINANCE CHARGE The dollar amount the credit will cost you.	AMOUNT FINANCED The amount of credit provided to you or on your behalf.	TOTAL OF PAYMENTS The amount you will have paid after you have made all payments as scheduled.
9.877%e	$342,935.38e	$164,571.86e	$507,507.14e

PAYMENT SCHEDULE:

NUMBER OF PAYMENTS	AMOUNTS OF PAYMENTS	WHEN PAYMENTS ARE DUE	NUMBER OF PAYMENTS	AMOUNTS OF PAYMENTS	WHEN PAYMENTS ARE DUE
106	1,454.02	03/01/93	360		
253	1,391.32	01/01/02			
1	1,377.06	02/02/23			

You should refer to the contract documents for information about nonpayment default, lender's right to accelerate the debt, prepayment, and assumption.

( ) This loan contains a variable rate feature. Variable rate disclosures have been provided earlier.

DEMAND FEATURE: (X) This loan does not have a Demand Feature.
( ) This loan has a Demand Feature as follows:

VARIABLE RATE FEATURE: (X) This loan does not have a Variable Rate Feature.
( ) This loan is an Adjustable Rate Loan.

SECURITY: (X) You are giving a security interest in the real property located at 4463 LOVEDAY STREET, SILVER SPRING, MD 20902

ASSUMPTION: Someone buying this property
(X) cannot assume the remaining balance due under current loan terms.
( ) may assume subject to lender's conditions the remaining balance due under current loan terms.

FILING / RECORDING FEES: $50.00

PROPERTY INSURANCE: (X) Property hazard insurance in the amount of $1710 with a loss payable clause to the lender is a required condition of this loan. The Borrower can purchase this insurance from any insurance company acceptable to the lender.

LATE CHARGES: If your payment is not received within 15 days, a late charge 5.00% of the overdue amount will be added.

PREPAYMENT PENALTY: You will not be charged a penalty to prepay this loan in full or in part. You may be entitled to a refund of part of the finance charge.
(If your loan is an FHA loan and you prepay on other than a regular installment date, you may be assessed interest charges until the end of the month.)

THIS DOCUMENT HAS BEEN CHECKED FOR ACCURACY BY _____

I / We hereby acknowledge reading and receiving a complete copy of this disclosure along with copies of documents referred to in this disclosure.

_____ BORROWER/DATE _____ BORROWER/DATE
_____ BORROWER/DATE _____ BORROWER/DATE

Application No. _____ Name __MILLER, THEODORE A. AND VICKI L.__

Property ___4463 Loveday Street_____Silver Spring, MD___

As required by the Real Estate Settlement Procedures Act of 1974 you are being furnished a "Good Faith Estimate" of settlement charges applicable to your loan request on the above referenced property. These figures are estimates only; and the items "#" may obviously vary. **"YOU MAY BE REQUIRED TO PAY ADDITIONAL AMOUNTS AT SETTLEMENT. YOU MAY WISH TO INQUIRE AS TO THE AMOUNTS OF SUCH OTHER ITEMS."**

Loan Application		Monthly Payment	
Amount	$ 171,000	Principal & Interest	$ 1422.29
Term	360 Mos.	Tax escrow	$ 128.00
Interest rate	9.375 %	Fire insurance	$ 25.00
Annual percentage rate (APR)	%	PMI	$ 48.00
		Other	$
		Total	$ 1575.29

Loan closing cost			Prepaid items		
Origination fee	$ 1710.00 *	1st year fire ins. Premium		$ 250.00 #
Construction fee Discount Points	$ 3420.00 *	Escrow:		
Title insurance	$ 600.00 #	Taxes 7 Mos. @ $ 143.00 =	$ 1001.00 #
Recording fees	$ 2850.00 #	F. Ins. 2 Mos. @ $ 21.00 =	$ 42.00 #
Pest Inspection	$ 35.00 #	PMI 2 Mo. @ $ 64.00 =	$ 128.00 #
Survey	$ 125.00 #	Interest Maximum 30 days		
PMI premium	$ 684.00 *	1 Days @ $ 43.00 day =	$ 43.00 #
Inspection Fee	$		$
Attorney fee	$ 250.00 #		$
Application fee (Includes credit rpt & Appr fee)	$ 225.00	Total	$ 1464.00
Total	$ 9899.00		

* Included in Prepaid Finance Charges for Regulation Z Disclosure

Sales price	$190,000.00
Less: Earnest money	$ 9,000.00
Application fee	$ 300.00
Loan Amount	$171,000.00
Seller's share taxes	$ (2,000.00)
	$
Plus: Estimated closing costs	$ 9,899.00
Prepaid items	$ 1,464.00
Buyer's share taxes	$ incl.
	$
ESTIMATED AMOUNT NEEDED AT CLOSING	$210,663.00

I am indicating below my preference of Attorney. Insurance agent. Surveyor. Title insurance company. and, if applicable. Private mortgage insurance company:

Attorney _____ TO BE DETERMINED

Fire insurance agent _____ TO BE DETERMINED

Surveyor _____ TO BE DETERMINED

Title insurance company _____ TO BE DETERMINED

Private mortgage insurance company _____ GENERAL ELECTRIC MORTGAGE INSURANCE COMPANY

All of the above have been clearly explained to me and by acknowledging receipt of this statement I understand the following:

- I have been advised that I have the right to file a written loan application
- I have been advised that I have the right to a copy of Raleigh Federal's written underwriting standards.
- This loan may be called, if there is any change in ownership. or recorded agreement to sell. and that my transfer of this loan is subject to the approval and consent of the lender.
- This loan may be paid in full at any time. without penalty. except current month's interest. Any other lump sum payments may be made in conformance with the amortization schedule.
- I have received the required HUD Guide Booklet.

Date: ___13/1/9 2___

_____ Loan Officer

_____ Applicant

_____ Applicant

FORM # ML-0017 (REV 1 87)

MORTGAGE INSURANCE APPLICATION

GE Capital
Mortgage Insurance

This Application must be filled out entirely before a commitment/certificate can be issued.

LENDER NAME AND ADDRESS

Dominion Bankshares Mortgage Corp.
12300 Twinbrook Pky.
Rockville, MD. 20852-0000
ORG B22432

Master Policy No. _____
Full 10 Digit Number

Borrower Name: <u>Theodore A. & Vicki L. Miller</u>
Base Loan Amount: $ <u>171,000</u> Base LTV <u>90</u> %

Front-End Zero (Financed Premium)
Premium Financed $ _____ Loan Term _____ Yrs.
Total Loan Amount $ <u>171,000</u> Total LTV <u>90</u> %
(Total LTV, including Financed Premium, must not exceed 95%.)

LOAN INFORMATION

Type of Certificate: <u>X</u> Primary ____ Pool ____ Both   If a Brokered Loan, Broker Name: _____

Property Use: <u>X</u> Primary Res. ____ Second Home ____ Investment   If Conduit Program, Conduit Name: _____

MORTGAGE INSURANCE INFORMATION

Standard Coverage:

____12% <u>X</u>17% ____20% ____22% ____25% ____30% ____Other ____%
____ Advantage to 75% Exposure   Premium financed ____ Yes ____ No

Annual Premium Plans:
<u>X</u> Standard
____ Front-End Zero (First-Year)
____ Front-End Lite
Renewals: ____ Amortized <u>X</u> Level

Single Premium Plan:
____ Single premium coverage
for ____ years
____ Front-End Zero (One-Time
coverage down to 80% LTV)

MORTGAGE INSTRUMENT DESCRIPTION (Detailed instructions appear on the BACK of this form.)

<u>X</u> Fixed Payment (For fixed payment loans only the top two lines of this section need to be completed.)
____ Balloon or call option: number of years _____
Non-Fixed Payment
____ Negative Amortization: ____ None ____ Potential
____ Fixed Rate, Non-Fixed Payment [GEM, Temporary Buydown, etc.]
____ Adjustable Rate Mortgage (ARM)

ARM Index:
____ 6 Mo. T. Bill—Auction Average (1D)   ____ FHLBB Monthly Median COF (3A)   Other _____
____ 1 Yr. T. Security—Constant Maturity (2A)   ____ FHLBB 11th District COF (3C)   _____

MAXIMUM GROSS MARGIN _____ % (MANDATORY FOR ALL ARMs)

Payment/Interest Rate Data:	Payment	Interest	
Initial Rate:	____%	____%	
Qualifying Rate:	____%		
Months until first Adjustment:	____	____	
Frequency of Adjustment:	____ mos.	____ mos.	
Per Adjustment Cap:	____%*	____%	
Lifetime Cap:		____%	
Prescheduled Payment Increase:	____%		

Buydown Data:
Amount of subsidy $ _____
Source: ____ Builder/Seller (S) ____ Borrower (B)
____ Employer (E) ____ Other (O) _____
Application of funds:
____ 3-2-1% (3) ____ 1-0% (1)
____ 2-1-0% (2) ____ Other (O) _____

*Including optional payment cap

DOCUMENTATION REQUIRED

<u>X</u> Signed Loan Application <u>X</u> Appraisal, Photos, Legal Description
<u>X</u> Credit Report <u>X</u> Good Faith Estimate
<u>X</u> V.O.E. <u>X</u> Sales Contract/Offer to Purchase
<u>X</u> V.O.D.

If Applicable:
____ Federal Tax Returns
____ Payment History on Present Mortgage
____ Lease Agreement
____ Gift Letter
____ Verification of "other" income (i.e. child support, alimony)

Lender represents and, except where prohibited by law, warrants that the statements and information contained in this Application and in all supporting documentation are accurate and complete and that the lender is not aware of any allowances or inducements that have been or are being given to the borrower(s) in connection with this transaction except those described in this Application and the supporting documentation, and acknowledges that GE will rely on such information and statements in issuing any commitment/certificate. This Application and all supporting documentation are hereby made a part of, and are incorporated by reference into, the Master Policy under which the commitment/certificate is issued.

LENDER RESPONSE:
Please complete for immediate commitment reply.

<u>Julie Davidson</u>   <u>555-8923</u>
Person to notify of disposition   Area code/telephone number

Authorized signature   <u>1/9/93</u>   Date

____ GE's PowerLine

Form 202 (REV. 5/88)

261

GE Capital
Mortgage Insurance

GENERAL ELECTRIC MORTGAGE INSURANCE CORPORATION   (The "Company)
PO Box 1415 Merrifield, Va. 22116
2000 Corporate Ridge
McLean, Va. 22102

COMMITMENT/CERTIFICATE OF INSURANCE

In consideration of the premium hereinafter set forth and in reliance upon the statements made in the application, the Company hereby issues this Commitment for Insurance to you, and tenders to you a Certificate of Insurance for the mortgage loan herein described subject to the terms and conditions of your Master Policy identified below, and subject to any Special Conditions that may be set forth below.

INITIAL PREMIUM	COMMITMENT EXPIRATION DATE	COMMITMENT EFFECTIVE DATE	MASTER POLICY NO.	COMMITMENT NO.
684.00	07/10/93	01/11/93	B2244322	81-0079234-5

INSURED'S NAME AND ADDRESS:	BORROWER NAME AND PROPERTY ADDRESS:
Dominion Bankshares Mortgage Corporation 12300 Twinbrook Pky. Rockville, MD 20852	MILLER, Theodore A. MILLER, Vicki L. 4463 Loveday Street Silver Spring, MD 20902

INSURED AMOUNT	SALES PRICE	APPRAISED VALUE	TERM OF LOAN	COVERAGE
171,000	190,000	190,000	360 months	Top 17%

INITIAL PREMIUM RATE	RENEWAL RATE	RENEWAL TYPE	PREMIUM PLAN	TERM OF COVERAGE
.40000	.340000	Level	500	1 year

PREMIUM SCHEDULE •   .40 of 1% of original loan amount for 1 year with annual renewal at
.34 of 1% of original loan amount for the next 9 renewal years.
Thereafter at .25 of 1% of original loan amount.

SPECIAL CONDITIONS •

Calculation assumes a term from closing of 360 months using initial principal and interest payment.

MORTGAGE INSURANCE INFORMATION •

TOTAL PREMIUM	BASIS PTS	MONTHLY PAYMENT/RATE			
$14,467.80	27	FIRST: $48.45	/ .34000 %	LAST: $35.63	/ .25000 %

PLEASE NOTE: Premium is due within 10 days of Loan Closing Date/Certificate Effective Date indicated below.

INSTRUCTION TO LENDERS: Please complete the following information relative to the closing of the loan and mail this Commitment together with your premium remittance to the Company. Insurance coverage as set forth above shall become effective as of the loan closing date or such later date as mutually agreed to by you and the Company. Any revision or modification of the terms and conditions set forth in this Commitment, or failure to satisfy any Special Conditions specified above, without prior written consent of the Company, will invalidate this Commitment and the related insurance coverage.

SECRETARY _____   AUTHORIZED REPRESENTATIVE _____

INSURED'S CERTIFICATION: By tender of premium and submission of this completed Commitment/Certificate, the Insured represents and certifies that the above loan transaction has been consummated in accordance with the loan documents provided to the Company by the Insured, any Special Conditions set forth in this Commitment have been satisfied, and the applicable premium has been paid.

LENDER'S LOAN NUMBER	LOAN CLOSING DATE/CERTIFICATE EFFECTIVE DATE	REMITTED PREMIUM	DATE OF SIGNATURE

CC (4/89)   **COMPLETE AND RETURN TO THE COMPANY**   BY: _____
AUTHORIZED REPRESENTATIVE OF LENDER

FannieMae

Compliments of
General Electric Mortgage Insurance Corporation

TRANSMITTAL SUMMARY

Lender Name	Lender Address		
Dominion, Bankshares Mortgage Corporation	12300 Twinbrook Parkway Rockville, MD		
Borrower Name		Lender Number	Lender Loan Number
MILLER, Theodore A. and Vicki L.			
Property Address		Contract Number	Fannie Mae Loan No.
4463 Loveday Street Silver Spring, MD 20902			

Section 1 - Loan Characteristics (Check all Applicable Categories)

Loan Type
- ☐ FHA
- ☐ VA
- ☒ Conv.

☒ 1st Mort.   ☒ Fixed Rate   ☐ Buydown
☐ 2nd Mort.   ☐ ARM Plan   ☐
No. _____

Loan Purpose
- ☒ Purchase
- ☐ Refinance
  If Refinance, Purpose

Occupancy
- ☒ Primary Single-Family Owner-Occupied
- ☐ Second Home
- ☐ S. F. Investment
- ☐ 2-4 Family Investment
- ☐ 2-4 Family Owner-Occupied

Loan Terms

Original Loan Amount	Initial Note Rate	Initial Monthly Installment	Date of Note	Term (months)
171,000	9.375	1,422.29		360

Section 2 - Underwriting Information

Sales Price	Appraised Value	Loan to Value
190,000	190,000	90.000

Does Fannie Mae have an interest in the first mortgage? ☐ Yes ☐ No
What is combined Loan-to-Value Ratio?

Property Type:
- ☐ Condominium Project Type
- ☐ PUD Project Type
- ☐ Cooperative Project Type
- ☐ De Minimus PUD
- ☒ Other

Appraiser Name & Company Name	Underwriter Name

Stable Monthly Income

	Borrower	Co-Borrower	Total
Base Income	$3936.42	$2214.50	$6150.92
Other Income	$	$	$
Positive Cash Flow (Subject Property)	$	$	$
Total Income	$3936.42	$	$

Ratios

Primary Housing Expense/Income	25.61 %
Total Obligation/Income	29.59 %
Investment Property Only	
Debt Service Coverage Ratio	

Proposed Monthly Payments

Borrower's Primary Residence

First Mortgage P&I	$ 1422.29
Second Mortgage P&I	$
Hazard Insurance	$ 25.00
Taxes	$ 128.00
Mortgage Insurance	$ 48.00
Home Owner Association Fees	$
Other: _____	$
Total Primary Housing Expense	$ 1575.29

Other Obligations

Negative Cash Flow (Subject Property)	$
All Other Monthly Payments	$ 244.91
Total All Monthly Payments	$ 1820.20

Section 3 - Lender's Underwriting Comments

Section 4 - Exhibits Submitted in Addition to Fannie Mae Standard Document Requirements

1.	4.
2.	5.
3.	6.

Section 5 - Lender's Contact (Person to Whom Correspondence Should Be Directed)

Name	Title	Telephone No.
Signature		Date

ISC/PFTSXX//1185/LASER
1008 (10/85)

Fannie Mae
Form 1008 Oct. 85

263

GLOSSARY OF REAL ESTATE AND MORTGAGE LENDING TERMS

18

Abstract of title   A written history of the title transaction or condition bearing on the title to designated real estate. An abstract of title covers the period from the original source of title to the present and summarizes all subsequent instruments of public record by setting forth their material parts.

Acceleration clause   A common provision of a mortgage, trust deed, and note providing that the entire principal shall become immediately due and payable in the event of default.

Accrued interest   The interest earned for the period of time that has elapsed since interest was last paid.

Acknowledgment   A formal declaration, attached to or a part of an instrument, made before a duly authorized officer (usually a notary public) by the person who has executed the instrument, who declares the execution to be a free act and deed.

Acquisition cost   The FHA-appraised value or purchase price (whichever is less) plus some closing costs.

Acre   A measure of land, 43,560 square feet.

Action to quiet title   A court action to remove any interest or claim to the title to real property, taken to remove a cloud on the title.

Administrator   A person appointed by a probate court to administer the estate of a person who died intestate (without a will).

Adjustment date   The date for periodic interest rate adjustments for an adjustable rate mortgage loan.

Adjustment period   The length of time between interest or payment rate change on an ARM.

Adjustable rate mortgage loan (ARM)   A type of alternative mortgage instrument in which the interest rate adjusts periodically according to a predetermined index and margin. This adjustment results in the mortgage payment either increasing or decreasing. In some situations, the adjustment is made to the outstanding principal.

Ad valorem   "According to the value, " used in connection with taxation.

Advance   In real estate, a partial disbursement of funds under a note. Most often used in connection with construction lending.

Advance commitment   A written promise to make an investment at some time in the future if specified conditions are met.

Adverse possession   The right by which someone occupying a piece of land might acquire title against the real owner, if the occupant's possession has been actual, continuous, hostile, visible, and distinct for a statutory period of time.

Affidavit   A sworn statement in writing before a proper official, usually a notary (see *acknowledgment*).

After-acquired property   Property acquired after the execution of a security agreement and which will serve as additional security for the underlying debt.

Agent   One who legally represents another, called a principal, from whom authority has been derived.

Agreement for sale   A written document in which the purchaser agrees to buy certain real estate (or personal property) and the seller agrees to sell under stated terms and conditions. Also called sales contract, binder, or earnest money contract.

Air rights   The ownership of the right to use, control, or occupy the air space over designated real estate.

Alienation   Transference of real property from one person to another.

Alternative mortgage instrument   Any one of the various new mortgage loans that is different from a traditional mortgage because the monthly payment, interest rate, term, or other provisions are changed in an agreed-upon manner.

Amenity   An aspect of a property that enhances its value. Examples are off-street reserved parking within a condominium community, the nearness of good public transportation, tennis courts, or a swimming pool.

American Land Title Association (ALTA)   A national association of title insurance companies, abstractors, and attorneys specializing in real property law. The association speaks for the title insurance and abstracting industry and establishes standard procedures and title policy forms.

Amortization   Repayment of a debt in equal installments of principal and interest, rather than interest-only payments.

Amortization schedule   A table showing the amounts of principal and interest due at regular intervals and the unpaid balance of the loan after each payment is made.

Annual percentage rate (APR)   A rate which represents the relationship of the total finance charge (interest, loan fees, points) to the amount of the loan.

Annual statement   An annual statement sent to mortgagors detailing all activity in their mortgage loan account, including all escrow activity.

Application   A form used to apply for a mortgage loan and to record pertinent information concerning a prospective mortgagor and the proposed security.

Appraisal   A report by a qualified person setting forth an opinion or estimate of value. Also, the process by which this estimate is obtained.

Appraised value   An opinion of value reached by an appraiser based upon knowledge, experience, and a study of pertinent data.

Appraiser   A person qualified by education, training, and experience to estimate the value of real and personal property.

Appreciation   An increase in value; the opposite of depreciation.

Appurtenance   Anything attached to the land and thus part of the property, such as a barn, garage, or an easement.

Assessed valuation   The value that a taxing authority places upon real or personal property for the purpose of taxation.

Assessment   The process of placing a value on property for the strict purpose of taxation. May also refer to a levy against property for a special purpose, such as a sewer assessment.

Assignee   The person to whom property or a right is assigned or transferred.

Assignment of mortgage   A document that evidences a transfer of ownership of a mortgage from one party to another.

Assignment of rents   An agreement between property owner and mortgagee specifically fixing the rights and obligations of each regarding rent transferred to a mortgagee if a mortgagor defaults.

Assignor   A person who transfers or assigns a right or property.

Assumption   A written agreement by one party to pay an obligation originally incurred by another.

Assumption fee   The fee paid to a lender (usually by the purchaser of real property) resulting from the assumption of an existing mortgage.

Assumption of mortgage   Agreement by a buyer to assume the liability under an existing note secured by a mortgage or deed of trust. The lender usually must approve the new debtor in order to release the existing debtor (usually the seller) from liability.

Attachment   A seizure of defendant's property by court order as security for any judgment a plaintiff may recover in a legal action.

Automatic guarantee   An approved mortgage lender can make a guaranteed Veterans Administration mortgage loan without any prior approval from the VA.

Balance sheet   A financial statement showing assets, liabilities, and the net worth as of a specific date.

Balloon mortgage   A mortgage with periodic installments of principal and interest that does not fully amortize the loan. The balance of the mortgage is due in a lump sum at the end of the term.

Balloon payment   The unpaid principal amount of a mortgage or other long-term loan due at a certain date in the future, usually the amount that must be paid in a lump sum at the end of the term.

Bankrupt   A person, firm, or corporation who, through a court proceeding, is relieved from the payment of all debts after the surrender of all assets to a court-appointed trustee.

Basis points   A basis point is $1/100$ of 1% interest; thus, 50 basis points equals $1/2$ of 1%.

Basket provision   A provision contained in the regulatory acts governing the investments of insurance companies, savings and loan associations, and mutual savings banks. It allows for a certain small percentage of total assets to be placed in investments not otherwise permitted by the regulatory acts.

Beneficiary   The person designated to receive the income from a trust, estate, or trust deed.

Bequeath   To transfer personal property by will.

Bill of sale   A document in writing that transfers title to personal property.

Binder, insurance   A written evidence of temporary hazard or title coverage that only runs for a limited time and must be replaced by a permanent policy.

Bi-weekly mortgage   A mortgage with payments due every two weeks totalling 26 payments a year.

Blanket mortgage   A lien on more than one parcel or unit of land frequently incurred by subdividers or developers who have purchased a single tract of land for the purpose of dividing it into smaller parcels for sale or development.

Blue Sky laws   State laws to regulate the sale of securities to avoid investments in fraudulent companies or high-risk investments without disclosure of the risks to the investor.

Bona fide   In good faith, without fraud.

Borrower   One who receives funds with the expressed or implied intention of repaying the loan in full.

Breach   Violation of a legal obligation.

Break-even point   In residential or commercial property, the figure at which occupancy income is equal to all required expenses and debt service.

Broker   The person who, for a commission or a fee, brings parties together and assists in negotiating contracts between them.

Building codes   Local regulations that control design, construction, and materials used in construction. Building codes are based on safety and health standards.

Bundle of rights   The total rights or interests a person has in property, e.g., the exclusive right of an individual to own, possess, use, enjoy, and dispose of real property.

Buy-down mortgage   A mortgage made by a lender with a below-market interest rate in return for an interest rate subsidy in the form of money received from a builder, seller, or in some situations, a home buyer.

Buy-sell agreement   An agreement entered into by an interim and a permanent lender for the sale and assignment of the mortgage to the permanent lender when a building has been completed. Often the mortgagor is a party to this agreement on the theory that the mortgagor should have a contractual right to insist that the permanent lender buy the mortgage.

Call provision   A clause in the mortgage or deed of trust giving the mortgagee or beneficiary the right to accelerate payment of the mortgage debt in full on a certain date or on the happening of specified conditions.

Capital   Money used to create income, either as investment in a business or income property. The money or property comprising the wealth owned or used by a person or business enterprise. The accumulated wealth of a person or business. The net worth of a business represented by the amount by which its assets exceed liabilities.

Capital (debt service) reserve fund   Security requirement established to provide a revenue bond program with reserves that would be available in the event of a shortfall in operating revenues. Typically, the requirement has been equal to maximum annual debt service, but is in some cases calculated as a fixed percent of the principal amount of debt outstanding.

Capital market security   Financial instrument, including both debt and equity securities, with maturities greater than one year. Those instruments with maturities of less than a year are traded in the money markets.

Capitalization   The process of converting into present value a series of anticipated future installments of net income by discounting them into a present worth using a specific desired rate of earnings.

Capitalization rate   The rate which is believed to represent the proper relationship between real property and the net income it produces.

Cap   A limitation on the interest rate increase of either the periodic or lifetime rate or both for an adjustable-rate mortgage.

Cash flow   The income from an investment after gross income is subtracted from all operating expenses, loan payments, and the allowance for the income tax attributed to the income.

Cash-on-cash return   The rate of return on an investment measured by the cash returned to the investor based on the investor's cash investment without regard to income tax savings or the use of borrowed funds.

Certificate of eligibility   A document used by the VA to certify a veteran's eligibility for a VA loan.

Certificate of occupancy   Written authorization given by a local municipality that allows a newly completed or substantially completed structure to be inhabited.

Certificate of reasonable value (CRV)   A document issued by the VA establishing maximum value and loan amount for a VA-guaranteed mortgage.

Certificate of title   A statement furnished by an abstract or title company or an attorney to a client stating that the title to real estate is legally vested in the present owner.

Certified Mortgage Banker (CMB)   A professional designation of the mortgage banking industry.

Chattel real   All estates in real property less than fee estates, such as a lease.

Chain of title   The history of all the documents transferring title to a parcel of real property starting with the earliest existing document and ending with the most recent.

Closing   The conclusion or consummation of a transaction. In real estate closing includes the delivery of a deed, financial adjustments, the signing of notes, and the disbursement of funds necessary to the sale or loan transaction.

Closing costs   Expenses incidental to a sale of real estate, such as loan fees, title fees, appraisal fees, and others.

Closing statement   A financial disclosure accounting for all funds received and expected at the closing, including the escrow deposits for taxes, hazard insurance, and mortgage insurance for the escrow account.

Cloud on title   Any conditions revealed by a title search that adversely affect the title to real estate. Usually they cannot be removed except by a quitclaim deed, release, or court action.

Coinsurance   A sharing of insurance risk between insurer and insured depending on the relation of the amount of the policy and a specified percentage of the actual value of the property insured at the time of loss.

Collateral   Any property pledged as security for a debt.

Collateralized mortgage obligation (CMO)   Issuer guarantees that a minimum repayment schedule will be met.

Collection   Procedure followed to bring the mortgage account current and to file the necessary notices to proceed with foreclosure when necessary.

Commercial loan   A mortgage loan on property that produces income.

Commercial paper   Short-term unsecured promissory notes of large firms sold to meet short-term capital needs.

Commission   An agent's fee for negotiating a real estate or loan transaction.

Commitment   A written promise to make or insure a loan for a specified amount and on specified terms.

Commitment fee   Any fee paid by a borrower to a lender for the lender's promise to lend money at a specified date in the future. The lender may or may not expect to fund the commitment.

Community property   In some western and southwestern states, a form of ownership under which property acquired during a marriage is presumed to be owned jointly unless acquired in such manner as to be legally considered as separate property of either spouse.

Common law   An unwritten body of law based on general custom in England and used to an extent in the United States.

Comparables   Also "comps," an abbreviation for comparable properties used for comparative purposes in the appraisal process; facilities of approximately the same size and location with similar amenities; properties which have been recently sold, which have characteristics similar to property under consideration, thereby indicating the approximate fair market value of the subject property.

Compensating balance   A demand deposit usually required by a commercial bank as a condition for extending a line of credit or a bank loan.

Compound interest   Interest paid on original principal and on the accrued and unpaid interest which has accumulated.

Condemnation   The court proceedings for taking private property under the right of eminent domain for public use with just compensation to the owner.

Condominium   A form of ownership of real property. The owner receives title to a particular unit and a proportionate interest in certain common areas. A condominium generally defines each unit as a separately owned space to the interior surfaces of the perimeter walls, floor, and ceilings.

Conduit An entity which issues mortgage-backed securities backed by mortgages which were originated by another, probably one or more of the traditional originators.

Constant The percentage of the original loan paid in equal annual payments that provide for interest and principal reduction over the life of the loan.

Construction contract An agreement between a general contractor and an owner-developer stating the specific duties the general contractor will perform according to blueprints and specifications at a stipulated price and terms of payment.

Construction loan A short-term, interim loan for financing the cost of construction. The lender makes payments to the builder at periodic intervals as the work progresses.

Construction loan agreement A written agreement between a lender and a builder or borrower in which the specific terms and conditions of a construction loan, including the schedule of payments, are spelled out.

Construction loan draw The partial disbursement of the construction loan, based on the schedule of payments in the loan agreement. Also called *takedown*.

Contract An oral or written agreement to do or not to do a certain thing.

Conventional loan A mortgage loan neither insured by FHA nor guaranteed by VA.

Convertible mortgage An adjustable-rate mortgage whereby the mortgagor can convert the mortgage to a fixed-rate mortgage during a predetermined time period.

Cooperative A form of multiple ownership of real estate in which a corporation or business trust entity holds title to a property and grants the occupancy rights to particular apartments or units to shareholders by means of proprietary leases or similar arrangements.

Corporation An artificial person created by law with certain rights, privileges, and duties of natural persons.

Correspondent A mortgage banker who services mortgage loans as a representative or agent for the owner of the mortgage or investor. Also applies to the mortgage banker's role as originator of mortgage loans for an investor.

Co-signer A person who signs a legal instrument and therefore becomes individually and jointly liable for repayment or performance of an obligation.

Cost approach An appraisal technique used to establish value by estimating the cost to reproduce the improvement, allowing for depreciation, then adding in the fair market value of the land.

Coupon rate   The annual interest rate on a debt instrument. In mortgage lending, the term is used to describe the contract interest rate on the face of the note or bond. The interest rate of a security which will be less than the rate of the underlying mortgages. GNMA MBS have a coupon which is 50 basis points less than the single-family mortgages in the pool.

Covenant   A legally enforceable promise or restriction in a mortgage. For example, the borrower may covenant to keep the property in good repair and adequately insured against fire and other casualties. The breach of a covenant in a mortgage usually creates a default as defined by the mortgage or deed of trust and can be the basis for foreclosure.

Credit deal   A mortgage made based primarily on the credit of a borrower or tenant with a net lease.

Credit report   A report to a prospective lender on the credit standing of a prospective borrower or tenant. Used to help determine creditworthiness.

Curtesy   The common law interest a husband had in the real estate owned by the wife at the time of her death.

Custodian   Usually a commercial bank which holds for safekeeping mortgages and related documents backing an MBS. Custodian may be required to examine and certify documents.

Debenture   An unsecured debt instrument backed only by the general credit standing and earning capacity of the issuer.

Debt coverage ratio   The ratio of effective annual net income to annual debt service.

Debt service   The periodic payment of principal and interest earned on mortgage loans.

Deed   A written legal document which purports to transfer ownership of land from one party to another.

Deed in lieu   A deed given by a mortgagor to a mortgagee to satisfy a debt and avoid foreclosure.

Deed of reconveyance   The transfer of legal title from the trustee to the trustor (the borrower) after the trust deed debt is paid in full.

Deed of trust   In some states it is the document used in place of a mortgage; a type of security instrument conveying title in trust to a third party covering a particular piece of property; used to secure the payment of a note; a conveyance of the title land to a trustee as collateral security for the payment of a debt with the condition that the trustee shall reconvey the title upon the payment of the debt, and with power of the trustee to sell the land and pay the debt in the event of a default on the part of the debtor.

Deed restriction   A limitation placed in a deed limiting or restricting the use of real property.

Default   Breach or nonperformance of a clause in either a note or mortgage which, if not cured, could lead to foreclosure.

Default point   See *break-even point.*

Defeasance clause   The clause in a mortgage that gives the mortgagor the right to redeem property upon the payment to the mortgagee of the obligation due.

Deficiency judgment   A court order to pay the balance owed on a loan if the proceeds from the sale of the security are insufficient to pay off the loan. Not allowed in all states.

Delinquency experience   The level of loans past due, expressed as a percentage of the total portfolio of loans. Most commonly, record-keeping for delinquent loans is according to 30-, 60-, and 90-day intervals.

Delinquent   The status of a mortgage with a payment past due.

Delivery   The legal, final, and absolute transfer of a deed from seller to buyer in such a manner that it cannot be recalled by the seller; a necessary requisite to the transfer of title; in mortgage banking, the physical delivery of loan documents to an investor or agent in conformance with the commitment.

Demand note   A note that is due whenever the holder demands payment.

Deposit   A sum of money given to bind a sale of real estate, or a sum of money given to assure payment, or an advance of funds in the processing of a loan. Also known as *earnest money.*

Depository Institutions Deregulation Committee (DIDC)   A committee established by the U.S. Congress in 1980 to oversee the orderly phasing out of interest rate ceilings in depository institutions.

Depreciation   A loss of value in real estate property brought about by age, physical deterioration, or functional or economic obsolescence. Broadly, a loss in value from any cause. The opposite of appreciation.

Depreciation allowance   The accounting charge made to allow for the fact that the asset may become economically obsolete before its physical deterioration. The purpose is to write off the original cost by distributing it over the estimated useful life of the asset. It appears in both the profit-and-loss statement and the balance sheet.

Developer   A person or entity who prepares raw land for building sites, and sometimes builds on the sites.

Development loan   A loan made for the purpose of preparing raw land for the construction of one or more buildings. Development may include grading and installation of utilities and roadways (see *construction loan*).

Disbursements   The payment of monies on a previously agreed-to basis. Used to describe construction loan draws.

Discount   In loan obligations, a discount refers to an amount withheld from loan proceeds by a lender. In secondary market sales, a discount is the amount by which the sale price of a note is less than its face value. In both instances, the purpose of a discount is to adjust the yield upward, either in lieu of interest or in addition to interest. The rate or amount of discount depends on money market conditions, the credit of the borrower, and the rate and terms of the note.

Discount point   See *point.*

Discounted cash flow   The present value of future cash flow determined by a given discount rate.

Disintermediation   The flow of funds out of savings institutions into short-term investments in which interest rates are higher. This shift normally results in a net decrease in the amount of funds available for long-term real estate financing. Also, the market condition that exists when this shift occurs.

Direct reduction mortgage   An amortized mortgage with principal and interest paid at same time, and with interest calculated only on the remaining balance.

Dower   The rights of a widow to a life estate in the real property of her husband at his death. Not allowed in all states.

Down payment   Cash portion paid by a buyer from his own funds, as opposed to that portion of the purchase price which is financed.

Due-on-sale clause   A type of acceleration clause calling for a debt under a mortgage or deed or trust to be due in its entirety upon transfer of ownership of the secured property.

Earnest money   See *deposit.*

Easement   Right or interest in the land of another entitling the holder to a specific limited use, privilege, or benefit such as laying a sewer, putting up electric power lines, or crossing the property.

Economic rent   The rent that a property would bring if offered in the open market at the fair rental value. Not necessarily the contract rent.

Economic value   The valuation of real property based on its earning capabilities.

Effective gross income (personal)   Normal annual income including overtime that is regular or guaranteed. It may be from more than one source. Salary is generally the principal source, but other income may qualify if it is significant and stable.

Effective gross income (property)   Stabilized income that a property is expected to generate after a vacancy allowance.

Effective rate   The actual rate of return to the investor. It may vary from the contract rate for a variety of reasons. Also called yield (see *yield*).

Eminent domain   The right of a government to take private property for public use upon payment of its fair value. It is the basis for condemnation proceedings (see *condemnation*).

Encroachment   An improvement that intrudes illegally upon another's property.

Encumbrance   Anything that affects or limits the fee simple title to property, such as mortgages, leases, easements, or restrictions.

Equal Credit Opportunity Act (ECOA)   ECOA is a federal law that requires lenders and other creditors to make credit equally available without discrimination based on race, color, religion, national origin, age, sex, marital status, receipt of income from public assistance programs or reliance on any consumer protection law. Also known as Regulation B.

Equity   In real estate, equity is the difference between fair market value and current indebtedness, usually referring to the owner's interest.

Equity of redemption   The common law right to redeem property during the foreclosure period. In some states the mortgagor has a statutory right to redeem property after a foreclosure sale.

Equity participation   Partial ownership of income property, given by the owner to the lender as part of the consideration for making the loan.

Escalator clause   A clause providing for the upward or downward adjustment of rent payments to cover specified contingencies, such as the provision in a lease to provide for increases in property tax and operating expenses.

Escheat   The reversion of property to the state if the owner dies intestate and without heirs.

Escrow   A transaction in which a third party, acting as the agent for the buyer and the seller, carries out instructions of both and assumes the responsibilities of handling all the paperwork and disbursement of funds.

Escrow analysis   The periodic examination of escrow accounts to determine if current monthly deposits will provide sufficient funds to pay taxes, insurance, and other bills when due.

Escrow payment   That portion of a mortgagor's monthly payment held by the lender to pay for taxes, hazard insurance, mortgage insurance, lease payments, and other items as they become due. Known as impounds or reserves in some states.

Estate   The ownership interest of an individual in real property. The sum total of all the real and personal property owned by an individual at time of death.

Estoppel letter   A statement that in itself prevents its issuer from later asserting different facts.

Eviction   The lawful expulsion of an occupant from real property.

Exclusive listing   A written contract giving a licensed real estate agent the exclusive right to sell a property for a specified time, but reserving the owner's right to sell the property alone without the payment of a commission.

Exclusive right to sell   The same as exclusive listing, but the owner agrees to pay a full commission to the broker even though the owner may sell the property.

Executor   A person named in a will to administer an estate. The court will appoint an administrator if no executor is named. Executrix is the feminine form.

Face value   The value of notes, mortgages, etc., as stated on the face of the instrument, and not considering any discounting.

Fair market value   The price at which property is transferred between a willing buyer and a willing seller, each of whom has a reasonable knowledge of all pertinent facts and neither of whom is under any compulsion to buy or sell.

Fannie Mae   See Federal National Mortgage Association.

Farmers Home Administration (FmHA)   An agency within the Department of Agriculture which operates principally under the Consolidated Farm and Rural Development Act of 1921 and Title V of the Housing Act of 1949. This agency provides financing to farmers and other qualified borrowers who are unable to obtain loans elsewhere. Funds are borrowed from the U.S. Treasury.

Federal Home Loan Mortgage Corporation (FHLMC)   A private corporation authorized by Congress to provide secondary mortgage market support for conventional mortgages. It also sells participation certificates secured by pools of conventional mortgage loans, their principal and interest guaranteed by the federal government through the FHLBB. Popularly known as Freddie Mac.

Federal Housing Administration (FHA)   A division of HUD. Its main activity is the insuring of residential mortgage loans made by private lenders. It sets standards for construction and underwriting. FHA does not lend money, or plan or construct housing.

Federal National Mortgage Association (FNMA)   A privately owned corporation created by Congress to support the secondary mortgage market. It purchases and sells residential mortgages insured by FHA or guaranteed by VA as well as conventional home mortgages. Popularly known as Fannie Mae.

Fee simple   An estate under which the owner is entitled to unrestricted powers to dispose of the property and which can be left by will or inherited; commonly, the greatest interest a person can have in real estate.

Fiduciary   A person in a position of trust and confidence for another.

Finance company   A limited-purpose financing entity organized and controlled by a builder for the purpose of facilitating the issuance of bonds.

Financial intermediary   A financial institution which acts as a middleman between savers and borrowers by selling its own obligations or serving as a depository and, in turn, lending the accumulated funds to borrowers.

Financing package   The total of all financial interest in a project. It may include mortgages, partnerships, joint venture capital interests, stock ownership, or any financial arrangement used to carry a project to completion.

Financing statement   Under the Uniform Commercial Code, this is a prescribed form filed by a lender with the registrar of deeds or secretary of state to perfect a security interest. It gives the name and address of the debtor and the secured party (lender) along with a description of the personal property securing the loan. It may show the amount of indebtedness.

Finder's fee   A fee or commission paid to a broker for obtaining a mortgage loan for a client or for referring a mortgage loan to a broker. It may also refer to a commission paid to a broker for locating a property.

Firm commitment   A lender's agreement to make a loan to a specific borrower of a specific property. An FHA or PMI agreement with a designated borrower to insure a loan on a specific property.

First mortgage   A mortgage having priority over all other voluntary liens against certain property.

Fixture   Personal property that becomes real property when attached in a permanent manner to real estate.

Floor loan   A portion or portions of a mortgage loan commitment that is less than the full amount of the commitment. It may be funded upon conditions less stringent than those required for funding the full amount. For example, the floor loan equal to perhaps 80 percent of the full amount may be funded upon completion of construction without occupancy requirements, but substantial occupancy of the building may be required for funding the full amount of the loan.

FNMA   See *Federal National Mortgage Association.*

Forbearance   The act of refraining from taking legal action despite the fact that a mortgage is in arrears. It is usually granted only when a mortgagor makes a satisfactory arrangement by which the arrears will be paid at a future date.

Foreclosure   An authorized procedure taken by a mortgagee or lender under the terms of a mortgage or deed of trust for the purpose of having the property sold and the proceeds applied to the payment of a defaulted debt.

Forward delivery   The delivery of mortgages or mortgage-backed securities to satisfy cash or future market transactions of an earlier date.

Front-end money   Funds required to start a development and generally advanced by the developer or equity owner as a capital contribution to the project.

Freehold estate   An estate in real estate that could last forever.

Freddie Mac   See *Federal Home Loan Mortgage Corporation.*

Futures contract   A contract purchased on an organized market (e.g., Chicago Board of Trade) either for the purchase of a GNMA Certificate at a specified price on a specified future date or for the sale of the Certificate at a specified future date.

Gap financing   An interim loan given to finance the difference between the floor and the maximum permanent loan as committed (see *floor loan*).

Garnishment   A proceeding that applies specified monies, wages, or property to a debt or creditor by proper statutory process against a debtor.

Government National Mortgage Association (GNMA)   On Sept. 1, 1968, Congress enacted legislation to partition FNMA into two continuing corporate entities. GNMA has assumed responsibility for the special assistance loan program and the management and liquidation function of the older FNMA. Also, GNMA administers the mortgage-backed securities program which channels new sources of funds into residential financing through the sale of privately issued securities carrying a GNMA guaranty. Popularly known as Ginnie Mae.

GNMA-backed bond   A "mortgage-backed bond" using GNMA Certificates as the collateral rather than the individual mortgages.

GNMA futures market   A regulated central market in which standardized contracts for the future delivery of GNMA securities are traded.

GNMA mortgage-backed securities   Securities guaranteed by GNMA that are issued by mortgage bankers, commercial banks, savings and loan associations, savings banks, and other institutions. The GNMA security holder is protected by the "full faith and credit of the U.S." GNMA securities are backed by FHA, VA, or FmHA mortgages.

GNMA II   Similar to GNMA certificates except that the mortgages within the pool may have interest rates that vary within 100 basis points.

Graduated payment mortgage   Residential mortgage which has monthly mortgage payments that start at a low level and increase at a predetermined rate.

Grantee   The person to whom an interest in real property is conveyed.

Grantor   The person conveying an interest in real property.

Gross rent multiplier   A figure used to compare rental properties to determine value. It gives the relationship between the gross rental income and the sales price. Synonyms are gross multiplier and gross income multiplier.

Ground rent   The earnings of improved property allocated to the ground itself after allowance is made for earnings of the improvement. Also, payment for the use of land in accordance with the terms of a ground lease.

Growing equity mortgage   Residential mortgage which has monthly payments increasing according to an agreed-upon schedule. This increased payment reduces principal, allowing the loan to be paid off sooner than a traditional mortgage.

Guaranteed loan   A loan guaranteed by VA, FmHA, or any other interested party.

Hard money mortgage   A mortgage given in return for cash, rather than to secure a portion of the purchase price, as with a purchase money mortgage.

Hazard insurance   A contract whereby an insurer, for a premium, undertakes to compensate the insured for loss on a specific property due to certain hazards.

Hedging   In mortgage lending, the purchase or sale of mortgage futures contracts to offset cash market transactions to be made at a later date.

Highest and best use   The available present use or series of future uses that will produce the highest present property value and develop a site to its full economic potential.

Holdback   That portion of a loan commitment not funded until some additional requirement such as rental or completion is attained (see *floor loan*). In construction or interim lending it is a percentage of the contractor's draw held back to provide additional protection for the interim lender, often in an amount equal to the contractor's profit given over when the interim loan is closed.

Home Owners Loan Corporation (HOLC)   An agency formed in 1933 to help stabilize the economy. The HOLC issued government-guaranteed bonds to lenders for delinquent mortgages and then refinanced home owner indebtedness.

Home owners policy   A multiple-peril policy commonly called a "package policy." It is available to owners of private dwellings and covers the dwelling and contents in the case of fire or wind damage, theft, liability for property damage, and personal liability.

Homestead estate   In some states, the home and property occupied by an owner are protected by law up to a certain amount from attachment and sale for the claims of creditors.

HUD   The Department of Housing and Urban Development, established by the Housing and Urban Development Act of 1965 to supersede the Housing and Home Finance Agency. It is responsible for the implementation and administration of government housing and urban development programs. The broad range of programs includes community planning and development, housing production and mortgage credit (FHA), equal opportunity in housing, and research and technology.

Hypothecate   To give a thing as security without the necessity of giving up possession of it.

Impound   See *escrow payment.*

Income and expense statement   The actual or estimated schedule of income and expense items reflecting net gain or loss during a specified period.

Income approach to value   The appraisal technique used to estimate real property value by capitalizing net income (see *capitalization*).

Income property   Real estate developed or improved to produce income.

Index   An economic measurement that is used to measure periodic interest rate adjustments for an adjustable-rate mortgage.

Industrial park   A controlled development designed for specific types of businesses. These developments provide required appurtenances including public utilities, streets, railroad sidings, auto parking, and water and sewage facilities.

Installment   The regular periodic payment that a borrower agrees to make to the mortgagee.

Installment sale   A disposition of real property or personal property by a nondealer if at least one payment is to be received after the close of the taxable year in which the disposition occurs. Under the installment method, gain on a sale is reported ratably as each installment payment is received.

Institutional lender   A financial institution that invests in mortgages carried in its own portfolio. Mutual savings banks, life insurance companies, commercial banks, pension and trust funds, and savings and loan associations are examples.

Insurance   A contract for indemnification against loss.

Insured loan   A loan insured by FHA or a private mortgage insurance company.

Interest   Consideration in the form of money paid for the use of money, usually expressed as an annual percentage. Also, a right, share, or title in property.

Interest rate   The percentage of an amount of money which is paid for its use for a specified time. Usually expressed as an annual percentage.

Interim financing   Financing during the time from project commencement to closing of a permanent loan, usually in the form of a construction loan or development loan.

Intestate   To die leaving no valid will.

Investor   The holder of a mortgage or the permanent lender for whom a mortgage lender services the loan. Any person or institution investing in mortgages.

Involuntary lien   A lien imposed against property without consent of an owner. Examples include taxes, special assessments, federal income tax liens, mechanics liens, and materials liens.

Joint tenancy   An equal undivided ownership of property by two or more persons whose survivors take the interest upon the death of any one of them.

Joint venture   An association between two or more parties to own or develop real estate. It may take a variety of legal forms including partnership, tenancy in common, or a corporation. It is formed for a specific purpose and duration.

Judgment   That which has been adjudicated, allowed, or decreed by a court.

Judgment lien   A lien upon the property of a debtor resulting from the decree of a court.

Judicial foreclosure   A type of foreclosure proceeding used in some states that is handled as a civil lawsuit and conducted entirely under auspices of a court.

Junior mortgage   A lien subsequent to the claims of the holder of a prior (senior) mortgage.

Kicker   A term describing any benefit to a lender above ordinary interest payments. It may be an equity in a property or a participation in the income stream.

Land contract   A contract ordinarily used in connection with the sale of property in cases where the seller does not wish to convey title until all or a certain part of the purchase price is paid by the buyer. This financing vehicle is often used when property is sold on a small down payment.

Landlord   Owner or lessor of real property.

Late charge   An additional charge a borrower is required to pay as penalty for failure to pay a regular installment when due.

Lease   A written document containing the conditions under which the possession and use of real or personal property are given by the owner to another for a stated period and for a stated consideration.

Leaseback   See *sale-leaseback.*

Leasehold   An interest in real property held by virtue of a lease.

Leasehold mortgage   A loan to a lessee secured by a leasehold interest in a property.

Legal description   A property description recognized by law which is sufficient to locate and identify the property without oral testimony.

Legal lists   A term describing investments that life insurance companies, mutual savings banks, or other regulated investors may make under a state charter or court order.

Lessee (tenant)   The person(s) holding rights of possession and use of property under terms of a lease.

Lessor (landlord)   The one leasing property to a lessee.

Leverage   The use of borrowed money to increase the return on a cash investment. For leverage to be profitable, the rate of return on the investment must be higher than the cost of the money borrowed (interest plus amortization).

Lien   A legal hold or claim of one person on the property of another as security for a debt or charge. The right given by law to satisfy a debt.

Limited partnership   A partnership that consists of one or more general partners who are fully liable and one or more limited partners who are liable only for the amount of their investment.

Line of credit   An agreement by a commercial bank or other financial institution to extend credit up to a certain amount for a certain time to a specific borrower.

Lis pendens   A notice recorded in the official records of a county to indicate that there is a pending suit affecting the lands within that jurisdiction.

Loan   A sum of money loaned at interest to be repaid.

Loan constant   The yearly percentage of interest which remains the same over the life of an amortized loan based on the monthly payment in relation to the principal originally loaned.

Loan submission   A package of pertinent papers and documents regarding specific property or properties. It is delivered to a prospective lender for review and consideration for the purpose of making a mortgage loan.

Loan-to-value ratio   The relationship between the amount of the mortgage loan and the appraised value of the security expressed as a percentage of the appraised value.

Loss payable clause   A clause in a fire insurance policy listing the priority of claims in the event of destruction of the property insured. Generally, a mortgagee, or beneficiary under a deed of trust, is the party appearing in the clause being paid the amount owing under the mortgage or deed of trust before the owner is paid.

MAI (Member, Appraisal Institute)   The highest professional designation awarded by the American Institute of Real Estate Appraisers.

Margin   The number of basis points a lender adds to an index to determine the interest rate of an adjustable-rate mortgage.

Marketable title   A title that may not be completely clear but has only minor defects that a well-informed and prudent buyer of real estate would accept.

Market approach to value   In appraising, the market value estimate is predicated upon actual prices paid in market transactions. It is a process of correlation and analysis of similar recently sold properties. The reliability of this technique is dependent upon the degree of comparability of each property with the subject property, the time of sale, the verification of the sale dates, the absence of unusual conditions affecting the sale, and the terms of the sale.

Market rent   The price a tenant pays a landlord for the use and occupancy of real property based upon current prices for comparable property.

Market value   The highest price that a buyer, willing but not compelled to buy, would pay, and the lowest a seller, willing but not compelled to sell, would accept.

Master servicer   For MBS, the master servicer is responsible for servicing and administering mortgage loans in a mortgage pool. This function may be contracted to the originator of each mortgage loan under the supervision of the master servicer.

Maturity   The terminating or due date of a note, time, draft, acceptance, bill of exchange, or bond. The date a time instrument or indebtedness becomes due and payable.

Metes and bounds   A description in a deed of the land location in which the boundaries are defined by directions and distances.

Modified pass-through   A variation of the "pass-through security" which guarantees and pays the investor the scheduled monthly principal and interest payment, irrespective of what amounts are collected from the pool mortgages.

Moratorium   A period during which a borrower is granted the right to delay fulfillment of an obligation.

Mortgage   A conveyance of an interest in real property given as security for the payment of a debt.

Mortgage-backed bonds   A "bond" or debt instrument which is backed by a pool of mortgages and for which the cash flow of the mortgages serves as the source of repayment.

MBS   Mortgage-backed securities of all types.

Mortgage-backed securities   Bond-type investment securities representing an undivided interest in a pool of mortgages or trust deeds. Income from the underlying mortgage is used to pay off the securities (see *GNMA mortgage-backed securities*).

Mortgage banker   A firm or individual active in the field of mortgage banking. Mortgage bankers, as local representatives of regional or national institutional lenders, act as correspondents between lenders and borrowers. Mortgage bankers need to borrow the funds they lend out.

Mortgage banking   The packaging of mortgage loans secured by real property to be sold to a permanent investor with servicing retained for the life of the loan for a fee. The origination, sale, and servicing of mortgage loans by a firm or individual. The investor-correspondent system is the foundation of the mortgage banking industry.

Mortgage broker   A firm or individual bringing the borrower and lender together and receiving a commission. A mortgage broker does not retain servicing.

Mortgage company   A private corporation (sometimes called a mortgage banker) whose principal activity is the origination and servicing of mortgage loans which are sold to other financial institutions.

Mortgage discount   The difference between the principal amount of a mortgage and the amount for which it actually sells. Sometimes called points, loan brokerage fee, or new loan fee. The discount is computed on the amount of the loan, not the sale price.

Mortgagee   A person or firm to whom property is conveyed as security for a mortgage loan.

Mortgagee in possession   A mortgagee who, by virtue of a default under the terms of a mortgage, has obtained possession but not ownership of the property.

Mortgage insurance   The function of mortgage insurance (whether government or private) is to insure a mortgage lender against loss caused by a mortgagor's default. This insurance may cover a percentage of or virtually all of the mortgage loan depending on the type of mortgage insurance.

Mortgage life insurance   A type of term life insurance often bought by mortgagors. The amount of coverage decreases as the mortgage balance declines. In the event that the borrower dies while the policy is in force, the debt is automatically satisfied by insurance proceeds.

Mortgage insurance premium (MIP)   The consideration paid by a mortgagor for mortgage insurance either to FHA or a private mortgage insurance (PMI) company. On an FHA loan, the payment is ½ of 1 percent annually on the declining balance of the mortgage.

Mortgage note   A written promise to pay a sum of money at a stated interest rate during a specified term. It is secured by a mortgage.

Mortgage portfolio   The aggregate of mortgage loans held by an investor or serviced by a mortgage lender.

Mortgagor   One who borrows money, giving a mortgage or deed of trust on real property as security (a debtor).

Mutual mortgage insurance fund   One of four FHA insurance funds into which all mortgage insurance premiums and other specified revenue of the FHA are paid and from which the losses are met.

Mutual savings bank   A state or federally chartered financial institution, located primarily in the Northeast, that is a heavy purchaser of mortgage loans in both the primary and secondary mortgage market.

Negative cash flow   Cash expenditures of an income-producing property in excess of the cash receipts.

Negative amortization   Also called deferred interest. A loan payment schedule which produces additions to principal, not a reduction, because the interest collected is insufficient to cover interest earned. The unpaid interest is added to the principal balance.

Net income   The difference between effective gross income and expenses including taxes and insurance. The term is qualified as net income before depreciation and debt service.

Net lease   A lease calling for the lessee to pay all fixed and variable expenses associated with the property. Also known as a pure net lease, as opposed to a gross lease. The terms net-net and net-net-net are ill-defined and should be avoided.

Net worth   The value of all assets, including cash, less total liabilities. It is often used as an underwriting guideline to indicate an individual's creditworthiness and financial strength.

Net yield   That part of gross yield that remains after the deduction of all costs, such as servicing, and any reserves for losses.

Nondisturbance agreement   An agreement that permits a tenant under a lease to remain in possession despite any foreclosure.

Nonrecourse loan   A loan not allowing for a deficiency judgment. The lender's only recourse in the event of default is the security (property), and the borrower is not personally liable.

Nontraditional mortgage investors   Those investors, such as pension funds, which traditionally had not invested in mortgages but instead looked to stocks and bonds.

Notice of default   A notice recorded after the occurrence of a default under a deed of trust or mortgage, or a notice required by an interested third party insuring or guaranteeing a loan.

Novation   The substitution of a new contract or obligation between the same or different parties. The substitution, by mutual agreement, of one debtor for another or one creditor for another whereby the existing debt is extinguished.

Obsolescence   The loss of value of a property occasioned by going out of style, by becoming less suitable for use, or by other economic influences.

Open-end mortgage   A mortgage with a provision that the outstanding loan amount may be increased upon mutual agreement of the lender and the borrower.

Option   A contract agreement granting a right to purchase, sell, or otherwise contract for the use of a property at a stated price during a stated period of time.

Origination   The process of originating mortgages. Solicitation may be from individual borrowers, builders, or brokers.

Origination fee A fee or charge for the work involved in the evaluation, preparation, and submission of a proposed mortgage loan. Limited to only one percent for FHA and VA loans.

Originator A person who solicits builders, brokers, and others to obtain applications for mortgage loans. Origination is the process by which the mortgage lender brings into being a mortgage secured by real property.

Overcollateralization Sufficient mortgages must be placed into a collateral pool so that their discounted value is sufficient to cover the bond, plus a reserve. Overcollateralization is usually defined as a percentage of the bond, such as 110 percent.

Package mortgage A mortgage or deed of trust that includes items which are technically chattels, such as appliances, carpeting, and drapery.

Par The principal amount of a mortgage with no premium or discount.

Partially modified pass-through A variation of the "pass-through security" which guarantees, to a certain extent, that monthly principal and interest payments will be made to the investor, even if not collected from the mortgage pool.

Participation certificate (PC) Mortgage-backed security issued by FHLMC which consists of mortgages purchased from eligible sellers. Called PC because seller retains some interest (5 or 10 percent) in the mortgages sold to FHLMC.

Participation loan A mortgage made by one lender, known as the lead lender, in which one or more other lenders, known as participants, own a part interest, or a mortgage originated by two or more lenders.

Pass-through security A form of a "mortgage-backed bond" for which the monthly collections on the mortgage pool are "passed through" to the investor.

Pay-through security A form of a "mortgage-backed bond" which is secured by a mortgage pool and for which the payment features closely resemble those of a "modified pass-through security." The bond is fully amortizing with scheduled principal and interest payments which closely track the scheduled collections on the collateral mortgage pool.

Percentage lease A lease in which a percentage of the tenant's gross business receipts constitutes the rent. Although a straight percentage lease is occasionally encountered, most percentage leases contain a provision for a minimum rent amount.

Personal property Any property that is not real property.

PITI (principal, interest, taxes, and insurance) The principal and interest payment on most loans is fixed for the term of the loan; the tax and insurance portion may be adjusted to reflect changes in taxes or insurance costs.

Plans and specifications Architectural and engineering drawings and specifications for construction of a building or project including a description of materials to be used and the manner in which they are to be applied.

Point   An amount equal to one percent of the principal amount of an investment or note. Loan discount points are a one-time charge assessed at closing by the lender to increase the yield on the mortgage loan to a competitive position with other types of investments.

Police power   That right by which the state or other government authority may take, condemn, destroy, impair the value, limit the use, or otherwise invade property rights. It must be affirmatively shown that the property was taken to protect the public health, public morals, public safety, or the general welfare.

Pool insurance   Pool insurance represents various forms of insurance which provide investors with additional safety by insuring against default by home owners to a certain percent of initial principal amount.

Preclosing   A transaction preceding the formal closing, often used to settle outstanding issues with the formal closing shortly thereafter.

Premium   The amount, often stated as a percentage, paid in addition to the face value of a note or bond. Also, the charge for insurance coverage.

Prepayment assumption   A calculated guess of how a portfolio of single-family loans will perform over time, relative to the incidence of recoveries of principal. The assumption is expressed as a percentage of long-term FHA experience.

Prepayment fee   A consideration paid to the mortgagee for the prepayment privilege. Also known as prepayment penalty or reinvestment fee.

Prepayment privilege   The right given a borrower to pay all or part of a debt prior to its maturity. The mortgagee cannot be compelled to accept any payment other than those originally agreed to.

Prepayment penalty   A fee charged a mortgagor who prepays a loan before it is due. Not allowed for FHA or VA loans.

Prepayment (recovery of principal)   Payment in full on a mortgage, due either to a sale of the property or to foreclosure and, in either case, before the loan has been fully amortized.

Primary loan insurance   Type of insurance for loans with minimal down payments, usually less than twenty percent. Typically, provided by the Federal Housing Administration or private mortgage insurance companies.

Principal   Amount of debt, not including interest. The face value of a note, mortgage, etc.

Principal balance   The outstanding balance of a mortgage, exclusive of interest and any other charges.

Priority   As applied to claims against property, priority is the status of being prior or having precedence over other claims. Priority is usually established by filing or recordation in point of time, but may be established by statute or agreement.

Private mortgage insurance (PMI)   Insurance written by a private company protecting the mortgage lender against loss occasioned by a mortgage default.

Pro forma statement   A financial or accounting statement projecting income and performance of real estate within a period of time (usually one year) based on estimates and assumption.

Purchase money mortgage   A mortgage given by the purchaser of real property to the seller as part of the consideration in the sales transaction.

Quit claim deed   A deed that transfers (with no warranty) only such interest, title, or right a grantor may have at the time the conveyance is executed.

Real Estate Investment Trust (REIT)   A financial institution which can own and hold mortgages on real estate and pass earnings from these assets on, free of income tax to the corporation, but taxable to shareholders.

Real Estate Mortgage Investment Trust (REMIC)   A type of mortgage-backed security that allows for income to be taxed only to the holders of the instrument.

Real estate owned (REO)   A term frequently used by lending institutions as applied to ownership of real property acquired for investment or as a result of foreclosure.

Real property   Land and appurtenances, including anything of a permanent nature such as structures, trees, minerals, and the interest, benefits, and inherent rights thereof.

Realtor   A real estate broker or an associate holding active membership in a local real estate board affiliated with the National Association of Realtors.

Recapture   An owner's recovery of money invested in real estate, usually referring to a depreciation allowance.

Recision   The cancellation or annulment of a transaction or contract by the operation of law or by mutual consent.

Reconveyance   The transfer of the title of land from one person to the immediately preceding owner. It is used when the performance of debt is satisfied under the terms of a deed of trust.

Record date   The date which determines who is the holder of record entitled to receive payment of principal, interest, and any prepayment from the servicer or custodian.

Recorder   The public official in a political subdivision who keeps records of transactions affecting real property in the area. Sometimes known as a registrar of deeds or county clerk.

Recording   The noting in the registrar's office of the details of a properly executed legal document, such as a deed, mortgage, a satisfaction of mortgage, or an extension of mortgage, thereby making it a part of the public record.

Recourse   The right of the holder of a note secured by a mortgage or deed of trust to look personally to the borrower or endorser for payment, not just to the property. In the secondary mortgage market, the forced repurchase of a defaulted mortgage by the seller.

Redemption period   That period of time in those states where it is allowed in which a foreclosed mortgagor has to buy back his property by paying principal amount and interest and fees.

Redemption, right of   The right allowed by law in some states whereby a mortgagor may buy back property by paying the amount owed on a foreclosed mortgage, including interest and fees.

Refinance   (1) The renewing of an existing loan with the same borrower and lender; (2) a loan on the same property by either the same lender or borrower; (3) the selling of loans by the original lender.

Release of lien   An instrument discharging secured property from a lien.

Remainder   That part of an estate that remains after the termination of a prior estate.

Rent   Consideration paid for use or occupancy of property, buildings, or dwelling units.

Reproduction cost   The money required to reproduce a building under current market conditions less an allowance for depreciation.

Residence   A place where someone lives.

Residential mortgage credit report   The more inclusive credit report required for mortgages sold into the secondary mortgage market. Verifies employment, address, and checks national repositories of credit.

RESPA   Real Estate Settlement Procedures Act.

Restrictive covenant   A clause in a deed limiting use of the property conveyed for a certain period of time.

Return on equity   The ratio of cash flow after debt service to the difference between the value of property and the total financing (see *cash-on-cash return*).

Reverse leverage   A situation that arises when financing is too costly. It results when total yield on cash investment is less than the financing constant on borrowed funds (see *negative cash flow*).

Reversion   A right to future possession retained by an owner at the time of a transfer of an owner's interest in real property.

Reversionary clause   A clause providing that any violations of restrictions will cause title to the property to revert to the party who imposed the restriction.

Right of survivorship   In joint tenancy, the right of survivors to acquire the interest of a deceased joint tenant.

Right-of-way   A privilege operating as an easement upon land, whereby a land owner, by grant or agreement, gives another the right to pass over land (see *easement*).

Sale-leaseback   A technique in which a seller deeds property to a buyer for a consideration and the buyer simultaneously leases the property back to the seller, usually on a long-term basis.

Sales contract   Another name for a sales agreement, purchase agreement, etc. Not to be confused with a land contract, which is a conditional sales contract.

Sandwich lease   A lease in which the "sandwiched party" is a lessee, paying rent on a leasehold interest to one party, and also is a lessor, collecting rent from another party or parties.

Satisfaction of mortgage   The recordable instrument given by the lender to evidence payment in full of the mortgage debt. Sometimes known as a release deed.

Savings and loan association   A mutual or stock association chartered and regulated by either the federal government or a state. S&Ls accept time deposits and lend funds primarily on residential real estate.

Secondary financing   Financing real estate with a loan or loans subordinate to a first mortgage or first trust deed.

Secondary mortgage market   An unorganized market where existing mortgages are bought and sold. It contrasts with the primary mortgage market, where mortgages are originated.

Secured party   The party holding a security interest or lien; may be referred to as the mortgagee, the conditional seller, or the pledgee.

Securities and Exchange Commission (SEC)   The federal agency which regulates securities and the securities business. It is involved in real estate and mortgage lending when MBS are issued.

Security   The collateral given, deposited, or pledged to secure the fulfillment of an obligation or payment of a debt.

Security instrument   The mortgage or trust deed evidencing the pledge of real estate security as distinguished from the note or other credit instrument.

Security interest According to the Uniform Commercial Code, security interest is a term designating the interest of the creditor in the property of the debtor in all types of credit transactions. It thus replaces such terms as chattel mortgage, pledge, trust receipt, chattel trust, equipment trust, conditional sale, and inventory lien (see *financing statement*).

Seller/servicer FNMA term for an approved corporation that sells and services mortgages for FNMA.

Servicing The duties of the mortgage lender as a loan correspondent as specified in the servicing agreement for which a fee is received. The collection for an investor of payments, interest, principal, and trust items such as hazard insurance and taxes on a note by the borrower in accordance with the terms of the note. Servicing also consists of operational procedures covering accounting, bookkeeping, insurance, tax records, loan payment follow-up, delinquency loan follow-up, and loan analysis.

Single-purpose issuer An entity, such as a "finance company, " whose single purpose is the accumulation of mortgages and the issuance and servicing of bonds.

Society of Real Estate Appraisers (SREA) The designation of an appraiser who is a member of the Society of Real Estate Appraisers. The designations are: senior residential appraiser (SRA), senior real property appraiser (SRPA), and senior real estate analyst (SREA).

Soft costs Architectural, engineering, and legal fees as distinguished from land and construction costs.

Special hazard insurance Special hazard insurance is a form of pool insurance which covers losses from such freaks of nature as earthquakes and floods. This insurance, typically one percent of the initial aggregate amount of the pool, is placed in a collateral pool as a whole.

Special limited obligation debt Bonds issued by a housing agency which are secured (as defined) only by the revenues and funds pledged in the specific indenture. Funds held by the agency for other programs or in general funds are not pledged for debt service.

Special warranty deed A deed containing a covenant whereby the grantor agrees to protect the grantee against any claims arising during the grantor's period of ownership. Often used during probate.

Specific performance A remedy in a court of equity compelling the defendant to carry out the terms of an agreement or contract.

Stand-by commitment A commitment to purchase a loan or loans with specified terms, both parties understanding that delivery is not likely unless circumstances warrant. The commitment is issued for a fee with willingness to fund in the event that a permanent loan is not obtained. Such commitments are typically used to enable the borrower to obtain construction financing at a lower cost on the assumption that permanent financing of the project will be available on more favorable terms when the improvements are completed and the project is generating income.

Stand-by fee   The fee charged by an investor for a stand-by commitment. The fee is earned upon issuance and acceptance of the commitment.

State (moral obligation) pledge   A security device frequently used by state governments to enhance the marketability of revenue bond debt. The pledge requires that notification of a shortfall in a bond program's debt service (capital) reserve fund be sent formally to the governor of the state. It is intended that the shortfall be included in the governor's next budget message to the legislature. There are state-to-state variations in the use of the pledge; however, none except Idaho's are legally binding.

Statute of frauds   A state law requiring that certain contracts be in writing. In real estate, a contract for the sale of land must be in writing to be enforceable.

Statute of limitations   A law that limits the length of time in which a lawsuit must be commenced, or the right to sue is lost. It varies from state to state.

Step-down lease   A lease calling for one initial rent to be followed by a decrease in rent over stated periods.

Step-up lease   A lease calling for one initial rent followed by an increase in rent over stated periods.

Straight bond   A form of a "mortgage-backed bond" which is required by a mortgage pool. The instrument is similar to corporate bonds, with scheduled periodic interest payments. Principal repayment is usually at the end of the bond term.

Straight pass-through   A variation of the "pass-through security" which pays principal and interest, as and when collected from the pool, to the investors.

Subject to mortgage   When a purchaser buys subject to a mortgage but does not endorse the same or assume to pay the mortgage, a purchaser cannot be held for any deficiency if the mortgage is foreclosed and the property sold for an amount not sufficient to cover the note (see *assumption of mortgage*).

Sublease   A lease executed by a lessee to a third person for a term no longer than the remaining portion of the original lease.

Subordinate   To make subject to, or junior to.

Subordination   The act of a party acknowledging, by written recorded instrument, that a debt due is inferior to the interest of another in the same property. Subordination may apply not only to mortgages but to leases, real estate rights, and any other types of debt instruments.

Subrogation   The substitution of one person for another in reference to a debt, claim, or right.

Takeout commitment   A promise to make a loan at a future specified time. It is commonly used to designate a higher cost, shorter term, back-up commitment as a support for construction financing until a suitable permanent loan can be secured.

Tandem plan   A mortgage assistance program in which GNMA agrees to purchase qualified, below-market interest rate mortgages at prices favorable to sellers. The mortgages purchased by GNMA are accumulated and periodically sold at auction as either GNMA securities or whole mortgages. As the subsidy cost of the program, GNMA absorbs the difference between the price it paid for the loan and the market price paid by the investor. If the seller or assignee assumes GNMA's obligation to purchase, then GNMA will pay the seller a differential of the excess of the specified purchase price over a published interim selling price (ISP). The term is also used to describe any of the many forms of special assistance programs sponsored by GNMA to affect mortgage finance activity and costs.

Tax deed   A deed on property purchased at public sale for nonpayment of taxes.

Tax lien   A claim against property for the amount of its due and unpaid taxes.

Tenancy   A holding of real estate under any kind of right of title. Used alone, tenancy implies a holding under a lease.

Tenancy at will   A holding of real estate that can be terminated at the will of either the lessor or the lessee, usually with notice.

Tenancy by entirety   The joint ownership of property by a husband and wife where both are viewed as one person under common law that provides for the right of survivorship.

Tenancy in common   In law, the type of tenancy or estate created when real or personal property is granted, devised, or bequeathed to two or more persons in the absence of expressed words creating a joint tenancy. There is no right of survivorship (see *joint tenancy*).

Tenant   One who is not the owner of, but occupies, real property under consent of the owner and in subordination to the owner's title. The tenant is entitled to exclusive possession, use, and enjoyment of the property, usually for a rent specified in the lease.

Term   The period of time between the commencement date and termination date of a note, mortgage, legal document, or other contract.

Testate   The estate or condition of leaving a will at death.

Title   The evidence of the right to or ownership in property. In the case of real estate, the documentary evidence of ownership is the title deed which specifies in whom the legal state is vested and the history of ownership and transfers. Title may be acquired through purchase, inheritance, devise, gift, or through foreclosure of a mortgage.

Title insurance policy   A contract by which the insurer, usually a title insurance company, agrees to pay the insured a specified amount for any loss caused by defects of title to real estate, wherein the insured has an interest as purchaser, mortgagee, or otherwise.

Trust deed   The instrument given by a borrower (trustor) to a trustee vesting title to a property in the trustee as security for the borrower's fulfillment of an obligation (see *deed of trust*).

Trustee   One who holds title to a real property under the terms of a deed of trust. With MBS, the party responsible for determining whether all other parties are performing as contractually required to do.

Underwriting   The analysis and matching of risk to an appropriate rate and term. The process of deciding whether to make a mortgage loan.

Unencumbered property   A property to which the title is free and clear.

Uniform Commercial Code (UCC)   A comprehensive law regulating commercial transactions. It has been adopted, with modification, by all states.

Usury   Charging more for the use of money than allowed by law.

Vacancy factor   A percentage rate expressing the loss from gross rental income due to vacancy and collection losses.

VA certificate of reasonable value   The VA issues a certificate of reasonable value at a specific figure, agreeing to guarantee a mortgage loan to an eligible qualified veteran buyer upon completion and sale of the house. The veteran must be aware of the VA's appraised value of the property.

Valuation   See *appraisal.*

Variable rate mortgage   A mortgage agreement that allows for adjustment of the interest rate in keeping with a fluctuating market and terms agreed upon in the note.

Vendee   The party to whom personal or real property is sold.

Veterans Administration (VA)   The Servicemen's Readjustment Act of 1944 authorized this agency to administer a variety of benefit programs designed to facilitate the adjustment of returning veterans to civilian life. The VA home loan guaranty program is designed to encourage lenders to offer long-term, low down payment mortgages to eligible veterans by guaranteeing the lender against loss.

Warehousing   The holding of a mortgage on a short-term basis pending either a sale to an investor or other long-term financing. These mortgages may be used as collateral security with a bank to borrow additional funds. A builder "warehouses" mortgages when he takes back a mortgage from a home buyer and holds the mortgage for a time period.

Warranty deed   A deed in which the grantor or seller warrants or guarantees that good title is being conveyed, as opposed to a quit claim deed that contains no representation or warranty as to the quality of title being conveyed.

Waste   Damage to real estate by neglect or other cause.

Whole loan   The entire mortgage loan package representing 100 percent ownership, and not individual ownership as in a mortgage pool.

Will   A written document providing for the distribution of property at death.

Wrap-around   A mortgage which secures a debt that includes the balance due on an existing senior mortgage and an additional amount advanced by the wrap-around mortgagee. The wrap-around mortgagee thereafter makes the amortizing payments on the senior mortgage. (An example is when a land owner has a mortgage securing a debt with an outstanding balance of $3,000,000. A lender now advances the same mortgagor another $1,500,000 and undertakes to make the remaining payments due on the $3,000,000 debt by taking a $4,500,000 wrap-around junior mortgage on the real estate to secure the total indebtedness.)

Yield   In real estate, the effective annual amount of income which is being accrued on an investment. Expressed as a percentage of the price originally paid.

Yield to maturity   A percent returned each year to the lender on actual funds borrowed considering that the loan will be paid in full at the end of maturity.

Zoning   The act of city or county authorities specifying the type of use to which property may be put in specific areas (see *restrictive covenant*).

INDEX